3D ANIMATION

for the

RAW BEGINNER

Using

MAYA

3D ANIMATION
for the
RAW BEGINNER
Using
MAYA

Roger "Buzz" King

CRC Press
Taylor & Francis Group
Boca Raton London New York

CRC Press is an imprint of the
Taylor & Francis Group, an **informa** business

A CHAPMAN & HALL BOOK

CRC Press
Taylor & Francis Group
6000 Broken Sound Parkway NW, Suite 300
Boca Raton, FL 33487-2742

© 2015 by Taylor & Francis Group, LLC
CRC Press is an imprint of Taylor & Francis Group, an Informa business

No claim to original U.S. Government works

Printed on acid-free paper
Version Date: 20140320

International Standard Book Number-13: 978-1-4398-5264-4 (Hardback)

Library of Congress Cataloging-in-Publication Data

King, R. (Roger), 1942-
    3D animation for the raw beginner using Maya / author, Roger King.
        pages cm -- (Chapman & Hall/CRC computer graphics, geometric modeling, and animation series)
    Includes bibliographical references and index.
    ISBN 978-1-4398-5264-4 (hardback)
    1. Computer animation--Amateurs' manuals. 2. Three-dimensional display systems. 3. Maya (Computer file) I. Title. II. Title: Three D animation for the raw beginner using Maya.

TR897.72.M39K56 2014
006.6'96--dc23   2014008500

Visit the Taylor & Francis Web site at
http://www.taylorandfrancis.com

and the CRC Press Web site at
http://www.crcpress.com

To my family—Wendy, Martina, Isabelle, and Julien—and to Alan Apt, technical book publisher and avid outdoorsman, who set me on the path of writing this book.

Table of Contents

Acknowledgments

Several of the models that appear in this book were created by other people. The three characters in the cabana scene were made from base characters bought from Daz3D. Some of the other smaller items in the scene, in particular the potted plants, chairs, table, and palm trees, are from Daz3D as well, as are a few of the textures used in the scene. Hiro, the character I covered in a pink material, is also a Daz3D character.

The terrain in the canyon scene was made by D&D Creations. I enjoy shopping on their site. Their work is awesome.

The photographer who shot the evergreen bush texture image is Tyler Olson. The photographer who shot the cactus texture image is Jens Ickler.

The cactus photograph was taken by my daughter Martina. The unit circle technique for teaching trigonometric functions was taught to me by my daughter Isabelle; she clearly went to a better high school than I did. My wife, Wendy, spent an enormous amount of time editing the manuscript. She also created the texture shown in Figures 9.15 and 9.16.

Faculty members always thank their students, and in this case it is quite sincere. I teach classes that are a mix of computing and fine arts students. My students are always fun to teach—and they have taught me a lot.

Sarah Chow, my editor, has been extremely patient with me and has been very responsive to my concerns and questions.

Autodesk freely hands out a student version of Maya and does not hobble it in any fashion. My university has had a many-seat lab and classroom license of Maya for several years. But it's very nice that my students can install a full version on their home machines and therefore do not have to camp out in the computer lab. I do, however, fully respect Autodesk's intellectual property rights. I personally own a commercial license, although some of the figures in this book were created with the student version of Maya. Given that Maya is the general-purpose animation application of choice all around the world, its commercial license fee is surprisingly low.

Finally, feel free to e-mail me at: buzz@3DbyBuzz.com.

Author

Roger "Buzz" King is a professor at the University of Colorado at Boulder, and teaches 3D animation for the Computer Science Department and the Alliance for Technology, Learning, and Society (ATLAS), an institute dedicated to the application of technology to the arts.

Over the years, he has trained several hundred animation students. He has made a number of Autodesk Maya training videos (http://3DbyBuzz.com), and he maintains a blog with Maya lessons (http://buzzking.me).

Dr. King has an A.B. degree from Occidental College in Los Angeles, and a Ph.D. in computer science from the University of Southern California.

He has performed research involving the management of animation media assets, data visualization, and the integration of complex data and multimedia. His research has been funded by the National Renewable Energy Lab, the U.S. Air Force, the U.S. Navy, the National Aeronautics and Space Administration (NASA), the Defense Advanced Research Projects Agency (DARPA), IBM, AT&T, the Department of Energy, and the Smithsonian. Dr. King was involved in the original development of the Encyclopedia of Life, which is dedicated to providing Web access to information about life forms on Earth. He has been an expert witness for the Federal Bureau of Investigation (FBI).

Dr. King has traveled widely around the world and has taught in India. He is a member of the board of advisors for a graphics start-up, and a cofounder of a second graphics start-up. He is currently focusing on product development and on his animation studio (http://BuzzWorks.buzz).

The Book's Web Site

Maya is a mature product and this book focuses on its stable, core capabilities. But Autodesk works hard at enhancing Maya with cutting-edge animation technology to keep it ahead of the competition. Inevitably, there are changes to Maya that impact even introductory books like this one.

So, on the book's Web site, http://3DbyBuzz.com, I will post revisions of the tutorials presented in this book to keep it up to date with new releases of Maya. I will also post any errata on the Web site.

On the Web site, there are a number of video tutorials on Maya, as well as a blog on which I post short lessons on Maya. That blog can be accessed independently: http://buzzking.me.

If you are an instructor using this book as a text, I would welcome the opportunity to interact with your students. My e-mail is buzz@3DbyBuzz.com. For that matter, if you are using this book personally, I would love to hear from you.

Thanks,
Buzz King

CHAPTER 1

Getting Oriented

FOCUS AND APPROACH OF THIS BOOK

This is a hands-on book and the chapters have a very prescriptive flavor. Section I uses an incremental, example-driven approach that illustrates the core concepts of 3D modeling, animation, and rendering. Then in Section II we gather up the concepts we have learned and put them together in a series of focused charts.

The book covers the principles of 3D animation. Our vehicle for doing this is Autodesk Maya, arguably the most popular and powerful general-purpose 3D modeling, animation, and rendering application that is available for purchase by the general public. As of the time of this writing, students can download it for free at: http://students.autodesk.com. (This is the full version of Maya, but it cannot be used commercially.) We take brief looks at other modeling, animation, and rendering applications. This book does not cover the myriad of technical and workflow issues that arise with large-scale team projects; rather, it is directed at people who are building small, animated projects on their own or in a small team environment. Character modeling is given only very brief attention.

This book is intended as a one-semester text for beginners with no experience with 3D modeling or animation. It targets the many computer-centric professions that demand solid "literacy" knowledge of 3D modeling and animation. These include a broad spectrum of disciplines, including engineering, advertising, desktop and Web application development, film, architecture, and product design. It is important to keep in mind, though, that Maya is not an engineering tool, and so this book does not cover computer-aided design (CAD); for that, a more appropriate tool to learn is Autodesk AutoCAD or SolidWorks.

Within the context of single person or small team projects, the focus of the book is on workflow within Maya and not on the workflow of a complete animated video project, which invariably demands several other applications besides Maya. Brief attention is given to the other applications that are necessary to complete a project; in particular, we look at the use of image editing applications and how they can be used to prepare textures for animated models, as this is a crucial step that affects the animator's workflow within Maya. We give less attention to audio editing and video editing, focusing mostly on how a soundtrack can be imported into Maya for the purpose of timing the movement in a scene. This way, when the soundtrack is integrated with the video image track in a video editor, the visual and audio tracks of the video will be properly synched.

Finally, we do not delve deeply into the mathematics inside Maya in this book. We do, however, provide intuitive descriptions of the mathematics and physics that underlies applications like Maya. Often these discussions are generalized and do not focus specifically on what is going on inside Maya.

In sum, we step through concrete Maya-based examples, as well as focus on the generic concepts that underlie the building of animated projects; and throughout, we give intuitive explanations of just what goes on inside an application like Autodesk Maya.

A Necessarily Nonlinear Approach to Learning 3D Animation

One of the greatest challenges in learning 3D animation is that it is far from a linear process. The animator does not move in a single thread through the various capabilities provided by Maya, first modeling, then adding materials and textures to the surfaces of models, then inserting lights that will make models visible, then animating models, then adding cameras so they can be used as rendering perspectives, and then rendering the frames (at perhaps thirty per second) that make up the animation.

Indeed, because of the extreme interdependencies between the capabilities provided by Maya, the overall process is highly iterative. The subtle, complex interaction of light and materials/textures/color in itself is enough to fill countless hours of experimentation. So, if the process of creating an animated project were viewed as a tree, with major branches labeled for the various processes of modeling, textures and materials, lights, cameras, and rendering, the animator would move laterally back and forth, and up and down, on these major branches.

In the examples presented this iterative approach will be taken. Small but complete examples will be created from the start. It is often necessary to put materials on models, add light, and then render them in the early stages of modeling, so the nascent models can be properly judged. Further, this book is intended for beginners, and it takes a lot of experience to be able to accurately imagine what a model will look like when it is placed under lights and is rendered.

Finally, there is another major reason for not using a strictly hierarchical approach to learning to do 3D animation: it would repeatedly dump too much out-of-context knowledge on the reader—and little of it would stick.

Perhaps the Most Important Principle

In order to make the discussions concrete the book is focused heavily on Maya, but intuitive observations that go beyond Maya and get at the heart of 3D modeling and animation will be presented.

Perhaps the most important principle of 3D modeling and animation for the beginner to keep in mind is this: If you build the various aspects of your animated project with your overall goals for that project in mind, you can avoid a lot of mistakes and thus minimize unnecessary painstaking iteration. Above all else, careful planning is the best way to create models that are easy to put materials on, and then to animate and render. It also simplifies the task of adapting models to other scenes and projects. This means that even as you begin to create the basic scenes and models for a project, you will already be thinking about materials, lights, textures, animation, and rendering.

Planning is key.

3DBYBUZZ.COM

On the Web site http://3DbyBuzz.com the reader will find a series of videos that for the most part follow the step-by-step tutorials in this book. The videos range from about eight minutes to about twenty-two minutes in length. They are, however, missing much of the conceptual material that appears in this book; they focus on "how-to-use-Maya," and contain only brief intuitive explanations about why we are performing each step.

Please note that the videos were not professionally made and were only meant for students in the author's animation classes. Also, they were made with various versions of Maya, including 2012, 2013, and 2014. Autodesk pulled most of its support of a modeling technique called subdivision out of Maya 2014, and so a few of the videos will only work with Maya 2013 and 2012.

This book should be current up to Maya 2014, and in several places, I have indicated things that have changed or been added to Maya 2015. Importantly, the vast majority of the changes in Maya 2015 consist of adding specialized, powerful capabilities and do not impact the content of this book, which is introductory in nature. If you go to http://3DbyBuzz. com, you will find a discussion on some of the changes that have been made in Maya 2015.

WHAT MAYA DOES AND DOES *NOT* DO

It's worth focusing briefly on the exact scope of Maya. Here's what it does *not* do: Maya is not a video editor and it is not an audio editor.

Maya allows one to model objects (like spaceships, chickens, skyscrapers, and washing machines). It allows one to place those objects in scenes by putting them into hierarchies, and then creating models out of these hierarchies. Materials and textures can then be added. Lights must be added, which is necessary because nothing can be seen if there is no light bouncing off those materials and textures. Models can be animated in Maya. And cameras can be placed in scenes; cameras within Maya are used to render animated scenes into a series of pixel-based images that can then be used to create a video with your favorite video editor.

Maya can also be used to simulate natural forces like wind and gravity. It can be used to create natural-looking clothing, hair, and fur. It provides facilities for modeling such things as fire, smoke, and water by using particle dynamics. Objects can be made soft or rigid, and can collide with each other. Particles can collide with objects and with each other.

Maya has even more capabilities, and so this book covers a lot of ground but always with the focus of presenting the key concepts and Maya capabilities that will get you started quickly.

A video editing program must be used to generate video from single images and to edit, cut, and paste video clips. A sound editor must be used to create the soundtrack, although a quick solution for the beginner is to use prerecorded sound, like a continuous piece of music. And generally, a raster image editor is needed to prep textures for objects.

The examples in this book are engineered to require only very basic knowledge of these other media applications. The reader will focus almost entirely on using Maya itself.

THE SPECIAL NEEDS OF GAMING

One last point: Maya is not a gaming engine and cannot be used to create interactive video games. Indeed, Maya is designed to create detailed, realistic models, rather than quickly rendered, angular models. The two renderers in Maya that we will use in this book are also not suitable for most game-based rendering tasks. This book does not cover interactive 3D graphics. But it is common for game designers to create models in Maya and then import them into their favorite gaming engine to create interactive animated games. One of the main challenges is to produce models that have as few polygon faces as possible in order to reduce the number of calculations that have to be performed to simulate the effects of light on those models. Often, game designers will use a low polygon count version of a given model when it is to be rendered from a distance and a high polygon count version of that model when it is to be rendered up close.

WORKFLOW WITHIN AND AROUND MAYA

What follows is an overview of Maya and how it is used to create 3D animated projects, along with the roles that are played by other applications in the larger 3D workflow. It might be best to read it quickly if you are just beginning to use this book, and then come back and look at this overview more carefully as you move through the book and work with the various tools inside Maya.

There are times when an animator might prefer to perform tasks in other applications, even when these tasks can be done with Maya alone. One of the most common complaints about Maya is that it is too complicated because it offers so much. Some artists have been moving much of their preliminary modeling to other applications that might be simpler to use or that offer different ways of creating models. Then, they import their models into Maya to continue crafting them, putting materials on them, and animating and rendering them.

Other Applications Commonly Used by Animators

There are certain effects that can be added to a scene with Maya or later in one's workflow by using a special effects video editor and/or compositing application. Such applications include Apple Motion, Adobe After Effects, and Autodesk Smoke. But in this book as much as possible will be done with Maya.

The Big Picture

As previously noted, the process of creating an animated project is extremely iterative. There is no single way to represent the overall workflow of producing a final video. So Figure 1.1 is a bit arbitrary, but it delineates a workflow that can be used as a template when creating simple projects.

In Figure 1.1, there is a box in the center of the diagram. It represents the tasks that can be done with Maya alone. Outside of the box are a number of applications and tasks that

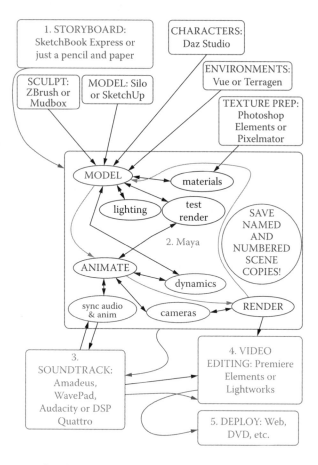

FIGURE 1.1   **(See p. CI-1 of Color Insert)** Overview of animation workflow.

In Figure 1.1, there is a box in the center of the diagram. It represents the tasks that can be done with Maya alone. Outside of the box are a number of applications and tasks that either must be added to the workflow or are optional. The diagram also includes media applications that are reasonably cost-effective for small-scale projects.

1. Storyboarding

The tasks in the workflow are in numbered boxes. 1 represents the preliminary phase, which consists of making rough drawings of the scenes that comprise the video. It is essential to have some sort of story or message in mind. Even if the final video is only a minute long, it should have a beginning and an end. Having a middle is a good idea, too. A rocket taking off, releasing its boosters, and then disappearing into the sky? An egg rocking back and forth, then a chick leg breaking through the shell, then the chick popping out and making its first squeak?

Maya and many of its competitors use a live action, movie-making metaphor. In particular, rendering is done from the perspectives of cameras. So, you might want to break your story down into a series of scenes and within scenes create a series of rough drawings. One approach is to create an image that details the initial view of every rendering camera of every scene you plan on creating. You could draw them with any vector application or by hand. You might want to draw, in some detail, a preliminary version of your main character or model. You might well end up pulling this reference image into Maya as an aid for modeling. This technique will be discussed later.

A good, free drawing program is Autodesk SketchBook Express, which is available for both Mac and Windows machines. You can also paint with this program.

If you have never drawn before, a good way to create a drawing is top-down. If you are drawing a couch, start with a box, using light strokes. Then incrementally add the curves to the sofa, using slightly heavier strokes. Each object needs to take up the right amount of territory in the overall drawing, and as you add to the drawing, each object must be in the proper visual relationship with objects that are already in the scene. You might want to roughly sketch all the objects as boxes, and then incrementally add the curves that each object needs.

And remember that you are drawing in 2-space. Some objects will be partially hidden. That fits right in with 3D modeling, because ultimately, the renderer will do the same thing by not rendering hidden parts of a scene as it turns the 3D scene into a 2D image.

Also, when you are drawing "organic" objects, such as plants or critters, it's good to think in terms of smooth curves that do not jerk back and forth. If you are drawing the curves of a car or a human, be smooth, and don't use any more curves than you absolutely need. This will make it easier to later model these curves with Maya. (And yes, a car is in many ways an organic object.)

2. Maya

Follow the arrow from phase 1 to phase 2. It's all about Maya. The details of this box will be discussed shortly; for now, we see that there are two basic roles that outside applications have. They can supply input to Maya or they can work with what comes out of Maya.

Importing into Maya   In particular, consider the four purple boxes at the top of Figure 1.1. There are a few types of applications that are often used to take on some of the modeling chores. Some animators prefer applications that have the feel of crafting a model almost as if it were clay; these include Pixologic's ZBrush and Autodesk Mudbox. These applications are commonly used for crafting organic characters.

There are also basic modeling applications that are simpler to learn and use than Maya. Nevercenter's Silo 3D is a clean, elegant subdivision modeler. SketchUp is extremely popular and is used heavily to create polygon models of human-made, angular things like buildings and furniture. Another one is FormZ's Bonzai. But again, we will do all our modeling in this book with Maya.

Poser is sometimes used to create bipeds and quadrupeds for importing into Maya. A popular program is Daz Studio; its human models are very detailed and lifelike. Daz Studio characters can be carefully individualized via the many (and easy to use) controls available in the Daz Studio interface. Poser comes with a lot of canned content, and there is a lot of material for it available for sale on the Web. Daz content, for the most part, has to be purchased on their site and does not come free, but on average, Daz content is excellent and surprisingly cheap as well. Also, Poser can use most Daz models.

I discourage the use of these programs in introductory 3D classes; it's a much better idea to learn to build your own characters, even if they are very simple. Or better yet, start out with an interior or exterior architectural project and not with the daunting task of creating lifelike people. But tucking a human next to a towering building makes it clear that this is no ordinary hut. By the way, Daz 3D also sells a relatively inexpensive, full-blown modeling, texturing, animating, and rendering application called Carrara.

Vue and Terragen are two programs that can be used to quickly create outdoor, natural environments. There are a lot of premade, animated environments available for Vue but not much available for Terragen. Terragen is less powerful than Vue and the interface is rather unintuitive; but it is much cheaper.

Before deciding to use an application to create material to import into Maya, it is critical that you test that part of your workflow and make sure you can cleanly move a model from the given application into Maya. This can be tricky. There are two popular ways of doing this. Sometimes you'll find a plug-in for Maya; they exist for Poser and Vue, in particular, so that you can call these programs from within Maya. Or, you can explicitly export and import. This second option can produce varying results. OBJ is a common 3D modeling standard and has been around a long time, but it is best for moving only wireframes and textures. Autodesk's FBX is much newer and can move complete, animated models intact, but the results can be highly imperfect.

Finally, note the purple box with the word TEXTURE PREP in it. It is difficult to produce complex textures with Maya alone, and a good, inexpensive application that runs on a Mac is Pixelmator. Photoshop Elements is much cheaper than the Pro version of Photoshop and yet it is very powerful.

One other technique is to use drawings or photographs as reference images. Many modelers start with hand-drawn sketches.

Importing from Maya into Maya   Unless your scene is very simple, you will most likely use multiple scene files to create a single integrated scene for rendering purposes. Perhaps the environment (such as the interior of a room or a downtown street) will be built in one Maya scene. Then other scenes will be used to create props, like sofas and streetlights.

You can save Maya files as .ma (for Maya ASCII) files or .mb (for Maya binary). A critical difference is that Maya ASCII files consist of code in text form, while Maya binary files are not readable as text. Some animators use .mb as their primary file format because sometimes binary files open more quickly but use .ma files as periodic backups. .mb files, if they become corrupted, are almost impossible to fix, but .ma files can be edited. You would need to know Maya's scripting language or get help from someone who does. As a long-term recovery mechanism, when you make models that you might use in the future as props for other Maya projects you can keep .ma versions of them, so that when you go back to them months or years later, they can be fixed if they have been damaged.

It's also a good idea to "build in the large" by modeling individual scenes, props, and characters close up to make sure that if you end up rendering them just a tad closer than you thought you would, they will still look good. Do not let the need to rescale an object when you import it stop you from modeling it in the best fashion you can. But do avoid having to rescale a model upward so much that previously unseen details suddenly loom large. By the way, Maya allows one to assign precise units to models to avoid imprecise rescaling. But this is beyond the scope of this book.

3. Soundtracks

There are two general classes of audio applications: (1) basic sound or "wave" editors, and (2) digital audio workstations (DAWs). DAWs are far more sophisticated and are used by musicians and sound engineers to blend multiple tracks, to program software instruments (as plug-ins to DAWs), and to inject special sound effects into music and soundtracks (also via plug-ins to DAWs).

Wave editors are sometimes limited to two tracks, which is all that is needed for a basic Maya project. They are geared toward editing and combining audio segments. Many audio editors support the same kind of plug-ins used in DAWs, and in particular, plug-ins that can clean sound are used frequently. Names to look for are iZotope and Wave Arts. The two most popular formats for plug-ins are VST (Virtual Studio Technology) and AU (Audio Units). Steinberg invented the VST standard. Steinberg produces a nice sound editor called WaveLab, and there is a reasonably cheap low-end version of this editor. Apple introduced the AU standard.

Maya can be used to sync sound with animation in Maya; this will be discussed later in the book. But the soundtrack must be created and edited outside Maya. I often tell my students to let the sound drive the animation, so you don't get caught up in making detailed edits of soundtrack segments. Sometimes it's best to just find a nice piece of music and time the action in your video to coincide to rises in amplitude in the sound (something that wave editors display visually).

Audacity is the best deal out there in free audio editing software. It is quite powerful and relatively easy to learn. It runs on Windows and Apple machines. Amadeus is a Mac application that is reasonably cheap and very nice. DSP Quattro is a full-blown professional editor but is surprisingly cheap given what it does. WavePad is very basic but easy to use and does not cost much.

Note: When you import your sound into Maya for timing with your animation, it must be in either AIF or WAV format. Also, if you are looking for special effects sounds (like a gun going off) to insert into your soundtrack, try audiomicro.com.

One of the nicest things about Audacity is that it has a native tool that can be used to clean sound of background noise. Since those of us doing super-low-budget animation projects cannot afford high-end microphones or professional sound studios, this can be an extremely valuable tool. Vendors of sound wave editors invariably make available at least one VST or AU plug-in with this capability but usually you have to pay extra for them.

To use a typical sound cleaning plug-in, place a microphone in a position to record your voice, a door closing, or whatever other sound you are capturing. But before you begin recording the sound you want, you record silence—which of course is not really silence. It is likely filled with rumbling sounds from a furnace or A/C, or the hum of computer fans, and so on. Then after you make the recording of your voice or sound effect, you tell the wave editor to take the sounds that are in the "silence" fragment and to remove the background noise in it from your entire recording.

4. Video

Maya renders images, not entire video segments. The images must be turned into video segments by a video editor. The soundtrack must be also imported into a video editor, so that the video editor can export a video with the sound properly synched. Within the video editor you are likely to also cut and paste various video segments rendered at different times.

Generally, you will want to use thirty frames per second when you render in Maya. You might need to change settings inside your video editor to match, so that it generates a video that uses the exact same frame rate as that used by Maya to generate individual images. If you try to make movements in a scene look faster by speeding up the frame rate within the video editor, your action will not look faster—it will look bad. The same is true for trying to slow action by having the video editor use individual images at a slower rate than they were generated within Maya. You should adjust the speed of your animation in Maya; get the timing right before you render individual images. Do not try to shortcut the process by changing the timing of your animation with the video editor—unless you are a pro and you really know what you are doing.

Adobe Premiere Elements is much cheaper than the Pro version of Premiere, and, like Photoshop Elements, it is very powerful. Another alternative is Lightworks; at the time of this writing, there is a Windows version with the planned release of a Mac version soon. Lightworks comes in a free and a paid (but inexpensive) version. One caveat: I have had multiple students tell me that it has an idiosyncratic interface.

5. Deploying Your Video

The last phase in the workflow diagram is deployment. You may simply want to burn a DVD with your video on it or upload it to Vimeo.com. There are a number of DVD burning applications out there; Roxio and Nero make popular commercial applications. There are also a lot of free applications for burning both playable and data discs.

Inside Maya

The blue ovals in the Maya box in Figure 1.1 represent the three core stages of creating an animated video: modeling, animating, and rendering.

The instruction in the circle is a reminder to create named versions of your .mb or .ma files frequently. Putting an integer in the name is best, so that you know the order in which they were made. This will facilitate going back to the latest correct version when you decide your model has become a mess, and this will happen with virtually all of your initial attempts to build anything nontrivial.

The black "test render" ovals are a reminder to test the interaction of your models, lights, and materials. All the black ovals are meant to underscore the relationship between materials and lighting, and the fact that we do not truly know what something will look like until we do a test render. Nothing can be seen until light hits the surfaces of your models.

The purple ovals describe three items that are particularly critical during the animation and rendering phases. Dynamics is a powerful form of modeling and animation that can radically increase render time. Also, rendering is done from the perspective of cameras, and cameras can themselves be animated. It has already been mentioned that audio and movement must be synched in Maya before being imported into your video editor.

Other Application Needs

Finally, you might find that your various applications conflict when it comes to media formats. So you might need a video format converter, an audio format converter, and/or an image converter. Be careful with audio and video converters. You need to check their output; sometimes these applications produce terrible results. I tend to use products made by Xilisoft.

WORKING WITH PREFAB CONTENT

Although the focus of this book will be on a "do-it-yourself from the ground up" approach to learning how to create, animate, and render 3D scenes, many animators use a class of applications that were once considered only for "hobbyists" but have been slowly emerging as tools suitable for professionals. They provide canned content that can be tailored and greatly abbreviate the time needed to put an animated scene together. As mentioned earlier, Poser and Daz 3D are the two most prominent vendors of inexpensive character content (and to a lesser extent, indoor/outdoor scene content), but there are a significant number of online stores that are not associated with any specific application and sell only content.

THE CABANA OF COOL CONCEPTS

Since the book is organized around a series of tutorials, the reader will have the satisfaction of starting to build models quickly and seeing what they look like when they are rendered.

Simple but complete Maya models will be built from the get-go. The tutorials will also return to various models and scenes and add to them.

There is another reason for proceeding in this example-driven way. Given the breadth and depth of the knowledge needed to learn 3D animation skills, it simply is not tractable to learn its basic concepts in a purely abstract setting. It is also true that the massiveness of the Maya interface needs to be introduced gradually.

The tutorials will specify precisely how to perform a wide array of tasks in Maya, and they will almost always explain why the tasks are being performed. Basic concepts will be explored in more depth as new material is presented.

It is necessary to develop a top-down view of the 3D animation world to eventually go beyond what is covered in this book. And so, in Chapter 16, the concepts that have been covered in the first fifteen chapters will be pulled together. A metaphor of a giant cabana is used to view this collected, organized body of concepts. Since reading abstract material—when the concepts they cover have already been seen in action—is a lot less painstaking than following the detailed tutorials step by step, the cabana will be viewed as a relaxing place we can go to at the end of the book.

The contents of the cabana should really be independent of any particular animation application. However, realistically, it is impossible to avoid a bias toward the way things are done with Maya; otherwise, the knowledge would be too abstract to absorb. Luckily, Maya is the industrial standard of the 3D world, and most of its competitors view the 3D world similarly to how Maya views it.

THE SMALL SUBSET APPROACH TO LEARNING 3D ANIMATION

Although Maya and its competitors are highly complex programs that take many years to learn, complete projects can be created with just a small subset of Maya's capabilities. In two of the charts in Chapter 17, suggested collections of core tools are presented.

Every Animation App Is Unique

Every 3D application has its unique capabilities and its own user interface idiosyncrasies. It's not a good idea to attack a new application by trying to find a way to get it to do exactly what you have done in an application with which you are already familiar. You have to be willing to invest the time in learning the unique aspects of a new application. Sometimes it is as simple as a given application supporting different kinds of lights or materials. Sometimes the difference is more fundamental and you need to be deliberately unbiased, so that you get the most out of every application you use.

HOW TO USE THIS BOOK

The tutorial-driven organization of Chapters 3 through 15 is well suited to students working inside or outside the classroom. It is strongly advised that students do not simply read these examples. Rather, students should be using Maya to follow the tutorials. There is something about the hand and eye aspects of using a complex application that can only be learned while doing. However, small mistakes on the part of the student, a minor change in the Maya preferences, or a small change to the Maya interface introduced by a new release of the application can completely stall a student. Rather than spinning one's wheels and getting frustrated when this happens, students should move on to the next example.

To the instructor: I have often stepped through these tutorials with my students in class. I teach in a laboratory setting where every student has a computer running Maya right in front of them. Students should be encouraged to install the free version of Maya and bring their machines to class.

The top-down coverage of major topics presented in Chapter 16 should give the instructor all that is needed to engineer a classroom experience that is a solid blend of example-driven and conceptual material. I recommend that the instructor who is not highly experienced in using an application like Maya start by reading Chapter 16.

Finally, as students go through the book mimicking the tutorials they should not feel they have to necessarily produce work of high artistic quality; getting through the examples with reasonable success is the only aim. Skill comes later, with repetition and patience. Incrementally, students will learn how to use Maya's tools in creative ways.

PREREQUISITES

This book is for anyone who wants to learn 3D animation. Students do not need a background in computer science, media arts, or mathematics. There is a minor use of scripting in Chapter 11 using the "Maya Embedded Language" (MEL). Even students who have never seen programming code before should be able to easily understand this material.

CONTENTS OF THIS BOOK

A quick overview of what is covered in each chapter follows. Although many of the terms will be unfamiliar to the new animator, the descriptions should help with using the book for guidance later.

Section I

In Chapter 2, the overall process of creating an animated project is introduced. We also examine the complex user interface of Maya as well as the basic types of 3D modeling supported in Maya: polygon and NURBS. The three critical operations of translate, scale, and rotate are introduced.

The basics of modeling, important terminology, and rendering are the main topics of Chapter 3. Students get started with the basics of NURBS and polygon modeling by building a glass bowl with NURBS, a hand with an index finger using polygon geometry, and a simple cactus using NURBS modeling. The need to add detail very carefully to a model is discussed. The process of rendering using raytracing, the two primary renderers available within Maya, and ways to enhance lighting, the importance of rooting objects in scenes by using shadows are all covered in Chapter 3, as well. We take a quick look at sculpting 3D models in Maya.

In Chapter 4, the focus is on further exploring the basics of NURBS and polygon modeling. First, a critical aspect of 3D modeling and animation is introduced: using hierarchies to control the unified movement of complex models. To illustrate this, the glass bowl gets some sorbet added to it and a walking cow cocks his baseball cap to the side. Then polygon modeling is explored in more detail by building a mailbox. The use of polygon modeling to create 3D writing is illustrated with our cow. After this a detailed polygon example consisting of building a Moai statue is presented. We also look at a critical issue for polygon modelers: ways to make an angular polygon model smooth. A handful of tools that can be used to clean up small problems with emerging models are covered. Finally, NURBS modeling is used to build the beginnings of a breadbox. As we go through these tutorials, we will begin to look at the task of putting materials on models.

Chapter 5 focuses largely on placing materials on models and on the various sorts of lights supported in Maya. First, we varnish a wood table. Then we look at lights in Maya and the two main ways in which Maya lights can cast shadows. After this, we construct a street and sidewalk scene out of cement and blacktop; we use this example to look at creating 3D objects using Maya's painting tool. Then we turn to the critical concept of prepping textures: we use an outside image editor to create a layered texture; after this, we take a quick look at the native capability within Maya to create layered textures. We look at a major distinction in Maya, and that is the difference between projection textures and normal textures. Then we tile a texture for our cactus. We create two stairs using NURBS modeling, connect the two stairs to the vertical face between them and carpet them. We show one way to ensure that an object's texture does not slip away from the object when it is moved. Finally, we build a simple ice rink out of multiple layers of polygon geometry so that we can experiment with creating a texture that looks like ice.

Particle dynamics and particle emitters are introduced in Chapter 6. As we do this, we build complete models and put textures on them, and animate some of our models. We start with a simple rocket and use a ramp shader to color the hardware particles that make up the rocket exhaust. We create a box of cold cereal and pour the Trix into a bowl to study software particles. Then we turn to the powerful capability of turning a polygon object into a dynamics effect as a way of creating cloth. To illustrate this, we make a Colorado flag flap in the wind—wind made by Maya. We wrap up Chapter 6 by returning to hardware particles to create a rainstorm.

Animating models is the main topic of Chapter 7. First, a can of Spam flies along a motion path and glides into the mailbox built in Chapter 5. The important topic of key-framing the action in a scene is covered; to illustrate this a camera is animated and we ride along as it follows a meandering river. Then we look at Maya's graph editor and create a simple movement cycle; we use the graph editor to iteratively repeat the cycle. Last, the topic of animating models by using skeletons is introduced; we build a simple leg and look at the two main ways to animate a skeleton. We distinguish between forward kinematics (FK) and inverse kinematics (IK).

Chapter 8 discusses some tools that can be used for both modeling and animation purposes by shattering the surface of an egg, and then using a blend shape to morph a tiny bird leg as a chick tries to break its way out. Then, we look at an alternate way to surface an object. Rather than using a material or a texture, we put Maya fur on the head of a character, add some Maya hair, then make use of Maya's ability to animate hair and to transfer this movement to the fur. After this, we examine another technique that spans both modeling and animation by using a bend deformer to roll up the cover of a swimming pool. We wrap up by using three different deformers: one to twist a piece of wood, another to squash a ball, and a third to damage our mailbox.

Chapter 9 returns to materials, and in particular, how to work with a texture (our cactus texture) without the seams between the tiles being too obvious. We look at how a seam-lessly tileable texture can be created by using Maya's painting tool. Three different ways of modeling a glass bottle will be compared. Next, we build a scene with a fluid pouring from a glass bottle into a drinking glass, and then we render it in a way that creates a sort of 2D effect. Last, there is a return to the street scene from Chapter 6 to add some nighttime fog, along with a pair of approaching headlights, built by making objects emit light—a power-ful way of introducing light into a scene.

Chapter 10 is dedicated mostly to a single example scene. We construct a closet, paint it white, and give it frosted glass doors. Moving the pivot point of a door to enable its proper movement is discussed, and we examine the notion of a bounding box and how every object in 3-space has one. We look at one of the key operations that an animator uses while building a model: how to add detailed geometry. Then, we return to the topic of making cloth by creating a shirt and placing it on a hanger inside the closet. To make sure it hangs properly, constraints are used to bind the shirt to the hanger, the hanger is turned into a passive collider, and gravity is used to pull the shirt downward. We create a camera for the closet scene and use an aim constraint to keep the camera focused on the closet, even as the camera moves. A simple soundtrack of the doors closing is synced to the motion of the doors. The important topic of generating multiple frames by using Maya's batch rendering capabilities is discussed. We return briefly to the graph editor in Maya to tailor the motion of one of the closet's doors. fcheck, Maya's utility for quickly creating test videos, is presented. The linking of lights to specific objects in a scene is discussed. The three-light paradigm inspired by the way film crews place lights while recording live action is presented.

Chapter 11 returns to animation, in particular, to the complex topic of creating skeletons to drive the movement of a living creature, as well as ways to both enable and limit the movement of an IK skeleton. A second major animation topic is introduced: collisions between rigid and/or soft objects. Specifically, a full human skeleton is generated and put inside a simple biped; we learn to use IK handles and effectors to move the skeleton in a natural way. An anime character from the Daz Studio application is bound to this skeleton. This character serves as a vehicle for learning how to insert solid objects under the skin of a character so that its limbs will bend naturally. A few other techniques for animating skeletons are examined, including the use of an aim constraint so that a character will follow a moving object, pinning and unpinning the feet of a character, and using Maya's sticky construct to limit the movement of a limb. Then we turn to the animation of rigid objects by animating a bowling ball and a few pins. The Moai from Chapter 4 is resurrected and the process of making it turn transparent is animated. Maya's scripting language, MEL, is used to animate the knobs on our closet door, create randomly flashing lights, and stretch a ball while it moves under the influence of gravity. Some aspects of MEL are briefly considered. We wrap up by using cloth to animate the movement of water.

Chapter 12 looks at some techniques for creating materials and placing them on models. Students create a cow and make it look 2D by using a specialized material provided by Maya. Some graffiti is spray-painted on a brick wall. Next, we make our last visit to the street scene from Chapter 5 to build a daytime horizon and sky, and then render it with what is arguably the better of two raytracing renderers in Maya—mental ray. We examine a powerful tool for speeding up the rendering process by baking a material on an object. We end by making our own, homemade, sky dome.

Chapter 13 focuses on the UV Texture Editor in Maya—a powerful facility for recasting the grid on the surface of an object so that it can be properly textured. We go back to the doorknobs from Chapter 11 and improve the material on the knobs by using the UV Texture Editor. Then we look at a few special ways that Maya can help animators improve the placement of materials.

In Chapter 14, the common problem of using multiple applications in a single workflow is examined, in particular, how to exploit plug-ins to support the use of other applications while working in Maya. These applications include ones that create natural terrains, create

3D characters, and sculpt organic models. And we look at the more limited sculpting capabilities of Maya. We also look at the use of second-party renderers via plug-ins. We examine the common need to minimize the number of polynomials on the surface of a polygon object so that it can be rendered quickly.

In Chapter 15, we look at a handful of special topics involving lights and materials. These include ambient occlusion, global illumination and final gathering, caustics, irradiance, using light to color glass, anisotropy, the penumbra and dropoff of a light, depth map and raytrace shadows, altering the resolution of shadows, and the mental ray sun and sky.

Section II

Chapter 16 covers the construction of the cabana, reuse as a tool for more quickly constructing scenes, the need for reference images, modeling and texturing with animation in mind, and the use of prefab content, in particular, characters. Also discussed is motion capture data for animating humans.

Chapter 17 contains a series of concise charts that distills the concepts and terms that we have studied in this book.

A MOTIVATIONAL EXAMPLE

To get started, we will look at a simple but fully fleshed out scene. The construction of this scene is fully within the abilities of anyone who has studied this book. The goal is to get an intuitive feel for what makes up a 3D scene. In the last chapter, we will return to the scene and discuss how to build it.

In Figure 1.2, we see what appears to be a poolside scene. Our eyes do not immediately go to the water, though. They focus on the large, boxy structure, with its shiny gold arches. We also quickly see the pattern in the blue material that makes up the front wall of the structure. We see pillars. Maybe we see the water next. Then we notice the contents of the structure: there are people in the scene. We take in the larger scene, the tiled ground,

FIGURE 1.2 **(See p. CI-2 of Color Insert)** The cabana with gold metallic arches.

the brick wall, the palm trees, and the sky beyond. Maybe we do not consciously realize that the coloring of the sky gives us the feel of warmth, and the apparent angle of the sunlight makes us think of sunset—the people are probably not there at sunrise. We see that the people are dressed casually. We might even notice that the girl is wearing a dress with a fatigue pattern on it. The other two characters are taller and might have gray hair. It all makes sense.

But unless we grew up on the Atlantic coast or have a habit of vacationing in fancy resorts, we have never seen a cabana. We have heard of them, of course. But if that's what this is, it's a bit over the top. It's huge and ostentatious. It certainly does not provide these people with privacy, but it does give them shade. They are probably on vacation. This cabana could indeed belong to a resort. The accompanying hotel is probably vast and ornate.

Let's break this down.

1. First, it is a complete scene. An "environment," as animators might call it, with an architectural model serving as the focus of the scene. It is fleshed out. This is important. What we are seeing is complete and very visual. The scene makes a strong impression on us. It's vibrant.

2. The structure is exotic. But the scene as a whole fits into our understanding of the world around us. It is grounded in reality but has its own unique look and feel.

3. There appears to be only one source of light—the sun. It seems to be low in the sky, and, ignoring the overall context of the scene, this suggests that the sun is just now rising or setting. The tall shadows of the two characters in the left half of the cabana also indicate that the sun is low in the sky. But on closer examination, there is something odd about the lighting in the scene. The overall scene is cast in soft shadows, but there are pronounced shadows of the man and child on the interior wall of the cabana. Why are they there? Without these shadows, the people in the cabana would appear to be floating in air. A tough choice has been made: a modest secondary light source has been introduced to enhance the shadows inside the cabana. The size of the rendering might make it difficult to detect this, but the table and chairs and the woman are also casting shadows created by this secondary light.

4. The reflections of the gold arches and furniture are bright, and they add a little majesty to the scene. All in all, the lights, shadows, and reflections give us a strong sense of depth. Also, the shadows don't blur together; we can tell exactly what object is creating each shadow.

5. We may wonder how the cabana is supported. The modeler has tried to suggest that it is structurally sound by showing us the internal wood walls and support beams.

6. The patterned material seems to be cloth. The cloth has some smooth curves where it comes down below the golden arches. This is fitting with our cabana concept. But the four corners of its roof are awfully sharp for something made out of cloth and held up with wood slats.

7. The scene is very pristine. We assume it was built the day before yesterday and these folks are the first guests to ever check into the luxury resort hotel. That's okay if we are going for a certain dramatic look and not trying to be too realistic. We could consider adding a bit of what animators call a "grunge" look, by dirtying up the tiles and the brick wall. The carpet inside the cabana must need nonstop maintenance, since it is exposed to the elements.

8. The placement of humans in the scene gives us an immediate, intuitive feel for just how large this structure is. Everything seems in proportion, including the potted plants, wall, and gate.

9. The scene has some character to it. It tells a story. This could be a family on vacation in an exotic locale.

So, that's our analysis. It highlights some of the things we need to keep in mind as we build animated scenes with Maya. Because this is an introductory book, we will be focusing on smaller parts of scenes, things that make up individual models, such as metal tables and pieces of clothing. But we will return to the cabana at the end of this book.

Before we continue, there are a few other things worth noting about the cabana scene:

1. The cabana's cloth is a dark color, so that the whitish pillars will stand out against the cloth.

2. The people are variations of stock characters from the Daz site, so we don't get any modeling credit for them. But nothing is wrong with plugging in prefab components, as long as they fit in style and nature in the environment in which we place them. The palm trees, potted plants, chairs, and table are also canned items from the Daz site. Most of them have had their textures changed, but they are actual geometry, not just images.

3. The geometry of this scene is actually simple. It is easy to model, and we'll realize this soon enough as we begin to look at 3D modeling.

4. The brick wall is just an image on a flat plane. It would not render nicely if we got close to it; but as something in the background, it is realistic enough. Likewise, the pillars have little sculpted or etched "geometry" to them, but there is an image pattern projected on them to give them a classical look. In general, what makes the scene are the "materials" in it, and some of them are quite detailed. There is a critical trade-off, though: using image textures (as materials on objects) to create the illusion of geometry is in general a quick thing to do. But a much more realistic effect can be obtained by creating true, detailed geometry.

5. The water is not geometry, either, and is simply two layered images. The one on top has a ripple painted on it and is very transparent. The bottom one has an almost-neon green color that shows through the upper, transparent layer. A casual observer might not guess at how this was done; the critical point is that this water is not animated.

FIGURE 1.3 **(See p. CI-2 of Color Insert)** The cabana with stone arches. (The cabana with yellow arches appears on the cover.)

6. Look at Figure 1.3. The only change is that the golden arches are now stone. Apparently, the artist is a sort of inverse alchemist. But more seriously, we see that indeed, materials are everything when it comes to recognizing the nature of things we see in a scene. The exact same geometric object can easily be made to look like gold or stone.

ART AND ENGINEERING

3D animation sits at the crossroads of art and engineering. It demands that the animator have strong analytic skills. Objects must be carefully built, oriented, and animated in 3-space with respect to the scene and to other objects in a scene. Some aspects of animation are best done with scripting code, and a strong intuitive sense of physics is needed in order to provide natural looking movement, deformation and collisions of objects, and particle emission and collision. In comparison to 2D animation, where the primary required skill is drawing, some forms of 3D modeling, such as constructing the exterior and interior of buildings, call for talents closer to CAD than free-form drawing. But even though 3D animation has a strong engineering aspect to it, you'll also have to develop your own voice as an animation artist.

Above all else, you must keep in mind that you are trying to convey a message, whether your video is one minute long or three hours long. Something must transpire between the first and the last frame.

It is also true that applications like Maya are used to make single-frame renderings without any animation, and even then, there is a message. You might create a model of a modern kitchen with the goal of making it look so real and so inviting that the viewer must have it.

A FINAL NOTE

Don't worry about the massiveness of Maya. A primary goal of this book is to carefully carve out a slice of Maya so that you can quickly get started making complete animated projects.

I

CHAPTER 2

The Maya Interface and Modeling Concepts in Maya

I N THIS CHAPTER, we take a quick look at the Maya interface. We consider the two primary ways you can model in Maya (and in many other 3D animation and modeling applications) and how 3D models are represented inside an application like Maya. Then we examine the core concepts that underlie the process of incrementally crafting a 3D model.

The Maya interface can be tailored. But changing default settings can have subtle and unexpected consequences. So, we will use Maya almost entirely with its default settings. This will help ensure that the examples in the book will behave the same way when you go through them on your Maya installation.

THE 3D WORLD OF MODELING AND ANIMATION

Within most 3D graphics applications, there are multiple coordinate systems you must keep in mind.

The first is the global (x, y, z) space; Maya calls this the *world space*, and its origin (0, 0, 0) is at the center of the Maya grid space.

The second is the (x, y, z) space of any given object within the global space; Maya calls this *object space*. We differentiate between these two so that we can manipulate 3D objects independently of where they are in the global space. The object space has an origin (0, 0, 0) associated with that object. It might be easy enough to guess where the origin is when the object is a cube or a sphere. But if an object is heavily morphed, it can become difficult to guess where Maya might be placing the origin.

There is a third (x, y, z) space assigned to each object. This is called *local space*, and it allows us to put objects in hierarchies and to use these hierarchies to control the movement of multiple, related objects. The local space of an object is the object space of its immediate parent in the hierarchy. Thus, an object can move independently, but it is also bound by the movement of its parent. So, we might have a car that has four wheels, and so we "parent" the wheels to the car meaning that the wheels are children of the car. We could use object space to make a given wheel rotate while the car is moving in a straight line. But if the car turns a corner, we need the wheel to move with the car; local space will make sure this happens.

There is also a completely different space, and it has only two dimensions. We call this *(u, v) space* and it refers to the surfaces of objects. For any given 3D object, we can assign its surface a (u, v) grid that we can then use to manipulate properties of the surface of that object. This is straightforward enough to visualize when considering a freshly made cube that has not been morphed yet. But, as we will see later, an object that has been heavily morphed can end up with a highly irregularly spaced (u, v) grid. It then becomes a little difficult to place a material on its surface and have that material look even; parts of it will be stretched thinner than other parts. Sometimes we choose to completely reassign a new (u, v) grid to the object before we put materials on it.

SEEING THE 3D WORLD THROUGH THE EYES OF MAYA

The reason this book focuses on Autodesk Maya is because it provides a broad set of capabilities and is also arguably the most important single application for the aspiring animator to learn. We need to keep in mind, though, that like most complex media applications, Maya provides a large set of tools but does not specify how to use these tools methodologically to get a job done. Nor does Maya guide the animator through the process of navigating its interface. Therefore, we will pursue both of these goals: learning the conceptual process of building an animated project with Maya, as well as becoming comfortable with its interface.

A Warning: The Maya Interface Can Be Intimidating, Don't Be Dispirited

Autodesk Maya is a true mega-app. The menu system of Maya dwarfs the famously inscrutable interface of Adobe Photoshop in its size and complexity. So, if you have no experience with 3D modeling and animation applications, Maya can be intimidating at first.

Luckily, given the goals of any particular animated project, there are many ways to get the job done with Maya. So, much of learning Maya lies in developing a familiarity with whatever set of tools in Maya fits your style and gets the job done. This means that an animator can be creating complete animated projects with Maya long before mastering its interface. That's what we'll do in this book—focus on the paths through Maya's interface that take us to a small, core subset of its critical capabilities that can be used to construct full 3D animations.

Also, there is a large set of shortcuts that can be used in Maya. These help to minimize keystrokes and shorten the distance your mouse has to travel to perform a series of tasks. Because we are focusing on basic skills, only a handful of these shortcuts will be presented. It is better for a beginner to learn how to properly use a sophisticated tool rather than to focus on how to use it quickly. Sometimes, forced patience leads to better results.

One important shortcut, however, is Control+Z. This undoes the previous operation. Maya maintains a huge undo stack, and the beginning animator will make heavy use of it. By the way, the undo stack in Maya works quite well, but it is dangerous to rely on it.

The Main Window

Figure 2.1 shows the Main Window in the Maya interface. The place to start is a small dropdown menu on the upper left of the window. This is the Main Menu Selector and right now it is set to "Surfaces." When you change the selection, some of the Main Menu items at the top of the screen will change. There is a rough correspondence between the value of the Main Menu Selector and the phase of the overall process of building an animated project in Maya. But the items at the left end of the Main Menu tend not to change (File, Edit, etc.).

It's time now to introduce a few formal words we will be using. *Tools* are the basic operations that can be used to craft an animated project in Maya. Maya also has its own database system and we use the word *object* to refer to any basic data item stored in its database. The properties of objects are called *attributes*. Not all objects correspond to things that are directly rendered. Maya manages many abstract objects, such as the assignment of a material to the surface of an object.

There are a few places in the Maya interface where shortcuts to various capabilities can be found. Some of the most heavily used are on the Shelf Tabs near the top of the Main

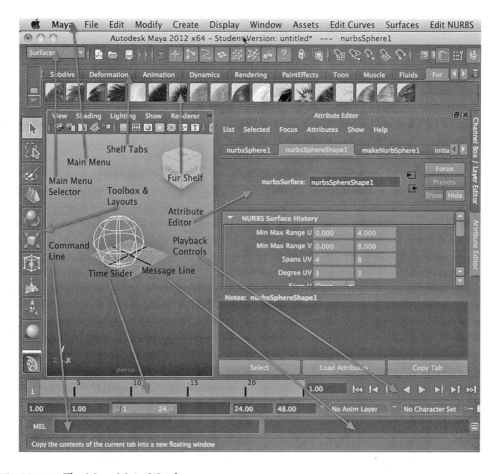

FIGURE 2.1 The Maya Main Window.

Window. By clicking on a tab, such as Fur, as seen in Figure 2.1, a number of options pop up. The Shelf Tabs are a way to quickly access tools that you otherwise would have to access by going up to the very top of the screen, clicking on menu items on the Main Menu, and choosing tools that appear in those dropdowns.

Some even more important shortcuts are on the left of the Main Window. There are two sets of them. The first is the Toolbox, which provides quick access to the Move (or translate), Rotate, and Scale tools, which are extremely heavily used in Maya. Below these shortcuts are layout choices, which are not shown in Figure 2.1. In the figure, the layout that is displayed shows the design area in the Main Window. We see a sphere. When using Maya, the animator will often break this area into four views, so that the developing scene can be simultaneously viewed from multiple perspectives.

That sphere in the design area is an object. The attributes of it are in the Attribute Editor (sometimes referred to informally as the Attribute Box), directly to the right of the sphere. Down below are four key areas. The lower left is home to the Command Line box, where scripting code can be entered. Right now, it is set to MEL, the Maya Embedded Language. Maya also supports Python scripting. Above the Command Line box is the Time Slider, which shows a series of frames. Twenty-five are showing; that's about a second's worth of animation. To the right of the Time Slider are the Playback Controls, which can be used to create and preview the motion in your scene, what we call the animation. Below the Playback Controls is the Message Line, where Maya provides various forms of feedback. It's a good idea to keep an eye on that box: if it turns red, it's bad news.

Figure 2.2 shows the Channel Box, which is more formally called the Channel Editor. You can toggle between it and the Attribute Editor with Control+A. The Channel Editor contains attributes of the object selected (the sphere) that can be used to animate the object. For example, we see that we can translate (or move), rotate, and rescale the sphere from frame to frame over the course of the animation.

A Note on Changing Geometry Modes

When we are working with Maya, we can select an object (such as the sphere in Figure 2.1) with a left click, and then right click. A menu called the Marking Menu then pops up. This lets us carefully control the way in which we manipulate an object. If the model is made of polygon geometry, the geometric modes include Edge, Vertex, Face, and Object. This is important: When we manipulate the sphere in Figure 2.1, the mode we are in will dramatically impact the sort of changes we make to the sphere.

Later, we will consider the mode choices that appear when we right click on a NURBS object.

The Hypershade

Figure 2.3 shows the second most frequently used window in Maya. It is the Hypershade. This is where we create materials and textures, and then assign them to objects. For now, we will only take a quick look at it. The left half of the window shows a number of materials and textures that we can put on objects. We can also create lights and other objects in this window. The right side of the window has a series of tabs. Right now, the Materials tab is selected. Below it is a box that is currently empty; we can use this area to carefully examine

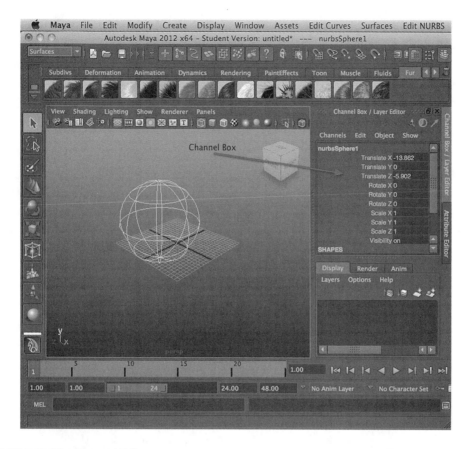

FIGURE 2.2   The Channel Editor.

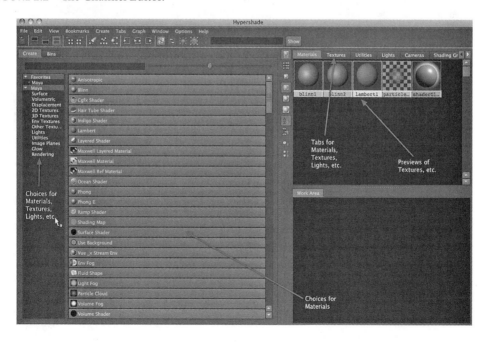

FIGURE 2.3   The Hypershade.

and control the way materials, textures, and other things are interconnected and assigned to objects like our sphere.

The name Hypershade, by the way, comes from "shader," which is another name for a material. In fact, shader is the more generic, commonly used term. A material can be complex. A "texture" is a simpler thing; a texture can be part of a material.

An Object and Its Attributes

In Figure 2.4 we see an object, a sphere, along with its attributes. One of them is the red material that has been assigned to it. It's a Blinn material, which, in its initial form, is very shiny. Later, you might be surprised at just how many attributes an object can have. In order to accommodate this, the attribute box groups the attributes in sets, each one marked by a tab.

The Render View for Creating Single Render Tests

Figure 2.5 contains the Render View, the window we use to set up test renderings. This window is used very heavily while building an animated project. The "camera action" icon at the far upper left is the Render Button, which we click to create a single-frame render.

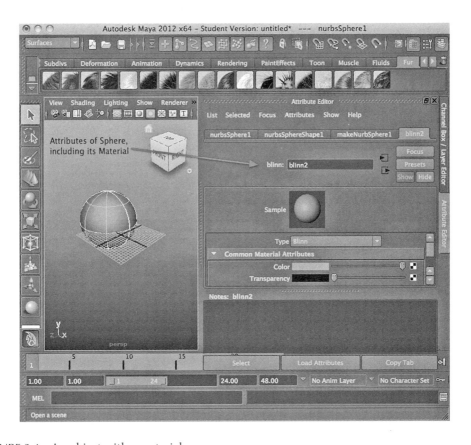

FIGURE 2.4   An object with a material.

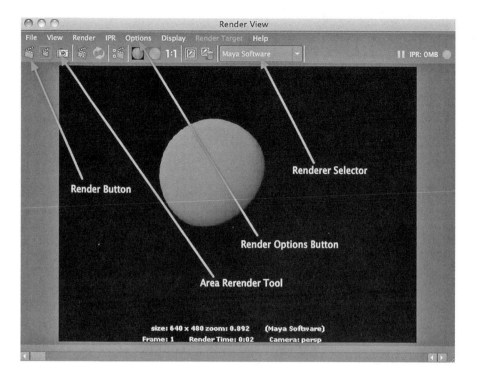

FIGURE 2.5   The Render View.

To the right of it is a similar icon, but with a red box (not evident in Figure 2.5) around it; this is the Area Rerender Tool. We use this to rerender a piece of a frame that has already been rendered and is showing in the Render View. Sometimes a frame takes a long time to render, and we only need to check out a piece of it to judge the effect of some change we have made.

The Renderer Selector is used to control the renderer that will be used. In Figure 2.5, the Maya Software renderer has been selected. We can also choose a renderer called mental ray (always written uncapped).

A number of other rendering settings can be changed by using the window that pops up when we select:

Options → Render Settings

In Figure 2.6, we see the settings. The left tab, Common, allows us to create settings that are independent of what renderer we are using. The right tab gives us access to settings that are renderer specific.

Notice that the second dropdown from the top is another way of choosing the renderer to use. This setting will always be the same as the setting chosen in the Render View.

The Render Format Selector lets us decide the format of the rendered frames. It is set to create the frame format that is used by Quicktime (.mov), the Apple video container standard. Below this is the dropdown that lets us control the naming of each frame ("name");

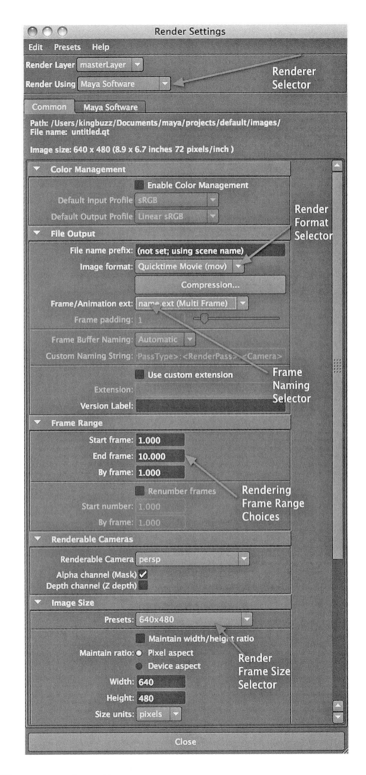

FIGURE 2.6   Common render options.

the ".ext" refers to the fact that the renderer will tack on the appropriate file format to each named frame.

Below that are settings that tell the renderer what frames to render. In this case, we have chosen to start with frame 1, end with frame 10, and do every single frame in between. Sometimes, we skip frames so we can quickly get an idea of how our rendering is going to look. To create a single-frame rendering, we can assign a 1 to all three settings in the Frame Range.

Renderings are always done from the perspective of a given camera. We have chosen "persp," the default camera provided by Maya.

Below that, we can set the pixel count—the resolution—of the rendered frame. It is set to 640 by 480 pixels, not very big but good for an animation that might be played on a notebook computer screen.

Figure 2.7 shows the Settings specific to the Maya Software renderer. We can set the Quality. The higher we set this, the better the individual frames, but the longer it will take to render. Low quality is what you would choose if you are just trying to see what the render will look like and you are not ready yet to create a production rendering.

Below this is a dropdown labeled Edge anti-aliasing. This is an important setting when it comes time to produce the set of frames that will make up our video. Anti-aliasing corrects the jagged edges around objects that we often see on renderings. The resolution of a rendered image might not be high enough to create edges that appear to be smooth, because any edge that is not perfectly horizontal or perfectly vertical will run at an angle across multiple rows of pixels. Anti-aliasing is a process that turns pixels along this jagged edge into colors that are in between the colors on the two sides of the edge. This causes us to see a sharp line.

Finally, notice that Raytracing is turned on. Raytracing is by far the most dominant technique used to render video, and it can create amazingly deep, detailed images. But raytracing can also demand a tremendous amount of CPU, GPU, and memory resources.

Render Settings and the Batch Renderer for Creating Multiframe Renderings for Video

For most of this book, we will be creating single-frame renders to examine our models. But in order to test the movement in a scene or to render a series of frames to create a final video, there are four things we need to do.

- First, we need to choose a naming setting (Frame/Animation ext) that has a pound sign (#) in it. This means that each image in the series of rendered images will have its sequence number embedded in its name. (To do a single-frame rendering, we choose a setting that does not have a # in it.)

- Second, we need to supply Frame Range settings where the End frame number is greater than the Start frame number. For a final rendering, we set the "By frame" number to 1.

- Third, we almost never want to use the default camera (persp), and so we need to change Renderable Camera to a camera that we have created. (Later we will create cameras.)

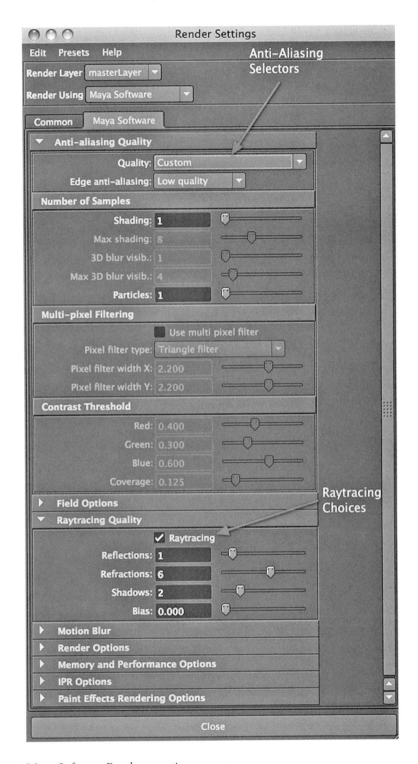

FIGURE 2.7   Maya Software Renderer options.

- Fourth, we must go to the Main menu at the top of the Maya interface and set the Menu Selector to Rendering. Then we choose:

- *Rendering Main Menu → Render → Batch Render*

This means that we will generate a series of renderings in "batch" mode.

How to Find Something in the Maya Interface

Here is a great way to look for something if you have forgotten where it is in the interface. Go to:

any Main Menu → Help → Resources and Tools → Find Menu

Then type in the name of the tool you are looking for or a word that appears in the name of that tool. This feature can prevent hours of frustration! By "any Main Menu," we mean that the Main Menu Selector can be set to any choice (Polygons, Animation, etc.).

Maya's Data Folders

When you install Maya, it creates a series of nested folders. The outermost one is called Maya. On both Mac and Windows machines, this is inside the Documents folder of some user. All of your working data for everything you do within Maya will be inside the Maya folder. This includes rendered images and textures. Only data that is not directly manipulated by Maya is outside this folder, and this includes soundtracks as well as videos that have been created from rendered images.

When you are creating a given 3D project, you will work inside a folder called projects, which is just inside the Maya folder. Both of these folders are created by Maya. The unit of working storage for the animator is the project, and within the projects folder Maya creates a folder called default, which refers to the default project. But you should get in the practice of creating your own project folders that are parallel to the default project folder—and not use the default one. To make sure you are always in the right place when Maya creates new data you should set your project each time you open up Maya. This is done by going to:

any Main Menu → File → Set Project

If you need to move your work from one machine to another, you need to move the entire named project folder (i.e., default, etc.). Also, there are times when you need to take files from outside Maya, in particular photographs used for textures, and use them within Maya; in these cases, the files must be placed somewhere in the Project folder or they will be lost if you ever move your project to a different machine. Losing texture images is an extremely common mistake.

While the larger unit of work within Maya is the project, the unit of modeling and animating is one level deeper in the Maya folder system. It is called the "scene," and scene files are located in a folder called scenes. Specifically, there is a folder named scenes inside every named project folder, and a project can have many scenes. There are also many other folders parallel to the scenes folder, which have names like "particles" and "images." Every time you save a scene file with a name, that file is saved inside the scenes folder.

A scene is the basic unit of work on which an animator focuses. When you look at the Maya Main Window, you are looking at the contents of one scene file, which is itself inside the folder called scenes. In other words, we work on scene files, not projects. The name of your project does not jump out at you, and so it is easy to make the mistake of putting a scene in the wrong project folder. Scene files end in .mb or .ma.

So for instance, we might have the following sequence of nested folders:

maya → projects → *les miserables* → scenes → *barricades.mb, inn.mb, prison.mb*

where the italicized words are names that you must create.

Finally, the rendered frames produced either by clicking on the "action render" icon on the top of the Render View window or by running the batch renderer will be automatically placed in the folder called "images" that will be inside the project folder.

Later, we will formalize a few notions relating to the projects, scenes, and models.

TWO KINDS OF MODELING IN MAYA

Maya's complexity goes way beyond the interface, especially when it comes to modeling. Much of this is because it offers multiple ways to get a given modeling job done. It supports two forms of 3D modeling—polygon and NURBS—and they are very different. In the Maya interface there are hundreds of modeling tools for each one.

A basic question is when to use polygon modeling and when to use NURBS modeling. It turns out that there are no rigid rules on when to use either of the two approaches. We'll suggest some subjective guidelines in this book, none of which are axiomatic. It's up to the beginner user to develop a personal style and workflow for using Maya.

Terminology

Let's cover a little more terminology. We have already covered Maya's notion of a project and a scene.

In Figure 2.4 the scene consists of a single unanimated sphere. If we stretched it out a bit, it might be an egg. Or we could turn it into an entire human being. We would probably call that egg or human a "model."

Consider Figure 2.8. This shows a window called the Outliner, and it can be found by going to:

any Main Menu → Window → Outliner

The Outliner helps us keep track of the structure of the contents of a scene. As it turns out, Maya does not actually have a formal notion of a model. It does have a semiformal notion of an "object," and objects are put into hierarchies. Generally speaking, each model is the root of some hierarchy in the Outliner. But other types of objects, for example, skeletons and materials, also appear in the Outliner.

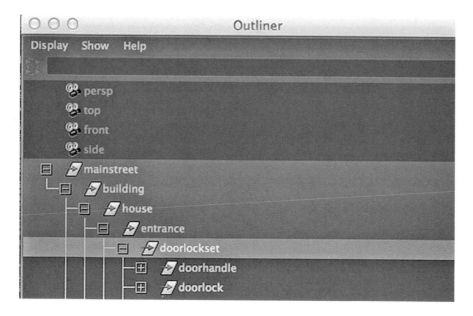

FIGURE 2.8 The Outliner window.

In the Outliner of Figure 2.8, we see that there is an object called mainstreet, and underneath it in the hierarchy is building, and within that, house, and so on. In Figure 2.8, we also see four default cameras that come with every scene. These cameras are objects, too.

The process of creating a model is called "modeling." When we create any kind of movement that takes place over a series of frames, we call this "animating." We can animate a scene by having a ball bounce over the course of some number of frames, or we might have the geometrical shape of the ball change over a series of frames because it is losing air. Or we might have both kinds of animation in a scene, as the ball squashes when it hits the ground. We can also animate a scene by having a camera wind along a country road; we might not have any other objects in the scene move.

We also use the term *animation* in a broader fashion to refer to the entire process of creating what will end up being an animated video.

In sum, the word *model* refers to an abstract notion inside the animator's head. The sphere is an object that might be the starting point of a human or an egg. In other words, an object, and not a model, is a specific thing that Maya keeps track of in its database. A model is an abstract thing that corresponds to whatever the animator is trying to build and then perhaps animate and ultimately render.

Meshes

We have all seen "wireframes" or "meshes" of objects, such as those in Figure 2.9. Consider the one in the upper left part of Figure 2.9, which can be completely specified by a set of points in 3-space, along with a list of the pairs of points that are connected by straight lines.

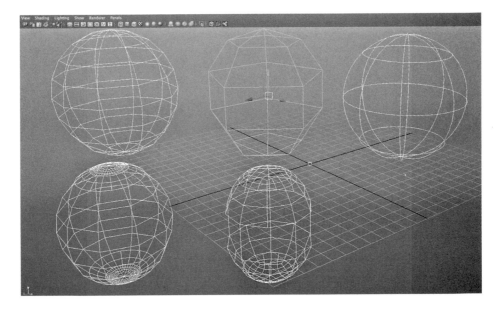

FIGURE 2.9   Polygons, NURBS, and subdivision.

(In Maya and in the animation world, we say vertex instead of point, and edge or curve instead of line.)

This is pretty impressive, because Maya does not need to store much data or perform any complex computations to keep track of the current state of a wireframe model. Basic wireframe modeling can usually be done even on a machine with a slow processor and not a lot of memory.

But underlying this simple mathematics is the assumption that we are creating a "polygon" object. This means that the object consists of a number of flat, 2D polygon "faces." The object in the upper left of Figure 2.9 will not look smooth when we put a material on it. The only way to make it look smooth is to increase the number of polygons until the sphere begins to look smooth to our eyes. Of course, the more polygons and the more vertices and edges, the more Maya has to keep track of as you craft your model.

Surface—And Not Solid—Modeling

Figure 2.10 shows the spheres with a Blinn material on them. In Maya, a model consists of a wireframe with an infinitely thin surface. In other words, the surface of a model is simply the properties that tell Maya how the model should look when light hits its surface. This is called "surface modeling."

But an engineer designing a bridge or a jet aircraft needs much more than that. Engineering design uses something called "solid modeling." This is necessary because engineers have to control the various properties of their models, such as thickness, cost, density, weight, and flexibility. It is also much easier to build a model using precise dimensions and angles with an engineering design application. While Maya is not an engineering

FIGURE 2.10   Polygons, NURBS, and subdivision—rendered.

design tool, you can indeed set the units of measurement. The way to do this in Maya is to go to:

any Main Menu → Window → Settings/Preferences → Preferences → Settings/Working Units

Vector versus Raster Graphics

Now, take another look at Figure 2.9. For now, ignore the two objects in the bottom row. Two of the spheres are polygon objects, chosen from:

any Main Menu → Create → Polygon Primitives → Sphere

But the one on the right was made using:

any Main Menu → Create → NURBS Primitives → Sphere

(In Maya, a "primitive" is a single, complete 3D object, like a sphere or a cube, that can be used as a starting point for a model.)

The sphere on the right in Figure 2.9 is made entirely out of curved lines. We cannot represent this model as a set of points with straight lines between them. We'll get back to this later, but for now we are going to step back and take a look at a critical distinction, and that is the difference between "vector" and "raster" graphics.

Vector graphics is what we use to specify wireframe models, regardless of whether they are models made entirely of straight lines, made entirely of curved lines, or are a hybrid of both. Vector graphics is line graphics. Often, vector images consist of lines with solid colors assigned to enclosed areas. Children's coloring books are vector based; they consist of lines, and the child typically fills each outlined region with a single color. We tend to make political maps in the same fashion, for example, Colorado is displayed as a rectangle filled with a single color.

Raster graphics, on the other hand, refers to the construction of images entirely as a grid of pixels. We also call these bit-mapped images. Digital photographs are raster images. Later, we will use raster images to create textures to put on models.

If we were to create a digital coloring book for children, we would have to take the line drawings of the coloring book and display them on the screen using a bit-mapped image. This is because our computer displays can only display grids of pixels. When a child assigns some color to an enclosed region, we would then assign the same value to every pixel on the screen that is in that region. The child would view the coloring book as a vector graphic, and internally, the coloring program would probably store it as a vector graphic, but the screen would actually display bit-mapped images.

Likewise, if you look at a political map of the United States on a computer display, it has been transformed into a raster image because, again, that's the only kind of graphics we can directly display on a computer screen.

We call this transformation from vector graphics to raster graphics "rendering." This process of turning line-based models into pixel-based models is how we turn animated wireframe models (with materials assigned to the surfaces of these models) into videos. We typically generate a series of pixel-based images that are then seen by the viewer at 24 to 60 (or more) images per second.

Polygon and NURBS Modeling

One of the two supported modeling techniques in Maya is based on building 3D models out of straight lines, and the second uses both straight and curved lines. The first is called "polygon" modeling because every surface is made of a patchwork of polygons, which means, of course, that they are 2D. We often call this patchwork a mesh. The second is called "NURBS."

The upper-leftmost image in Figure 2.9 is a polygon model. The upper rightmost is a NURBS model. The one in the upper middle is also a polygon object. But it has fewer vertices and edges, thus fewer polygons. The two polygon objects will not render as smooth spheres. But the one in the upper right will.

Now look at the two in the second row. These are what you get if you select the left and middle sphere in the top row (one at a time) and then go to:

any Main Menu → Modify → Convert → Polygons to Subdiv

This converts each of the two polygon objects into subdivision objects that are shown immediately below the respective polygon objects. The one on the bottom left has more or less the same overall shape as the one above it, but there is a lot of dense geometry on the top and bottom of it. This is caused by the denser geometry on the top and bottom of the polygon object in the upper left. The one in the bottom middle looks terrible. That's because it started out with less dense geometry in its polygon form (upper middle).

Now, look at Figure 2.10. The sphere on the bottom left looks nice and smooth. That's because it was converted to subdivision modeling. Subdivision modeling in Maya is a render-time capability. It tells Maya to recursively subdivide each polygon face in the mesh until the resulting rendering looks smooth. The geometry of the object in the lower left is identical to the object in the upper left in Figure 2.9. The change only happened at render time.

Now, look at the bottom right sphere. Its polygons have been recursively subdivided at render time as well. But it looks like an egg.

First notice that the NURBS sphere does not need to be rendered to make it smooth.

But why is the bottom-right object egg shaped? It started out as a sphere formed from the Polygon Primitives on the Create menu. If you look closely, the upper-middle object is also nonspherical. It is also true that the top-left one and bottom-left one are not quite spherical. But the difference is so slight we don't notice it. Only when the density of edges and vertices is sparse, do we notice that the model and the rendering are imperfect spheres.

There are two lessons here. First, polygon objects need to be smoothed before rendering them, and converting to subdivision is one way to do it. Second, polygon objects are always approximate, and wherever the density of geometry is greater on an object, the object is closer to the smooth, organic object it is supposed to represent. The problem with the bottom-right object is that its geometry is not very dense at all, especially in the middle of it, and so it does not render as a true sphere when it is subdivided at render time. In short, the polygon object in the top middle is not a sphere, and the conversion to a smooth subdivision rendering only accentuates this fact. By the way, the Create menu allows us to choose how dense we want the geometry to be in the polygon objects we create.

Finally, there is another way to smooth a polygon object, and that is to do it at modeling time and not at rendering time. Select the sphere in the upper middle of Figure 2.9, and then go to:

Polygons Main Menu → Mesh → Smooth

The result will be quite similar to the bottom right: only the object will be smoothed geometrically and not just smoothed at render time. This is done by increasing the number of vertices and edges until the model appears to be smooth.

Choosing between Polygon and NURBS Modeling

The two kinds of modeling each have pros and cons. Polygon models are simple to specify internally and if you are careful not to make models that are dense in polygons, they render quickly. NURBS models are more difficult to model internally and demand that Maya perform some mathematics to create the curved lines. This in itself impacts rendering times only slightly. But there is another factor that can have a modest impact on rendering times: the current generation of graphics cards, for the most part, want polygons (in particular, triangles) in order to render a scene. This means that the software has to turn a NURBS model into a polygon model in order to render it. This may well not deter the animator who is making a playable, noninteractive video. Rendering time tends to be the bottleneck in video games because scenes must be rendered in real time in order to respond to user input. Angular, low-vertex/edge-count polygon models tend to be used in games.

Thus, outside of gaming, the choice between polygon and NURBS modeling is really up to the animator who is creating the model. It is not even true that organic models (like humans or horses) should be done with NURBS; the fact that a polygon model must be smoothed is far from the dominating factor in making the decision. It's really just a matter of preference as to which form of modeling feels best to an individual animator.

NURBS Modeling Modes

When we right click on a NURBS object to select the mode in which we want to work, we discover that the modes have different names than what we see in polygon modeling. This underscores the difference between straight and curved line modeling. Surface Point and Control Vertex are similar, but Surface Point refers to NURBS geometry and Control Vertex refers to polygon geometry. Notice that NURBS surfaces are made up of "patches."

MAYA IS ALWAYS RENDERING

Look again at the spheres in Figure 2.9. They look like vector-based objects, but this is not really true. They have actually been rendered, because they are being viewed on a raster computer screen as a grid of light-emitting pixels. So, while we are creating models and Maya is showing us how our models are progressing, they are actually being crudely rendered in real time. There is no way to natively display vector-based models on a conventional display. But, even simple models quickly outpace this quick-and-dirty rendering, and so we must render them in the Render View if we want to see what they will really look like. This is particularly true if we use light effects, particle dynamics effects, or any form of smoothing that does not actually alter the geometry of the object being displayed.

SUBDIVISION IS ALIVE AND WELL

For its 2014 release of Maya, Autodesk dropped most of its subdivision support. But in its 2015 release, it has introduced a new subdivision capability based directly on a highly regarded, publicly accessible standard produced by Pixar. Ultimately, lots of powerful capabilities, such as rendering NURBS models without converting them to polygon models, will be put into future generations of graphics cards, radically reducing render time.

One popular 3D modeling and animation application, MODO by Luxology (now part of The Foundry), makes heavy use of subdivision. A low-resolution (low vertex/edge/face count) model is converted to a smooth subdivision model at render time. Subdivision still offers a powerful option for creating smooth, organic models using basic polygon modeling.

CUDA

There are other technologies that already provide for far more hardware efficiency at render time. The CUDA (Compute Unified Device Architecture) standard can be found in NVIDIA graphics cards. CUDA-compliant GPUs contain a programming environment that provides a platform that shifts many computations formerly performed in software on the CPU to the GPU. A sort of competitor to CUDA is OpenCL, which also supports a language that can be used to speed the process of rendering. It should be noted that both CUDA and OpenCL are in fact parallel programming platforms that can be used for more general purposes and not just for graphics capabilities.

Otoy's Octane Renderer (which is supported by Otoy's plug-ins for various 3D applications, including Lightwave, 3ds Max, ArchiCAD, Autodesk Softimage, Blender, and Rhino) is based on CUDA—and is very fast. All of these are popular 3D applications, and given Otoy's wide product coverage, Octane promises to be very successful commercially. It also has plug-ins for Poser and Daz Studio, two popular character modeling and animation applications used both by hobbyists and professionals making simple animated scenes.

CURVED LINES, BEZIER, AND NURBS

Consider Figure 2.11. The line on the right is straight and the one on the left is curved. The straight line is specified by a start-vertex and an end-vertex. Although we build 3D models in Maya, all of the lines, curved or straight, are in 2-space. Indeed, this is true for the NURBS model in Figure 2.9. The vertices in all our models are in 3-space, however, and this is how we build 3D wireframes. In other words, we can shift to drawing a curve on a different plane in order to make a series of curves that span 3-space.

Notice that in Figure 2.12 there is a series of straight lines outside of the curved line. These straight lines are used by Maya to create curved lines. The series of straight lines are only there to help us define the curved line.

In Figure 2.11, the straight lines have been removed by Maya. This is because we hit the Enter key after laying down the last straight line. (Enter always ends the use of a tool in Maya.) The vertices at the intersections of these straight lines are called "control" vertices (CVs) and there are two kinds of them in the series of straight lines: begin/ end control vertices and internal control vertices. The reason for the two kinds of vertices and for the straight lines has to do with the mathematical complexity of specifying a curved line. The curved line is completely defined by the location of the begin vertex and the end vertex, along with the four other vertices. Notice that only the endpoints are on the curve and that the others are outside the curve. This is by design.

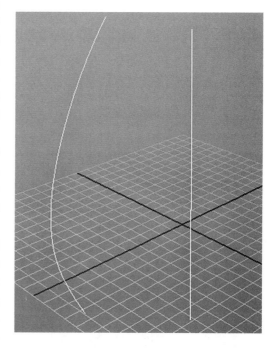

FIGURE 2.11   A curve and a line.

Let's compare the mathematics used to define straight lines and the mathematics used to define curved lines. Consider Figure 2.13. It tells us what we need to know to specify a

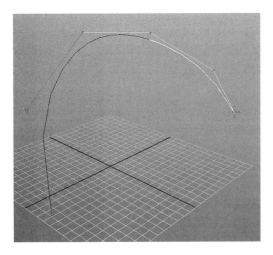

FIGURE 2.12   Making a NURBS curve.

1. A set of points, P. Each point p_i can be defined as (x_i, y_i, z_i).

2. A set of lines, L. Each line l_{ij} connecting p_i and p_j can be defined as a pair of two points (x_i, y_i, z_i) and (x_j, y_j, z_j).

FIGURE 2.13   Straight-line math.

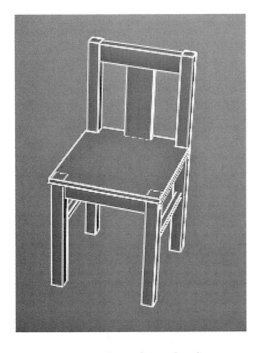

FIGURE 2.14   A chair of straight edges.

polygon object in 3-space. Remember that we work within a global grid in 3-space that we label (x, y, z). The horizontal axis is x, the vertical axis is y, and the depth axis is z. All we need are a set of points and a set of straight lines, each defined by a start and end point to define a polygon object. It's that simple. In Figure 2.14, we see a fairly complex object that is made entirely out of straight lines.

Now look at Figure 2.15. Bezier is a technique similar to NURBS, and since it is a bit simpler to understand, we will describe it here, instead of NURBS. Bezier curves are also supported in Maya (although NURBS are used for most purposes), and in Microsoft Word, SketchUp, and a large number of other applications. It is the default standard for curve specification in not-too-high-end modeling applications.

Bezier was a French engineer who designed cars. He had a problem: How can you completely specify the shape of a curved line that is going to make up one of the curves in the body of a car? If you specify a curved line simply as a series of points, you would have to put them very close together if you want the factory workers to produce cars with exactly the right curves in them. Suppose that Bezier did indeed use pencil and paper to design a curved line that runs down the entire length of a car. He would have needed to do more than put the points on the curve close together. Unless he drew it on a giant piece of paper, the curve would have had to been scaled up. These two things—making the shape of a curve unambiguous and being able to scale a curve up to any size—are the problems that Bezier attacked.

There is a third capability that we might well demand. We need to be able to fine-tune a curve. That means we would have to specify a curve in a way that would allow

$$x[t] = x_0 + 3t(x_1 - x_0) + 3t^2(x_0 + x_2 - 2x_1) + t^3(x_3 - x_0 + 3x_1 - 3x_2)$$

$$y[t] = y_0 + 3t(y_1 - y_0) + 3t^2(y_0 + y_2 - 2y_1) + t^3(y_3 - y_0 + 3y_1 - 3y_2)$$

$$0 \leq t \leq 1$$

FIGURE 2.15   Bezier polynomials.

localized changes to the shape of the curve without redrawing or redefining the entire curve.

Bezier made a discovery. He could specify a curve with very few points, scale a curve up to any size, and fine-tune a curve quickly and easily.

Look at Figure 2.15 again. It's more complicated than specifying a straight line, but it's radically better than specifying a huge number of points for a curved line. Remember that although we are modeling in 3-space, all of our lines are in 2-space. So, all we need is a way to calculate as many x and y coordinate pairs as we need for a given curve. True, we would probably want more coordinate pairs the larger we scale a curve up, but it would still be a modest number of calculations to create a smooth curve. So, Bezier's technique allows us to scale a curve up as large as we want to without creating a computational bottleneck and without losing any accuracy. Bezier could draw a simple curve on a piece of paper, then just give the factory a handful of CVs and two polynomials, and boom—a car-sized curve could be created in a precise fashion.

There are two polynomials in Figure 2.15. One specifies the x coordinate and the other specifies the y coordinate. We can quickly calculate as many (x, y) points on the curve as we want by using the two polynomials, one for the x-axis and one for the y-axis. It is a very compact mechanism, as the polynomials are simple and quick to calculate. This means that a curve can be easily scaled to whatever sized device is being used to display the curve, and we can adjust the constants in the polynomials to adjust a curve.

Let's go back to Maya terminology. Points are vertices. There are really two kinds of vertices in a curve: the vertices along the curve and the control vertices used to calculate the vertices along the curve. For polynomials of degree 3, like the polynomials in Figure 2.15, we need four control vertices, two of which are the end vertices and two of which are not on the curve. In Figure 2.16, we see a basic

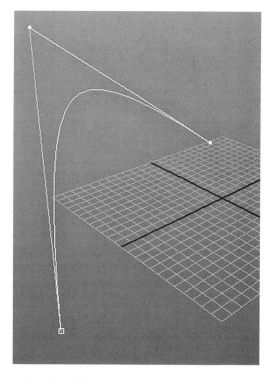

FIGURE 2.16   A Bezier curve.

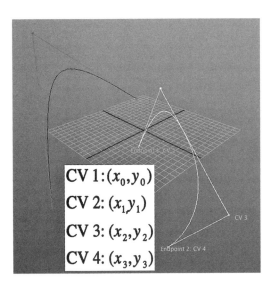

CV 1: (x_0, y_0)

CV 2: $(x_1 y_1)$

CV 3: (x_2, y_2)

CV 4: (x_3, y_3)

FIGURE 2.17   An annotated curve.

Bezier curve. Notice how elegantly we can visualize the relationship between the single center control vertex and the shape of the curve. By moving around the vertex in the upper left, we change the shape of the curve below it. There is another curve in Figure 2.17 (which has been annotated), and it has two internal CVs. By moving them around, we can smoothly change the shape of the curve below it. The point is that the polynomials remain the same; all we have to do is create the CVs and move them around, and thus allow the polynomials to dynamically create the precise curve we want.

CORE TOOLS: TRANSLATE, SCALE, AND ROTATE IN MAYA

There are three basic tools that we use while we are crafting a model and/or animating a scene. Maya also employs them under the covers, often without us being explicitly aware. These are the basic 3D primitive operations for moving an object, scaling an object, and rotating an object. (The Move tool is more generally known as Translate. But we'll use Maya's term and just call it Move from now on.)

Remember that objects in Maya consist of vertices in 3-space, along with straight or curved lines that connect these points. To make our discussion simpler here, we will think only about straight line (polygon) geometry, but our discussion can be extended to involve NURBS curves along with their control vertices.

Consider Figure 2.18. In the upper left is a basic Maya modeling primitive, a cube. (It has already been scaled along the y-axis.) To the right is the same cube after it has been rescaled along the x-axis. The dotted part shows the outline of the original cube. The lower right of the figure shows the cube from the upper left before and after it has been translated (moved) through 3-space. In the lower left of the figure we see the cube from the upper left before and after it has been rotated around the y-axis. In the white box in the very upper right is the mathematics behind all of this. I have taken these equations directly from Jones (2001). Let's take an intuitive look at this.

Some Trig

For now, ignore the equations to the left of Figure 2.19. To the right of Figure 2.19 is a diagram that my daughter Isabelle helped me engineer. There is an orange circle. In light blue are the x-axis and y-axis. They meet at the origin of the circle, at (0,0). The black lines are equal in length and each of them is the radius of the circle (half the diameter).

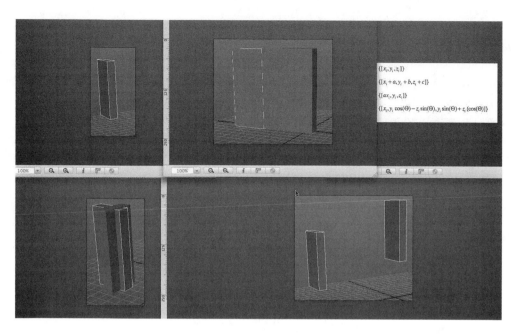

FIGURE 2.18   Translate, rotate, and scale with equations.

The point of this diagram is to focus on two particular triangles in the image. They are in the upper right of the circle. The first has a black line as its hypotenuse, a red line for its vertical edge, and a green line for its horizontal edge. The second triangle also has a black line as its hypotenuse, and has a yellow line for its vertical edge, and a combined green and brown line for its horizontal edge. The two triangles have identical hypotenuses, which are the length of the radius of the circle.

For each of these triangles, let's call the angle from the horizontal axis to the hypotenuse θ. For the triangle with the red vertical edge, this value is about 75 degrees. For the triangle with the yellow vertical edge, this value is perhaps 30 degrees. Let's define two operators: $\cos(\Theta) = f_d/h$ and $\sin(\Theta) = g_d/h$, where the length of the black lines = length of the hypotenuse = h, length of the red line = g_1, length of the yellow line = g_2, length of the green line = f_1, and length of the concatenated green/brown lines = f_2.

a set of vertices: $\{[x_i, y_i, z_i]\}$
translations: $\{[x_i + a, y_i + b, z_i + c]\}$
scalings: $\{[ax_i, by_i, cz_i]\}$
rotations: $\{[x_i, y_i \cos(\theta) - z_i \sin(\theta), y_i \sin(\theta) + z_i \cos(\theta)]\}$

$\cos(\theta) = f_d/h$
$\sin(\theta) = g_d/h$
black lines = hypotenuse = h
red = g_1, yellow = g_2, green = f_1, green|brown = f_2

FIGURE 2.19   **(See p. CI-1 of Color Insert)** Translate, rotate, and scale.

As the angle from the y-axis becomes larger, the value of sin(Θ) becomes larger and the value of cos(Θ) becomes smaller.

What this tells us is that these two values track the effect of increasing or decreasing the angle of rotation. Think of it this way: the black edges mark the size of the angle from the horizontal axis. There is a vertex where the red edge meets the top black edge, and a vertex where the yellow edge meets the lower black edge. Call these vertices vertex Red and vertex Yellow. Now imagine you start at vertex Yellow and rotate it upward to meet vertex Red. Now, assume that h is equal to 1, that is, the radius of the circle is 1. This would mean that $\cos(\Theta_1) = f_1$, $\cos(\Theta_2) = f_2$, $\sin(\Theta_1) = g_1$, $\sin(\Theta_2) = g_2$.

We see that vertex Yellow is at (f_2, g_2) and that vertex Red is at (f_1, g_1). In fact, as we move from the smaller value for Θ to the bigger value for Θ, the increase of sin(Θ) tells us the location of g_2 and the decrease in cos(Θ) tells us the location of f_2.

This means that taking the sine and cosine of angles can tell us how to compute the rotation of a vertex in 2-space, assuming that the center of rotation is (0, 0).

Translation, Scaling, and Rotation in 3-Space

The mathematics for rotating an object in 3-space is a bit more complicated. But the principle is the same. Let's step back, though, and look at the left of Figure 2.19. Here, we see equations that pertain to objects in 3-space, not in 2-space, like the circle at the right of the figure.

We assume that an object is represented by a set of vertices in 3-space, $\{[x_i, y_i, z_i]\}$, and that its center is at [0,0,0]. The translation of this object in 3-space, the scaling of an object in 3-space, and the rotation of an object around the x-axis can be calculated as shown in Figure 2.18. The reason that the third equation seems a little complex is that our tool needs to know something about the angle through which the object is being rotated. We looked at our circle to get an intuitive feeling for why there are sines and cosines involved in the equations relating to rotation.

While these three tools represent basic and key components of the mathematics inside a 3D modeling application, the job of calculating the shape of a model under development is actually much more complex than this. The reason is that often we do not treat every vertex in an object equally. For example, sometimes we translate a single vertex in 3-space, and instead of doing the same with the vertices that are connected to this vertex via edges, they remain fixed, and we stretch the edges instead. We will see that Maya offers an extremely complex set of modeling tools, but we should keep in mind that translation, scaling, and rotation underlie much of what is going on inside its geometry engine.

In Sum

The primitive operations that underlie much of what we do in 3D modeling consist of translation (move), rotation, and scaling. We use them to incrementally craft models out of objects, place objects in geometric relationships to each other, and to animate objects in our scenes. Often the objects involved do not get directly rendered and consist of things like cameras and lights.

REFERENCE

Jones, H. 2001. *Computer Graphics through Key Mathematics*. London: Springer.

CHAPTER 3

Modeling, Creating Materials, and Rendering

W E WILL BEGIN WITH a high level look at modeling, focusing on some suggestions for how to get organized as you begin the process. Then we will look at a few modeling examples in detail. Along the way, we will take our first look at putting materials on models and rendering them. We start with the task of building 3D models.

MODELING AS A SUBJECTIVE PROCESS

There is no single method by which you should model. There are almost always many ways of obtaining a desired result. And, since Maya is a vast application that was built incrementally over a number of years (and is still being built), it has many idiosyncrasies that animators have learned to live with, and in fact, have found creative ways of exploiting. As you gain experience and confidence, you will develop your own style—and often the most astonishing models are made in some unorthodox ways.

So everything that follows is only meant as a possible way to proceed when you create your first models. I would suggest that you start with human-made objects in the real world, things that are naturally angular, and as a result, are easily modeled with polygon modeling. There is nothing you cannot build with polygon modeling, although some animators prefer to use subdivision or NURBS when making smooth, organic objects.

First, we will consider some basic modeling guidelines, and then we will look at examples that will help make the overall process tangible.

Deliberate Modeling

A common mistake made by novice animators is to create "accidental models." This is what happens if you don't model with step-by-step discipline, crafting your models carefully. The result is often a model that seems random and inelegant. If it was meant to model something that appears in the real world, it is obviously flawed. If it was meant to capture an otherworldly vision in the mind of the modeler, that vision seems muddled. A common symptom is surface geometry that seems unnecessarily noisy and that does not seem to have any functional or artistic purpose.

The way to avoid this is to plan and to have a specific modeling vision in mind. That means you need to choose your type of geometry carefully. You might think that you could begin a given model with either a polygon or NURBS sphere. But the surface geometries of these two starting points are extremely different, and the tools available in Maya vary dramatically in their nature and effect. That initial decision has to be made with a modeling plan in mind.

Models and Objects

Maya's notion of an object is broad. Everything in your scene is an object or made from objects, including lights and materials. Let's focus on objects that appear in a scene and have 2D (like planes) or 3D geometry. Models that we build in Maya are typically made up of such independent pieces of geometry.

Try the following:

any Main Menu → Create → Polygon Primitives → Sphere

and use this tool to create a sphere by clicking and dragging.

Now try the following:

RMB (right mouse button) hold → (Edge|Vertex|Face|Object)

Choosing Object means that we are going to manipulate the entire sphere. If we choose Edge, Vertex, or Face, we will go into modes that let us select specific pieces of that sphere.

But note that there is no "model" mode. What makes up a model is a creative decision, one that exists only in the mind of the animator. Models in Maya are made up of objects that are usually arranged into a hierarchy, and the choices you make when deciding what object is the parent of what other objects are fundamental to your scene.

You will find that polygon modeling lends itself to a natural component-based approach to building models, with clearly defined, hierarchical internal boundaries between objects that form a given model, and this is a key reason why polygon modeling remains a favorite.

Top-Down Modeling

You should not take on a scene that will have models that are too complicated or too numerous for you to finish in an elegant, complete fashion. So instead of trying to create an entire house, you may want to build a living room. And remember to draw your scene out by hand or with a vector drawing program first.

A good thing to do if you are a beginner is to rough out your model first and then to model in a top-down fashion. Usually, it's best to break the scene into individual models that represent real items in the world. Each model should be formed from the object components that the item has in the real world. So, we start with the room itself, a cube, perhaps with one wall missing, to create a sort of stage on which to build the scene. That cube should be carefully scaled to the proportions envisioned for the room.

Models can contain other models. We might put down another, much smaller cube for the sofa and position it carefully in the room. Initially, this cube is simply a placeholder. The same approach is taken to add a couple of stuffed chairs and a coffee table. We would likely add some smaller models later, like lamps and books, things to give the room a fleshed-out feeling. Incrementally these placeholders can be transformed into real furniture, or the pieces of furniture might be built in another scene and imported. Either way, we must begin with a good visual sense of the overall geometry of the room.

The coffee table is likely to be composed of four individual legs and a top, all made from polygon cubes. The legs will have to have materials assigned to them separately, each with its own wood grain—just like in the real world. After all, the table is built out of pieces of wood, not carved out of a solid block of wood.

The same do-it-naturally approach should be taken when adding light to the scene. The scene is by its very nature artificial, and so lights may illuminate specific aspects of it; the initial lights could be a lamp on an end table and soft light coming from the television. Perhaps the sun or a streetlight might stream in through a window. These things add more models to the room.

Adding Detail with Precision

As you craft a given model, like a sofa or a lamp, be careful to add detailed geometry in the form of vertices and edges, only where it is needed. This will make your job of adding materials and animating models easier. It will also result in models that are easier to adapt and reuse.

Perhaps the tabletop has a wood perimeter with tiles and grout in the center. Initially, you might only add the edges you need for the perimeter. Or you might build up the perimeter with the intention of dropping tiles into the center. Later, you will decide on the number and shape of those tiles.

Choosing the Model Hierarchy

When you decide to move your table to a different place in the room, you want the legs to go with the top. The legs can be "parented" to the top. This is different than "combining" the several objects that make up the table into a single object. By leaving the legs as independent objects, we could more easily animate our table by letting the legs fold up, as a card table's legs fold.

To make one (polygon) object the child of another, first, go to:

any Main Menu → Window → Outliner

Select the (polygon) object and with your MMB (middle mouse button) drag and drop it onto the (polygon) object you want to serve as the parent.

To combine multiple objects into a single object, select the first object, then with your Shift key down, select the next, and with your Shift key still down, continue selecting until you have selected all of the objects. Then choose:

Polygons Main Menu → Mesh → Combine

(From here on out we will refer to this process of selecting multiple objects at once as a "Shift-select.")

FIGURE 3.1 The layers icon.

Building Models in Separate Scenes and Using Display Layers

You might also want to create each model in its own scene, and then import them into the living room scene. It's a good idea to keep your work area uncluttered by not trying to create too many objects/models in the same Maya scene. Models can be rescaled after they are imported into a scene. It's their relative proportions that are important initially.

You can also selectively make objects invisible in a scene by arranging the objects in your scene into layers and only showing specific layers.

Let's suppose we have a scene with two horses in it, and they are partly obscuring each other. We can create what are called "display layers" in this scene by clicking on the icon on the far upper right of the Main Window; see Figure 3.1. Then we Shift-select the objects we want in the layer (in this case, one of the horses), then select the Layers tab at the bottom right of the Main Window, and then click on Create Layer from Selected. See Figure 3.2, where we have placed the green horse in a layer by itself. You can now toggle on and off the visibility of that layer by clicking on the V associated with that layer, as seen in Figure 3.3. (The horse used in Figure 3.2 is a base model provided with Autodesk Mudbox.)

In general, you can use display layers to selectively conceal and reveal parts of a complex scene you are working on.

Create Versions of Models That You Can Retreat To

Finally, a beginner should always keep a series of versions of each model. It's good to number them: sofa1, sofa2, and so on. Then when you discover that your sofa has become a lumpy bathtub, you can go back to an earlier version and remodel from there.

In Sum

Modeling demands planning:

1. Choose a type of geometry (polygon, NURBS, or a mix) with a modeling plan in mind.

2. Rough out your model first.

3. Add detail (vertices/edges/polygons) only where it is needed in order to flesh out the 3D model.

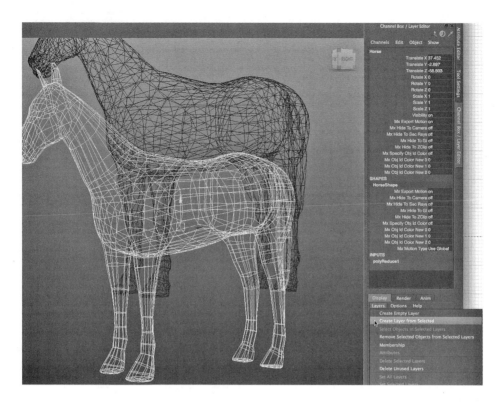

FIGURE 3.2   Putting a horse in a layer.

4. Create an object hierarchy with animation in mind. This will also make it easier to apply materials to selected objects later.

5. Keep named, enumerated versions of your scene file so you can retreat when your modeling goes awry.

More on Layers in Maya

There are actually three kinds of layering of scenes that can be done with Maya. We have looked at display layers. The other two can be found in the Main Window, in the same place as display layers. In Figure 3.4, we see a set of double doors. We will make a render layer out of one of them.

Using render layers lets us put various objects in a scene into different layers, and

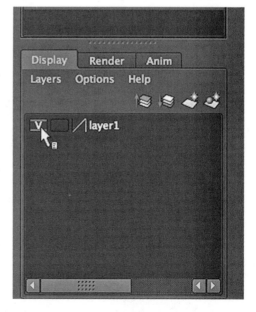

FIGURE 3.3   Toggling a layer on and off.

FIGURE 3.4 **(See p. CI-5 of Color Insert)** The closet.

then decide which layers we want to render. We can remove items in a scene that might be time consuming to render, and focus on more quickly rendered items. We can render one layer of a scene and finalize that layer, and then continue to rerender other layers until we like them. We can also use render layers to render different parts of our scene with different renderers. And we can use multiple render layers so that we can carefully control the light and color effects in a scene. Using render layers usually causes us to have to compose multiple layers into a single layer in our video application or in a more specialized "compositing" application.

Figure 3.5 shows a render layer being used to render only the right-hand door.

Animation layers are the third kind of layer technology in Maya. They can be used to blend different forms of animation in a single scene. They also allow us to carefully reuse existing animation in a new context. Figure 3.6 is a look at where to create animation layers, but going any further with this topic is out of the scope of this book.

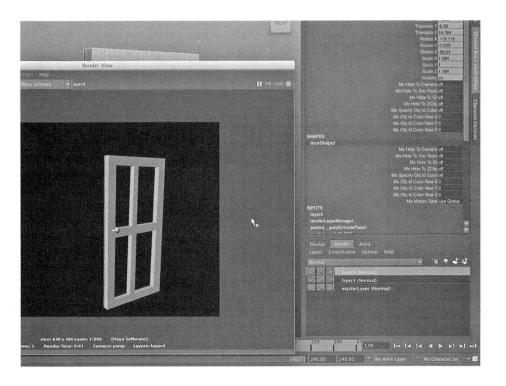

FIGURE 3.5 Render layer controls.

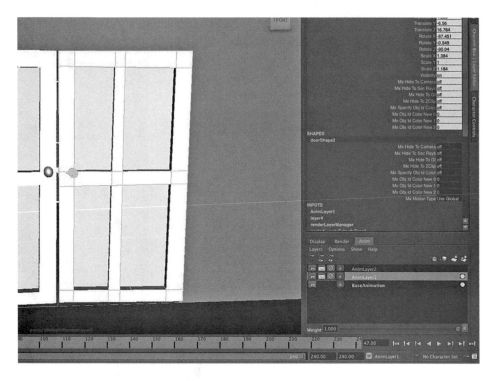

FIGURE 3.6   Animation layer controls.

USING CURVED LINES AND MENTAL RAY TO MAKE A NURBS GLASS DISH

We are going to take on the task of modeling glass in Maya. It involves the delicate interplay of curved line modeling, materials, and lighting effects. This will be the first example of how intimately modeling is tied to other functions in Maya.

From Curved Lines to Smooth Surfaces

Because we can build something simple with NURBS almost magically, we will not use polygon modeling for our first model. We will use NURBS, and we will see an elegant model appear in a few simple steps. The example we will use will highlight an essential distinction between polygon and NURBS modeling. Polygon modeling is all about making 3D models out of meshes of 2D surfaces, namely polygons. NURBS is all about creating surfaces out of lines in 2-space and putting surfaces together to make 3D objects.

We have already looked at the way that many animation (and other) applications model curved lines. Now, we are going to see a few ways in which curved lines can be used to create 3D models in Maya. In particular, we will learn a fundamental difference between modeling with straight lines and modeling with curved lines. With straight-line modeling, we generally start with a basic 3D object, like a cube or a sphere, and incrementally craft it into a spaceship or a jar of jam. Often, but not always, with curved-line modeling, we start with curved lines and use those to create smooth, curved surfaces in 3-space, which we then knit into 3D models.

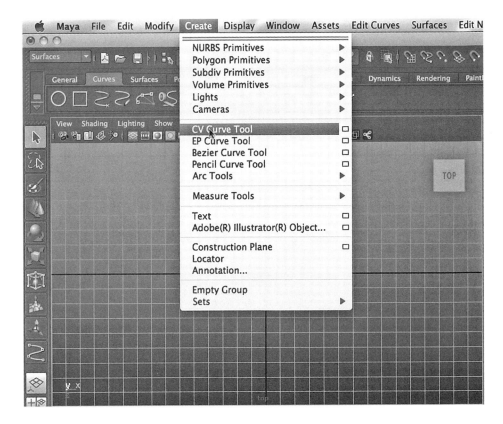

FIGURE 3.7 The curve tool.

In other words, NURBS (and Bezier) modeling often uses 2D curved lines, and not 3D objects, as basic modeling primitives. So, that's where we will start. In Figure 3.7, we see the menu selection for creating a NURBS curve (i.e., by creating control vertices [CVs]). We have set the Main Menu Selector in the upper left of Figure 3.7 to Surfaces. The tool is simple: It works with a series of clicks, each one of which lays down a CV. Every time you double back you start creating a new NURBS curve, but they are all connected. This means that there will be multiple begin and end vertices within the continuous series of curves.

The tool can be found at:

any Main Menu → Create → CV Curve Tool

Creating a Series of NURBS Curves

In Figure 3.8, the curve is being laid down in the lower-right-hand window. That's because this is the view that is in the x-y plane. When you pull open the four-way view in Maya, you can manipulate your scene in any of the four windows. (Hitting the space bar will toggle the interface between the single perspective and the four-way view. Hitting the space bar and the right mouse button simultaneously will reveal a set of menus that provide shortcuts to many of the tools in Maya.)

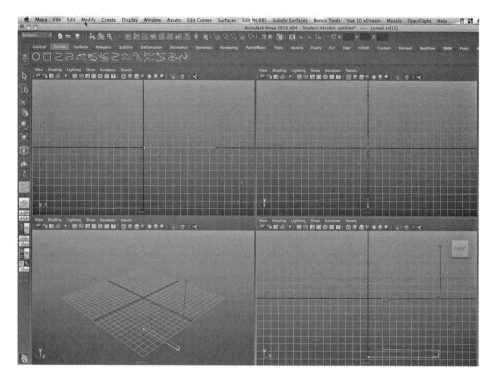

FIGURE 3.8   A series of NURBS curves.

We start at the upper right of the lower-right window and end the series of curves by ending on the y-axis. In Figure 3.8, we can see the series of curves being laid down. Near the turns, where we double back and make a new curve, we have to lay down the points very close together if we want the CVs to be close to the resulting curve.

Why build these curves on the x-y plane? In Figure 3.9, we have laid down the last CV on the y-axis and then hit Enter. This ended the process of laying down CVs and the green line in Figure 3.9 is the resulting series of curves. The CVs that are not on the series of curves are gone from view and only the NURBS curves remain. Interestingly, if we look at Figure 3.10, which is the perspective from above, we see only a single line, reinforcing the fact that our curved lines are all in a single plane.

But we picked that plane very carefully.

Revolution!

Now comes the magic. With the curves selected, we go to:

Surfaces Main Menu → Surfaces → Revolve

The result is shown in Figure 3.11. We have taken the series of NURBS curves and revolved them around the y-axis. And in a flash, we have a dish, which is just a NURBS surface that happens to wrap back on itself.

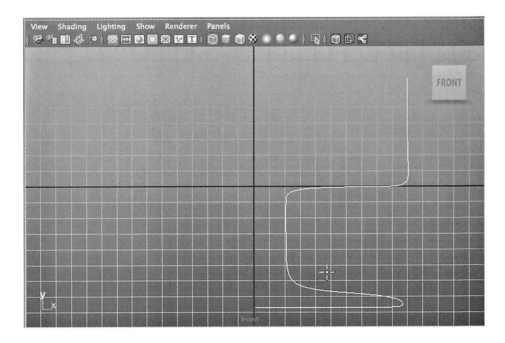

FIGURE 3.9　The curve up close.

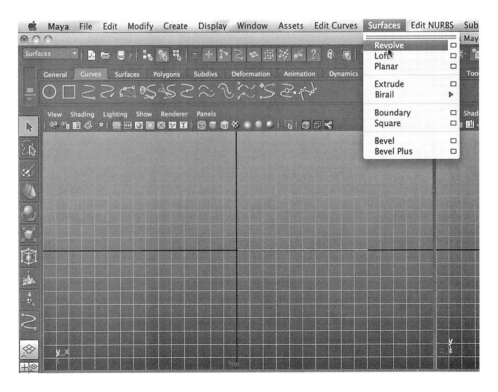

FIGURE 3.10　The Revolve tool.

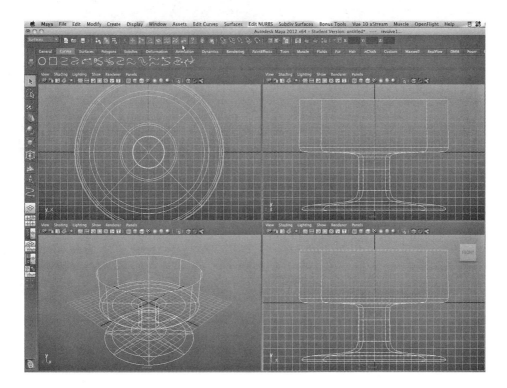

FIGURE 3.11 The revolved curve.

The dish nicely illustrates the overall philosophy of NURBS modeling in Maya. The focus is on making surfaces, not necessarily on making enclosed objects. So, we can make car fenders, bubble-shaped skylights, and other objects that do not need to be enclosed. Keep in mind that these surfaces, like everything we make with Maya, will not have any thickness; if we view the car fender from the perspective of someone lying on his back underneath the car and looking directly at the edge of the fender, it will look like it is made out of incredibly thin paper. A bubble-shaped skylight will look okay because it will be framed in. Later, we will look at using NURBS to make surfaces that are not enclosed.

We will see later that even when you start with a canned NURBS cylinder, it actually consists of multiple surfaces, namely, circular surfaces in 2-space for the top and bottom and a third surface for the body of the cylinder. This third piece is a curved surface that wraps back on itself. But a polygon cylinder consists of a single, enclosed object made up of vertices and straight lines.

Putting a Glass Material on the Dish

Remember that Maya is a surface modeler, and the models we create consist of "wire-frames" that are a set of vertices in 3-space, along with a set of straight and/or curved lines that connect these vertices. To give the appearance of a three-dimensional solid, we put an infinitely thin surface on the wireframe.

To understand how this works, we need to also remember that when Maya makes a quick and dirty render for us in the Main Window while we are crafting our model, as

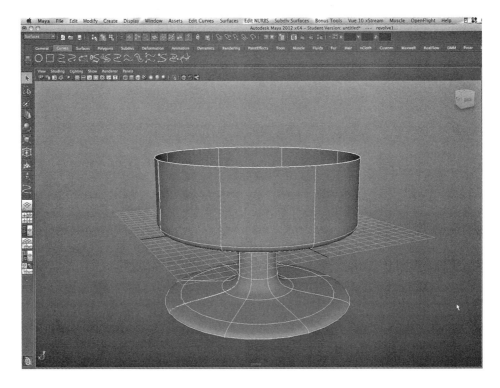

FIGURE 3.12   Smooth shaded dish.

well as when mental ray or the Software Renderer creates a full rendering, we are actually taking our 3D vector-based model and converting it to a 2D grid of pixels, a raster image. In other words, Maya assigns color and transparency properties to the grid of pixels that make up the display in a way that simulates the appearance of a 3D scene.

Now look at Figure 3.12. This is the view we get by going to the menu in the design area (*View, Shading, Lighting, Show, Render, Panels*) and choosing:

Shading → Smooth Shade All

This gives us a fast rendering of our dish with a Lambert surface on it—the material that Maya assigns by default to new objects. But we will not keep this material; shortly, we will look at creating a render of our model, complete with a material.

Two Software Renderers

We noted earlier that there are multiple renderers that come with Autodesk Maya. In this book, we will make use of three of them: the Maya Software renderer, mental ray, and the Maya Hardware renderer. Right now, we will focus on mental ray, which comes with a number of powerful materials. There is one particular material that we will use repeatedly in this book. One thing it is good for is making glass.

Figure 3.13 shows how to get to the Hypershade, a key window that allows us to construct materials and apply them to models. Figure 3.14 shows the Hypershade. There is a

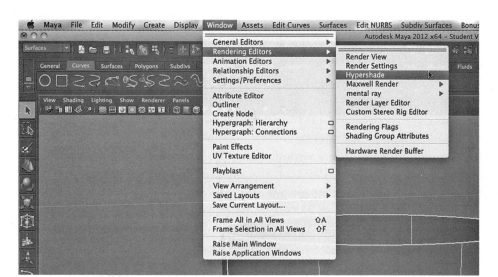

FIGURE 3.13   Opening the Hypershade.

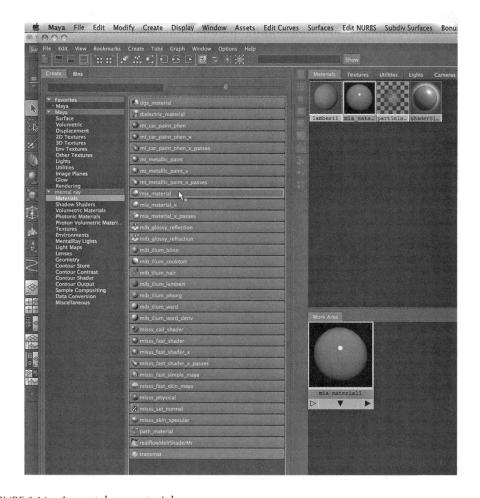

FIGURE 3.14   A mental ray material.

series of menu choices along the left part of the window. They are broken into two basic categories: selections that pertain to the Maya Software renderer and selections that pertain to the mental ray renderer. Usually, if you choose something from the Maya Software list, the result will render reasonably with the Maya Software renderer or with mental ray. However, if you choose items from the mental ray list (the bottom part of the selection list), you generally have to use mental ray to do your rendering; the result is usually unsatisfactory if you use the Maya Software renderer.

When you are working with any combination of 3D modelers and renderers, you should choose your materials and renderer as a symbiotic pair. We can use the Maya Software Renderer's materials with mental ray because, over the years, mental ray has been incrementally and deeply embedded in Maya. More generally, second-party renderers that are being used with a given modeling application tend to come with their own materials. They often will not work with the materials native to the modeler.

And just to clarify some language: mental ray is also a software renderer. Both of these renderers perform complex calculations in software, in combination with lower-level calculations that are performed in the graphics card. This is in contradistinction with the Maya Hardware renderer, which does most of its work in the graphics card. This means that the Maya Software renderer and mental ray tend to have much longer running times per frame than the hardware renderer. But they can do beautiful things; mental ray in particular can produce stunning visual effects.

Mental ray is generally considered superior to the native Software Renderer in Maya. And because mental ray is now an integral part of Maya, it is fairly easy to use.

A library of materials also comes with mental ray, which is equipped with presets that allow you to easily tailor a partially transparent or highly reflective material to look exactly the way you want.

Two Important Perspectives

Within an animation application like Maya, there are two distinct perspectives that have to be taken into account when rendering a scene. Before we begin, remember that all rendering is performed through the eye of some camera. We will assume one camera and one light source in this discussion.

The first perspective is that of the viewer, who is always looking through a camera. Before any cameras are created, the animator is using the default camera. The camera will see any rays of light that are reflected from or refracted through surfaces and into the camera's field of vision. This controls what is rendered.

In Maya, the field of vision has a precise definition. The field of vision is usually modeled as two rectangular planes, one closer to the camera and one that is farther away. This second plane is larger. They are parallel to each other and perpendicular to a straight line emanating directly from the camera. The camera will see anything that lies in the rectangular tube that connects the two planes; in other words, objects in front of the first plane or behind the second plane will not be rendered. This shape (the field of vision) is often called a frustum. The two planes that define the field of vision are called the near clipping plane and the far clipping plane.

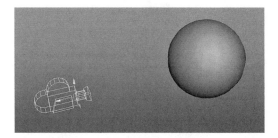

FIGURE 3.15   A camera and a clipping plane.

In Figure 3.15, we see a camera and a sphere. In Figure 3.16, we are looking from the perspective of that camera. It sees the sphere. The far clipping plane is at 10,000. But in Figure 3.17, the far clipping plane has been set to 10 and so the camera no longer sees the sphere. This is because the far clipping plane now lies between the front clipping plane and the sphere. The sphere is now outside the frustum.

Note that units in Maya can be set by going to:

any Main Menu → Window → Settings/Preferences → Preferences → Settings

The default is centimeters. Thus, our far clipping plane is at 10,000 centimeters.

In keeping with the live action metaphor, we say that we "dolly" the camera as we move it forward and backward along the z-axis; on a Mac, we hold down the Command key and use the right mouse button to dolly. To "track" means to move the camera from side to side on the x and y axes; we can do this by holding down the Command key and using the middle mouse button. To "tumble" the camera means to rotate it; this is done by holding down the Command key and using the left mouse button. The focal length of a camera

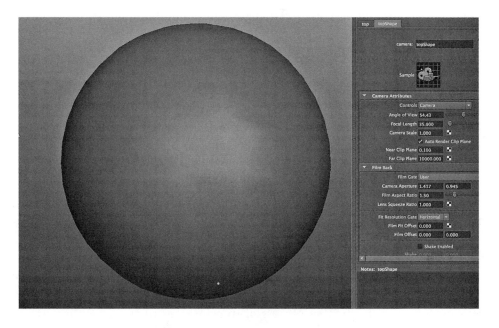

FIGURE 3.16   The perspective of the camera.

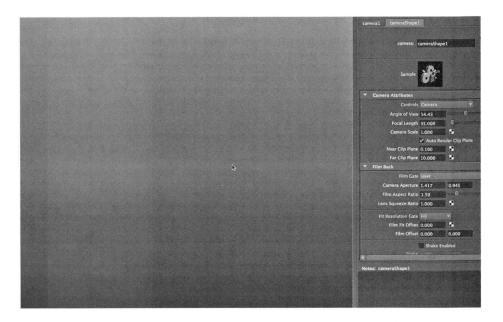

FIGURE 3.17   Pulling the clipping plane close.

can be changed, too; this changes its angle of view. In this way, we can "zoom" the camera forward without moving it. A number of camera tools can be accessed under the View menu in the design area of the Main Window (see Figure 3.18).

The second perspective that must be considered belongs to the light source. Light moves out from the source in rays. In many animation and rendering applications we call them photons and conceive of them as massless particles moving in straight lines. Those photons continue to move in straight lines until they hit something. Then they reflect off or refract through the object they hit. When it reflects, a photon may bounce off at the same angle it hit. Or it might fragment into many smaller rays of light that bounce off in different directions; this creates "diffuse" light.

The reason we need to consider both the view of the camera and of the light is that we can change attributes of either one to change the look of rendered images. This reinforces the fact that light, materials, and the renderer are all tightly interconnected.

Rendering by Tracing Rays

The process of rendering is artificial, in that the camera (and therefore the rendering perspective) is not a human eye powered by a human brain, and the rendered images created by mental ray are only 2D grids of pixels. The people who eventually view our video will not be sitting inside the 3D scene in Maya. They see only grids of pixels flying by at perhaps thirty per second.

Mathematically, the internal representation of a Maya scene is full of depth, as it is constructed from 2D vector graphs in 3-space. But all of the nice 3D vector properties of the scene were destroyed during that process of transforming what we built in our vector-based 3D scene into a rendered 2D system of pixels.

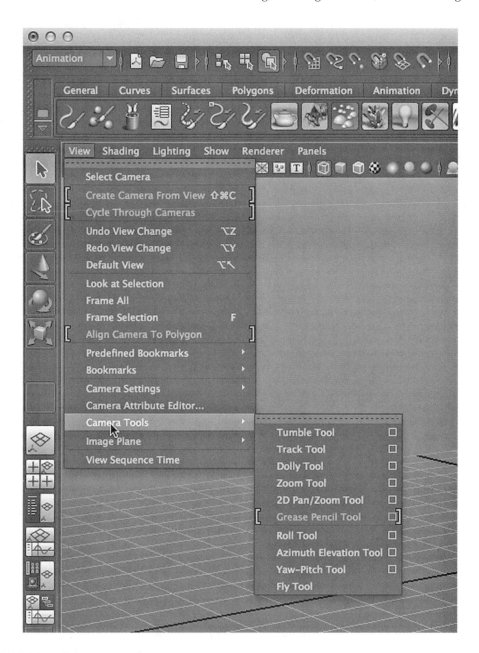

FIGURE 3.18   Camera controls.

The job of the renderer is to trick our brains into seeing that missing depth by providing the illusion of depth. It does this by simulating the behavior of light in 3-space.

Keep in mind that the renderer has to create this illusion with only one tool: the light properties of each pixel on the 2D grid. So the renderer has a lot of work to do. It must calculate, from the perspective of the eye (camera), what is visible in the field of view. And this can be very complex to calculate, since there might be multiple light sources hitting multiple objects, and since the light continues to reflect and refract, going off in multiple directions. The one thing that the renderer can do to save a bit of time is to determine what we call "hidden surfaces," and not performing any calculations about their light properties.

This process of calculating the movement of light in a renderer like mental ray is called "raytracing."

Here is the major point. The more calculations that go into tracking light rays as they reflect and refract, the more mental ray is able to simulate and recapture the sense of depth in a scene by carefully assigning each pixel on the display its own individual light properties. This means that sometimes, in order to get the apparent 3D visual result we want, each frame might take a long time to render because it involves tracking photons as they bounce many times around the scene. At some point, we stop calculating the movement of light rays as they move through a scene. This can be carefully controlled by choosing:

any Main Menu → Window → Rendering Editors → Render Settings

For mental ray, choose raytracing. For the Maya Software renderer, choose Raytracing Quality.

This is the frustrating part for us as we learn to use Maya on a conventional desktop or notebook computer. At render time, we find ourselves having to compromise between visual quality and computational tractability. Rendering, not modeling, is what demands a lot of memory, powerful processors, and a high-end graphics card.

Renderers like the Maya Software Renderer and mental ray are called "photorealistic" because the main goal of using one of them is to create a rendering that is as close as possible to what looks like a photograph of the real world. Most renderers used with 3D modeling software are considered photorealistic and use raytracing, but it is not true that raytracing and photorealism are the same thing. In principle, raytracing is just one technique that can be used to create realistic renderings.

There are times when 3D modelers might want to use nonphotorealistic renderers. We might, for example, want to turn a scene into something that looks like a line drawing and use it in a product development document. Or, we might want to "toon" the scene by flattening it into a 2D image; we will look at a way to simulate tooning in Maya later in this book. (But we still use a photorealistic renderer.)

One last remark: As we will see later, it is not always best to calculate raytracing as far as possible, as this sometimes washes out shadows. Somewhat ironically this has the opposite effect from what we desire—by removing the visual sense of the geometric relationships between objects in a scene.

Glass in mental ray

In Figure 3.19, we are selecting a material from the mental ray list. It is called mia_material, and it can be easily tailored to create different looks. This material, along with the others that begin with "mia" can be used to create almost any sort of reflective or semitransparent

FIGURE 3.19   A mia_material.

effect. They are used heavily for modeling human-made objects, such as buildings, glass, and automobiles.

Presets are a set of attribute values of the material that are used to create various visual characteristics. The many presets that come with these materials save us a lot of painstaking work. In general, crafting materials is well worth a significant effort, as the complex interplay between light and the surfaces of objects has everything to do with the visual impact of a scene. Painstaking, elegant modeling can be completely lost to the viewer if the materials on those models are poorly engineered.

Some of the more critical attributes that these presets control involve:

1. *Color*—There are separate color settings for light that is refracted, reflected, or diffuse.

2. *The index of refraction of light through a material*—This controls the angle of light as it is bent as it goes through an object. Visually, transparency is closely related to the refractive nature of a material.

3. *Reflectivity of a material*—Car paint is very reflective. So is glass. A sponge is not.

4. *Diffuseness*—Visually, this is related to reflection. The higher the diffusiveness level of a material, the more light is fragmented into multiple, less powerful rays that go off in multiple directions, thus causing the material to have a softer look. Our car paint will not have much in the way of diffuse reflections. Our sponge will. Frosted glass results in more diffuse light than smooth glass.

5. *Translucency*—This involves both reflection and refraction. It measures the effect of light bouncing around at different angles after it has entered an object. This gives an object a feeling of having a partially clear subsurface.

6. *Ambient occlusion*— "Occlusion" is related to the word *exclusion*, and it refers to the process of some wavelengths of light being removed to create shadow effects.

In Figure 3.20, the dish has been selected in the Main Window; then:

RMB (right mouse button) hold → Assign Material to Selection

The material has been applied to the dish.

Now we need to tailor the material. Notice that the assignment of the material to the dish causes an object (that is not rendered) to be created. So, the dish, the material, and the assignment of the material to the dish are all separate objects. And, in particular, we can change the attributes of the material at any time, and it will automatically take effect on any object to which it is assigned. In Figure 3.21, we have selected the material so that its attributes pop up in the Attribute Editor. Then we choose:

LMB (left mouse button) → Presets

Now we choose:

LMB (left mouse button) → GlassThin → Blend 90% (see Figure 3.22)

Before we can render our scene, we need to fill in the other half of the light/materials partnership by creating at least one light in our scene. The "default" light is created for every scene so that the modeler can do test renders before creating any lights. However, since renderings using this light might not be at all indicative of what a final rendering with a permanent light will look like, it is best to stop using the default light early in the process. In Figure 3.23, we are creating a spotlight. Spotlights are often used as a way of

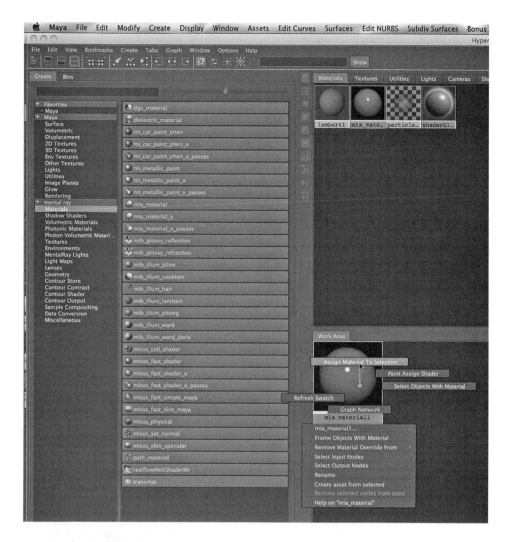

FIGURE 3.20   Assigning a material to the dish.

putting direct light on a particular part of a scene or model; the Cone Angle attribute of a spotlight will narrow the area that it illuminates in a scene. You have to be careful with them, though; using a lot of spotlights can wash out parts of a scene and can lead to unnatural shading effects by having light coming from too many sources. In Figure 3.24, we are increasing the intensity of the light beyond the default intensity. We are also increasing the width of the cone by using a slider.

The Background

Sometimes it's easier to get a glass material looking good by having other objects around or behind the glass object in order to accentuate the visual impact of light refracting through glass. In Figure 3.25, a polygon plane is being created to use as a background. In Figure 3.26, we see the Hypershade; a Ramp texture is being created. This is under the Maya Software renderer set of choices. It is not shown, but the plane has been positioned more or less

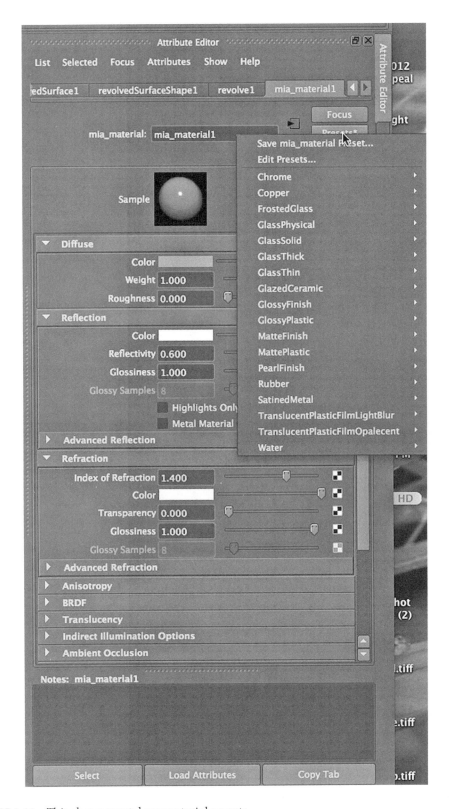

FIGURE 3.21 This shows mental ray material presets.

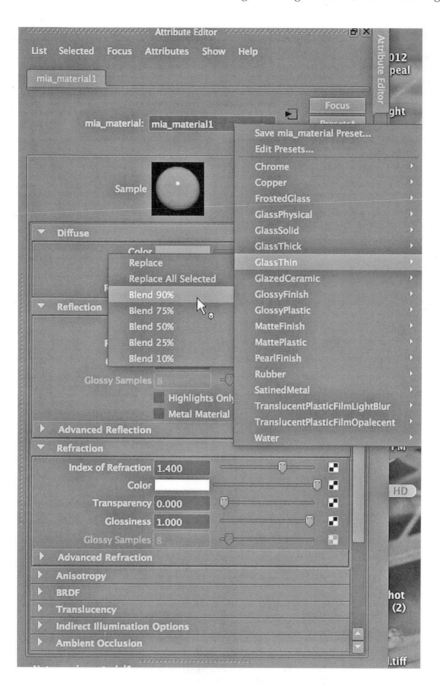

FIGURE 3.22   Selecting presets.

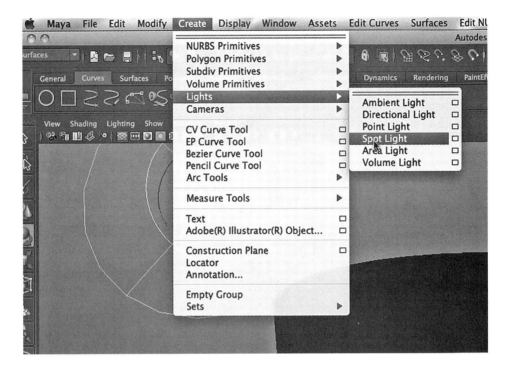

FIGURE 3.23   Creating a light.

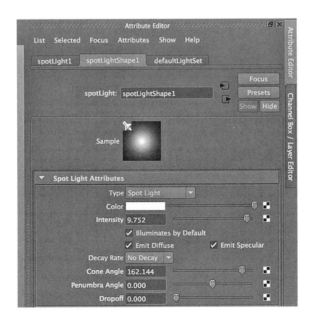

FIGURE 3.24   Raising the intensity and cone angle.

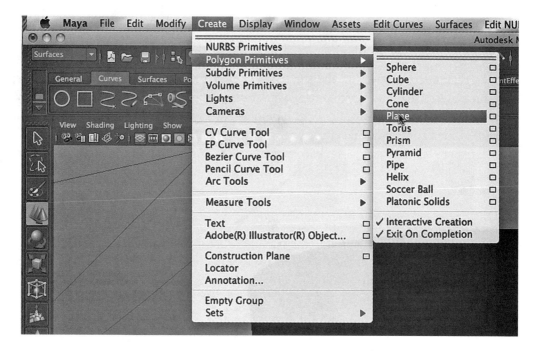

FIGURE 3.25   Creating a background plane.

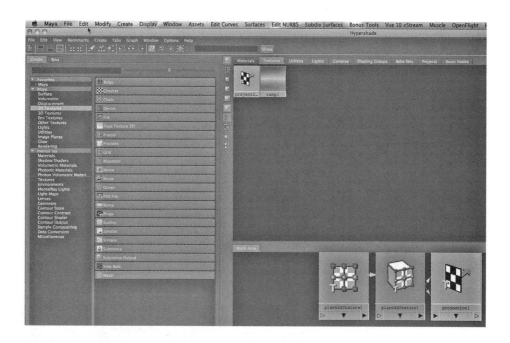

FIGURE 3.26   Creating a texture for the plane.

parallel with the x-y plane, and then placed behind the glass dish. Also, the spotlight has been positioned to the front-left of our dish.

In Maya, there is a 2D ramp texture as well as a ramp material, and both allow us to create a gradient color effect on the surface of a model. Compared to the ramp texture, the ramp material gives us more control over crafting a gradient surface. Ramp materials and textures are in some ways the duct tape of surfacing; they can be used to create an extremely wide variety of visual effects.

In Chapter 6, we will take a closer look at creating and tailoring a ramp material or texture.

In Figure 3.27, we have selected the background plane in the Main Window, and then we have gone to the Hypershade window and chosen:

RMB → Assign Texture's Material to Selection

We are thus assigning the material to the plane. We are using the default colors and other attributes of the texture, since we are simply using it to draw out the refractive appearance of glass. The stripes of the ramp texture highlight the effects of reflected and refracted light by warping the lines in the texture.

Figure 3.28 shows the scene with the texture applied to the background. Notice that it appears green in the Main Window. Maya uses this green color frequently to tell us that it cannot accurately display the material in the Main Window—and so we have to render it to see what it looks like.

Figure 3.29 shows our glass. What is not apparent is that it took several seconds on my MacBook Pro to render this. Keep in mind what this would mean if we were rendering a video at thirty or so frames per second, and all we had to work with was a general purpose desktop or notebook machine.

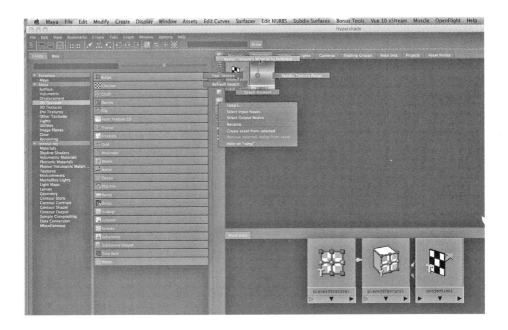

FIGURE 3.27 Assigning a material to the plane.

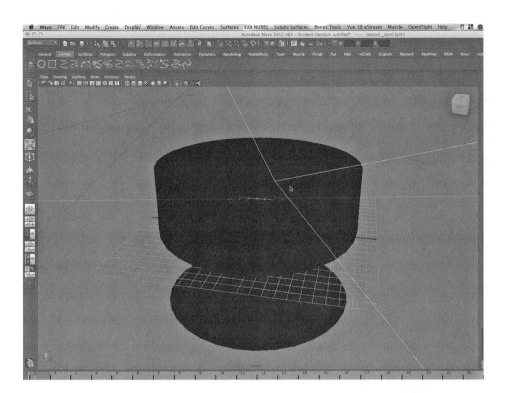

FIGURE 3.28   Dish scene with background.

One more thing to note: Select the ramp texture in the Hypershade, then choose:

RMB → Graph Network

We see the ramp texture and how it is connected to other objects in the scene. Specifically, we see that Maya has created a place2dTexture1 object in the Work Area. This is in keeping with Maya's policy of creating objects, both renderable and nonrenderable.

The place2dTexture object is the object that ties the ramp to the background plane. Why? This is what allows us to tailor how the texture is placed on the plane. If you select the place2dTexture object, you will find its attributes in the Attribute Editor in the Main Window. As we move on in this book, you might want to look at the Work Area as you build materials.

More mental ray Computations: Quality

There are a few options that have been added to the process of raytracing in mental ray. They increase the computational time, but sometimes they can significantly heighten

FIGURE 3.29   **(See p. CI-6 of Color Insert)** Rendered dish.

the effect of a mental ray material. Figure 3.30 shows the Quality tab of the mental ray rendering options. We get to this by going to:

> *any Main Menu → Window → Rendering Editors → Render View → mental ray* (in the dropdown) *→ Options → Render Settings → Quality tab*

Then we adjust the Quality slider to the right and increase the Min Samples to 2. This essentially increases the level of anti-aliasing. The anti-aliasing setting for the Maya Software renderer is shown in Figure 2.7.

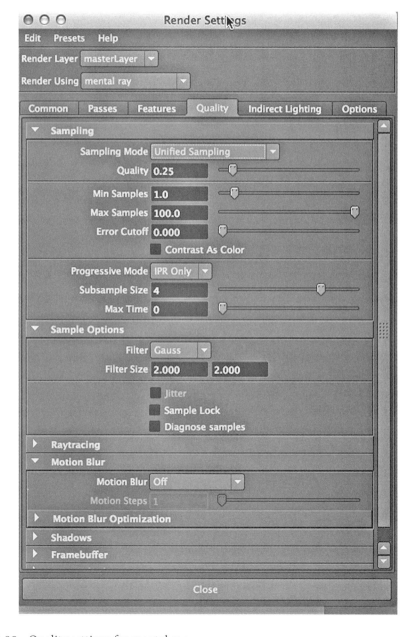

FIGURE 3.30   Quality settings for mental ray.

More mental ray Computations: Indirect Lighting

There is a set of other lighting effects that are known informally as Global Illumination and Final Gathering. These are effects that enhance indirect lighting, that is, the light in a scene that does not come directly from a primary source of light.

Figure 3.31 shows us the Indirect Lighting tab of the mental ray render options. We have checked Global Illumination and Final Gathering.

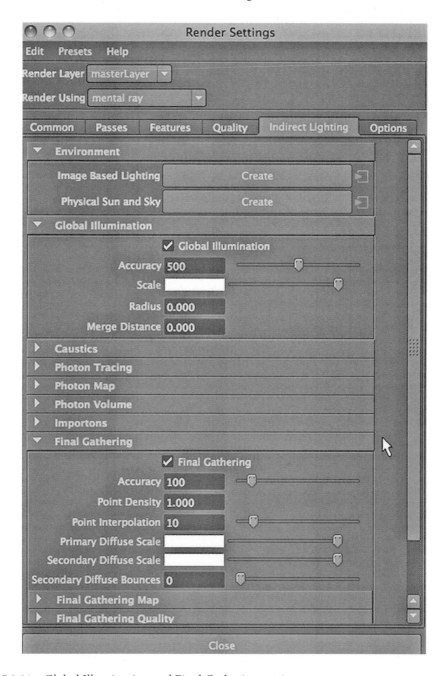

FIGURE 3.31   Global Illumination and Final Gathering settings.

Global Illumination calculates the effects of diffuse light. This is light that has hit a surface and then bounced off in multiple directions because the surface is not perfectly smooth and reflective. Global Illumination tells the renderer to do some extra calculations to determine the effects of this added light.

Final Gathering is a more localized effect. It tends to remove small dark areas that did not receive light during the raytracing or Global Illumination processes. It works by adding extra light to the scene, in particular light that does not come from a preexisting light object in the scene (like a spotlight or a directional light). It also softens shadows. Final gathering uses less computational time than Global Illumination and adds small-scale details to the rendering of a scene.

There is a third option under Indirect Lighting in the mental ray tab. It is called Caustics. Later in this book, we will look at applying Caustics to a glass model. Caustics is used to model light that bounces off smooth, polished surfaces, and thus creates what is known as "specular reflection." It also includes light that refracts through semitransparent surfaces. In either case, this is in contrast to diffuse light, which is light that bounces off nonsmooth surfaces; rays of diffuse light are broken up into a larger number of smaller reflections when they hit an object.

In sum, Global Illumination and Final Gathering simulate the effects of diffuse light, while Caustics simulates the effects of light bouncing off very smooth, reflective surfaces.

There are Final Gathering attributes that belong to our mia_material. This underscores the fact that the overall appearance of an object can be carefully tuned by adjusting the attributes of both lights and materials.

In some cases, Final Gathering, Global Illumination, and Caustics can wash out desirable shadows, making the scene look flat, because objects are no longer rooted to the scene via shadows. Of course, one way to repair this damage is to shut off these options.

Shadows as Roots of Models

Let's take a closer look at the role of shadows with respect to rooting models in a scene. A shadow that begins at the base of a model, such as at the feet of a human, will make it clear that the object is making contact with the ground. If a shadow is present but does not touch the model, then it will make the object appear to be in the air, like a bird.

Often, the worst situation is if the model seems to cast no shadow at all; this can trigger an ambiguous response in the viewer's mind because the model seems to be floating (but not flying) through a scene.

As another example, if a pool ball is sitting on a table and it does not cast a shadow on that table, then it will not appear to be touching the felt. Since we know from our experience with the real world that the pool balls must be making contact with the table, the scene seems unrealistic and unfinished.

mental ray's Advantage

Glass is a delicate balance between materials and light. The mental ray renderer does a particularly good job of performing the raytracing calculations that draw out the effects of light that is reflected off and refracted through a semitransparent material-like glass.

The Renderer's Main Job

Keep in mind that no matter what renderer we choose, when we render a scene, we are trying to retrieve that sense of 3D depth that exists mathematically in our 3D vector-based models but can be stolen when we translate a scene into a 2D grid of pixels. And what gives that 2D grid a sense of depth? Light. This is what holds the entire scene together. A renderer uses light to calculate iterative sequences of reflections and refractions. This is why semi-transparent objects like glass can add powerfully to a scene.

Equally important is the selection of camera positions that are used to render a scene. The correct rendering perspective is critical. If we render a creature with the face, torso, and feet directly facing the viewer, we tend to lose some of the sense of depth. The same can happen if we look directly at a house. Angles are usually better.

USING POLYGON EXTRUSION TO (START TO) MAKE A HAND

We are going to shift to polygon modeling. Our goal will be to learn how polygon modeling is often performed. We will also make some comparisons between polygon and NURBS modeling, to help us develop an intuitive feeling for these two very, very different modeling technologies.

Polygon Modeling: Basic Shapes

Perhaps the most straightforward yet highly versatile modeling technique is polygon modeling. Every object is made up of a patchwork of polygon faces, mostly triangles and "quads" (four-sided polygons). Using polygons with more than four edges can lead to undesirable rendering effects as well as models that are difficult to refine or tailor for different uses. Polygon modeling is particularly suited to human-made things, such as houses and spaceships and interior scenes, where there are sharp boundaries between objects that make up models (like the doors, windows, walls, and roof of a house) and where models are more likely to have sharp edges.

We often build a single model, especially a nonorganic one, out of multiple basic shapes, and often a nonorganic model is built out of the same set of components as the real-world item it represents. Thus, the body panels of a car, its wheels, windshield, bumpers, tires, and so on might be created separately and then put together. This makes it a lot easier to create a car model from a set of blueprints (which can often be found on the Web and downloaded for free). This also makes the model look more realistic, since all the seams are in the right places. And it makes the model easier to animate; we can open car doors and roll the wheels simply by moving various parts with respect to each other.

Recursive Refinement

"Organic" (or smoothly curved) models that often represent living things, such as human-oids and rats, can also be made with polygon modeling. One of the nice things about polygon modeling is that we often start with a basic shape, like a cube or a cone, and incrementally transform it into a complex model; this leads to a seamless model that can be animated quite naturally. So, we might start with a single 3D primitive, like a cube, and craft a human hand. After all, our fingers are not detachable like the legs of a table.

Of course, we could model a living thing out of multiple basic shapes, and we can craft a human-made object out of a single basic shape. The more complex an organic creature, the more overwhelming it might be to try to craft it out of a single initial basic shape. And there are a lot of human made things that don't have obvious discrete components. Consider a coffee mug with a handle.

Two crucial polygon modeling techniques will be employed next. One consists of carefully inserting added geometry where detailed modeling needs to be performed. Without changing the outward shape of an object, we surgically increase the vertex, edge, and polygon count where it is needed. The second technique consists of manipulating this new detailed geometry, often by using an Extrude tool. These steps are frequently recursive in nature. We will start with a polygon basic shape from the Create menu, visualize what we want that basic shape to morph into, and accordingly add appropriate detailed geometry. Then we focus on specific pieces of this new geometry and further refine them.

One significant issue is that our polygon hand will not start out smooth. Later in this book, we will look at a few alternatives for smoothing polygon models, but for now we simply note that our angular hand will need some work to make it smooth.

The Hand

We are going to create the beginnings of a human hand. Figure 3.32 shows us how to create a basic polygon shape, a cube. You might notice that we are on the Polygons setting of the Main menu selector, but the Create menus for the two basic modeling methods (polygon

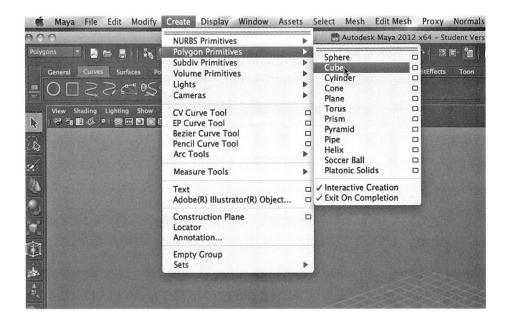

FIGURE 3.32   Creating a polygon cube.

and NURBS) are available on all Main Menu selections. However, other polygon modeling tools are available only with the Main Menu selector set to Polygons.

Because polygon modeling often uses this "basic shape" approach to modeling, there are more basic shapes available as starting points on the Create dropdown than there are for NURBS.

Look at Figure 3.33. The cube is created in two steps: one click and drag to lay down a rectangle, and another click and drag to pull the rectangle into a 3D object. Already, this cube (which is not really a cube, since it varies in size across the three dimensions) has been crafted with a human hand in mind. The shape resembles the palm of a hand.

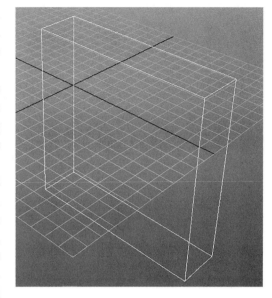

FIGURE 3.33   A polygon cube.

With this object selected, we go to the Attribute Editor and prep it for five fingers by increasing the subdivisions across the x-axis; this is shown in Figure 3.34. The result is shown in Figure 3.35.

Now, we go to:

Polygons Main Menu → Edit Mesh → Extrude

(Remember that mesh is another word for the polygon-based surface that makes up a polygon model.)

In Figure 3.36, we have selected Extrude. With the object in the scene selected, we choose:

RMB → Face

We are in Face mode (see Figure 3.37), which means that we will apply the Extrude tool to individual faces (or polygons). In Figure 3.38, we hit the space bar to go to the multiview layout. Then we go to the upper-right view, so that we can carefully extrude a finger up the y-axis. We repeat the Extrude tool as seen in Figure 3.39. Now, we have the first bone of the finger, along with the middle knuckle.

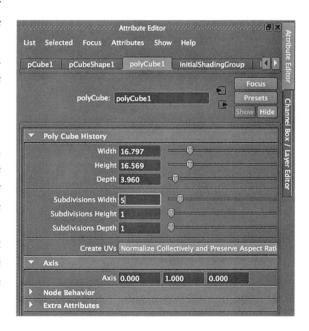

FIGURE 3.34   Five subdivisions for fingers.

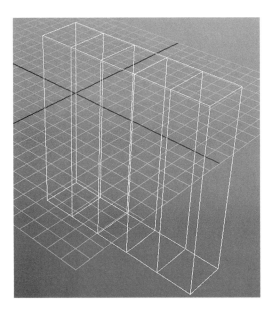

FIGURE 3.35   Five fingers.

FIGURE 3.36   Extrude tool.

Figure 3.40 shows us how to quickly add geometry to the knuckle, so that we can make it look rougher than the other parts of the finger. If you select the little box at the right side of any tool selection in Maya, you will pull up its settings. We do this, and in Figure 3.41, choose 1 for the Division level and below it, quads. We see the result: There is now one level of new divisions and there are four quads in the division in Figure 3.42. (The word *quad* is used for any four-sided polygon, but in this case they are also rectangles.) In Figure 3.43, we right click and select Vertex so we can rough up the knuckle a little.

We use the Move tool, shown in Figure 3.44, to pull out the center vertex, dragging four edges with it, which pull out to make a sort of bump. This is shown in Figure 3.45.

Figure 3.46 shows our hand with a single finger. This one starts out with an extrusion for the first knuckle. Until now, we have ignored that first knuckle and assumed that it will be part of crafting the palm of the hand. There are a number of ways of creating hands with polygon extrusion, and in particular there are no set ways for placing the first knuckle, roughening the knuckles, or creating fingernails. In Figure 3.46, we see that the tip of the finger has been prepped for a nail by extruding the top face of the tip along the y-axis. This is done by pulling on the green arrow in the figure, instead of using the move tool to pull the face, as we did to create the bone sections and knuckles.

There are also multiple ways of creating thumbs. In our example, the thumb is being treated like any other finger, but we would have to pull it out to the side to separate it from the other four fingers.

Often, the thumb is created as an extrusion from the side of the palm, not from the top of the palm like the other four fingers.

So, in sum, we see that the "basic shape" approach to polygon modeling starts with a single polygon primitive, like a cube or a sphere, and then the model is incrementally crafted from that primitive.

USING NURBS LOFTING AND EXTRUSION TO MAKE A SAGUARO CACTUS

To illustrate the differing philosophies that underlie polygon and NURBS modeling, we are going to go back to curved-line modeling. We will look at a few more modeling techniques that can be

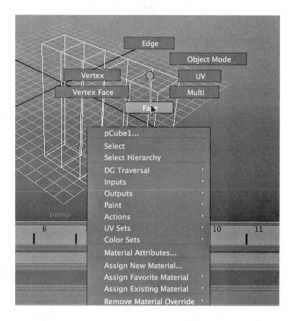

FIGURE 3.37   Face mode.

used with NURBS in Maya. We are going to look at extrusion again, but this time in the context of NURBS modeling.

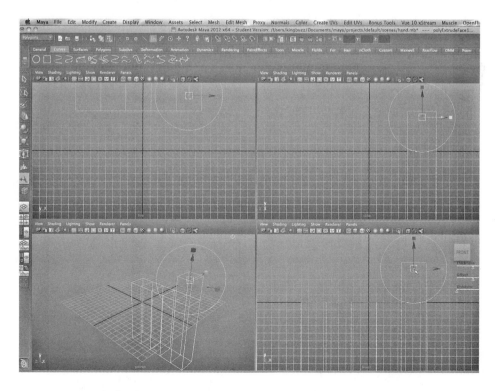

FIGURE 3.38   Extrude finger.

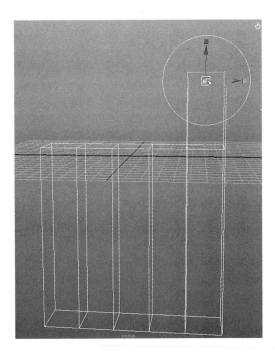

FIGURE 3.39   Extrude knuckle.

With our hand, we started out with a complete "solid," an enclosed cube, and as we extruded our finger we continued to maintain an enclosed model. But when using extrusion with NURBS modeling, we are going to start out with lines and create surfaces from them. We will see that our surfaces are not necessarily completely enclosed. In fact, we will have to take some action at the very end to finish up our cactus so it does not have any holes in its surface.

Again, there are no ironclad axioms in 3D modeling. As we finish our cactus, we will make use of completely enclosed NURBS primitives (spheres). Correspondingly, we often create objects with polygon modeling that are not completely enclosed. A living room might start out with five separate planes arranged in a box with one end left open to allow for room to

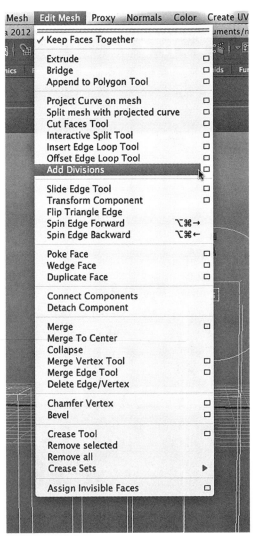

FIGURE 3.40   Add Divisions tool.

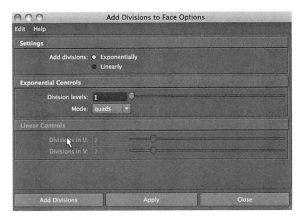

FIGURE 3.41   Divisions settings.

manipulate lights and cameras. We might also punch a hole in a cube to make a door or a window.

In this example, we also look at another modeling technique, one that can be used with both of Maya's modeling mechanisms (polygons and NURBS). It's called sculpting, and it provides a way to carefully craft an irregular surface, like a sculptor working with clay.

Using Reference Images

We have seen that we can create 3D surfaces by revolving a line in 3-space. There are other ways that we can use curved lines to create organic surfaces with Maya.

Figure 3.47 shows a photograph of a saguaro cactus, taken by my daughter Martina. They are big, old, and majestic. Later, we will look at putting a material on our saguaro.

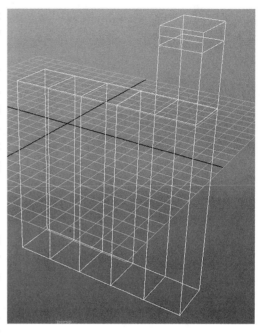

FIGURE 3.42   Divisions on knuckle.

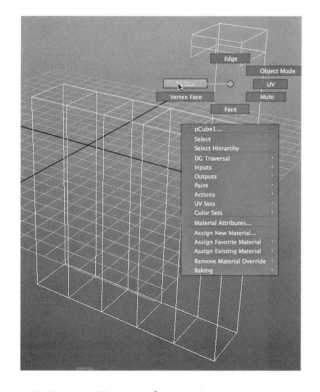

FIGURE 3.43   Vertex mode.

FIGURE 3.44   Move tool.

FIGURE 3.45 Knuckle bump.

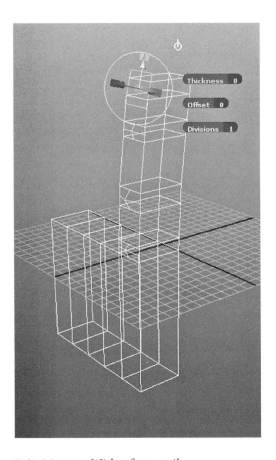

FIGURE 3.46 With a fingernail.

FIGURE 3.47 A saguaro cactus.

You can import reference images into a scene as "image planes" (in Maya parlance). You associate these images with cameras. We will look at creating and using cameras in later examples, but for now, you can go to:

any Main Menu → Create → Cameras → Camera

This creates a camera. We then select it and go to its attributes in the attribute box, and choose:

Environment → Image Plane → Create

We left click the manila folder icon that pops up, then choose an image file from the file system. We then go to the design area and choose:

Panels → Perspective → (select the new camera)

(The default name will be camera1 if this is your first camera in this scene.) You will see your image.

Then, you can select:

Panels → Layouts → Two Panes Side by Side

You will find your work area broken into two pieces. On one of them choose:

Panels → Perspective → camera1

On the other choose:

Panels → Perspective → persp

These two pieces of the work area are showing in Figure 3.48. And on the far right of Figure 3.48, we see the attributes of the image plane that has been created for the camera.

You can break the work area into more than two panes if you have other reference images. Many times it's best to find at least one more image taken from a 90-degree angle with respect to the first image. You then create another camera and assign the second image to it as an image plane.

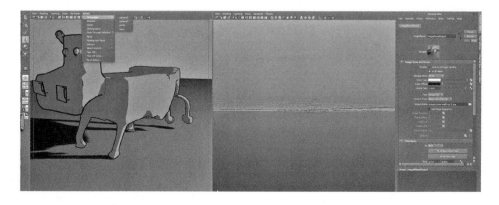

FIGURE 3.48   Two windows—reference image and persp view.

Or, you can use a single panel in the work area, the one showing the image plane from the perspective of a camera, and create your model in front of the image that is projected by the camera.

Give it a try.

Let's go back to our cactus reference image. We don't need to import it into our scene, because our model is going to be simple, and there's no need to see it from multiple perspectives.

One good reason to have a reference image is to use it to identify key visual properties of the object you are modeling. This is particularly useful with an object that does not have the sorts of complex geometry we often find with human-made things. With organic models, it's often simple geometric cues that trigger the right response from your viewer. You don't want someone to have to study your model for several seconds to figure out what it is. For example, the trunk of the cactus widens at the bottom, as we would expect. The various branches tend to be wide at the bottom as well, but each branch seems to start from a fairly narrow base and then quickly swells outward and upward.

NURBS Extrude

Ever seen rain gutters being manufactured right on the back of a truck? They are called seamless gutters, because they can be tailored to fit the dimensions of your house perfectly. The gutters are not prefab sections bolted together, so leaks are less likely to develop. Instead, the gutter guy extrudes the gutter using the cross-sectional shape of the gutter. We will do that to get our cactus started.

We will begin with a line again, since this is NURBS modeling. But this time, we want to make it a straight line. Go to Create, then EP Curve Tool, as shown in Figure 3.49.

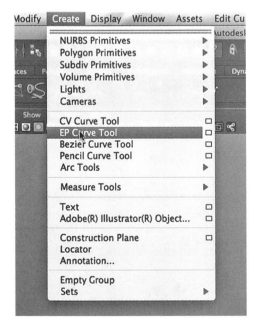

FIGURE 3.49   EP Curve Tool.

Create a line that goes up and down, that is, in the direction of the y-axis. Do not make it perfectly straight, but only lay down a few points. Organic things are rarely ruler straight, but our cactus wants to grow upward toward the sun. The line should look like the one in Figure 3.50. Now, as in Figure 3.51, go back to:

Create → NURMS Primitives → Circle

Create a small circle, like the one in Figure 3.52. This is actually a NURBS curve that happens to end where it begins, creating a loop. Put that circle flat along the x-z plane, as seen in Figure 3.52. Shift-select the circle, and then the line.

Now, as shown in Figure 3.53, go to:

Surfaces Main Menu → Surfaces → Extrude

The result should look like Figure 3.54.

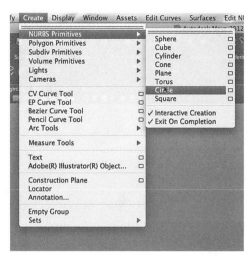

FIGURE 3.51   Creating a circle.

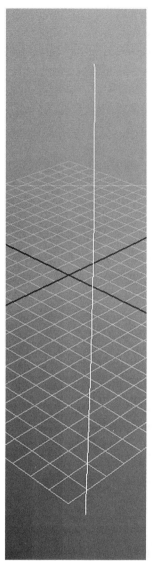

FIGURE 3.50   A curve for a cactus.

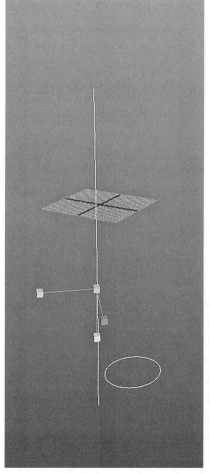

FIGURE 3.52   A circle and line.   FIGURE 3.53   Extrude tool.

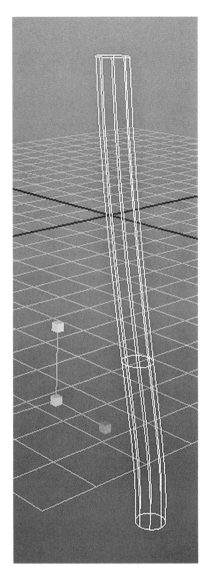

FIGURE 3.54   Extruded cactus.

Our developing cactus now has a tubelike appearance. But it is not a true cylinder. There is no top and no bottom; it is simply a circle extruded along a line. You must always know and understand the process by which your geometry was made, or later when you flesh your model out or try to adapt it in some way to use it in another scene, it will misbehave and not do what you want it to do.

Sculpting

In both modeling techniques (polygon and NURBS), there is a tool called Sculpt Geometry. It behaves differently, depending on the modeling technique you are using. It is a free-hand tool that can be used to make local but gradual changes in the shape of an object. It has a world of uses. You can put dents in a warrior's helmet, give a landscape a hilly appearance, or create eye sockets.

As seen in Figure 3.55, with the cactus selected, choose:

RMB → Object Mode

Figure 3.56 illustrates going to Edit NURBS (notice that we need to have the Main Menu selector set to Surfaces to see our NURBS-specific tools), and choosing Sculpt Geometry Tool. Make sure you click on the little box to the right of this selection. We want to see the settings for this tool. What pops up should look like Figure 3.57.

There is a lot here, so let's focus on just a few things right now. The sliders toward the top of the window control the size of the area that your sculpt tool will affect. The one marked Radius(U) controls the upper bound of the distance over which the tool will affect a model; Radius(L) is the lower bound. Set these sliders about the way they are set in the figure. Below the sliders are a series of icons; the one on the left, the fuzzy circle, means that we want the edges of our sculpting areas to be organic and gradual. The square means that we want sharp, angular sides to our sculpted area. The ones in between are more organic but not as gradual as the leftmost setting. Choose the one on the far left. Below these are a series of icons that control the resulting geometry each time we click on the surface of our cactus. Choose the second one from the left.

In Figure 3.58, the red lines indicate that we have our sliders set to create a large area over which our sculpting clicks will impact. This is because we want to gently widen the

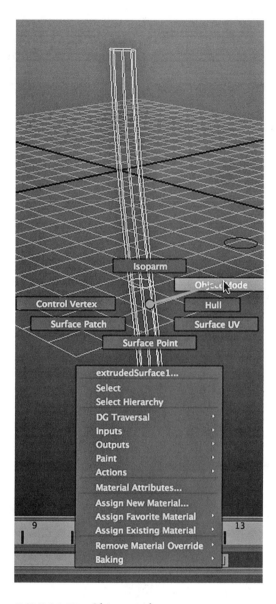

FIGURE 3.55   Object mode.

FIGURE 3.56   Sculpt geometry tool.

base of the cactus. Click a couple of times and get the bottom of the cactus to puff out just a bit. Try for a result like that shown in Figure 3.59.

The sculpting tool uses an engine inside Maya that is also used for painting. It is called Artisan, and it uses a paintbrush metaphor that allows us to craft geometry in a way that is reminiscent of creating something with our bare hands. (Later in this book, we will look at painting 2D and 3D objects into scenes using Artisan.)

One last thing to note: Sculpting can be used in polygon modeling, but with polygon modeling we will still have to address the issue of smoothing the surfaces of models.

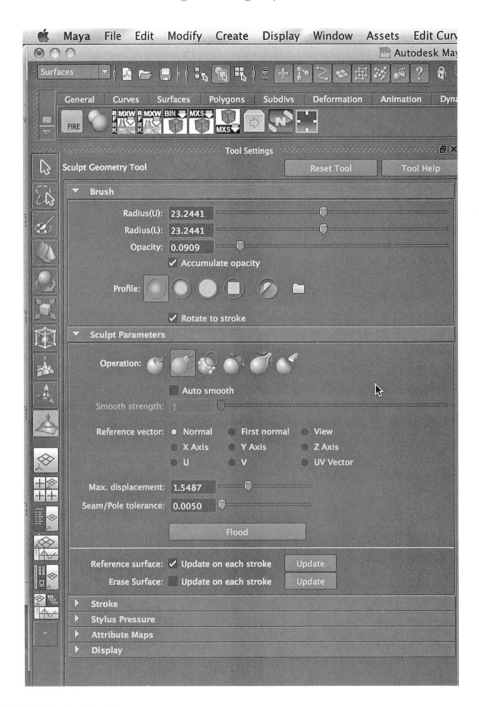

FIGURE 3.57   Sculpt settings.

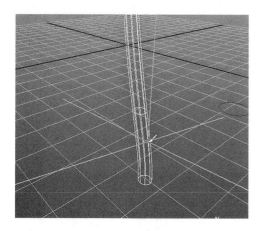

FIGURE 3.58 Sculpting area.

Lofting

Like extrusion, lofting is a core NURBS tool. Lofting allows us to create a series of curves and then to create a surface by sweeping across them. Notice that we are making a NURBS surface, even though this looks a bit like a cylinder. Maya will remember how this surface was created and you need to remember, too.

Lofting can be used to create the hull of a ship, by lofting through a few U-shapes with the ones in the middle bigger than the ones on the end. It can be used to create a rain gutter, as an alternative to using extrusion; we would just use open curves instead of the circle we used to create the trunk of the cactus.

Create three circles, as shown in Figure 3.60. Make the middle one bigger. We are going to loft a branch of our cactus, and you might remember that the branch, where it meets the trunk, is small. Do not flip any of these circles upside down. Orient them all the same way and stack them as in the figure. If you turn one of them upside down with respect to the other two, the lofting process will create a bizarre result. Go into the four-way view, as seen in Figure 3.61, and move the circles so that they are in the positions seen in the figure.

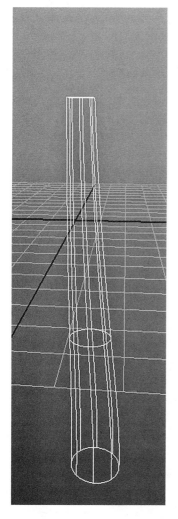

FIGURE 3.59 Widened base.

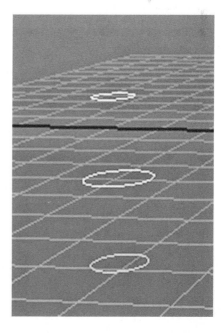

FIGURE 3.60 Circles for a branch.

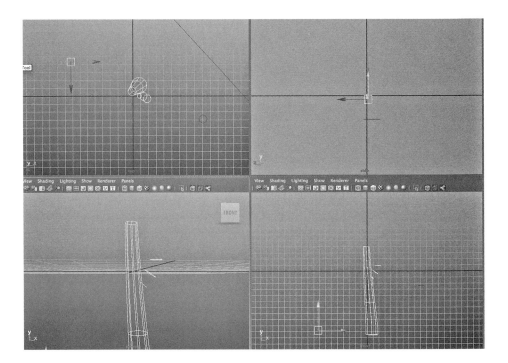

FIGURE 3.61   Circles situated in 3-space.

(Here is a bit of advice for lining up objects in Maya. First, create objects on planes and always move them with the Move tools arrow so they slide directly across some axis. If you want to go to the lower left, for instance, go lower, then go to the left. If you always do this and never cut across at an angle, you will end up with objects that sit on planes and they will be far easier to line up in the four-way view.)

Projection

Now Shift-select the trunk, then the bottom circle. This is shown in Figure 3.62. Go to:

   Edit NURBS → Project Curve on Surface (see Figure 3.63)

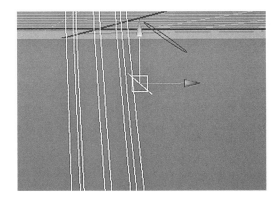

FIGURE 3.62   Project setup.

This is another key NURBS tool—one that lets us project a curve onto an object. The result is shown in Figure 3.64. The shape of the circle will be deformed, but make sure that the projected circle on the side of the trunk has not become a narrow ellipse.

Loft Again

Now, Shift-select the circles in either top down or bottom up order and go to:

Surfaces → Loft (see Figure 3.65)

The result is shown in Figure 3.66. We have put a branch on our cactus.

This series of steps, creating circles, projecting one of them, and then lofting through them all can be used to put an arm on a human torso. Or we could put fingers on a hand and create a hand using NURBS instead of polygon modeling, as we did previously.

The last thing we will do is put two completely enclosed NURBS spheres into the ends of the trunk and the branch (see Figure 3.67).

FIGURE 3.63   Project tool.

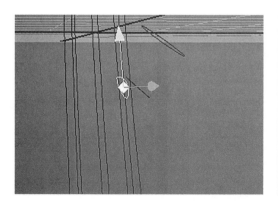

FIGURE 3.64   Project result.

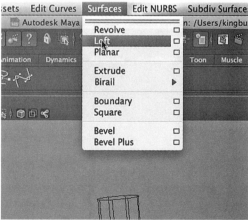

FIGURE 3.65   Loft tool.

FIGURE 3.66   Lofting result.

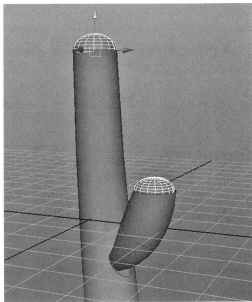

FIGURE 3.67   Two spheres for ends.

In Sum

A common approach to polygon modeling is to craft a model from a small number of objects that start out as basic primitives, like spheres or cubes. In NURBS modeling we often use curved lines to create smooth surfaces that are then arranged to make an enclosed object. But we can create objects out of polygon faces and we can create objects out of NURBS primitives, such as spheres and cubes, as well.

CHAPTER 4

Hierarchies of Objects, a Polygon Example, Detailed Polygon Modeling, and a NURBS Example

IN THIS CHAPTER, we will continue to look at modeling. We take the approach of incrementally digging more deeply into both polygon and NURBS modeling. Our goal is to become comfortable with both, with a bit of a bias toward polygon modeling, as it is a core 3D technique with which every 3D artist needs to be familiar.

We first examine a few semiformal and conceptual issues in Maya, then we build a polygon model, take a high-level look at the process of creating another polygon model, and study some techniques for performing various detailed polygon modeling tasks. And finally, we look at constructing a NURBS model.

BASIC CONCEPTS

Modeling Hierarchies

We have been informally using the word *model* to refer to the goal of the 3D modeling process. Of course, one must have a specific end point in mind. Although any complex model (and many simple ones) will evolve during the process of creating it, you don't want to be making incidental models by continuing to semirandomly massage an object until it finally looks like something interesting.

Perhaps a more critical notion is what gives a model its identity in the eyes of the modeler. The quick answer is that it is at the root of an object hierarchy.

Objects

First, remember that the word *object* has a specific meaning inside Maya, and it refers to an item stored in the Maya database. Objects can be things that are directly rendered or they can be abstract. In either case, they have attributes. Maya does, however, hide the specifics of its data management from us, and so it's actually difficult to know precisely what is an object and what is not.

We have also used the term *object* in a somewhat informal way to refer to pieces of a model or early stages of a model.

Either way, models are made up of objects.

A model might be made of other models, as well. A model of a house might have smoke coming out of the chimney, and that smoke effect might be a model that was made earlier and then imported into the scene containing the house by going to File on the Main Menu and selecting Import.

Formal Notions

The word *model* does not have a precise meaning in Maya, although we will continue to say that a model is made of objects arranged in a hierarchy.

There is a formal notion in Maya, though, of a project, as each project is a specific folder in the Maya file directory. In this book, when we talk about scenes we will usually be referring to a specific .mb or .ma file within a Maya scenes folder, which is within the Projects folder. So a scene is also a formal notion.

Maya binary files are encoded as bit files. Maya ASCII files consist of code. As an experiment, you might try storing a scene as an ASCII file, and then look at the vast amount of code that must be generated to create even a simple model. This will give you a sense of the astonishing amount of computational power hidden inside Maya.

A .ma or a .mb file can be imported into an open scene, and so our smoke effect might be stored as its own .ma or .mb file.

We might reasonably conclude that a scene is a precise thing that contains one or more models, and that a model is made up of objects.

Hierarchies

Remember the cactus we made from NURBS curves. In Figure 4.1, we choose:

any Main Menu → Window → Outliner

This window allows us to take various objects in a scene, give them names, and put them in a hierarchy. You can also give objects names by using the Attribute Editor. And of course, it is always a good idea to give the objects in your scene meaningful names.

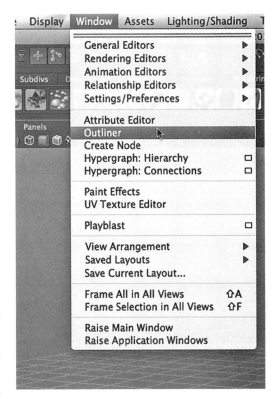

FIGURE 4.1   The Outliner.

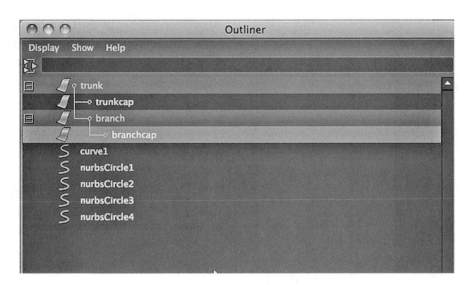

FIGURE 4.2   Cactus hierarchy.

In Figure 4.2, the NURBS surfaces that we created have been renamed in the Outliner; they are now called "trunk" and "branch." The two NURBS spheres have been renamed "trunkcap" and "branchcap."

Notice that the curve we made with the EP tool is called curve1, which is not renamed. The circles that were used for extrusion and for lofting are not renamed either, although perhaps they should have been. All of these objects started out at the same level in the Outliner.

The trunkcap object has been selected and, using the middle mouse button (MMB), dropped on top of the trunk object. This has put the cap underneath the trunk in the hierarchy of objects that make up the cactus. Likewise, the cap of the branch has been MMB dragged onto the branch, and the branch has been MMB dragged onto the trunk. This has placed those objects in their positions in the hierarchy. Why use the Outliner to create a hierarchy of objects? This is a critical concept in 3D modeling.

Doing this means that if we move the body of the cactus, the caps of the trunk and branch will remain in place, and the branch will maintain its position with respect to the trunk. In other words, if we translate the trunk in 3-space, the other objects will translate in 3-space but strictly with respect to the location of the trunk.

In Figure 4.3, only the trunk has been selected, but the entire cactus has been highlighted; this is because the objects now form a single hierarchy and will move as a unit if the root, the trunk, is moved.

Models can be built out of objects or out of other models. To a nonanimator, the branch of our cactus would probably not be viewed as an independent model, but we might want to give it a name and look at it as a reusable component as we build a desert scene—and so maybe it is a model as far as we are concerned. We would then make it a root of its own hierarchy and make a copy of it every time we want to put a branch on a particular cactus model.

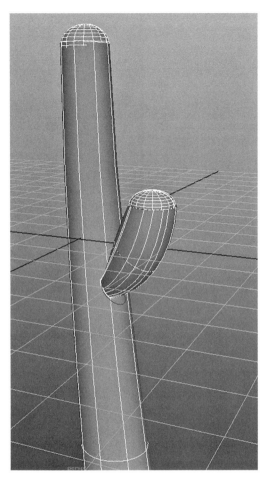

FIGURE 4.3   The NURBS cactus.

If you make use of the Outliner in your modeling, animating a scene will become much easier, as objects will move appropriately with respect to each other. It also helps later if you want to reuse a model in a different scene or project.

Another Example

If you look at Figures 4.4, 4.5, and 4.6, you can see that there is now some sorbet in our glass dish. The sorbet should certainly stay there when someone picks the dish up to eat, so the sorbet is a child of the glass dish.

Both of these examples show why it is so critical to rename things. In a complex scene, you might have so many different objects that it would be impossible to identify them later if you kept using the Maya default names. Some people like to embed the origins of a model or object in its name so that they don't start expecting it to act like it was made in some other fashion.

FIGURE 4.4   Dish and sorbet.

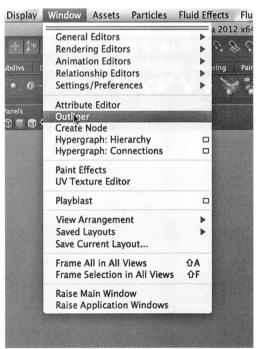

FIGURE 4.5   Dish and sorbet Outliner selection.

So, our cactus trunk might be called "trunk_NURBS_extrude."

Extending the Notion of a Hierarchy

The Outliner actually keeps track of a much larger notion of a hierarchy. If you open the Outliner window and select Show, and then select Objects, you will see that everything else in your scene sits in one hierarchy or another. This includes lights, cameras, and other objects that we have not yet discussed, such as joints and inverse kinematics (IK) handles (both of which are used in skeletons to animate organic models).

You can select any object in your Outliner window and it will be highlighted in your scene. Thus, the Outliner provides a quick way to locate objects in your scene if you have remembered to name them logically.

And, remember that what constitutes a model is in the eye of the beholder. The 3D artist uses the Outliner to put together objects that visually convey the model in the artist's mind. That hierarchy also facilitates the processes of putting materials on the model and animating it.

FIGURE 4.6   Dish and sorbet outliner.

The Importance of the Outliner

Later in this book, we will build a cow that looks like a 2D (and not a 3D) model. In Figure 4.7, we see a preview of him. I have put a cap on him. His cap moves along with him as he walks because the cap has been MMB dragged to the body of the cow in the Outliner, making the cap inherit the movement of the cow. The relevant fragment from the Outliner is overlaid to the upper right of the cow in the figure.

FIGURE 4.7   A cow with a red and yellow hat.

FIGURE 4.8   A cow with a cocked cap.

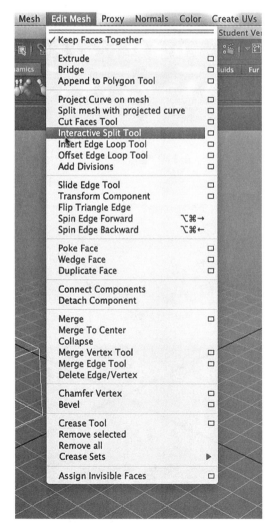

FIGURE 4.9   Interactive Split tool.

But the cap can still move independently. Indeed, our cow has decided his hat would look cooler cocked to the side. So, as he walked along, he has reached up and rotated it (see Figure 4.8).

USING BEVEL, EXTRUDE, DETACH, AND COMBINE TO MAKE A MAILBOX

We will make a mailbox and focus on elegance as we model it. How can we build a simple but nice looking model with a small set of tools and a small number of modeling steps?

A Working Set of Polygon Modeling Tools

We have taken a look at polygon modeling (with our hand example) and noted that extrusion is a key polygon modeling tool. We will make use of polygon extrusion again, along with two other key tools: Bevel and Interactive Split. We will also add tools called Detach Component and Combine.

We can do a lot with a handful of carefully chosen tools. And, we can incrementally build this working set of tools over time.

Creating a New Edge

In Figure 4.9, we have selected a polygon cube in the scene and then chosen:

Polygons Main Menu → Edit Mesh → Interactive Split Tool

(Note that in Maya 2015, the Interactive Split tool has been absorbed into a new tool called the Multi-Cut tool.)

In Figure 4.10, we see two views of it: one from Maya's "persp" view (bottom of the figure) and one from the top orthographic view. Orthographic images in the design area are most useful if the object in the scene is lined

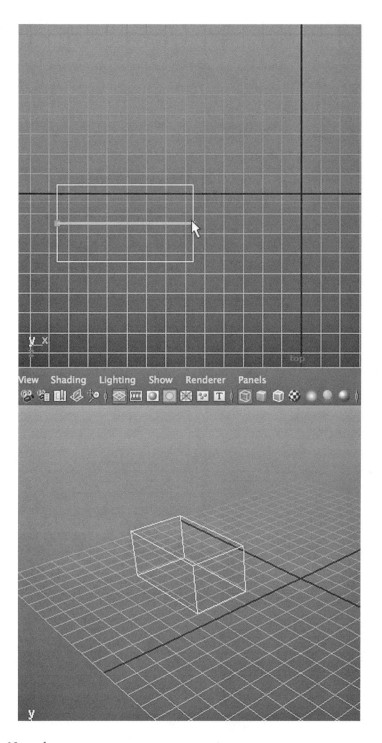

FIGURE 4.10 New edge.

up with the World axes of Maya. For example, if we are building a car, and if we precisely line the car up from front to back along the y-axis, the orthographic views will provide perfectly proportioned views of the car rather than angled images that are difficult to manage visually. Similarly, reference images are often orthographic; we would make use of a front, side, back, and top drawing from the blueprint of a 1965 Pontiac GTO to model one precisely.

With two left clicks and a tap of the Return button on the keyboard, we have added an edge to the top polygon in the cube. This gives us a bit of added geometry—without changing the shape of the object—to work with.

Beveling

Now, we are going to work with this edge. Remember that in polygon modeling we are responsible for smoothing our model; Maya does not do it for us. One of the ways to smooth an object is to bevel edges. In Maya to bevel an edge refers to turning a line into a plane. By repeated beveling, we can incrementally create what a carpenter would call a beveled, or smoothly rounded edge. In Maya, we can easily perform multiple bevels at once, allowing us to quickly smooth an edge.

The Bevel Tool is shown in Figure 4.11. But first, as seen in Figure 4.12, we select our developing model in the Main Window and then right click, and choose Edge. Once we are in Edge mode, we select one of the original top, longer edges of the model. This is *not* the center edge we just added. That new edge is only to provide a breaking point for two sets of beveling we are going to perform.

Then, we choose the Bevel tool. The result is shown in Figure 4.13. The Bevel Tool has created an abstract object called polyBevel2, and its attributes appear in the attribute box, as seen in Figure 4.14. Critical numbers in this attribute box are Offset, Segments, and Smoothing Angle. In particular, the reason there are 12 bevels in Figure 4.14 is because Segments is set to 12. Now, we select the other original long edge on the top of the model and bevel it with the Bevel Tool. The result is shown in Figure 4.15.

It's already starting to look like a mailbox.

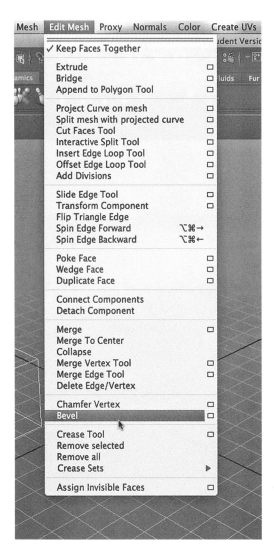

FIGURE 4.11 Bevel tool.

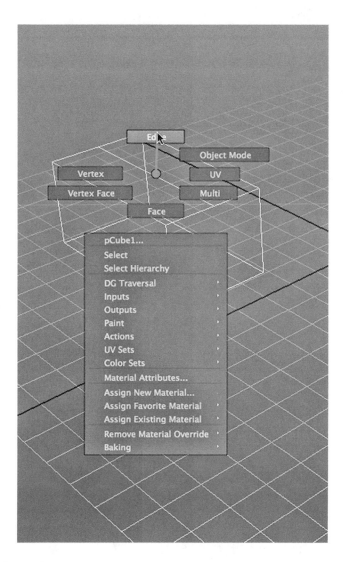

FIGURE 4.12   Edge mode.

Extrusion

In Figures 4.16 to 4.20, we go into Face mode with a right click, then Shift-select the three faces that make up the opening of the mailbox, extrude those faces, then go to the attributes of the extrusion object and set the Divisions to 1 and the Thickness to .2. You can see that the mailbox is now a little longer, and an edge has been created that goes all around the mailbox. As with the bevel tool, the extrusion tool has created an object; this is not the actual geometry of the extrusion but rather the abstract extrusion object itself. (The other attribute values of the extrusion object are the defaults on my Maya setup.)

In Figure 4.20, we see what will be the opening of the mailbox.

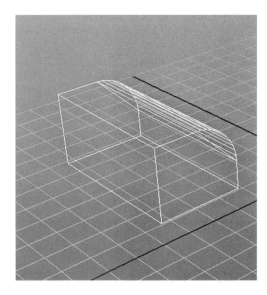

FIGURE 4.13   Beveling one side.

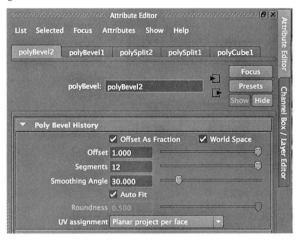

FIGURE 4.14   Bevel settings.

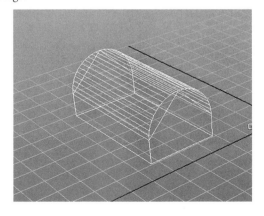

FIGURE 4.15   Both sides beveled.

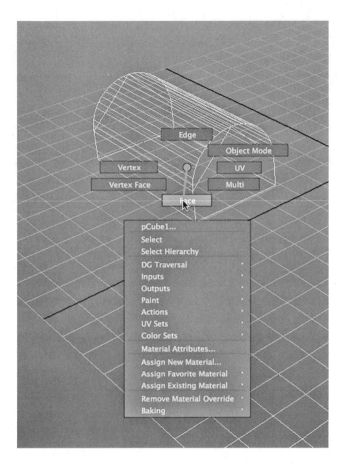

FIGURE 4.16   Face mode.

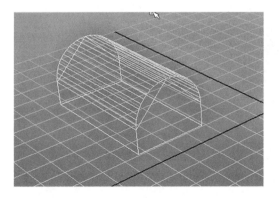

FIGURE 4.17   Faces selected.

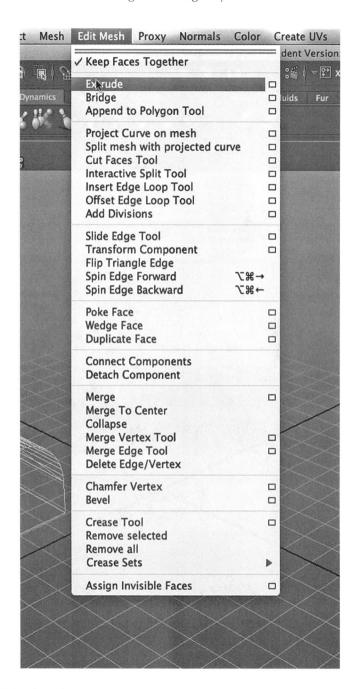

FIGURE 4.18 Extrude tool.

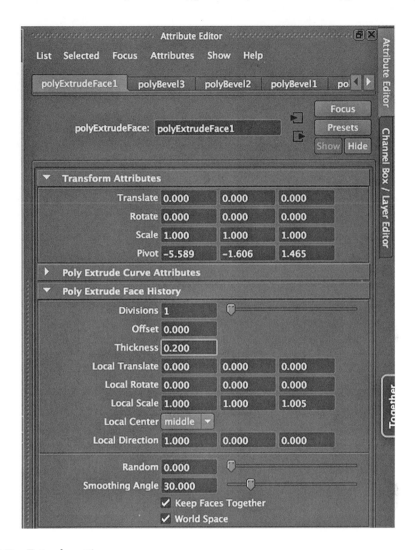

FIGURE 4.19 Extrude settings.

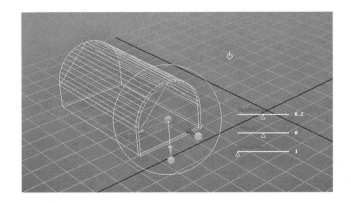

FIGURE 4.20 Extruded mailbox.

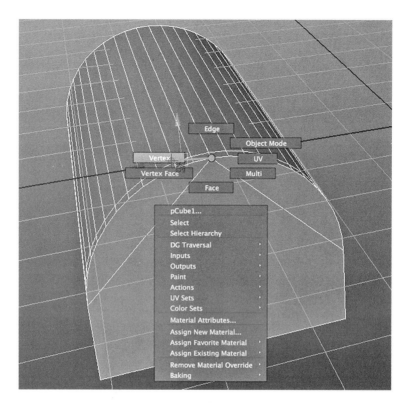

FIGURE 4.21   Vertex mode.

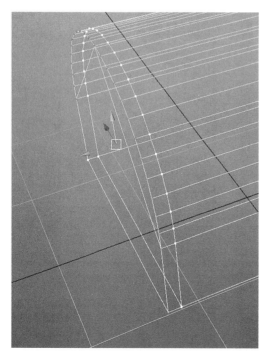

FIGURE 4.22   Selected vertices.

Detach

In Figures 4.21 to 4.24, we go into Vertex mode with a right click, Shift-select a set of vertices, and then detach them. The result, in Figure 4.24, is the door to the mailbox. In Figure 4.25, it has been placed up against the bottom front edge of the mailbox, so that we can later animate it as a door.

The Detach tool leaves the object intact, in the sense that it is still one, single object. It might be that we should have made the lid an independent object whose parent in the Outliner is the mailbox itself. Then the lid could have been opened and closed independently but would have always remained with the mailbox if it were moved.

The Clip

In Figures 4.26 and 4.27, we create two polygon planes and then use the Combine tool

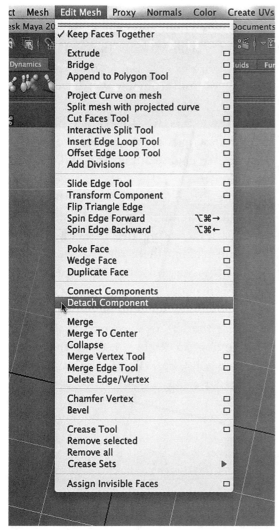

FIGURE 4.23   Detach tool.

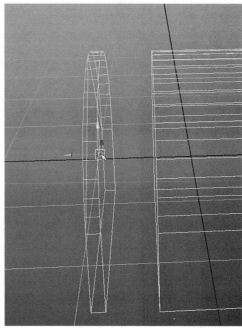

FIGURE 4.24   After detach.

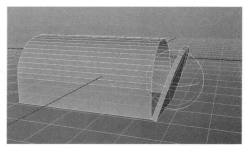

FIGURE 4.25   With door placed.

to make an L-shaped clip out of them. The Combine tool creates a single, integrated object, so we only use it when we no longer want to morph or animate the two pieces individually.

In Figure 4.28, we have placed the clip up against the door, and have made the box the parent of the clip. So, the clip will stay in place when we move the box.

There is more work that needs to be done, but with a few simple tools we have modeled something that is unmistakably a mailbox, shown in Figure 4.29.

BEVELED LETTERS

We used beveling to help build the mailbox. Beveling also plays a role in a toolset that is used to create 3D text. As seen in Figure 4.30, it can be found by going to:

any Main Menu → Create → Text

FIGURE 4.26   Two planes selected.

This pulls up the window in the left half of Figure 4.31. There are four different kinds of text to choose from. The first two use NURBS curves and the second two make use of polygon geometry. We have chosen polygon geometry, with beveling used to make the letters 3D. This choice has made the window in the right half of Figure 4.31 pop up. We choose a font, and make it bold and 16 pitch.

In the left window, we type in the letters we want to appear. Figure 4.32 shows the result after creating two lines of beveled text and placing them on a vertical plane behind the cow, which we will study later. Later in this book, when we look at creating the cow, we will see how we have given the cow and the letters that comical 2D look. The version of Figure 4.32 in the Color Insert (p. CI-3) best illustrates the 2D effect and the lettering.

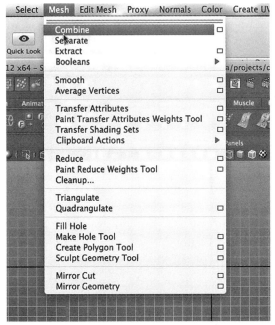

FIGURE 4.27   Combine tool.

FIGURE 4.28   Clip parented to box.

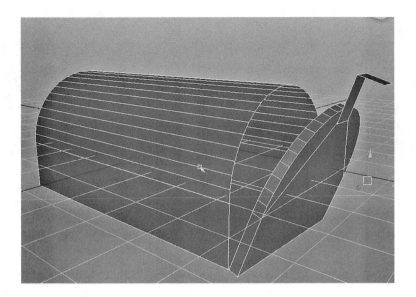

FIGURE 4.29   The mailbox.

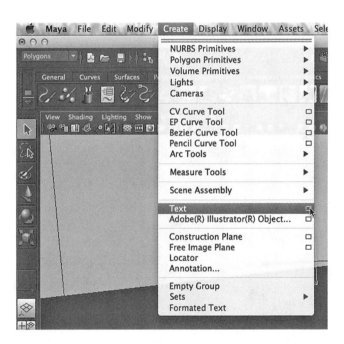

FIGURE 4.30   Creating text.

MAKING A POLYGON MOAI

The following is an overview of the process of crafting a simple but complete model by starting with a concept. We use a small set of Maya polygon modeling tools. At the end of the example, we will smooth our model by making quick use of subdivision modeling. We will also look at rendering the model.

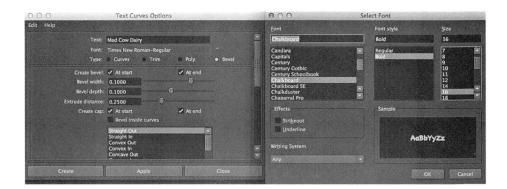

FIGURE 4.31   Choosing Bevel and Chalkboard.

Rapa Nui

There is an island in the Pacific Ocean about a five-hour jet plane ride from the coast of Chile. It is called Rapa Nui. (It is sometimes called Easter Island because a Western explorer "discovered" it on Easter Sunday.) Between 1000 and 1600 A.D., the indigenous people, also called Rapa Nui, made statues called Moai, which represented their ancestors. Rivalry between clans led in part to larger and larger statues being made over time. The average height of the 900 or so Moai on the island today is about 14 feet, though they range up to 30 feet tall. Most were carved out of volcanic tuff, entirely in the quarry. When a Moai was complete, it would be cut out of the quarry. It would then be upended and "walked" using ropes to an ahu, an altar where it was placed. The last detail added were its eyes, white coral with obsidian or red scoria pupils, and at this moment the spirit entered the Moai.

During the 17th century, the society was in crisis, and all of the Moai were knocked down during wars, though some of them have been stood back up since then. The eyes are gone on almost all of them—stolen or eroded away. The statues share a common style that is striking, almost intimidating. Some are just heads, some have complete bodies, and some even include a cylindrical stone on top, which represents the topknots in which the men tied their hair.

FIGURE 4.32   **(See Color Insert on p. C-3)** The Mad Cow Dairy.

A Modeling Exercise: Making a Moai on Your Own

Since a Moai is a specific art form, it is best to start with one or more reference images. Rapa Nui is a popular tourist destination, and so there are many images of Moai on the Web.

The following is an overview of constructing a Moai using polygon modeling. You can probably follow the steps in the example by looking at Figures 4.33 to 4.75

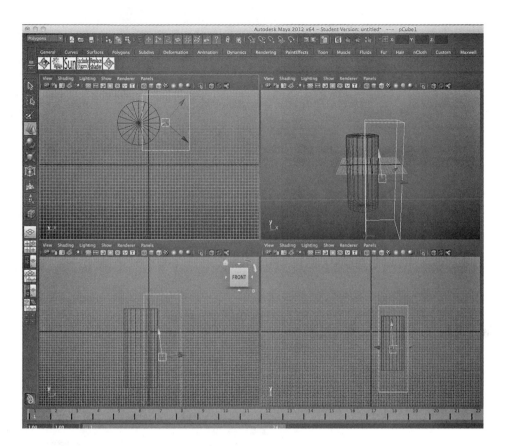

FIGURE 4.33   Boolean setup.

(Figure 4.61 is also in the Color Insert). They illustrate the process of building a Moai using a small number of polygon tools.

Don't be afraid for now, though, to simply look through the images to get an intuitive feeling for how Maya can be used to incrementally craft a model. That is the real goal, to see the granularity and succession of the steps. You can always try to build your own Moai after you have covered more of this book.

Making a Moai with Polygon Modeling

Roughly speaking, a Moai looks like a cylinder with a flat back, and so I started with a polygon cylinder, lined up a tall cube, and used it to cut off the back of the cylinder by performing a Boolean difference. This tool is found by Shift-selecting the cylinder, then the cube, and then choosing:

any Main Menu → Mesh → Booleans → Difference

I then used a combination of extrusion, and pulling on faces and edges, as well as rotating faces.

A hint: Remember that by using the right mouse button, you can move between vertex, edge, and object mode; this menu, called the Marking Menu, is shown in Figure 4.36.

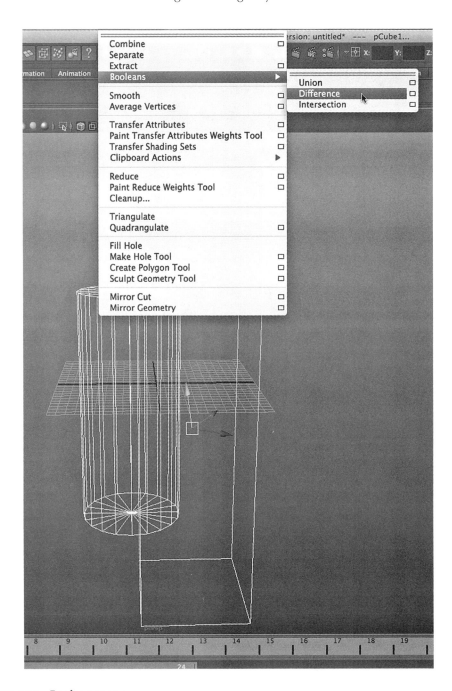

FIGURE 4.34   Boolean menu.

I also inserted edges to create new detailed geometry that would let me pull out features of the Moai. Note the use of the Insert Edge Loop tool in Figure 4.37. This creates an entire loop of edges around an object.

Another hint: Remember that by hitting the space bar, you can pull up a helpful set of shortcuts to various tools. This is used in Figure 4.57.

Smoothing and Rendering

The very last thing I did with my model before putting a material on it was to convert it to subdivision to smooth it and thereby simulate a bit of a weathered look. We can go to:

any Main Menu → Modify → Convert → Polygons to Subdiv

This completely changes the nature of the geometry of a model. The overall geometric effect can be rather unpredictable on a model that has a low vertex/edge/polygon count. On denser geometry it makes less radical changes to the original polygon object, but still, until you are familiar with how models tend to look after being con-

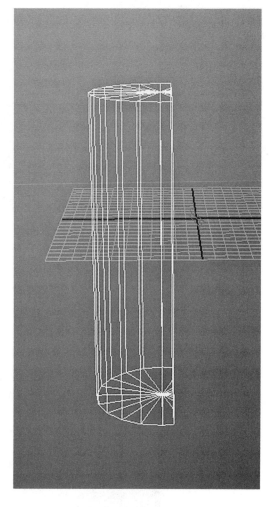

FIGURE 4.35   Boolean result.

verted to subdivision, the process can be quite unpredictable. Also, although subdivision support has been all but removed from Maya, the conversion to subdivision capability has remained, presumably because people use it as a smoothing technique (see Figure 4.76).

My finished result is shown in Figure 4.77. It uses a canned Maya material with only a bit of tweaking. I also created a Blinn material; see Figure 4.78 for the settings of that material. I then applied that finish to the Moai to make a steel version (see Figure 4.80).

SMOOTHING A POLYGON MODEL: MANY CHOICES

Maya has an explicit Smooth tool for polygon models, and it creates a result similar to the conversion to subdivision tool. Autodesk's advice is that the Smooth tool is preferable for conversion to subdivision.

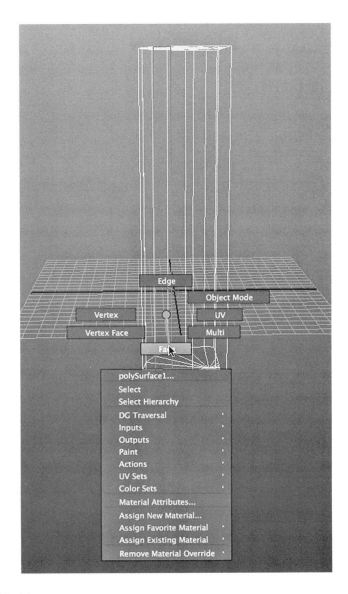

FIGURE 4.36   Marking menu.

Smooth Tool

That Smooth tool can be found by going to:

Polygons Main Menu → Mesh → Smooth

There are also more localized, surgical techniques for smoothing a polygon model.

Using the Smooth Tool Locally

First, it's important to note that we do not use the Smooth tool on entire objects. We can go into Face, Edge, or Vertex mode with a right click and carefully choose the polygons

FIGURE 4.37   Inserted Edge Loop tool.

we want to smooth. In fact, the Smooth tool was used locally on various parts of the face shown in Figure 4.81.

Next, we consider a couple of other smoothing options.

Adding Faces and Manipulating New Faces, and Beveling Edges

We have looked already at using beveling to smooth a model. (Remember the mailbox model.) This is a bit similar to using the Smooth tool, as it is another way of adding faces and giving them different angles. In Figure 4.81, we have already beveled the left, vertical edge of the nose.

Another way of smoothing is by manually adding faces using a tool like the Insert Edge Loop tool, as discussed earlier. The angles of these new faces can then be manipulated with the Rotate tool, and by using the Move tool on vertices, edges, and faces.

The Insert Edge Loop and Interactive Split tool (and the new Multi-Cut tool in Maya 2015) are good for surgically inserting detail into an object so that the rest of the object's surface will still have a mesh that is less dense, making it easier to manipulate on a larger scale. The Insert Edge Loop tool is particularly good for another task, that of adding a

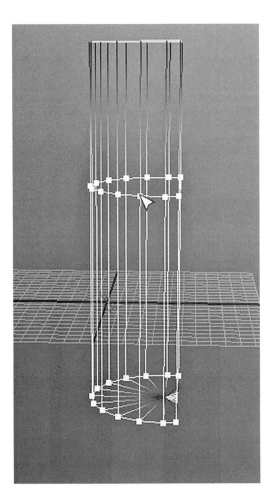

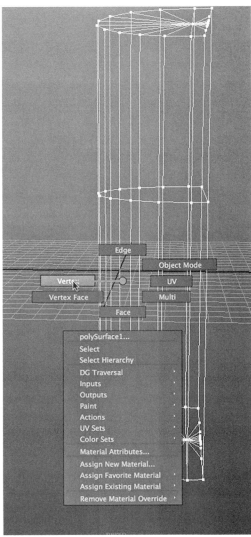

FIGURE 4.38   Edge loop.   FIGURE 4.39   Vertex mode.

series of edges around an object, so that a smooth extrusion can be performed later. We might put edge loops around the eye of a human so that the eye socket can be pushed in, or we might put a series of edge loops around the tip of a baseball bat that it can be smoothly pulled outward. In both cases, we are likely to want at least two or three concentric edge loops to support a gradual extrusion.

Manipulating Normals to Smooth Edges

In Figure 4.82, we are selecting the polygon "Soften Edge" tool. This does not actually alter the geometry. Here's how it works.

In geometry, a "normal" is a line that is at 90 degrees to the tangent of a curve or to a straight line running across the surface of a plane. On a given polygon face, all normals

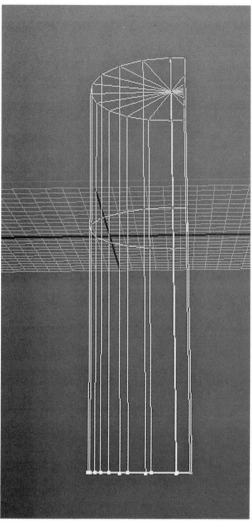

FIGURE 4.40   Vertices selected.

FIGURE 4.41   Move tool.

are parallel. So, we can informally refer to a normal as a single line that emanates from a face at 90 degrees. When renderers calculate the effects of light hitting reflective surfaces, they use the normal on each face to decide how to perform this calculation. Consider a polygon cube with exactly six faces. Now consider two neighboring faces and the edge that connects them. On one side of the edge, the normal of that face is at 90 degrees to the normal on the neighboring face. So, light bouncing off these two faces emanates in two very different directions.

Consider Figure 4.83. First, I went to Preferences for Maya, as shown in the top of the figure, and chose Polygons under the word Display. Then I checked the Normals Box in the top center of the Preferences panel. This causes Maya to display the normals for each object.

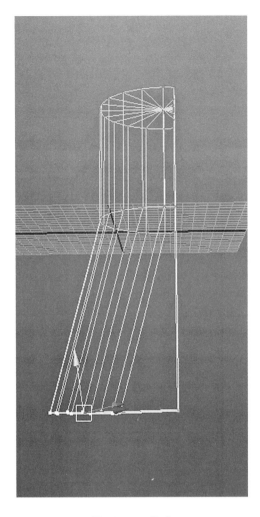

FIGURE 4.42 Vertices pulled.

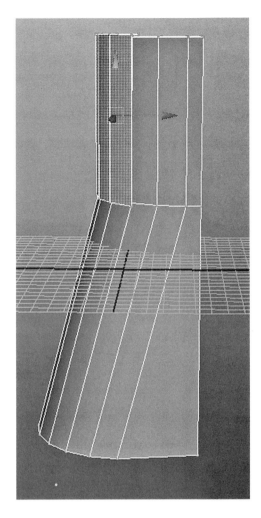

FIGURE 4.43 Face mode.

I then created a polygon sphere and a polygon cube. Their normals are indicated by the straight lines emanating from the objects. If you look at the angles of the normals (with respect to World Space) of the cube, you can see that it only has six unique values, one for each face.

But mathematically, a sphere has an infinite number of unique normals. Maya only keeps track of hundreds or thousands, but it is easy to see that the angles of the normals on a sphere change very slowly as we proceed over the surface of the sphere.

On the cube, all we have to do is cross an edge to get a sudden, 90 degree change in the orientation of the normals. (After checking off the Normals box in the Preferences panel, normals will be shown for new primitives, not for ones already created in the scene.)

Figure 4.84 is a composite image; in the top part, we have gone into Edge mode with a right click, selected a single edge, and then chosen:

Polygons Main Menu → Normals → Soften Edge tool

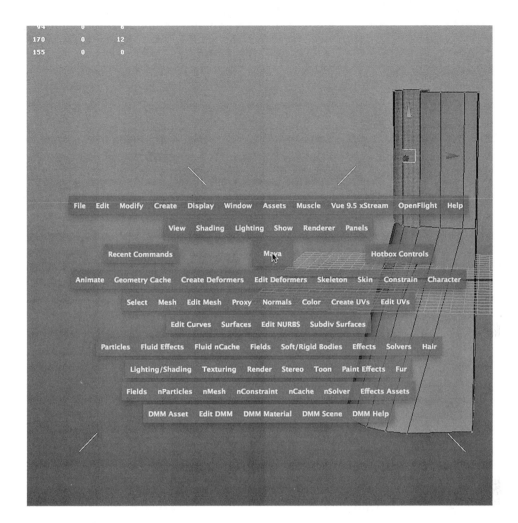

FIGURE 4.44   Shift hold menu.

The resulting render is at the bottom of Figure 4.84. The cube is unchanged geometrically; the apparent smoothing of the object is only a render-time artifact.

When we use the Soften Edge tool, it leaves the geometry alone but alters the normals information associated with the object. In a sense we trick Maya into thinking that there is no hard edge by gradually changing the apparent angles of the normals on either side of the edge. So instead of looking like they suddenly change by 90 degrees when we cross over the edge, they seem to change in value gradually, more like the normals on the surface of the sphere.

We can use the technique shown in Figure 4.84 to soften a vertical edge on the Moai's nose. The rendered result is subtle but can be seen in Figure 4.85. Look at the vertical edge running along the left side of the Moai's face. Again, we have not changed the geometry; rather, we have manipulated the normals information by using the Soften Edge tool.

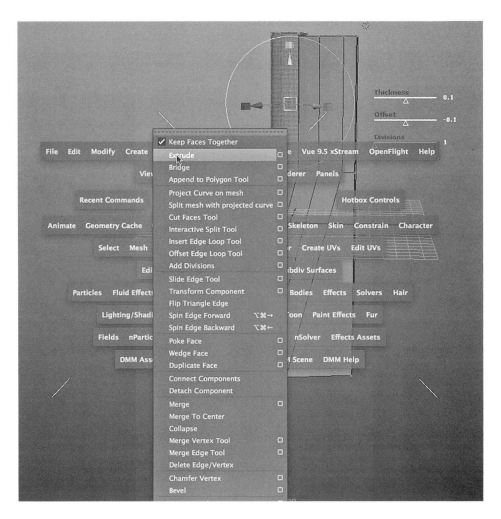

FIGURE 4.45   Extrude tool.

Smoothing with mental ray, without Changing the Geometry

There is a similar technique that only works with the mental ray renderer and not with the Maya Software renderer.

Figure 4.86 shows a wireframe of the Moai model. With a right click, we have gone into Object mode, and then selected the Moai. All we have done after this is hit the 3 key, and the immediate result is shown in Figure 4.87.

Let's look at the rendered version. Figure 4.88 shows the Moai rendered before hitting 3 and Figure 4.89 shows the render of the Moai after hitting 3. (Figure 4.89 happens to show the left side of the face, not the right.) We can see by looking at the Moai's jawline that the model has been significantly smoothed. (We can go back to the way the Moai looks in Figures 4.86 and 4.88 simply by hitting the 1 key.)

However, there is no actual change in the geometry. If you render the scene with the Maya Software renderer, it will not be smoothed.

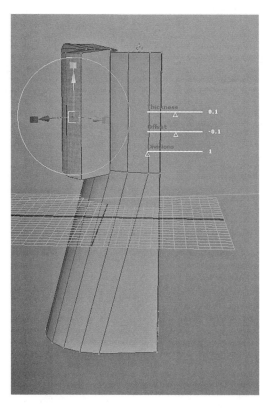

FIGURE 4.46   After extrude.

SURGICALLY MENDING AN IMPERFECT MODEL

Frequently, the long process of manipulating one or more geometric objects into a maturing model creates unexpected, flawed geometry. There are many reasons for this. If you are using Maya 2014 or earlier, the problem could be due to having used one of the Boolean operators, which tend to create odd artifacts in models. The problem could also be the result of having to shift course and morph a model in ways we had not envisioned. It is a good idea to have a game plan on how locally damaged models can be mended. (It should be noted that in Maya 2015, the implementation of the Boolean geometry operators has been improved.)

Merging Edges in a Single Piece of Geometry

We created a lid for the mailbox in Figure 4.29 by selecting a ring of vertices and separating the object into two pieces. The mailbox remained one object.

The problem is that the bottom edge is separated from the rest of the mailbox (see Figure 4.90). Perhaps we should have left the bottom of the ring of vertices connected so that we could more naturally animate the opening and closing of the mailbox. So, to reconnect the bottom of the lid to the mailbox, we select the series of edges that run across

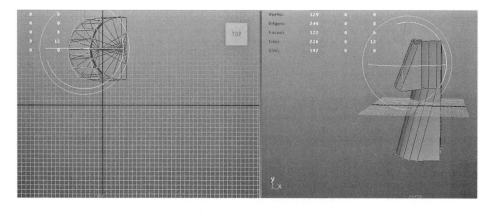

FIGURE 4.47   Rotate.

 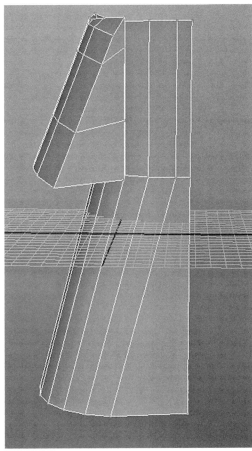

FIGURE 4.48   Inserted edge loop.   FIGURE 4.49   Set for nose and brow.

the bottom of the lid and select the corresponding series of edges along the bottom of the mailbox, and as seen in Figure 4.91, we choose:

Polygons Main → Edit Mesh → Merge Edge Tool

We hit Enter. Figure 4.92 is a closeup of the two edges before this process, and Figure 4.93 is afterward.

Removing a Face with Merge to Center

There is another powerful surgical tool on the same dropdown menu. We get to it by selecting:

Polygons Main Menu → Edit Mesh → Merge to Center

Figure 4.94 shows a set of double doors. (In Chapter 10, we will create them.)

FIGURE 4.50 Extruded and rotated nose.

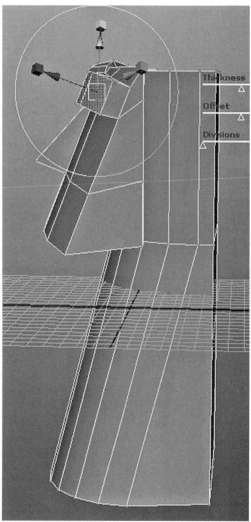

FIGURE 4.51 Extruded for head.

Perhaps we need a pair of doors that do not have windows in them. If we have glass paned doors, we do not have to model two new doors from scratch. Instead, we select four edges around the upper left window. Then we choose:

Polygons Main Menu → Edit Mesh → Merge to Center (see Figure 4.95)

The result is shown in Figure 4.96, and a render of the result is shown in Figure 4.97. We have taken a loop of edges, and by merging them, removed one of the glass panes in the doors.

Filling in a Hole in a Polygon Model with a Bridge Tool

Here, we look at another tool that can be used to fix a hole in a model.

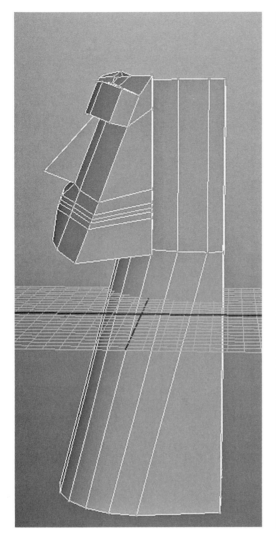

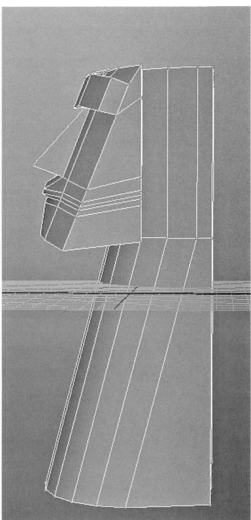

FIGURE 4.52 Pulled faces for mouth.   FIGURE 4.53 Pulled upper lip.

Consider the Moai in Figure 4.98. There is a missing polygon on the side of the nose. So, we right click and go into Edge mode, as seen in Figure 4.99. Then we select two edges, as shown in Figure 4.100. We select:

Polygons Main Menu → Edit Mesh → Bridge

In Figure 4.101, we succeeded in filling in the hole, but there are now multiple faces where we only want one (see Figure 4.102). So, we hit Control+Z until we undo the Bridge operation. Then we select the Bridge tool again, and this time click on the little box to the

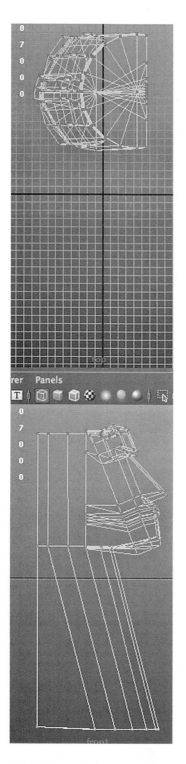

FIGURE 4.54 Side and top views.

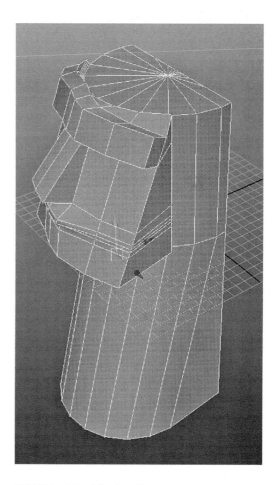

FIGURE 4.55 Moai so far.

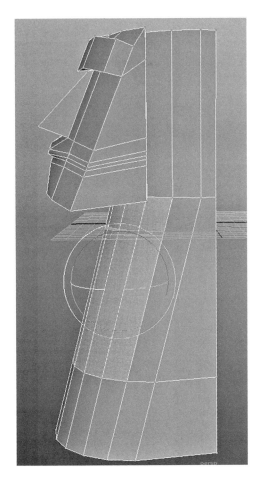

FIGURE 4.56   Edge loop for belly.

right of the tool's name and pull up its settings, shown in Figure 4.103. We change the number of divisions to 0 and try again.

It worked, and Figure 4.104 shows the result. One caveat: When you use the Bridge tool, all selected edges must be on the same object.

MAKING SMALL AND GRACEFUL CHANGES TO A MODEL

Often, we need to make small-scale and precise changes to a model to get just the right look. And even if a given object seems to render the way we want, it's good to make its geometry clean and elegant. That will ensure having no odd rendering results when we move an object, change its lighting, or move the rendering camera.

Sliding an Edge

Figure 4.105 shows a rendering of the Moai. Although we want this statue to look worn, the crease in the smile does not look good. In Figure 4.106, we see the problem: edges that are poorly lined up. Two tools can be used in concert to clean this up. The first is the standard Move tool, with the right click mode set at Edge. The other can be found at:

Polygons Main Menu → Edit Mesh → Slide Edge Tool

Figure 4.107 shows the dropdown containing this second tool. By moving and sliding edges, we can straighten the lines of edges around the mouth. The resulting geometry is shown in Figure 4.108. The resulting render is shown in Figure 4.109.

There is a significant difference between the Move tool and the Slide Edge tool. Figure 4.110 is a closeup of the left cheek of the Moai. Figure 4.111 is the corresponding rendering. In Figure 4.112, we have used the Move tool to push three edges to the right. The resulting (not very nice) rendering is shown in Figure 4.113.

We undo this by using Control+Z or by choosing:

any Main Menu → Edit → Undo

We repeat this until we are back to the state of our model depicted in Figure 4.110.

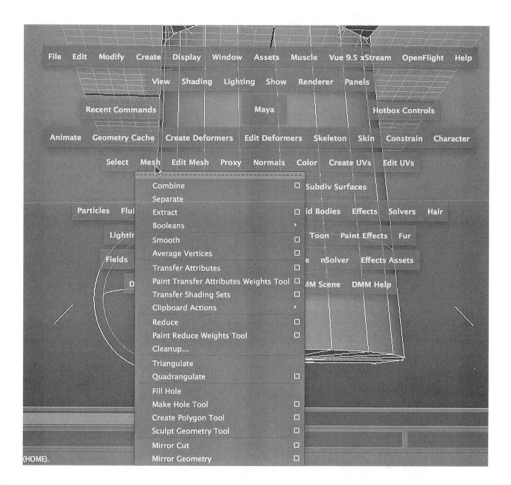

FIGURE 4.57   Mesh menu.

Now, we use the Slide Edge tool instead. This allows us to move the same edges over without pulling the cheek outward (see Figure 4.114). The smooth, proper rendering is shown in Figure 4.115.

The point is that the Slide Edge tool will constrain the movement of a series of edges to the original plane in which they are situated. When moving edges around, it's important to carefully select the right tool, Move or Slide Edge.

Soft Move

In Figure 4.116, we are selecting the Move tool, and by clicking on the little box on the menu selection, we pull up the settings of this tool, as seen in Figure 4.117. We click on Soft Select. Maya uses a spectrum of colors (yellow to orange to red to black) to indicate that if we move the component we have selected (in this case, the vertex with the box around it), we will move neighboring components as well. As we move from yellow to black, we are making the changes smaller in scale, to give us a gradual change in the geometry.

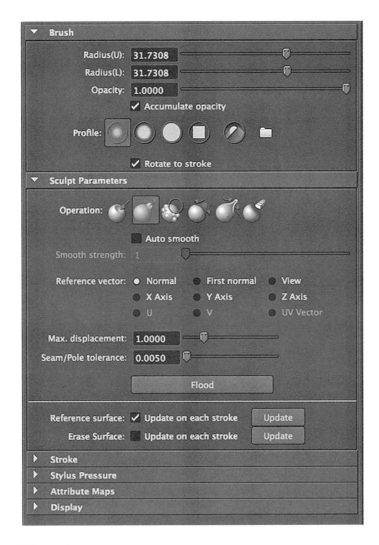

FIGURE 4.58   Sculpt tool.

In Figure 4.118, we show this selected vertex more clearly. We then move it. The result is shown in Figure 4.119: the upper part of the left line along the face has been molded in a graduated, smooth fashion. Yellow (white in Figure 4.117) indicates the most significant movement of vertices, while black indicates the smallest movement of vertices. Keep in mind that we are manipulating the angles between faces and altering the geometry of the wireframe.

Aligning Objects

Often, we want to line up two or more objects either in relationship to each other or with respect to World Space. Maya provides a handful of tools to do this; they can be found on the Modify dropdown in the Main Menu. We have seen that objects should almost always

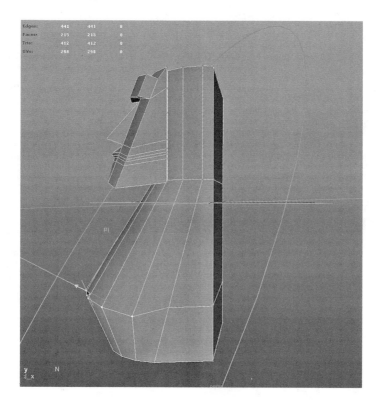

FIGURE 4.59   Sculpt on vertices.

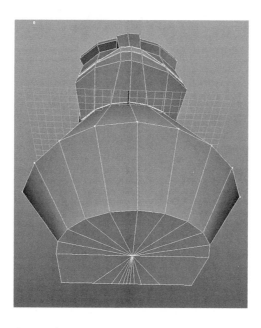

FIGURE 4.60   Bottom-up view.

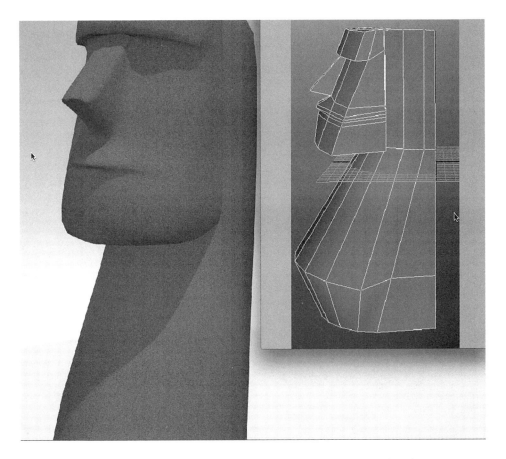

FIGURE 4.61 **(See p. CI-4 of Color Insert)** Moai wireframe and Moai rendered.

be moved directly along the x, y, or z axis, and not slid around freely in 3-space. Similarly, it is good practice to always place objects carefully in 3-space and to move them in a precise fashion with respect to each other. This will greatly facilitate animating objects in 3-space without getting unexpected behavior.

Figure 4.120 shows us the Modify dropdown on the Main Menu. With the two statues selected, we choose:

any Main Menu → Snap Align Objects → Align Objects

We click the little box to the right of Align Objects to get the settings for this tool; up pops the window we see in Figure 4.121. In Figure 4.122, we check off the World Y and the World Z boxes, meaning that we want the two Moai statues snapped into alignment with each other across the y-z plane. The result can be seen in Figure 4.123.

In Figure 4.124, we see some shortcuts for alignment tools; they are on the top left of the Main Window and have magnets in their icons.

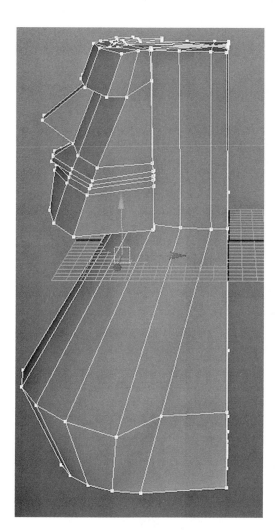

FIGURE 4.62   Pulling nose vertices up.

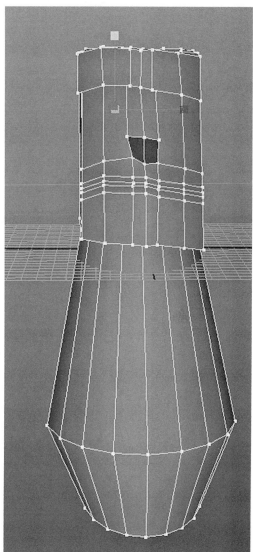

FIGURE 4.63   After scaling down width.

Also, Maya allows us to create a primitive (sphere, cube, etc.) by using the left mouse button to place and then scale the primitive. But that tends to put it in a random location that might make it clumsy to work with later. In Figure 4.125, we see how the Translate attributes of a just-created object (in this case a polygon cube) can be used to center it in World Space.

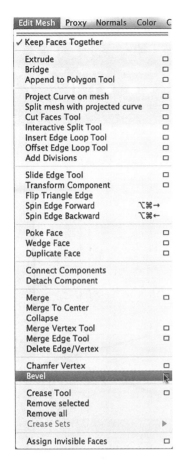

FIGURE 4.64   Bevel tool.

USING THE SWEEP OF A CYLINDER AND RESIZING TO MAKE A BREADBOX

We will turn back to NURBS modeling and highlight another reason why NURBS is about modeling surfaces, not necessarily enclosed objects. Even when it looks like we're working with a complete 3D primitive, the truth is somewhat different.

A NURBS Surface

A mailbox of the sort we modeled previously and the bread-box we are about to make are very similar looking objects. But because of the difference in the mechanisms used to open and close the two boxes, we will take a completely different approach to modeling our breadbox. NURBS modeling has a few unique, elegant capabilities that make the process of modeling and animating very fluid. Next, we look at a powerful attribute of NURBS surfaces called a "sweep."

In Figure 4.126, we are creating a NURBS primitive, a cylinder. The result is shown in Figure 4.127. As a reminder about the nature of models made out of NURBS surfaces, notice that in Figure 4.128 the two ends are separate objects and can be moved independently. So, our cylinder is really three NURBS surfaces.

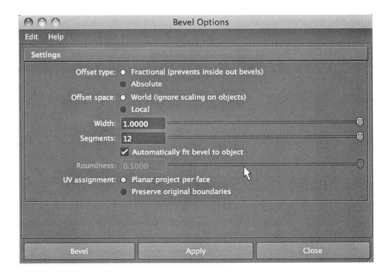

FIGURE 4.65   Bevel settings.

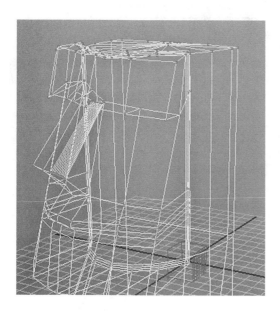

FIGURE 4.66   After beveling.

FIGURE 4.67   Rendered beveled nose.

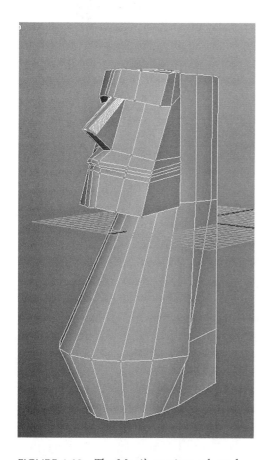

FIGURE 4.68   The Moai's vertices selected.

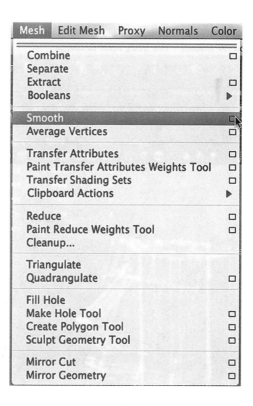

FIGURE 4.69   Smooth tool.

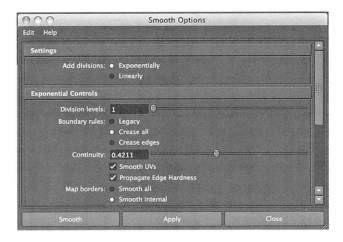

FIGURE 4.70   Smooth settings.

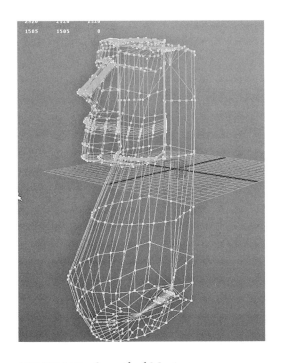

FIGURE 4.71   Smoothed Moai.

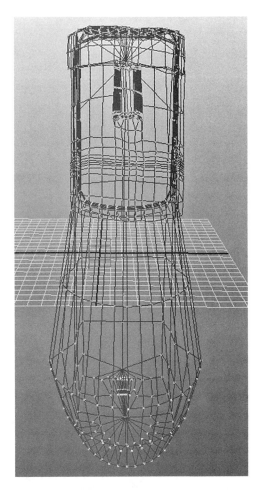

FIGURE 4.72   After cleanup—adjusting edges and vertices.

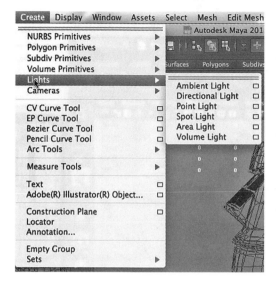

FIGURE 4.73   Light menu.

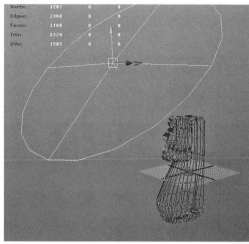

FIGURE 4.74   With spotlight.

The Sweep of a NURBS Surface

Consider Figure 4.129, which shows the attribute box of our NURBS cylinder. Notice the Start Sweep and End Sweep attributes. The settings in the figure cause the surface to "sweep" back on itself and make the tube-shaped part of the cylinder. In Figure 4.130, we have stopped the sweep at 180 degrees. This should reinforce the fact that with NURBS, we are working with surfaces—always.

By the way, if you create a NURBS sphere, you can use the sweep of it to create an eye that is blinking.

Nested Objects

Sometimes, when creating an organic object like an alien that does not represent anything in the real world, we get inspired and want to move in a quick, fluid fashion. We eyeball the dimensions of the model and manipulate vertices, edges, and faces sloppily. But when an object must be morphed in a precise way, the Attribute Editor provides us with ways of controlling sizes, distances, angles, and so forth. Often it is well worth your while to stop, take a few moments, and be careful about what you are doing.

When you want to scale an object, you can click on the Scale tool in the Toolbox and use the red, blue, and green boxes on the tool to scale an object in the x, z, and y dimensions, respectively.

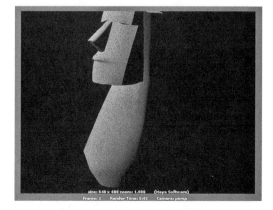

FIGURE 4.75   Rendered smooth with light.

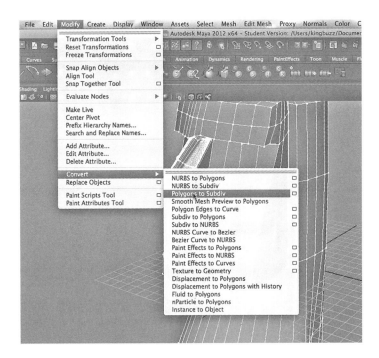

FIGURE 4.76   Convert Polygons to Subdiv.

For example, in Figures 4.131, 4.132, and 4.133, we are first copying the cylinder, and then pasting it in place, and then precisely scaling it down in the x and y dimensions by 5 percent. This is because we want to create two nested objects. There are many times when you want to do this, in particular, sometimes a thick glass can be more naturally modeled by putting one glass container inside another. This causes light to refract twice, creating the illusion of a thick surface.

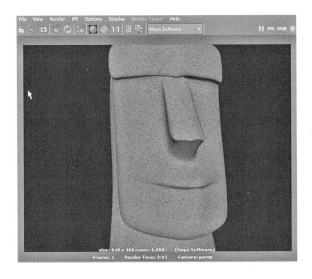

FIGURE 4.77   Subdiv render.

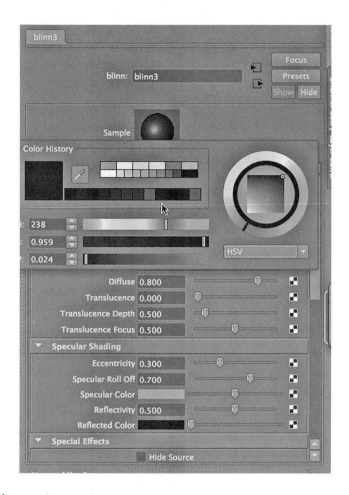

FIGURE 4.78   Blinn settings.

In Figure 4.134, we have centered the smaller cylinder inside the larger one.

Finishing the Geometry of the Breadbox

In Figure 4.135, the sweep of the inside cylinder is set to 115 degrees. In Figure 4.136, there is a plane that will serve as the bottom of the breadbox. In Figure 4.137, the pieces have been put together. (But they are all still separate objects and not in a hierarchy.) In Figures 4.138 and 4.139, the lid of the box is highlighted. In Figure 4.140, we are opening and closing the breadbox by using the Rotate tool on the lid. In Figure 4.141, we see the breadbox closed.

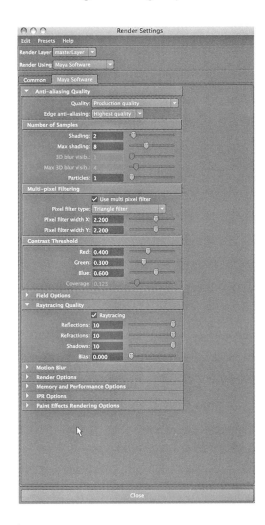

FIGURE 4.79   Render settings.

FIGURE 4.80   **(See p. CI-4 of Color Insert)** Metallic finish.

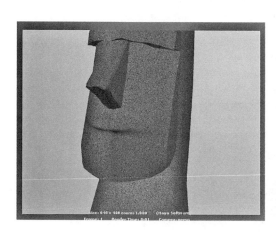

FIGURE 4.81   Smooth original.

FIGURE 4.82   Soften edge.

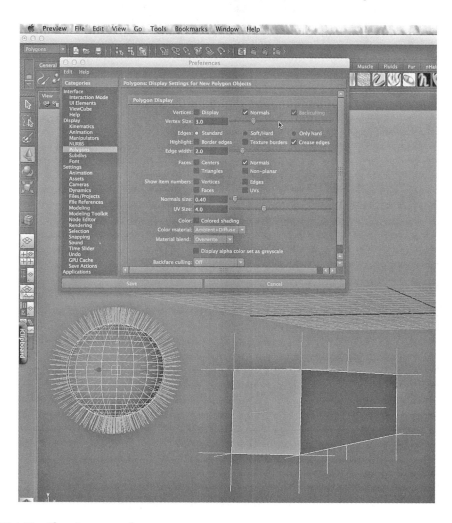

FIGURE 4.83   Showing normals.

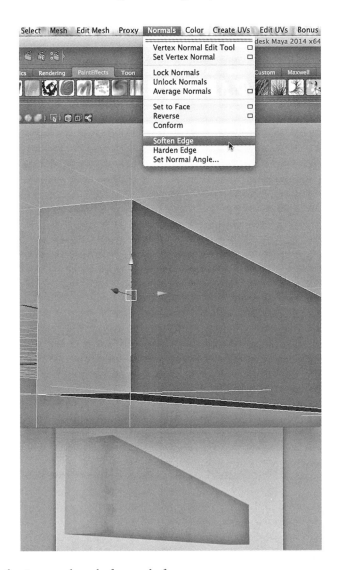

FIGURE 4.84   Softening an edge—before and after.

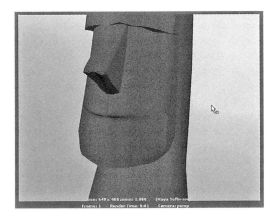

FIGURE 4.85   Smoothed render.

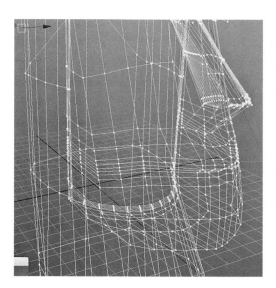

FIGURE 4.86   Moai not smoothed.

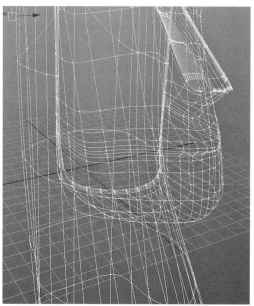

FIGURE 4.87   Moai smoothed.

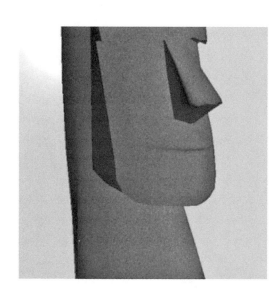

FIGURE 4.88   Rendered not smoothed Moai.

FIGURE 4.89   **(See p. CI-4 of Color Insert)**
Final Moai rendered.

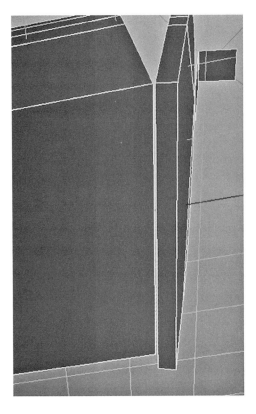

FIGURE 4.90 The detached lid.

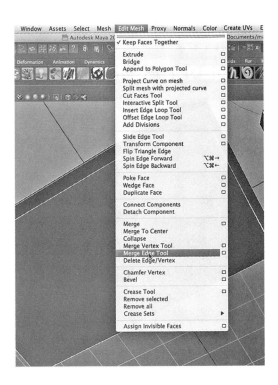

FIGURE 4.91 The Merge Edge tool.

FIGURE 4.92 Before merging.

FIGURE 4.93 After merging.

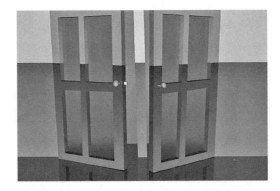

FIGURE 4.94   The doors.

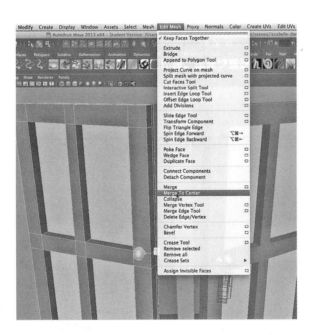

FIGURE 4.95   The Merge to Center tool.

FIGURE 4.96   One pane gone.

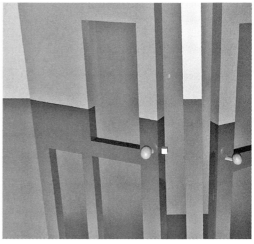

FIGURE 4.97   The re-engineered door.

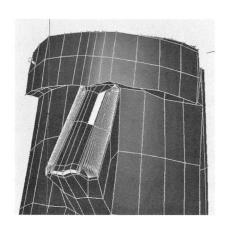

FIGURE 4.98   A missing face.

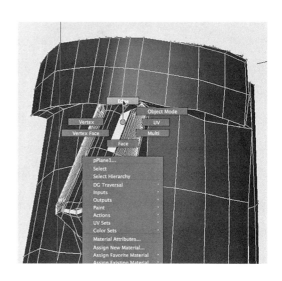

FIGURE 4.99   Edge mode.

FIGURE 4.100   Two edges selected.

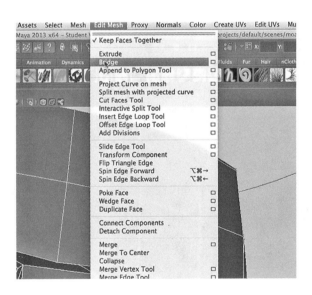

FIGURE 4.101   Bridge tool.

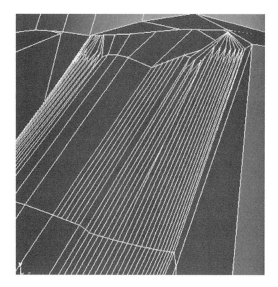

FIGURE 4.102   The result—too many faces.

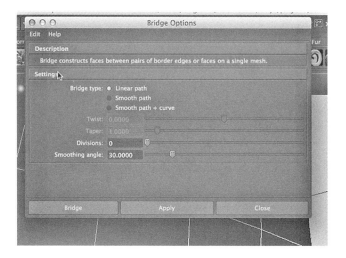

FIGURE 4.103   Bridge tool settings.

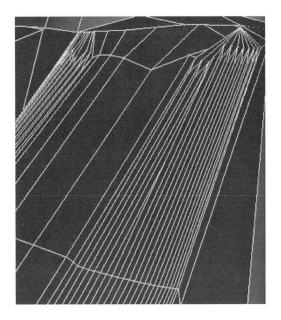

FIGURE 4.104 The correct result.

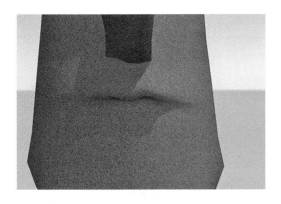

FIGURE 4.105 A twisted smile.

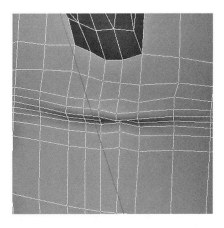

FIGURE 4.106 The problem—twisted lips.

FIGURE 4.107   The Slide Edge tool.

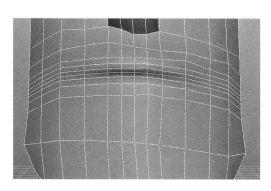

FIGURE 4.108   The fixed geometry.

FIGURE 4.109   A better Moai render with cleaned-up lips.

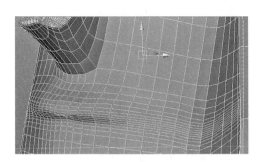

FIGURE 4.110   The left cheek of the Maoi.

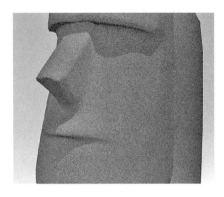

FIGURE 4.111   The rendering of the left cheek.

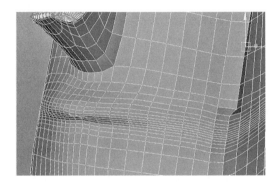

FIGURE 4.112   Moving a series of images with the Move tool.

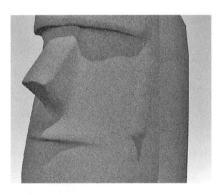

FIGURE 4.113   The resulting, damaged Moai rendered.

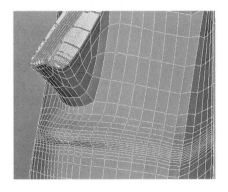

FIGURE 4.114   Using the Slide Edge tool instead.

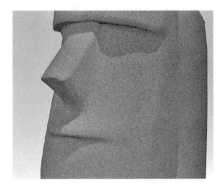

FIGURE 4.115   The resulting render with the jawline moved gracefully.

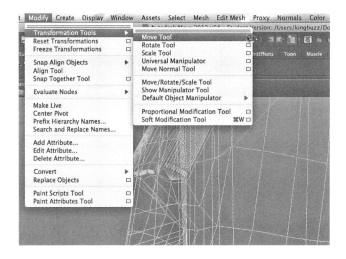

FIGURE 4.116   Move tool.

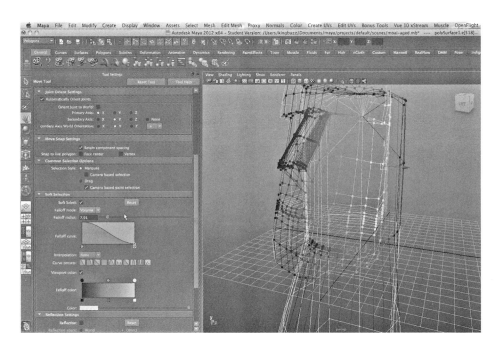

FIGURE 4.117   Soft select.

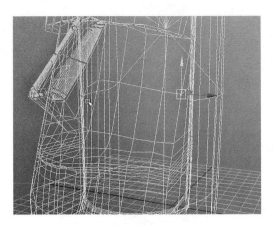

FIGURE 4.118   One vertex to move.

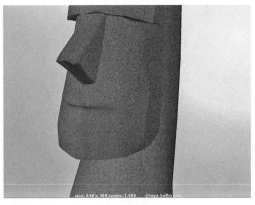

FIGURE 4.119   Rendering after soft moving of the vertex.

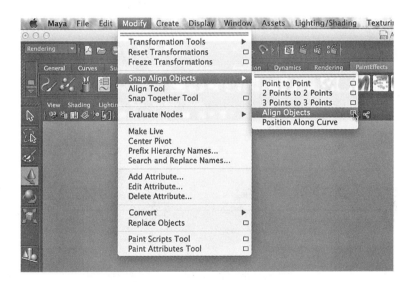

FIGURE 4.120   The Snap Align tool.

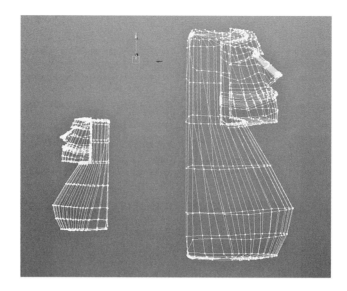

FIGURE 4.121   Two statues in 3-space.

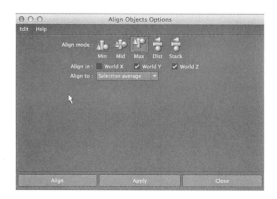

FIGURE 4.122   Choosing an alignment plane.

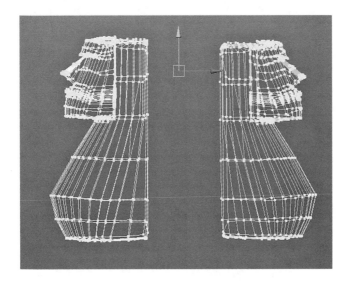

FIGURE 4.123   The aligned Moais.

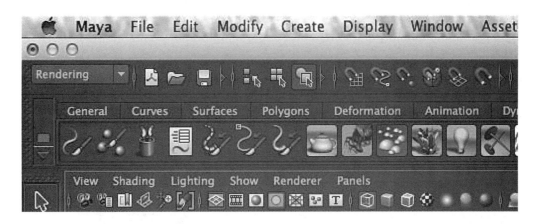

FIGURE 4.124   The "magnet" icons.

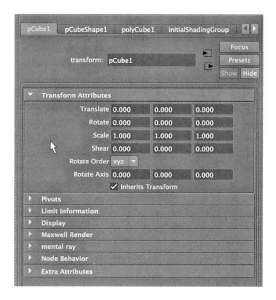

FIGURE 4.125   Centering an object.

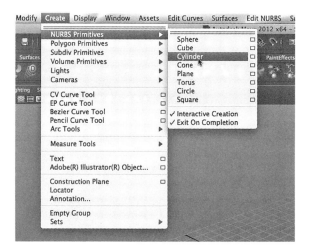

FIGURE 4.126   Creating a NURBS cylinder.

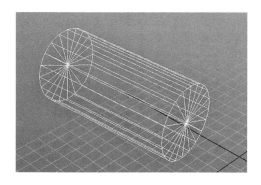

FIGURE 4.127   NURBS cylinder.

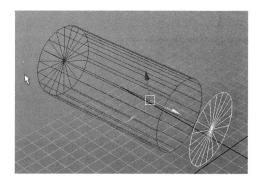

FIGURE 4.128   Cylinder with a separated end.

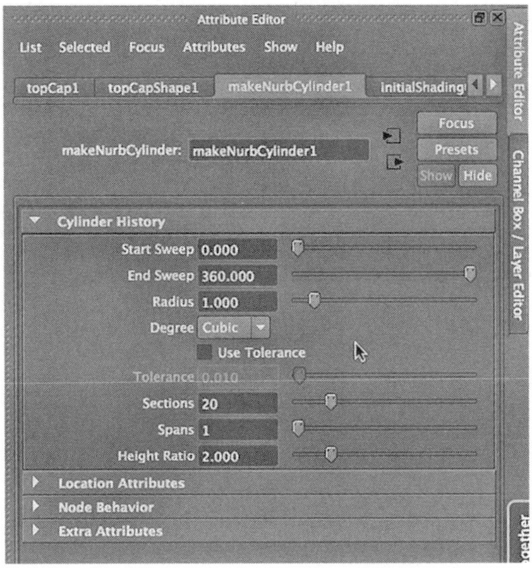

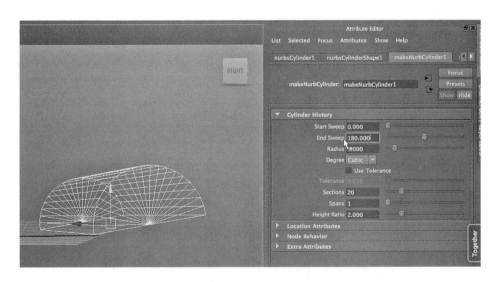

FIGURE 4.129   Attribute editor of cylinder.

FIGURE 4.130   180 degrees of sweep.

FIGURE 4.131   Copy tool.   FIGURE 4.132   Paste tool.

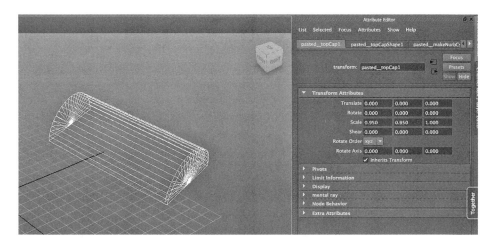

FIGURE 4.133   Scaled down inside.

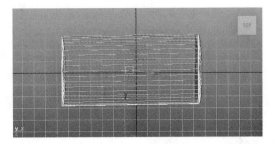

FIGURE 4.134   Inside centered.

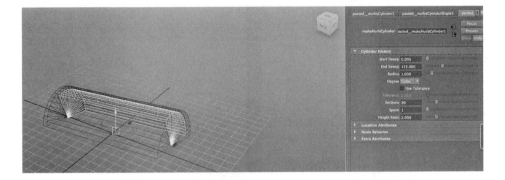

FIGURE 4.135   Inside sweep.

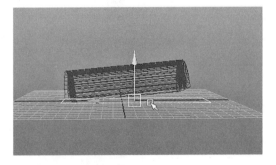

FIGURE 4.136   Placing and sizing the bottom.

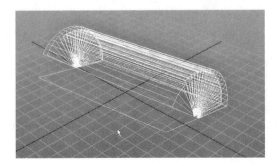

FIGURE 4.137   The breadbox so far.

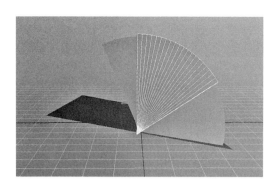

FIGURE 4.138   The breadbox lid.

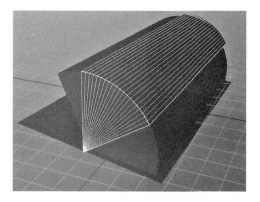

FIGURE 4.139   Another view of the lid.

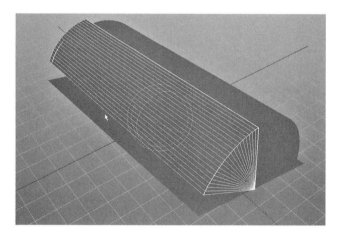

FIGURE 4.140   The breadbox closing with the Rotate tool.

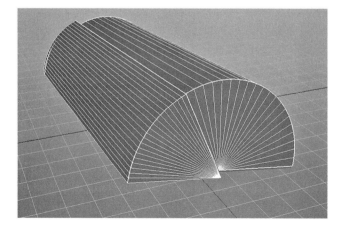

FIGURE 4.141   The breadbox closed.

CHAPTER 5

Materials, Bump Maps, Lights, Projection versus Normal Textures, Connecting NURBS Surfaces, and Layered Textures

Now, we will take a deeper look at some of the topics we have already covered, starting with putting materials on objects. We will look at the difference between a material and a texture, and at creative ways that images can be used to create a material. Because materials and lights are so intimately connected, we will also take a look at the sorts of lights that are available in Maya.

And we will consider the steps involved in creating a complete environment and not just an isolated model. We will build a road and a sidewalk.

In this chapter, we will take another look at NURBS modeling by putting two stairs together. We will look at doing this in NURBS modeling and in polygon modeling. We will go back to the topic of texturing by putting carpet on the stairs.

The Bottom Line

Materials will make or break a good model. It is not the wireframe that viewers see when they watch your animation. They see the materials—and they have everything to do with the success or failure of your models.

WORKING WITH MAYA MATERIALS TO MAKE A TABLETOP

The Maya Software renderer comes equipped with a number of textures. They have very suggestive names, like Wood and Tree Bark and Leather. But these names are only approximations of their overall appearance; these textures rarely deserve their names when used right out of the box. Their attributes must be manipulated to make them look good on your model. You can also use these textures in very creative ways; don't be limited by the name given to a texture.

When using the mental ray renderer, remember that it also comes armed with a number of materials. The mental ray materials come equipped with many preset options, and these presets can save you a lot of time. We will take a look at creating glass with a mental ray material and discover that this material comes ready to model a variety of sorts of glass.

Ways to Surface a Model

There are multiple ways of putting surfaces on a model or sections of a model. We will look at three of them in this book. The first is to create a material object, often called a "shader." The second is to put a texture on a model without using a material. The third is to use the Maya Paint tool to brush on a texture. We will start by looking at a commonly used and very powerful technique: creating a material and then using a texture as an attribute of that material.

Textures and Materials for the Maya Software Renderer

We have talked a bit about materials and textures. A material object is more complex than a texture and is a way of organizing a set of other objects that make up the surface properties of a model (or piece of a model). Maya comes packaged with two sets of materials.

The ones that are tailor-made for the Maya Software renderer can be seen by clicking on the word Surface near the top of the list on the left-hand side of the Hypershade. One of them, Lambert, is used as the default material on an object that has not yet been assigned a material by the modeler.

The second set of materials can be seen by clicking on the word Materials about halfway down the list on the left side of the window. These are intended for use with the mental ray renderer.

Also, if you look below the word Surface, you will see a list of other things that can be created in the Hypershade window. In particular, there are two kinds of textures listed there: 2D and 3D. There are three kinds of textures under these two headings.

The first kind is 2D bit mapped textures, which are always listed within the 2D Textures menu selection. These are essentially images.

The second kind of texture is a 2D "procedural" texture, and this is code. A procedural texture is a program that places the texture on a model mathematically, as opposed to a bit-mapped texture, which is simply an image. The Maya interface does not carefully distinguish between 2D bit-mapped and 2D procedural textures. One bit-mapped texture that we will make heavy use of is called a File texture. This is a general-purpose texture that can be used to create a texture out of a bit-mapped image imported into Maya from the outside.

The third kind of texture is a 3D procedural texture. While there are nonprocedural (bit-mapped) 2D textures, all 3D textures are procedural. We can visualize a 3D procedural texture this way: a program creates a cloud of texture. The model is then placed in this cloud, and wherever the texture touches the surface of the object, it sticks.

Textures can be used in combination with materials in a number of creative ways, and this is where we will begin.

Bump Maps

There are two basic ways to make the surface of a model appear rough or irregular. The first is to manipulate the geometry of the model's surface. The second is to use a material or texture to create the illusion of an irregular surface. The first way can demand more modeling time and it can also increase rendering times, as light will reflect and refract in a complex fashion when it strikes the irregular geometry. But a "bump map"—the most common approach to using a material to create the illusion of shadows—can be easy and effective.

In Figure 5.1, a Blinn material has been created in the Hypershade and its attributes are showing in the Main Window. Blinn is the workhorse of the native Maya materials, engineered to work with the Maya Software renderer. It is highly reflective right out of the box and can be used for a wide variety of surfaces, in particular glass (the transparency needs to be cranked up) and car paint. We are going to use it to create wood that looks varnished.

The color of the Blinn material has been set to a medium brown. (Click on the Color attribute box to pull up the color selector.) Two other things have been done. In the Hypershade is a set of 3D textures. One of them is called Wood. An instance of this has been created. Then, with the Blinn material selected and its attributes showing in the Main Window, the middle mouse button has been used to drag the wood texture into the box labeled Bump Mapping; once that has been placed there, the box has been clicked to finish the assignment. That creates an attribute of the Blinn material called a bump map, and its value is the wood texture. This in turn causes the bump3d1 and the wood1 tabs to appear in the attribute

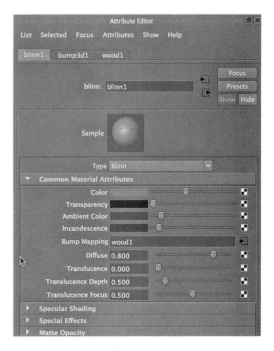

FIGURE 5.1 A Blinn.

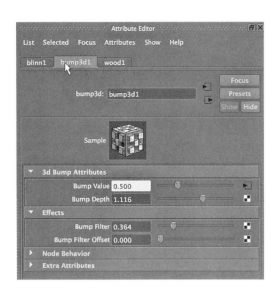

FIGURE 5.2   A bump map.

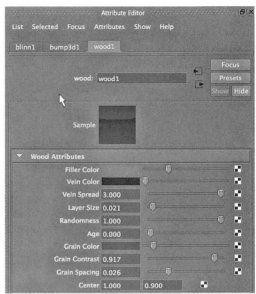

FIGURE 5.3   The wood texture.

box of the Blinn material. In truth, the bump map creates a number of new attributes for the Blinn material.

(A middle mouse button drag is a common shortcut in Maya for moving an object from one window to another.)

In Figure 5.2, the Bump Value attribute has been left at .5, the default on my installation of Maya. The Bump Depth has been modestly increased above the default of 1.0. In Figure 5.3, the Filler Color attribute of the wood was changed to black (by clicking on the color box and using the Color Selector) and a bit of the black was taken off the Vein Color by moving the lever a bit to the right. Adjustments have been made to some of the other sliders as well.

What we are doing here is telling Maya to use the Blinn as the material, but to use the wood texture to give the surface of our object the appearance of having a fine-grained relief. The Blinn surface, however, remains smooth, and so we will not be adding to the render time of our object. The Blinn material's highly reflective quality makes it a good choice when modeling a varnished surface. The color of the Blinn controls the color pattern on the object, and this is why we are using the wood texture as the color of the Blinn.

By selecting the tabletop on the design window and right clicking on the Blinn in the hypershade, we can assign it to the tabletop. The tabletop itself is just a simple stretched-out, flattened polygon cube.

Finishing the Table Scene

Three more things have been done to flesh out the scene. Four elongated polygon cubes have been used for the legs, and they have a Blinn finish with a steel-like color assigned to them. The legs have been parented to the tabletop in the Outliner.

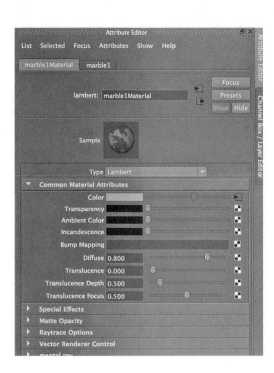

FIGURE 5.4　The marble material.

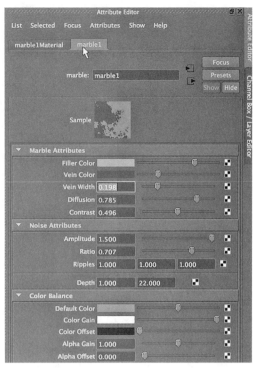

FIGURE 5.5　Marble attributes.

Second, a polygon plane has been created for the floor. An instance of the 3D Marble texture has been created. Its Filler and Vein colors have been altered, along with some other attributes, and it has been assigned to the plane. See Figures 5.4 and 5.5 for the settings of the marble texture.

Finally, a bright spotlight has been placed to the upper right of the scene. The resulting render is shown in Figure 5.6.

Materials or Textures?

A common question is when to use a texture and when to use a material. It may seem simpler to create a file texture or use one of Maya's textures, and in either case, place it directly on the surface of an object. The answer is that often we do indeed simply put a texture on the surface of an object. But if we assign a texture as the Color attribute of a material, we will have a more sophisticated shader object that we can use. Materials have more

FIGURE 5.6　**(See p. CI-3 of Color Insert)** Table render with shadow.

attributes than textures. We also can use textures as bump maps, but only if we apply them to materials. Of course, simplicity is best, so if all we are doing is making a flat wall in the background look like it was made out of bricks, we might just use a photograph of a brick wall as a texture.

LIGHTS

This is a good time to pause and look at the kinds of lights that Maya provides. You can create them from the Create menu dropdown on the Main Window:

any Main Menu → Create → Lights

They can also be created in the Hypershade. Below, we look at most of the kinds of light supported by Maya and at the role of light in a scene.

Ambient Light and Shadows

Ambient light models the light that you find in a room with the blinds closed. It is light that has been evened out, so that its source probably cannot be identified. It can also be used to model outdoor light in an area that is shaded from direct sunlight. One problem with ambient light is that it can wash out shadows, and as we discussed earlier, shadows are necessary to properly root models.

Try creating a polygon cube in a scene. Then go to the cube's attribute box. Click on the second tab from the left. You will find a set of attributes called "Render Stats." If you uncheck Casts Shadows, this cube will not cast any shadows. If you uncheck Receive Shadows, it will not allow any shadows to be cast on it. These attributes can be used to carefully control the shadowing effects of a complex scene. But keep in mind this option is meant to compensate for the inherently artificial nature of a 3D scene. Sometimes we simply have to manually control various factors in a scene to make everything fit together the way we want it to.

Directional Light and Shadows

Directional light is meant to model light from the sun. The angle of the light icon (which looks like a set of arrows) controls the angle of the sunlight. The idea is that light from the sun is coming from so far away that the rays seem perfectly parallel. The problem with directional light is that it, too, can wash out shadows in a scene. Like ambient light, you often have to keep its Intensity slider (see the DirectionalLightShape tab in the attribute box) far to the left.

Point Light and Shadows

Point light emits from a single vertex in 3-space and cannot be angled in any way. Point lights can be placed inside frosted glass orbs to simulate a light bulb, or inside the shade of a table or floor lamp. To get good, localized shadows with a point light, you should experiment with the Intensity and the Decay Rate attributes of the light.

Spotlights and Shadows

A spotlight has to be carefully positioned and carefully angled. It also has a Cone Angle attribute that is critical for controlling the area illuminated by the light. Spotlights are great for creating noticeable shadows, and like point lights, the Intensity and Decay rate are important attributes. Instead of using a point light in a table or floor lamp, a spotlight can mimic the coned light effect created by a shade.

Area Light

Area light is emitted at a right angle and evenly from a single surface of one object. It can be used to simulate light coming in through a window or from a fluorescent fixture.

mental ray Light Shaders

In the Hypershade, there are several shaders that can be found by clicking on mental ray Lights. These can be assigned to Maya lights; they add attributes to Maya lights, thus making them more powerful.

mental ray 2D and 3D Lights

If you create an area light, select it, and then select:

Attribute Editor → mental ray → Area Light

and check the Use Light Shape, you will find a dropdown called Type, with a number of choices. They include rectangle, disk, sphere, and cylinder.

If you check off sphere or cylinder, the light will become a 3D object that emits light. Instead of having all of the light emitted from a fixed distance, light is emitted from a source that varies in distance from the objects receiving the light. There is a growing feeling that this sort of 3D light creates a much more natural light source and much more natural shadows because most lights in the real world are indeed 3D.

Consider Figures 5.7 and 5.8. In both pictures we have double doors with frosted glass. In Figure 5.7, there is a mental ray planar light shining directly onto the double doors; the light is coming in at 90 degrees to the blue wall around the doors. In

FIGURE 5.7 **(See p. CI-5 of Color Insert)** Mental ray planar light.

FIGURE 5.8 **(See p. CI-5 of Color Insert)** Mental ray spherical light.

Figure 5.8, the planar light has been turned into a spherical light; the shadows are less sharp, we don't have the odd dark circles around the two doorknobs, and maybe the shadows look more natural.

Depth Map versus Raytraced Shadows

Raytracing attributes can be set in the render options for both the Maya Software renderer and mental ray. There are also raytracing attributes associated with most of the lights that can be created under the Create dropdown in the Main Window. (They are also available in the Create dropdown in the Hypershade.) For example, in the Attribute Editor for a spotlight there are a set of attributes under Shadows; they include two checkboxes, one for Use Depth Map Shadows, and one for Use Raytrace Shadows.

The difference between Depth Map Shadows and Raytrace Shadows is key. Depth Map Shadows are created by calculating the movement of light only until it hits an object in the scene. This creates sharp shadows because, wherever light is blocked, a shadow is created. With Raytracing Shadows, more computational time is invested in calculating the effect of light reflecting around the area on the edge of the shadow. These shadows are more gradual.

A sharp, depth map shadow from a spotlight can give a stark feeling to a scene. A raytracing shadow can look more gentle and calming.

Figure 5.9 shows the dish that we created in Chapter 3. It has a mental ray mia_material on it, set to GlassThin.

Next, the floor and the wall have been given the checkerboard 2D texture from the Hypershade. There are two lights in the scene: one coming from the upper right and another coming from the upper left. Both are spotlights. The light on the right is far brighter than the one on the left. When we render the scene (with the mental ray renderer), we would expect to get a shadow cast to the left.

Figure 5.10 illustrates what happens when we check Use Depth Map Shadows for the light on the right.

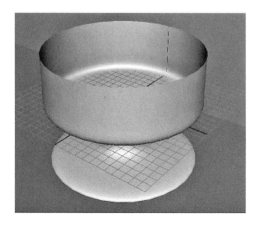

FIGURE 5.9   Glass model.

FIGURE 5.10   **(See p. CI-6 of Color Insert)** Glass bowl with depth map shadows.

Now, if we go back to the attributes of the light on the right, and check the Use Raytrace Shadows checkbox, we get Figure 5.11.

Notice that the single pass depth map algorithm creates large, black shadows, even though the dish is made of glass. The raytrace shadows in this example look more natural, as we assume that light can go through the rim of the dish and partially wash out the shadow on the left side of the dish.

FIGURE 5.11 **(See p. CI-6 of Color Insert)** Glass bowl with raytrace shadows.

The Varnished Table

We return to our table example, shown in Figure 5.6, and consider its shadows. The varnished table is illuminated almost entirely by a single, narrow spotlight. We wanted the bright spot in the center of the rendered image, at the edge of the table, to highlight its polished finish. The floor, on the other hand, is receiving less direct light, and therefore the viewer's eye is pulled toward the table, which is what we want.

There is a sharp, depth map shadow coming off the leg in the upper left of the rendering. This is the result of a point light in the scene. The point light is below the level of the table and coming in at about the same angle as the spotlight. Without this shadow, the table would not look rooted to the granite floor.

One more thing: Notice the reflection of the granite floor in the flat side of the leg. This is due to the high reflective nature of the granite and the leg, and also helps visually situate the table with respect to the floor.

BEING CREATIVE WITH TEXTURES FOR BUMP MAPS: MAKING A ROAD AND A SIDEWALK

Now we consider a couple more materials that make use of bump maps. We will also see in this example that we cannot be artificially limited by the name or the original source of a texture when we are looking for just the right bump map effect. Maya's materials and textures can be used creatively.

More Bump Maps

We have looked at using a bump map to give a Blinn finish the appearance of having a wood-like grain. Now we will use bump maps again; this time, we will put together multiple models and materials in order to craft an integrated environment. Our goal is a city street, with pavement, a sidewalk, some grass, and a light pole, which will serve as the sole source of light in the scene.

In Figure 5.12, blinn2 is our asphalt and blinn4 is our cement. Figure 5.13 shows the two textures that were used as bump maps; file1 is a file texture and rock1 is a canned Maya

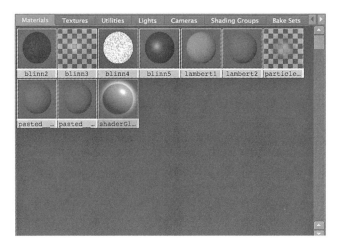

FIGURE 5.12   Asphalt and cement materials.

texture. Figure 5.14 shows the assignment of file1 to the bump map of blinn4. Figure 5.15 shows the Bump Map attribute settings; note the Bump Depth setting. Figures 5.16 and 5.17 display the file texture itself. Interestingly, the .jpg used for the texture is labeled "Stone." This texture seems to be a photograph of a slate-like stone, but it has an irregular, small-grained appearance that can be used to simulate cement.

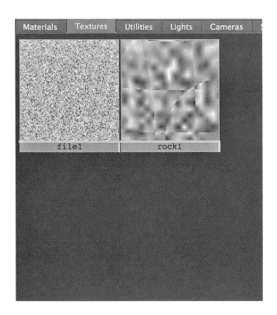

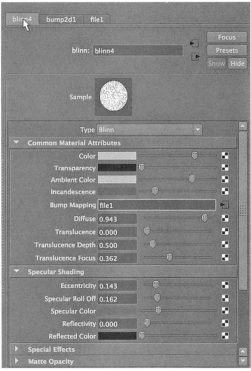

FIGURE 5.13   Asphalt and cement bump map textures.

FIGURE 5.14   Assigning a bump map.

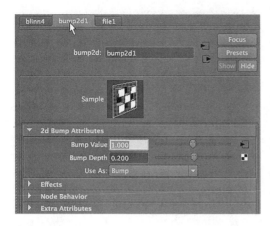

FIGURE 5.15 Bump map attribute settings.

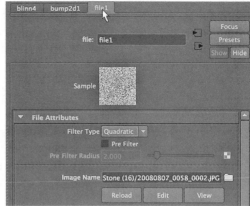

FIGURE 5.16 The file texture for the bump map.

Figure 5.18 shows the Blinn used for the asphalt. It is black, with a cranked up diffuse setting (scattering reflected light). The Blinn itself gives the asphalt a wet, new look. Older asphalt would demand a softer material, like a Lambert. In Figure 5.19, we see a more aggressive Bump Depth setting, compared to the cement material. Figure 5.20 displays the settings for the rock texture. Again, we see the importance of experimenting with textures when using them as bump maps. The rock texture is a 3D texture, and with a Grain Size set higher than the default, it makes a nice asphalt.

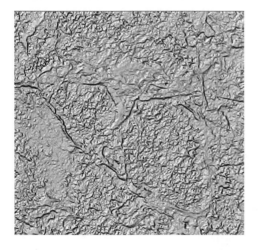

FIGURE 5.17 The file texture up close.

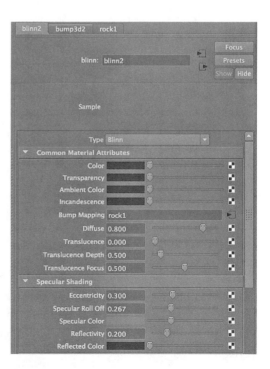

FIGURE 5.18 The asphalt Blinn.

FIGURE 5.19 Bump depth settings.

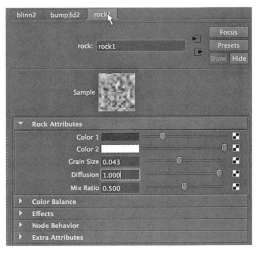

FIGURE 5.20 Rock texture settings.

Completing the Scene: Creating a Light Pole and Painting 3D Geometry to Make Grass

In Figure 5.21, we see a render of the entire scene. Under the grass is a flattened polygon cube with a Lambert material that has been assigned a brown color to simulate dirt.

FIGURE 5.21 **(See p. CI-13 of Color Insert)** Cement and asphalt rendered.

The grass was created easily, because it was taken from the Visor window. The Visor gives us access to a painting tool in Maya, along with a vast amount of prefab painting content. The painting tool is used to "paint" onto an object in a scene. With Maya you can paint in 2D or in 3D. In this case, the grass is 3D polygon geometry (and not just a 2D texture or a material). The grass is called GrassCarpet. It was found by going to:

any Main Menu → Window → General Editors → Visor

This is how the grass was created. Once the Visor was open, the dirt was selected, and then we chose:

Visor Window → Paint Effects → grasses → grassCarpet.mel

This 3D paint effect is written in Maya's scripting language, so there is a .mel at the end of the name of the grass. The painting tool creates a 3D clump of grass with every click of the left mouse button. Note: The painting tool has a tab in the Shelf and can also be found by going to:

any Main Menu → Window → Paint Effects

By the light pole are a few tulip flowers from the Visor; each of them was a click with the painting tool.

There is a point light inside the sphere that forms the light orb. The Intensity setting is 2.4. The glass orb uses blinn3 (in Figure 5.12). The Transparency setting is fairly high and the Color slider is far to the right (making it whiter). Notice that a largely (but not completely) transparent Blinn, combined with a white light, nicely simulates a frosted glass orb.

Painting is a powerful tool in Maya and we will look at it in more detail later. We will also come back to this scene and turn our clear night into a foggy night.

CREATING A LAYERED TEXTURE IN PIXELMATOR

The workflow of a 3D artist almost always involves some sort of bit-mapped image editor. The premiere one—and the most expensive—is Adobe Photoshop. We will look at a much cheaper competitor, and with it we will examine the issue of prepping images outside Maya in order to use them as textures within Maya.

Photographs for Textures

There are a number of sites that sell photographs and other bit-mapped images that can be used for textures. Sometimes they are completely free or free if you are willing to put up with a watermark. Two popular animation magazines that give away high-quality images to subscribers are *3D Artist* and *3D World*. It is a good idea to incrementally build up a library of images.

There are three things to keep in mind. The images need to be fairly high definition. Second, textures are much easier to work with if they can tile "seamlessly" (the texture when tiled from right to left and/or top to bottom does not produce visible seams). We will look at tiling textures later in this chapter and at how to improve the tiling in Chapter 9. The third issue is that while you may want to take photographs of stone walls, sandy beaches, brick siding, sedimentary layers, old barns, sheet metal buildings, and so forth, to use as textures, it can be difficult to get a properly proportioned image. If you are standing on the ground and take a picture of the brick side of a building, you are going to be looking upward, and this will cause the image to be distorted.

Materials and textures are critical for making models look realistic. They often determine the emotional impact of a model. They can also be used to draw the focus of the viewer to a specific aspect of a scene.

Working outside of Maya

Although Maya supports a wide variety of materials, it does not come with a library of bit-mapped images that can be used as file textures. But Maya does help out when it comes to prepping images for use as textures. In truth, though, it is not as rich in functionality as stand-alone image editors, and many animators do not make much use of it.

The industry standard, Adobe Photoshop, is overkill for many of us and can be almost as difficult to learn as Maya. An alternative is Corel PaintShop. This is a Windows-only application, and it is also fairly complex. A lot of photograph management applications, like Photoshop

Essentials, Apple Aperture, and Adobe Lightroom, also have extensive capabilities for editing images. A free application that is surprisingly powerful is Paint.net. GIMP is a Unix app that has been extended over the years so that it challenges Photoshop in its complexity and power. GIMP runs on Mac and Windows machines. On Macs, there are a number of fairly new, lightweight applications. My favorite, which we will look at here, is Pixelmator.

There are a few other kinds of applications that I find very useful. In particular, there are applications that can grab the color signature of something on your screen and tell you what that color is in terms of CMYK or RGB numbers. This makes it possible to capture a color in a bit-mapped image or on another model in your scene, and then match or contrast that color carefully. I use a program called Pochade (on Macs); another Mac application is called Colors.

You might want to go even further and get a program that can help you design sets of colors that go well together. I use the Mac application ColorSchemer Studio.

A third sort of application to consider is one that can be used to add pixels to an image, thus allowing you to enlarge it without blurring it. I use Perfect Resize, which runs on Mac and Windows machines; another choice is iResize.

Finally, remember that .jpg images are often compressed and of poor quality. Tiff images are, on the other hand, mostly uncompressed and tend to produce nicer results. So pay attention to what formats an application can export. Sometimes it helps to obtain a dedicated program that converts images into various formats. I use GraphicConverter.

The Uses of Bit-Mapped Images

There are times when the best way to model a real-world object is to use a photograph of the real thing. Using a photograph of a Monarch butterfly as a file texture can turn two planes into beautiful wings.

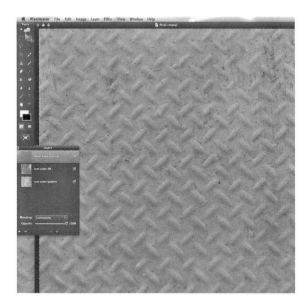

Often, we want to use layers to combine images in various ways. A layer can be used to change the color or apparent texture of an image. Layers can be used to simulate secondary effects, like rust and dirt; surfaces that do not look freshly made and completely clean often look more realistic.

Blending Layers

When using two or more layers to create an image, each layer is used with a specific "blend mode." Consider Figure 5.22. This is what we will produce by blending layers: a textured metal with rust and multiple, partial layers of old paint. (This material can also be seen in Figure 5.31, in the Color Insert.)

FIGURE 5.22   Rusty metal.

For our example, we need to understand two terms that relate to the blending of multiple texture layers. Luminosity refers to the property of emitting light, and in Maya the "luminosity" refers to the lightness properties of an image that is being used as a layer. "Darker color" is used to compare pixels that are positioned in the same place on multiple layers, and allows us to select the color that is the darkest.

The word "mode" is used to refer to the way we are making use of a given layer; for example, the darken (or darker) mode or the luminosity mode. We will use one layer to control the apparent relief of our final texture and two others to control its coloring.

Rusty, Painted Metal

Figure 5.23 shows the creation of a new Pixelmator file. The images that will be used in this example are high definition, and Figure 5.24 shows the controls for the width, height, and pixel count of the resulting file. Figure 5.25 shows us the base layer. It is a textured sheet metal that is painted blue. In Figure 5.26, we are creating a layered image, and we are specifying that the resulting image will have the luminosity of the base image. Figure 5.27 shows the first layer above the base layer, a light blue metal surface that is very rusty. In Figure 5.28, we are using it as a darkening layer. In Figure 5.29, we have another rusty looking image; it appears to have originally been painted white. In Figure 5.30, we see that we are using it as a darkening layer as well.

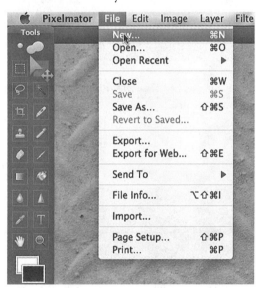

FIGURE 5.23   A new project in Pixelmator.

The resulting exported .tiff image is shown in Figure 5.31 (Figures 5.25, 5.26, 5.27, 5.28, 5.29, and 5.31 are in the Color Insert). The base layer has to be the layer at the top of the list (in Figures 5.26, 5.28, and 5.30), but the order of the two darkening layers does not matter. Also notice that the color of the base layer is effectively gone, but the final image has the texture and luminance of the base layer.

LAYERING CAPABILITY NATIVE TO MAYA

There is a layering capability that is native to Maya. In Figure 5.32, a layered texture is being created in the Hypershade. We will turn this into a two-layer texture.

FIGURE 5.24   New project settings.

FIGURE 5.25 **(See p. CI-7 of Color Insert)** Base texture.

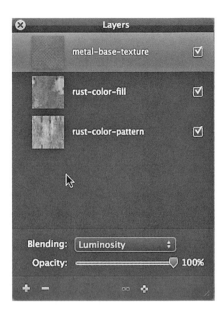

FIGURE 5.26 **(See p. CI-7 of Color Insert)** Stamped metal texture as base texture.

FIGURE 5.27 **(See p. CI-7 of Color Insert)** Rusty metal texture.

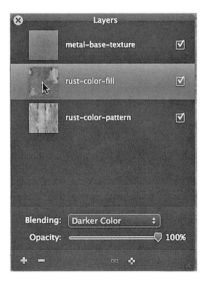

FIGURE 5.28 **(See p. CI-7 of Color Insert)** The rusty metal as a darker color.

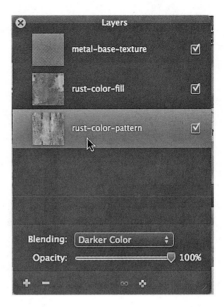

FIGURE 5.29 **(See p. CI-7 of Color Insert)** Rusty metal texture number 2.

FIGURE 5.30 Using rusty metal number 2 as a darker color.

FIGURE 5.31 **(See p. CI-7 of Color Insert)** The final result—three-layered texture.

FIGURE 5.32 Creating a Maya layered texture.

After clicking on the black and white icon to the right of the color slider in the attribute box for the layered texture, the menu in Figure 5.33 appears. We then select File in this menu and create a file texture using a rendered image of a cartoon cow. Then we set this first layer to the blend mode Illuminate using the Blend Mode dropdown (see Figure 5.34).

FIGURE 5.33 Creating a file texture for the color of the first layer.

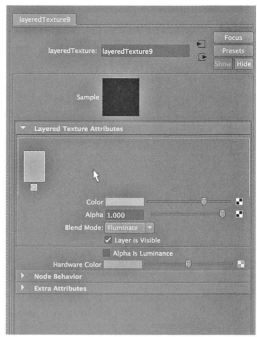

FIGURE 5.34 Setting the layer to Illuminate mode.

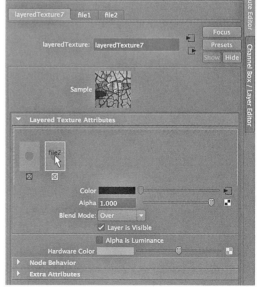

FIGURE 5.35 Using cracked dirt as the second layer.

In Figure 5.35, we have created another file texture and assigned an image of cracked dirt to it. Then, using the middle mouse button, we drag this file texture from the Hypershade and drop it just to the right of the first layer. A second box then appears in the attribute editor of the layered texture; this is layer 2. We then set this layer to Over as its mode.

(In Figure 5.36, we see the Work Area in the bottom half of the Hypershade; it shows how the two layers have been put together to create the layered texture.)

Next, we create a rectangular plane in the Main Window. Then we select the plane in the Main Window and go to the Hypershade; we right click on the layered texture in the Hypershade and assign it to the plane.

The rendering of the plane is shown in Figure 5.37. The rendered image of the cow has been used as the coloring for the layered texture, and the dark pattern of cracks in the dirt has been used as an overlay. The net effect is a sort of mosaic cow.

Brief Note: Various Color Systems

Maya uses the generally accepted red, green, and blue (RGB) color system designed specifically for computer display technology. But there are other systems. In the production of physical objects, product designers often use a cyan, magenta, yellow, and black (CMYB) system; computer printers use this system. The CMYB system is called "subtractive," in that as we blend more colors together, the result gets darker. But on computer displays we want a system where colors become brighter as you blend them together (otherwise known as being "additive"); the RGB system has this property because it is based on light, not pigments. Another additive system, one that is based on pigments and that we all learn in school, uses red, blue, and yellow—the "primary" colors.

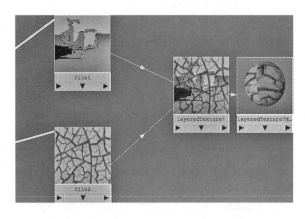

FIGURE 5.36   The view from the Hypershade.

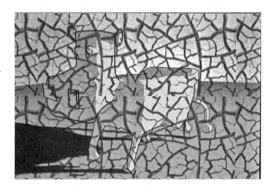

FIGURE 5.37   Mosaic cow render.

CYLINDRICAL PROJECTION OF AN IMAGE TEXTURE ON THE CACTUS

There are two windows that can be used when putting a material or texture on an object. The first is the Main Window, which we will look at now. The second is the UV Texture Editor, which we will look at later.

Projection or Normal Texture?

Let's look at the process of creating a 2D file-based texture in Maya. In the next example, we will create a file texture to place on our cactus. When creating a file texture, it is important to assign a value to a setting that controls the way the texture can be manipulated. To do this, go to the Hypershade and choose:

Create → 2D Textures → File

But don't click on File before looking at the three radio buttons at the bottom of the list of 2D textures. Make sure that the 2D Projection radio button has been selected. If not, then instead of clicking on File, click on the Projection radio button, and then go back to click on File in the list of 2D textures.

We set this radio button because we do not want the placement of the texture to be a property of the object on which we are placing the texture. This has two consequences. First, we can reuse the same texture on multiple objects and it will behave consistently. The second is that we are given controls inside the Main Window of Maya that allow us to manually place the texture on the object—this is called projecting—and we can choose from a handful of projection types. The idea is to choose a type that resembles the overall geometry of the object being textured. We can also go into Face mode and assign the texture to a given object face by face.

Another radio button is Normal, which we will choose when we discuss the UV Texture Editor window. In this case, the placement of the texture on an object is tied to the properties of the object itself.

Before we continue, let's step back and look at an important concept. It has to do with the definition of normals, in the sense of the perpendicular lines that extend from the surface of an object. Suppose we were to make a real-life polygon sphere and give it a highly reflective finish, perhaps by using car paint. We remember that each face (each polygon) would have a single normal. If we directed a strong light at the sphere, the normals would control the angle of reflection and this would reveal the flat nature of each face. If we were to repeatedly divide the polygons that make up the sphere's mesh, this would increase the number of faces significantly. Eventually, the normals of any two neighboring faces would not be that different, and our sphere would begin to look smooth.

Let's get back to our projection file texture. The way that our brains turn the coloring of a texture into something that simulates the look of relief on the surface of an object is by differentiating darker and lighter parts of the surface, giving the appearance of shadows on the surface.

But more times than not, we discover a problem. When we place the texture on the surface of an object, the way it is laid down is related to the varying density of the (u, v) space of the object. If the vertices of the (u, v) space are not evenly spaced around the surface of the object, the texture will end up being laid down in an uneven fashion. This will give an impression of relief (of shadowing) that is not what we want.

How do we compensate for this? There are two choices: alter the (u, v) space of the surface of the object so that the texture lays down properly or apply the texture in an uneven fashion that happens to compensate for the irregular grid of the (u, v) surface.

In Maya, we must choose which way we want to do this. A "projection" texture is used when we want to vary the way the texture is laid down. A "normal" texture is used when we want to adjust the (u, v) grid of the surface of the object.

Another way of looking at it is that when we use a projection texture we use the texture to create normal information that gives an object the appearance of relief. If we use a normal texture, we manipulate the (u, v) grid so that we can assign new normal information to the object's surface. In either case, the coloring of the texture gives the object the appearance of relief. But in the first case, the texture drives the process. In the second case, the object drives the process—and this is why we can more easily reuse a projection texture on multiple objects than we can a normal texture.

We have looked at another way to alter the apparent surface geometry of a model without actually changing its geometry. Instead of using textures, we used bump maps assigned to materials. A bump map in essence perturbs the mathematical formulation of normals on the surface of the object. It is another way of using the normals of an object to give it an apparent texture but without assigning color.

Later, when we look at the UV Texture Editor, we will see that we can use it to carefully craft the way a texture or material is programmed to map onto a surface. It will be important that we start by making sure our texture is a Normal texture.

(There is a third kind of texture, a Stencil texture. This allows us to use a texture as a mask to remove some of the surface appearance of the material on the object.)

Projecting Textures

Let's get back to our cactus. Perhaps the most basic way to put a surface on a model is to use a 2D file texture (that has been created with the Projection radio button selected) and to project it onto the model. No material (or "shader") needs to be created by the animator, and this method of placing a texture on a model has a straightforward visualization since we are given interactive controls.

Conversion to Polygons

We used NURBS modeling to create a cactus in Chapter 3. In Figure 5.38, we have opened the cactus scene and are selecting everything in the scene, that is, the four parts of the cactus model, the trunk, the branch, and the two spheres that act as caps on the trunk and the branch. In Figure 5.39, the NURBS model is being converted from NURBS to polygon geometry. This is a significant transformation: The curved surfaces and lines are gone, and the model is now made up of a grid of flat polygons.

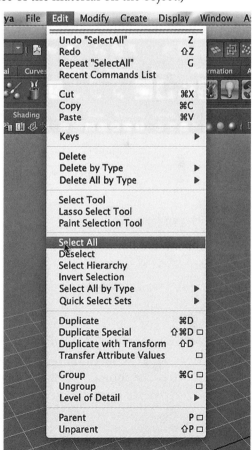

FIGURE 5.38 Select all.

FIGURE 5.39   Convert to polygons.

If you take a NURBS model and convert it into a polygon model, the model will not have the geometry it would have had if it had been built from scratch with polygon modeling tools. It will have more or less the same outward shape, but the layout of vertices and edges will be different. In general, this is true for all of the conversions you see in Figure 5.39. The difference can be so significant that some animators make use of the unusual placement of geometry that occurs when a model is converted from one kind of modeling to another. In other words, the conversion process might make the geometry (the density and placement of vertices and edges) in a certain area of the surface of the object more advantageous for some specific modeling purpose.

Why are we doing this conversion? We are sticking to the basics in this book, and that means that we will focus mostly on putting materials and textures on polygon models. Later, when we work with the UV Texture Editor, we will be using techniques that are only available with polygon models.

Types of Projections

Figure 5.40 shows the projection object that is created by Maya when, in the Hypershade, the texture is assigned to the trunk of the cactus. We will get to the process of assigning the texture in a moment, but for now note that in this figure the Proj Type has been set to Cylindrical. Other choices include Planar and Spherical. The idea is to pick a projection type that matches the overall geometry of the object to which you are assigning the texture. In our case, the trunk of the cactus is clearly cylindrical. (The way to get to the window seen in Figure 5.40 is by clicking on the projection object in the Hypershade.)

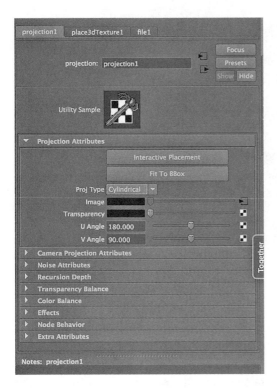

FIGURE 5.40   Cylindrical texture.

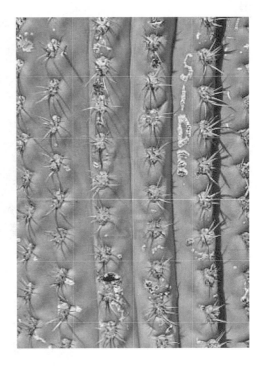

FIGURE 5.41   Patch of cactus whole.

There is an obvious limitation to using the projection type technique for placing a texture on an object. If the geometry varies significantly from the projection type chosen, the result might be quite messy. This is a reason to think about the future task of texturing as you are crafting models.

Tiling

In Figure 5.41, we see a patch of a cactus. This is what we will use to build our texture. There are a number of problems that can occur when attempting to use a file texture. Is the image dense enough in pixels? Will the texture look natural if it is stretched as it is applied to the model? This is usually not the case, and so the texture must be repeated in a grid. This is called "tiling," and there are two places where this can be done: inside Maya and inside your image editing application (such as Pixelmator).

Our goal is to create a bigger rectangle of cactus material than we see in Figure 5.41. We will grow it along both the u and the v axes. In Figure 5.42, we see a tiling created with Pixelmator. The seams between the fifteen segments are clearly visible.

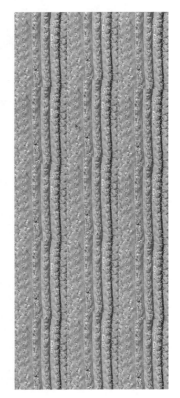

FIGURE 5.42   Tiling.

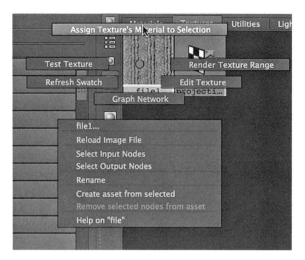

FIGURE 5.43   Assign texture.

Adjusting the Projection of a Texture

In Figure 5.43, the texture is being assigned to the trunk of the cactus. (As a reminder, this is done in the Hypershade.) After this, a cylindrical mapping is chosen, as shown in Figure 5.40.

There are two primary ways that a texture can be adjusted as it is placed on a surface. The first is to adjust attributes that control the placement. The second is to do this indirectly by using the Interactive Placement tool. We will use both techniques. In Figure 5.44, Interactive Placement is being chosen.

In Figure 5.45, we see the icon that appears in the Main Window as a result of selecting Interactive Placement. This tool can be manipulated to adjust the way the texture is projected. We will use the Scale Tool, as shown in Figure 5.46, to adjust the projection. In Figure 5.47, we see that the projection has been enlarged along the y-axis to cover the entire trunk.

The result is shown in Figure 5.48, and the news is not all good. The problem is that the texture is much too large grained, making the rendering look like a closeup of a baby cactus. So, we discover that it is often easier to adjust a projection of a texture by

FIGURE 5.44   Interactive placement.

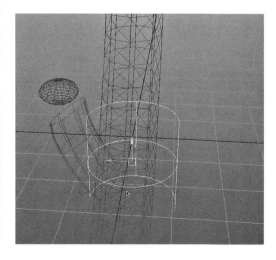

FIGURE 5.45   Placement icon.

making use of the attribute box. In Figure 5.49, the Repeat UV values have each been changed from 1 to 3. The result is shown in Figure 5.50, and things look better.

By the way, the default Repeat value of a projection texture is higher than that of a Normal texture. This helps prevent us from forgetting what kind of texture we are making.

In Chapter 9, we will try to make the patchwork appearance in Figure 5.50 less obvious.

STITCHING NURBS SURFACES TO MAKE CARPETED STAIRS

We now look at a key issue in NURBS modeling: the connecting of independently created surfaces. The overall philosophy of working with NURBS models is to think in terms of straight and curved lines that form the borders of surfaces. We have seen that the NURBS cylinder is actually three separate surfaces. We have seen that a NURBS surface can be created by revolving a curve through 3-space. We have looked at extruding and lofting of lines to create NURBS surfaces. And we have seen that NURBS surfaces have sweeps that allow us to carefully adjust the number of degrees in 3-space that a NURBS surface covers.

FIGURE 5.46 Scale projection tool.

The focus on individual surfaces rather than on working with premade, single-object 3D wireframe models as we often do in polygon modeling leads to an obvious question: How do we put individual NURBS surfaces together to create larger surfaces?

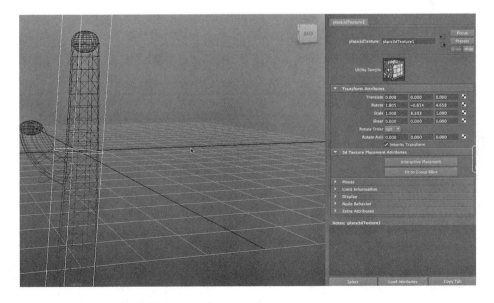

FIGURE 5.47 Texture rescaled.

FIGURE 5.48 A cactus with badly scaled texture.

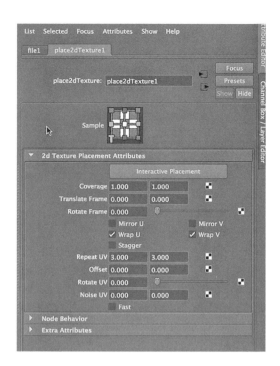

FIGURE 5.49 Repeat UV values.

Before we look at this, remember that we can and do work with polygon surfaces that are not completely enclosed in 3-space. And we work with completely enclosed basic shapes in NURBS modeling. So, there is no sharp divide between straight- and curved-line modeling that says that polygon modeling is used only with enclosed surfaces like cubes and that NURBS modeling is only used on objects that are not completely enclosed.

Isoparms

In Figure 5.51, we have a NURBS plane. In Figure 5.52, we have three NURBS planes: two that are horizontal and one that is vertical. The horizontal surfaces are two stairs and they

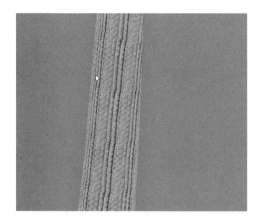

FIGURE 5.50 Cactus rerender.

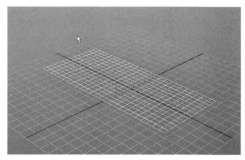

FIGURE 5.51 A NURBS step.

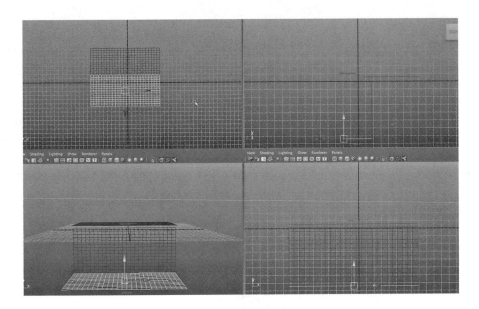

FIGURE 5.52   Two steps.

need to be connected via the vertical plane. We want to make the connection smoothly curved, as this is carpet we are modeling, not metal or wood. In Figure 5.53, we have selected the top plane and right clicked, and then chosen Isoparm mode. Notice that we are not selecting Edge mode like we might in polygon modeling, although for many purposes, NURBS isoparms can be treated like polygon edges.

Let's go over the difference between a curved line and an isoparm. In particular an isoparm is a more narrowly defined geometric concept. An isoparm is a line across a NURBS surface where the u or v value in 2-space is constant. Thus, the horizontal hoops in a NURBS sphere are isoparms, but in the vertical direction we single out half-hoops that go from top to bottom as isoparms. (You have to look at the surface without considering its orientation in 3-space, because u, v values are local to a given surface.)

In a sense, an isoparm creates a NURBS cross-section. Try creating a NURBS sphere primitive with the Create menu. Go into isoparm mode and click on some of the curved lines. You will discover that only the curved lines that have a constant value for u or v are actually isoparms. At first glance,

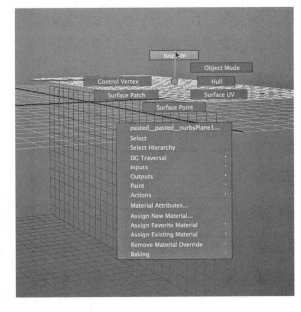

FIGURE 5.53   Isoparm mode.

this seems to not be true, however, as there are fully connected curves that wrap entirely around the sphere from top to bottom, but they are actually made up of two isoparms.

Why don't two of these curves form an isoparm? The answer lies in the following: When we are manipulating the sweep of a NURBS sphere, the two parts of one of those loops that look like they should be isoparms do not remain in the same plane. And they have neither a constant u value nor a constant v value. This is because a seemingly enclosed NURBS primitive (sphere, cylinder, etc.) can be opened up, and which axis is used to unfold the primitive controls which curves are isoparms. A default NURBS sphere in Maya, for instance, has a sweep that opens the sphere from top to bottom. This causes horizontal hoops on a sphere to be isoparms, but only half-hoops are isoparms in the vertical direction.

Connecting Stairs

In Figure 5.54, we have selected two isoparms: one from a vertical face and one from a horizontal face. The bottom face is tucked just a bit under the horizontal face; this is because we want to model the way carpet rolls back up under a stair. We then select:

Surfaces Main Window → Edit NURBS → Stitch → Stitch Edges Tool

We see this in Figure 5.55. The result is seen in Figure 5.56. Maya has connected the two NURBS surfaces by creating a smooth curved surface between them. The geometry of the connecting surface can be tailored with the settings of the tool.

Putting a Material on the Stairs

To carpet our stairs, we first create a file as a projection texture and use a photo of carpet as the texture image. In Figures 5.57 through 5.59, we use interactive planar placement to put a carpet texture on the stairs. This is done by projecting the carpet texture three times: one on the vertical plane between the two stairs and once on each of two horizontal planes that make up the two steps. We select the plane we want to texture, then go into the Hypershade and right click on the texture, and then choose Assign Texture's Material to Selection. The rendered result is shown in Figure 5.60. There is a hidden imperfection there; the carpet texture underneath the lip of the stair is stretched.

Using the Append to Polygon Tool for Connecting Two Stairs

We have connected two carpeted stairs and have created a horizontal offset for each under the top step, so that the carpet will tuck under the lip of each step. We used NURBS tools to do this. Here we take a quick look at doing a similar thing with polygon modeling.

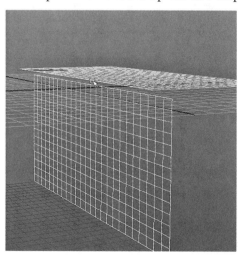

FIGURE 5.54   Two isoparms selected.

FIGURE 5.55   Stitch tool.

First, we create the two planes needed for two steps. Importantly, we must use the Combine tool and create one object out of the two. This tool is found by choosing:

Polygons Main Menu → Mesh → Combine (see Figure 5.61)

The planes are not connected yet, but they are one object. Now, we select:

Polygons Main Menu → Edit Mesh → Append to Polygon Tool (see Figure 5.62)

Then we select the two edges of the two polygons that are closest together (see Figure 5.63). We hit Enter, and the two planes are connected by an angled polygon, creating the offset of the carpet from the front of one step to the top of the other. The result is shown in Figure 5.64.

USING A FILE TEXTURE AS A MATERIAL'S COLOR AND MAKING A MATERIAL STICK

We are going to look at another creative way to make use of a texture: substituting it for the color attribute of a material. We will also look at one way to prevent a texture from wandering once it is applied to an object.

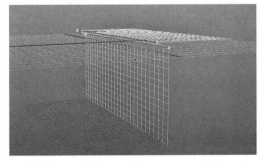

FIGURE 5.56   Stitch result.

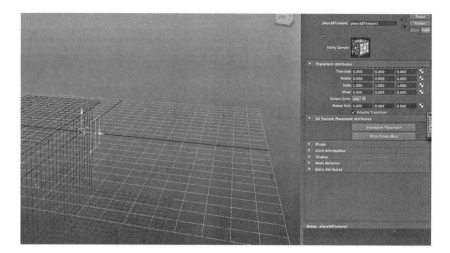

FIGURE 5.57   Texture placement.

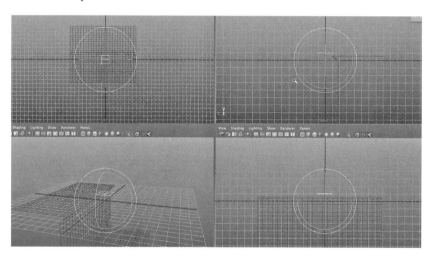

FIGURE 5.58   Texture rotated.

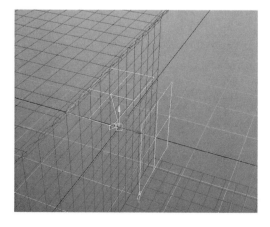

FIGURE 5.59   Two placements.

A Texture as a Color of a Material

The color attribute of a material can be manipulated by assigning a file texture to it, and then leveraging other attributes of the material to create a combined effect.

Assigning an Image to a Material's Color Attribute

In Figure 5.65, we have created a Blinn material and have clicked on the checkerboard icon to the right of its Color attribute. We have then chosen File when the Create Render Node panel has popped up.

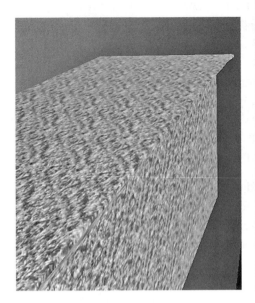

FIGURE 5.60   Carpet rendered.

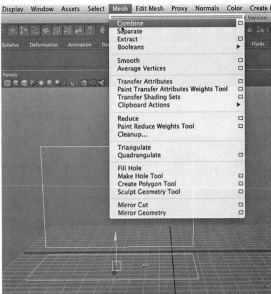

FIGURE 5.61   Combine tool.

In Figure 5.66, we are selecting the image that will serve as the texture. In Figure 5.67, a texture file that we have already used is selected; it is the rusty panel of blue painted metal. In Figure 5.68, we are assigning this Blinn material to an object in the scene. (It happens to be a face of a cube.)

In Figure 5.69, we see the system of nodes that have been created in the Hypershade.

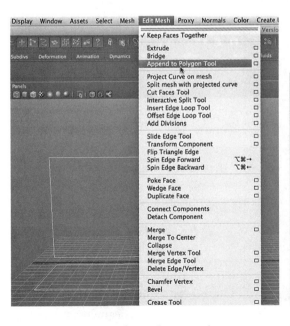

FIGURE 5.62   Append to polygon tool.

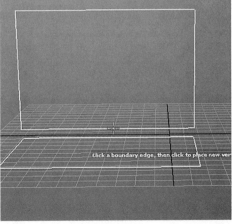

FIGURE 5.63   Selecting two edges.

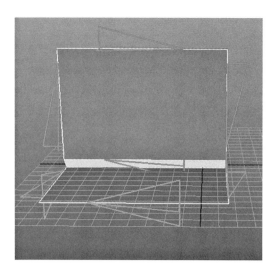

FIGURE 5.64   The result—two faces connected by one face.

Adjusting and Fixing the Material Placement

The resulting render is shown in Figure 5.70. The pattern is repeated too frequently. In Figure 5.71, we are adjusting the placement.

In Figure 5.72, we are parenting the cube to the place3dTexture1 node so that the texture will not float away when we move the cube.

Adjusting the Material's Ambient Color Attribute

The resulting render is shown in Figure 5.73. The texture is approximately to scale with the face of the cube. But it looks flat, lifeless. In Figure 5.74, we are changing the Ambient color to something warm, a soft yellow. We have also adjusted the Ambient slider to tune the exact shade of the yellow. The result is shown in Figure 5.75.

USING POLYGON FACE EXTRUSION AND A FILE TEXTURE AS A LAMBERT COLOR TO MAKE AN ICE RINK

Extrusion is the Leatherman Tool of 3D polygon modeling. It is extremely versatile. All it takes is a little creativity on the part of the modeler and it can produce quick solutions to a wide array of modeling problems. Next, we will look at extrusion again and use it in a way very similar to how we used NURBS extrusion earlier.

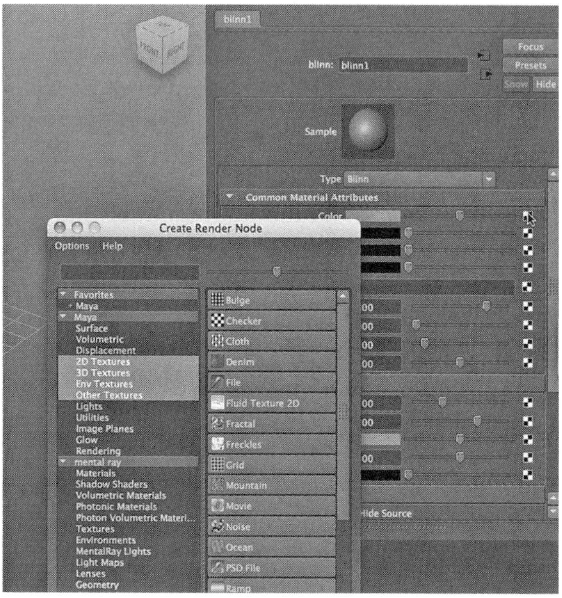

Extruding the Wall

In Figure 5.76, we have laid down a curve with the EP Curve tool. (It is under the Create dropdown on the Main Menu.) Then we created a plane that is tall and narrow. In face mode, the plane was selected, and the curve was Shift-selected. Then, we chose:

Polygons Main Menu → Edit Mesh → Extrude

The settings of this tool are shown in Figure 5.77. Divisions is set to 15, and that is how many segments we have in our wall (see Figure 5.78). Since this

FIGURE 5.65   Using a texture as a color.

is a polygon tool, the segments are angular. The Taper slider in Figure 5.77, by the way, would make the wall wider and taller as we moved through the extrusion. With it set at 1, the wall keeps the same thickness and height all the way around.

Polygon extrusion, as opposed to NURBS extrusion (or NURBS lofting), can be used to create angular ductwork, fences, and rain gutters.

Using a File Texture for the Fence

The wall was made by placing a projection texture on the extruded face and carefully adjusting it using the Interactive Placement tool. The texture consists of a photograph of a fence that tiles right to left quite seamlessly. Because I was told that nobody but nobody builds an ice rink with a wooden slat fence, the scene was

FIGURE 5.66   Selecting the manila folder.

also rendered with the wood texture changed to a mia_glass with a GlassThin preset. The glass happens to leverage the fact that the fence is 3D. The fence consists of

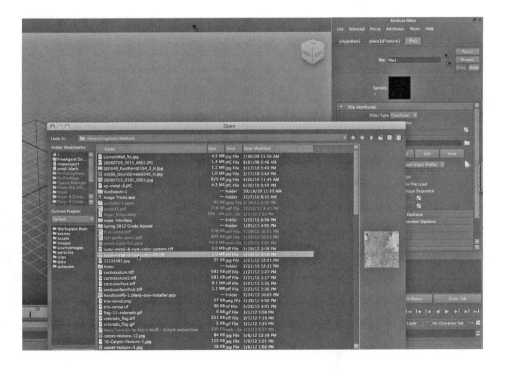

FIGURE 5.67   Selecting the texture image.

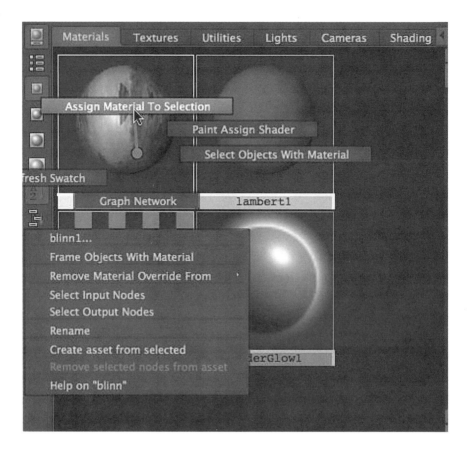

FIGURE 5.68   Assigning the texture.

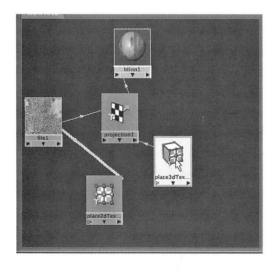

FIGURE 5.69   The Hypershades object network.

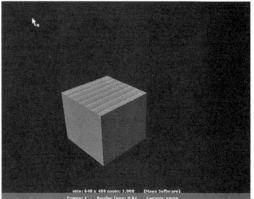

FIGURE 5.70   Initial render.

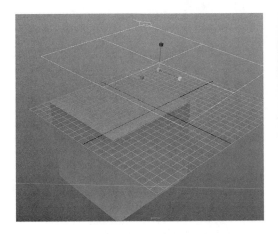

FIGURE 5.71 Resizing the texture projection.

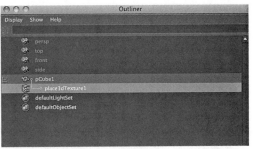

FIGURE 5.72 Making the texture stick.

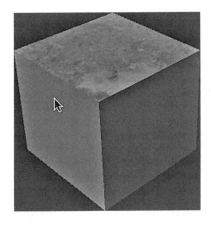

FIGURE 5.73 The render with texture resized.

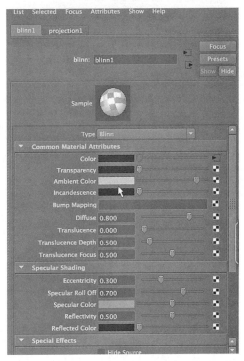

FIGURE 5.74 Adding ambient color.

sections of stretched cubes, and the double thickness of the glass makes the Plexiglas look more solid.

Using Two Layers for Ice

The ice consists of two horizontal polygon planes. The bottom one is a Blinn with a soft blue color. The top one was given a nonzero transparency so that the blue of the Blinn would bleed through.

The top material is a mia_material with Roughness (under Defuse) of .7, a white colored Reflection Color, transparency of .6 and Glossiness of .5 (all are under Reflection). And under Refraction, an Index of Refraction of 1.5, a very light blue color, Transparency

FIGURE 5.75   Final render—a brighter face.

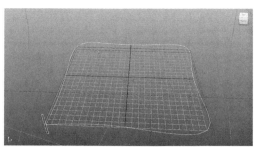

FIGURE 5.76   Face and EP curve.

of .6, and Glossiness of .16. Most significantly, it is a Glossy Samples setting of 8 that created the rough texture of the ice. In Figure 5.79, we see the resulting renders, with a wood fence during the day and a Plexiglas fence in the evening.

Textures versus Geometry: Bump Maps versus Displacement Maps

We have seen that there are multiple ways to make use of bit-mapped images in Maya, including using them directly as textures, or as the bump map attributes of materials, or as the color attribute of a material. As it

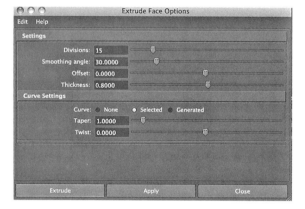

FIGURE 5.77   Extrude settings.

turns out, there is another way to use an image: as a displacement map. Like bump maps, displacement maps do not alter the geometry of an object, but they can sometimes provide a much more realistic simulation of geometric detail.

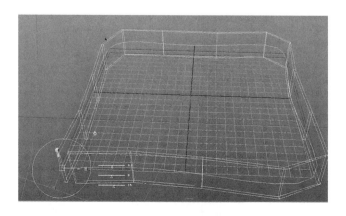

FIGURE 5.78   Rink wall.

BUMP MAPS VERSUS DISPLACEMENT MAPS IN MAYA

Now, we compare the use of bump maps and displacement maps in Maya.

Bump Maps

Bump maps simulate fine-grained geometry by manipulating the normals information derived from a texture to create the illusion of texture on a model.

Figure 5.80 shows a Blinn material with a checkerboard bump map applied to it. This was made by first creating a Blinn material in the Hypershade, then creating a checkerboard texture in the Hypershade. With the material selected, the texture was middle mouse button dragged to the Bump Mapping box in the attribute editor.

Displacement Maps

Figure 5.81 shows another Blinn

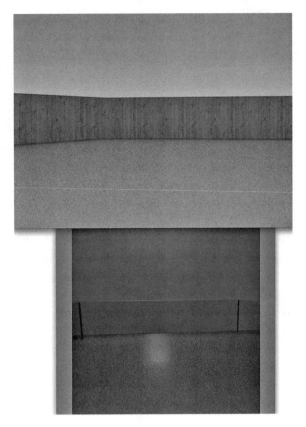

FIGURE 5.79 **(See p. CI-13 of Color Insert)** Ice rink—day and night.

material, but this time, instead of using a bump map, we are using a displacement map. We don't do this by selecting the material itself. Rather, we go to the Hypershade and choose the Shading Groups tab (instead of the Materials tab). We select the second Blinn. We then create another checkerboard texture and drag it to the Displacement Map box in the attribute editor of the Blinn Shading node.

To emphasize this distinction, Figure 5.82 shows the various tabs in the Hypershade window. The two Blinns are labeled blinn3 and blinn6, and Maya provides different icons for the two of them. The first icon gives us a hint that a bump map has been applied. The second icon is more abstract and indicates that we are using a different technique, namely, displacement mapping.

The Resulting Render: Comparing Bump Maps to Displacement Maps

Remember that the glass dish is simply a revolved curve and has completely smooth geometry. Figure 5.83 shows two versions of the polygon glass dish in the same rendering. They are identical geometrically. On the left, a bump map has been used to create the feeling of detailed, striated geometry. On the right, a displacement map has been used instead.

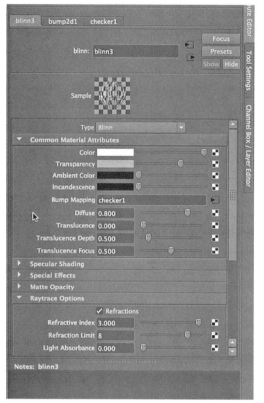

FIGURE 5.80   The bump map.

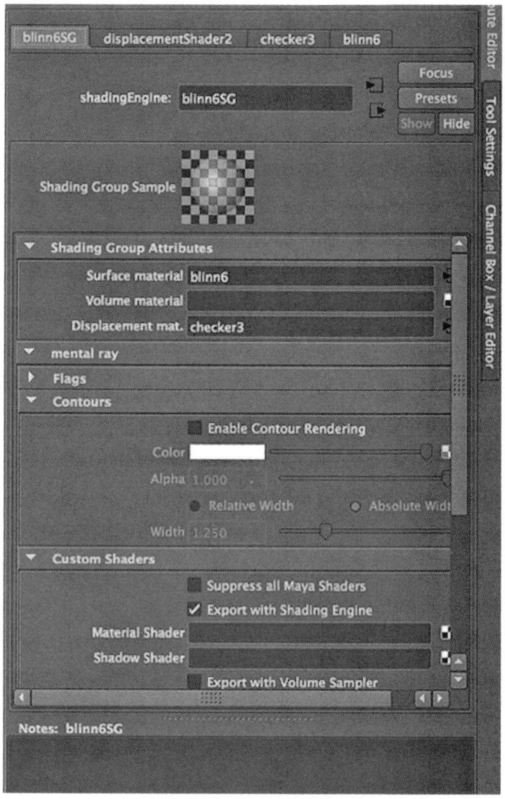

FIGURE 5.81   The displacement map.

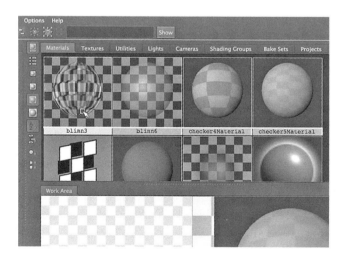

FIGURE 5.82   The shaders for the two glasses.

FIGURE 5.83   **(See p. CI-6 of Color Insert)** Bump map versus displacement map.

The scaling of the textures are identical on the two glass dishes. The main difference is that in one, the texture serves as a bump map, and in the other it serves as a displacement map.

The bump map creates an illusion of texture but does not give us internal shadows (shadows cast by an object on itself) or the sorts of light refractions that true, geometrically thick and detailed glass would.

The displacement map, on the other hand, does much better. However, it too is only a simulation, although one that demands more computational time. At the point of rendering, Maya has done an approximate job of computing the detailed geometry that would have existed if the model actually had 3D surface detail in the shape of the displacement map. We thus get a rendering that far more effectively gives the illusion of 3D geometry.

Notice the depth of detail on the dish on the right. The top of the dish gives a mottled look to the checkerboard that is reflected back to the viewer, while the one on the left simply bends the lines in the checkerboard. And the base of the right dish looks like true geometry, whereas the one on the left looks like there are simply dark lines drawn across the glass. We are getting what appears to be the sort of internal shadows we expect with true geometry.

All in all, the displacement map gives us a much richer sense of thick, cut glass.

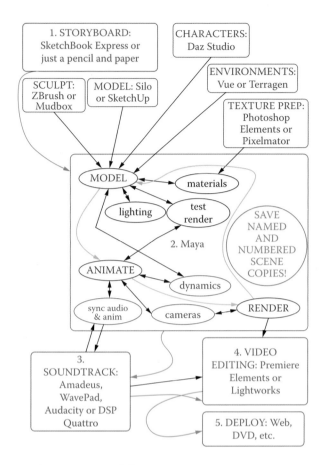

FIGURE 1.1   Overview of animation workflow.

a set of vertices: $\{[x_i, y_i, z_i]\}$
translations: $\{[x_i + a, y_i + b, z_i + c]\}$
scalings: $\{[ax_i, by_i, cz_i]\}$
rotations: $\{[x_i, y_i \cos(\theta) - z_i \sin(\theta), y_i \sin(\theta) + z_i \cos(\theta)]\}$

$\cos(\theta) = f_d/h$
$\sin(\theta) = g_d/h$
black lines = hypotenuse = h
red = g_1, yellow = g_2, green = f_1, green|brown = f_2

FIGURE 2.19   Translate, rotate, and scale.

FIGURE 1.2   The cabana with gold metallic arches.

FIGURE 1.3   The cabana with stone arches.

FIGURE 4.32   The Mad Cow Dairy.

FIGURE 5.6   Table render with shadow.

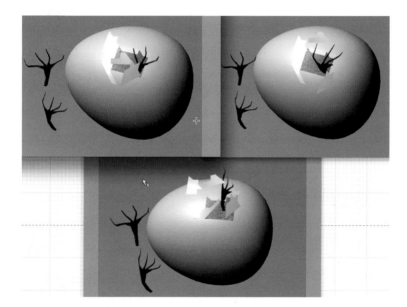

FIGURE 8.38   The chick breakout.

FIGURE 9.35   Stylized glass and bottle render.

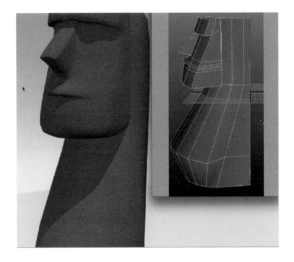

FIGURE 4.61   Moai wireframe and Moai rendered.

FIGURE 4.80   Metallic finish.

FIGURE 4.89   Final Moai rendered.

FIGURE 12.23   A complex material and light effect.

FIGURE 3.4 The closet.

FIGURE 5.7 Mental ray planar light.

FIGURE 5.8 Mental ray spherical light.

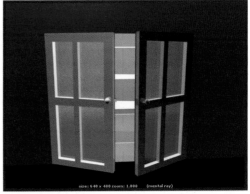

FIGURE 10.51 Left door illuminated.

CI-6

FIGURE 3.29   Rendered dish.

FIGURE 5.10   Glass bowl with depth map shadows.

FIGURE 5.11   Glass bowl with raytrace shadows.

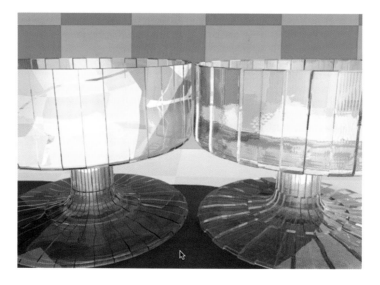

FIGURE 5.83   Bump map versus displacement map.

FIGURE 5.25 Base texture.

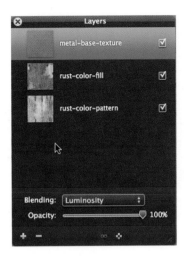

FIGURE 5.26 Stamped metal texture as base texture.

FIGURE 5.27 Rusty metal texture.

FIGURE 5.28 The rusty metal as a darker color.

FIGURE 5.29 Rusty metal texture number 2.

FIGURE 5.31 The final result—three-layered texture.

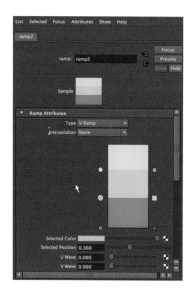

FIGURE 6.18　Classic Trix rendered.

FIGURE 6.17　The ramp texture for the per particle attribute.

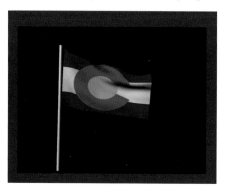

FIGURE 6.33　Rendered earlier frame.

FIGURE 7.14　Approaching the canyon.

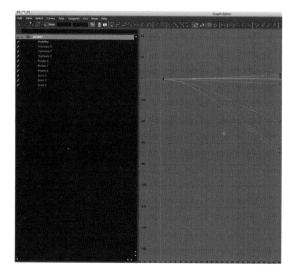

FIGURE 7.24　Graph Editor.

FIGURE 10.21　The cloth T-shirt rendered.

FIGURE 9.4   Bush texture number 1.

FIGURE 9.5   Bush texture number 2.

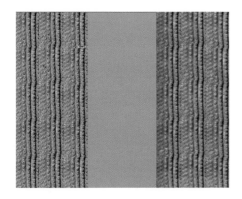

FIGURE 9.10   Rusty metal number 1—compare.   FIGURE 9.11   Rusty metal number 2—compare.

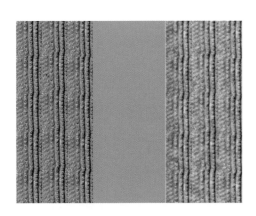

FIGURE 9.12   Bush number 1—compare.

FIGURE 9.13   Bush number 2—compare.

FIGURE 9.24   Three glass bottles rendered.

FIGURE 15.45   Render with jagged shadow.

FIGURE 15.47   Depth Map render.

FIGURE 15.49   Raytraced Shadow rendered.

FIGURE 15.51   A bottle in the Sun.

FIGURE 15.29   Rendering the colored glass.

FIGURE 15.35   Anisotropy of 1.

FIGURE 15.36   Anisotropy of 10.

FIGURE 15.37   Anisotropy of 100.

FIGURE 15.38   Anisotropy of .1.

FIGURE 15.41   Penumbra 10 and Dropoff 0.

FIGURE 15.42   Penumbra 0 and Dropoff 0.

FIGURE 15.43   Penumbra 10 and Dropoff 94.

FIGURE 5.21   Cement and asphalt rendered.

FIGURE 5.79   Ice rink—day and night.

FIGURE 12.22   The street on the horizon.

FIGURE 14.8   Generated terrain from Terragen.

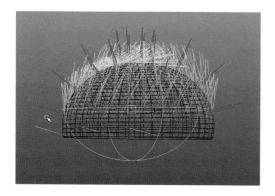

FIGURE 8.28   Resized sphere.

FIGURE 8.30   Pink man with punk yellow hair.

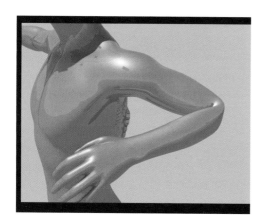

FIGURE 11.13   A folded elbow.

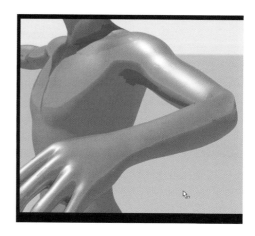

FIGURE 11.18   An improved elbow.

FIGURE 13.20 Doorknob render with blue and white texture.

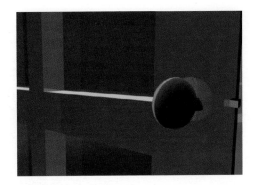

FIGURE 13.25 Doorknob render after Cylindrical Mapping.

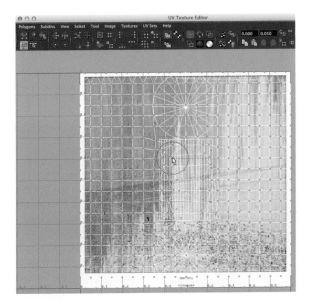

FIGURE 13.27 UV texture being smudged.

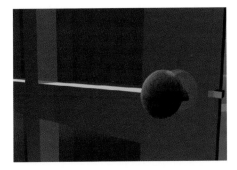

FIGURE 13.28 A final doorknob with new texture mapping.

FIGURE 15.17   Render without Caustics.

FIGURE 15.20   Render with Caustics.

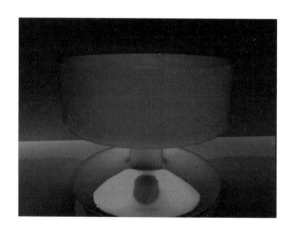

FIGURE 15.25   Irradiance glow.

FIGURE 15.33   A bowl colored by light.

CHAPTER 6

Particle Dynamics

WE ARE GOING TO shift focus now and cover an aspect of Maya that can be used to simulate particle dynamics. Maya has engines that can simulate two different aspects of real-world physics. The first involves the emission of particles, their semirandom behavior, and their interaction with each other and with objects in a scene. The second involves the physics of colliding objects, which we will look at in Chapter 11.

Particle dynamics are useful for situations where a large number of small objects are needed to properly construct a scene. In short, particle dynamics can scale to many hundreds or thousands of individual particles. This capability can be used to model smoke, fire, rain, and water. Particle dynamics can be used to make realistic cloth as well. Particles can be used to create effects where each particle is visually distinct or where the particles seem to form an organic mass where the boundaries of each particle cannot be identified visually. When we use particle dynamics, we tend to call the model a "special effect."

The general idea is to create an object, often called an "emitter," which will generate many geometrically identical objects. Typically, we also include a random factor that causes individual particles to have semi-independent movements and visual qualities, as we are often trying to model a chaotic effect.

We can program the emitter to incrementally produce particles over the course of some number of frames; this is how we might produce rain. But when modeling an ocean, we might want to generate all the particles but not render them or their movement until the complete body of water has been made.

USE EMITTERS SPARINGLY

There are some complications that occur when using particle dynamics in an animated project. Perhaps the most significant is that particle dynamics can radically increase render times. Imagine an ocean scene created with an emitter. Water scenes are often impressive visually; the surface can be alive with whitecaps, ripples, and waves. But this means that the position and appearance (how it reacts to light) of every single particle could potentially change in every single frame. For many of us who are creating animated scenes on desktop or notebook computers, rendering massive particle effects can be intractable. A minute-long water effect could take many hours or days to render.

In Maya, some particle effects can be rendered using the Maya software renderer or mental ray. There are also particles that are rendered with the hardware renderer, which pushes most of the job of rendering to the graphics card, thus making the process somewhat faster. Sometimes this makes the difference between an undoable and a doable effect.

SAVING RENDER TIME

In Maya, you can render a scene in layers, just as we saw earlier that you can choose to only display certain layers at a given time. By using render layers, you could render a particle effect once and not have to rerender it every time you rerender other objects in the scene. Layers also allow you to use different renderers for different parts of a scene.

You can create render layers in a scene by clicking on the icon on the far upper right of the Main Window, and then choosing the Render tab at the bottom of the right-hand side of the window. Of course, you need to compose the rendered layers into a single video, and this is done outside of Maya.

When doing one frame test renders, you can choose to rerender only a piece of a frame, by using the second icon in from the left at the top of the Render View. It has a red box around it. This is particularly useful when rendering particles.

In addition to the Display and Render tabs, there is one called Anim, which is for layering animation. This is a complex task and is not covered in this book.

ROCKET POLLUTION AND HARDWARE PARTICLES

In Maya, there are two different settings on the Main Menu Selector for creating a particle effect. Dynamics has been in Maya for a long time and nDynamics is somewhat newer. First, we will use Dynamics, and later we will look at nDynamics. These two dynamics systems overlap significantly in their capabilities, with nDynamics being in many cases more powerful and easier to tailor. It is often easier to produce visually impressive results with nDynamics.

We are using a cylinder to host our emitter. A NURBS cylinder was chosen because it consists of three pieces: two disks and a tube. This way, the bottom disk can be selected and Maya will default the placement of the emitter to the center of the disk. We can imagine that our cylinder is a rocket, but we will only concern ourselves with the disk at the bottom of it.

In Figure 6.1, we see a particle emitter being created. In the dropdown, we see two choices for creating an emitter. One is to make a stand-alone emitter not attached to any other object in the scene, and the other is to create an emitter and plant it on the surface of an object. Since we are trying to make a rocket take off, we will create a surface emitter. To do this, we must first select an object in the scene.

So, we select the bottom disk of our rocket, and then, choose:

Dynamics Main Menu → Particles → Emit from Object

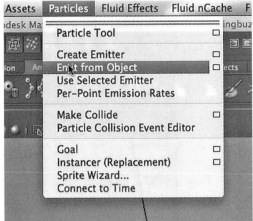

FIGURE 6.1   Emitter menu.

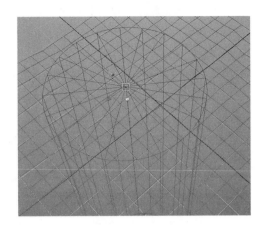

FIGURE 6.2   Emitter on the rocket.

In Figure 6.2, we see that Maya creates a small icon and places it where the emitter is attached to the object.

The Attributes of the Emitter and the Particles

In Figure 6.3, we are adjusting the attributes of the emitter. We will focus on three basic attributes for now. The first is the Direction Y setting. Notice that it is set to a negative one: we want our particles to fall downward, toward the earth. That is because our rocket trail needs to come out of the rocket's bottom. The second is the type of emitter. Our setting is Directional. Other choices for settings include Omni (all directions) and Surface (generating particles from the entirety of some surface). The particle rate is the final attribute we will look at here; 100 is fairly low, but it was chosen to decrease rendering time.

In Figure 6.4, we see that each particle has attributes as well. One fundamental setting is Particle Render Type, which happens to be set to Points. Particle Render Type defines the geometry of the particles and how they are rendered. Points are rendered with the hardware renderer. Some of the choices include "s/w" in their names; these are rendered with software. Particles that

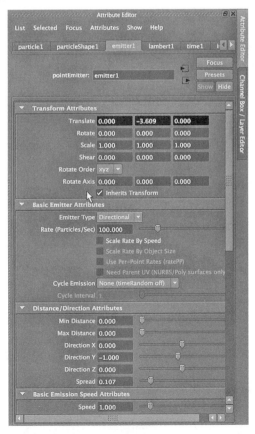

FIGURE 6.3   Emitter attributes.

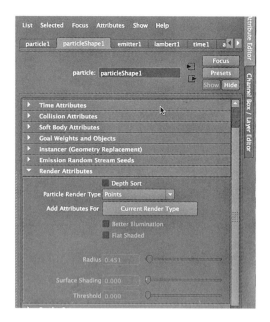

FIGURE 6.4   Particle attributes.

FIGURE 6.5   The hardware particles.

are rendered by hardware have no geometric existence. They are points in the (x, y, z) grid that are, in a sense, infinitely small. Hardware particles only possess properties that tell them how they should visually react to light and how they should move.

Next, we want to give our particles some color. So we go the Hypershade and create a Blinn material and choose black for its color. Then, in the Main Window, we use the Playback controls to run about a hundred frames. Particles are emitted, as shown in Figure 6.5. As in Figure 6.6, we select the particles and go to the Hypershade, right click on the Blinn and assign it to the particles. They will now render black.

It is not necessary to select all the particles to do this—you can generate just a small number and then assign the material. All particles emitted later will have the same material.

Figure 6.7 is a rendering of the particles. These are hardware particles, so we must render them with the renderer called Maya Hardware. We can see the large particulate pollution spewing from our rocket. If we had wanted our rocket to emit software particles that had true geometry and could be rendered with the Maya Software renderer or mental ray, we would have had to choose a particle type with "s/w" next to it.

USING SOFTWARE PARTICLES IN nDYNAMICS TO CREATE TRIX

Now, we will look at using software-rendered particles. We will create particles that have actual geometry. Thus, we will be using 3D geometry to specify the appearance of each particle, but their movement will be defined by the same mathematics of particle dynamics we would use for hardware-rendered particles.

FIGURE 6.6   Assigning a black Blinn to the particles.

nDynamics in Maya

The *n* in nDynamics stands for Nucleus, and you can access it by selecting nDynamics in the Main Menu Selector. This is an alternative dynamics system in Maya, and to distinguish it, the Maya interface uses the terms nParticles, nCloth (which we will look at momentarily), and so on.

In the Dynamics system, a particle does not modify its behavior in response to the movement of other particles. In particular, they cannot collide. But in nDynamics, the movements of particles can be dynamically affected by each other, and in particular, two particles can collide. Particles can even be set to react if they come within a specific distance from each other.

Particle Dynamics Engines and Solvers

Applications like Maya include complex systems that contain mathematical subsystems that simulate the physics of the real world.

FIGURE 6.7   The hardware rendered particles.

Specifically, there is usually a "solver" that takes the current properties of the particles and of the scene as a whole, and then computes—for every frame—the positioning and appearance of every particle.

In modern particle dynamics systems, such as nDynamics in Maya, there are a variety of settings that control the behavior of the solver by specifying the way particles interact with geometric objects in the scene. We can control the properties of natural forces in the scene, such as gravity and wind, and how they affect the particles. We can also adjust the speed of particles, the rate at which they are emitted, the direction in which they move, how far they move, and how long they exist in the scene after they are emitted.

We start to see why dynamics effects can require so much rendering time.

Emitting Trix into the Glass Bowl

In Figure 6.8, we see the glass bowl that we created earlier. Our goal is to pour Trix out of a box and into the bowl. In Figure 6.9, nDynamics is being selected on the Main Menu selector. Figure 6.10 shows an nParticles emitter being created; you can set the particle type being created, and we have chosen Balls. The emitter is set to Directional for the Emitter Type, so that the balls of cereal will tumble in an orderly way out of the box.

Colliders

It is common for a scene to have both standard geometric models and dynamics effects in it. These two parallel worlds typically come into contact with each other. This means we are going to have to have our particles interact with the glass bowl.

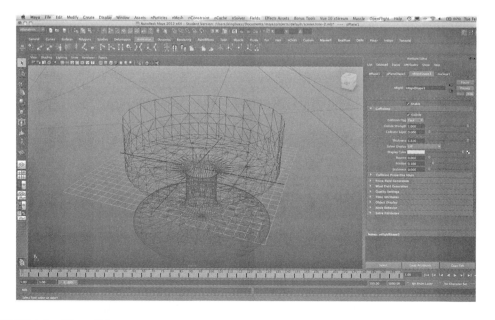

FIGURE 6.8 Glass dish.

In Figure 6.11, we are turning the glass bowl, which is selected in the Main Window, into a "passive collider" by selecting:

nDynamics Main Menu → nMesh → Create Passive Collider

The various passive collider attributes of the dish are visible in Figure 6.8. As a passive collider, the glass bowl will sit still, and our Trix will pour into it, then bounce, and then stay inside the confines of the bowl. If an object like the glass bowl is not turned into a collider, the cereal would pass right through it.

FIGURE 6.9   The nDynamics menu.

Scaling the Trix

First, though, we need to rescale the Trix. We do this by running the animation using the Playback controls on the bottom right of the Main Window. Then we select some of the particles. We go to the attributes of the particles (see Figure 6.12) and set the x, y, and z scaling factors to two.

FIGURE 6.10   Emitter menu.

Ramp Textures

We are going to create a ramp texture for our cereal and do so in an unusual way. But first we take a look at the process of creating a ramp texture and adjusting its attributes. Ramp textures (and materials) allow us to create multicolored surfaces that can be used in a wide variety of ways, and so they are heavily employed.

Figure 6.13 shows a ramp texture that has just been made by selecting Ramp under 2D Textures in the Hypershade. In Figure 6.14, its colors are being adjusted. The default colors are blue, green, and red, with the colors gently blended between them.

To remove an existing color, we select a box with an *x* in it to the right of the color.

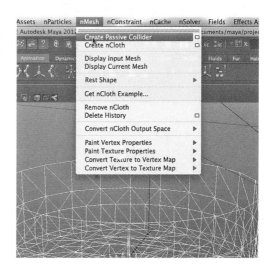

FIGURE 6.11   Passive collider.

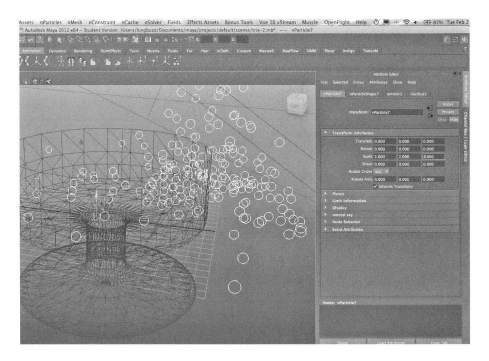

FIGURE 6.12   Scale particles.

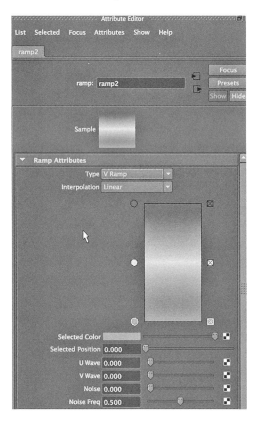

FIGURE 6.13   The default ramp colors.

FIGURE 6.14   Adjusting a ramp's colors.

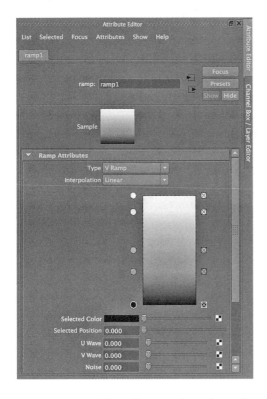

FIGURE 6.15   After adjusting the colors of a ramp.

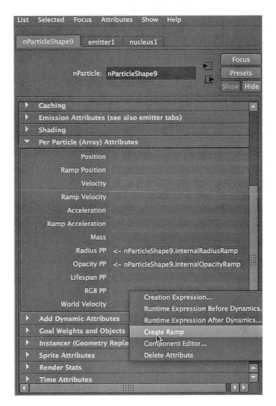

FIGURE 6.16   Creating a per particle attribute.

To change an existing color, we click on one of the circles to the left of the original color. To create a new color, we click on the inside of the ramp texture (the rainbow itself); a new circle and a new *x* box will appear. The colors that we will use in our ramp texture are shown in Figure 6.15.

The Trix's Ramp

For the Trix example, we need to create a ramp that contains the colors that we find in Trix. We will use the original three Trix colors from 1955 (according to *Wikipedia*): orangey orange, lemony yellow, and raspberry red.

But in order to make each piece of Trix, which is an independent sphere, have its own separate color instead of each having all three colors of the ramp, we have to create the ramp texture in a special way. We cannot simply swipe some Trix objects and assign the ramp to them, like we did when we assigned a black Blinn to the particles of rocket exhaust. In Figure 6.16, we have gone to the attribute tab for the shape of the particles. There is a set of attributes under Per Particle (Array) Attributes. We go to RGB PP (meaning color channels per particle) and right click. We choose Create Ramp. Then Maya

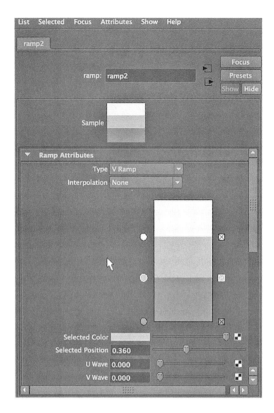

FIGURE 6.17 **(See p. CI-8 of Color Insert)** The ramp texture for the per particle attribute.

FIGURE 6.18 **(See p. CI-8 of Color Insert)** Classic Trix rendered.

makes a new ramp for us, and we find it in the Hypershade. It has already been attached to the balls of cereal.

We adjust the colors as seen in Figure 6.17. Note that we adjust the Interpolation attribute to None, so that the colors of the rainbow don't blend together.

Gravity

There are some useful settings that you will find on the nucleus1 tab that can be seen in Figure 6.12. In particular, we can program the way the emitted particles will interact with natural forces, like gravity and wind. In this case, we select the particles and choose:

nDynamics Main Menu → Fields → Gravity

This will pull the cereal downward toward the bowl. This gravity field will not affect any other objects or particle emitters we place in the scene.

Action!

Then we go back to frame 1 and play the scene. Fifty frames were used in this example. The emitter, which has been placed at the opening of the tilting Trix box, begins to create particles. They fall and collect in the bowl, as can be seen in the rendering of Figure 6.18.

A file texture consisting of a photograph of a Trix box was used as a projection texture on the cereal box.

An Aside

Another interesting use for particles is to model the stars in the sky. We simply generate as many stars as we want, using the settings of the emitter to space them out as they are emitted.

CREATING A CLOTH FLAG WITH nDYNAMICS

There is a clever technique used in Maya to simulate cloth, and it consists of bridging the gap between polygon modeling and particle dynamics.

nDynamics Meets Geometry

The goal is to create natural looking cloth, and we will have to enable it to interact with objects in the scene. You could imagine doing this by taking a polygon surface and subdividing it until the polygons were very small and then mechanically reshaping the polygon surface so that it drapes. But then, we would still face the intimidating process of animating that cloth so that a dress, for example, moves as the wearer walks, sits down, and so on.

Maya uses a very different technique, one that produces excellent results with minimal effort. It transforms the vertices in a polygon surface into nDynamics particles. This is a powerful and broadly used technique, because it gives us the modeling power of polygon modeling as well as the scalability of particle dynamics.

Now we will make a simple nCloth model.

How does it work? First, an nCloth model must be made out of a polygon surface. When Maya transforms a polygon surface into nCloth, it creates a system of connections (called "links"). These links contain information about the distance between the vertices in the nCloth. There are also "cross links" that contain information about the angles between links. Together, the links and cross links keep track of the precise shape of the cloth, and since the vertices connected by links and cross links are nDynamics particles, the cloth can change shape from frame to frame.

nCloth can be used to create a wide variety of materials that must gracefully fold under the power of forces like gravity and wind; examples include soft plastics and aluminum foil.

A Flag

In Figure 6.19, we create a polygon plane. You can see in the figure that there is already a cylinder in our scene; it will be our flagpole. In Figures 6.20, 6.21, and 6.22, we see the geometry of the flag increasing in density. This is important because we want our cloth to be smooth. This will also increase render time, of course.

In Figure 6.22, the flag has been lined up against the pole.

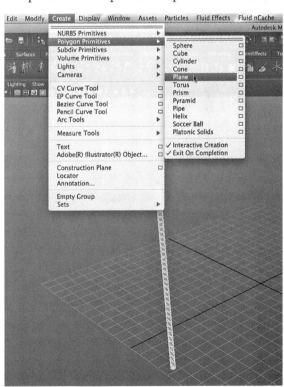

FIGURE 6.19   Polygon plane menu.

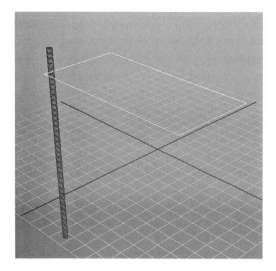

FIGURE 6.20   Pole and flag.

FIGURE 6.21   Subdivisions of the flag.

Then, we right click, go into Object mode, and as in Figures 6.23 and 6.24, we choose:

nDynamics Main Menu → nMesh → Create nCloth

Before doing this, the pole's geometry had to be made denser. The density of the horizontal geometry of the flagpole was increased to create vertices along the length of the pole that could be attached to the flag. This can be seen in Figure 6.25.

To attach the flag to the pole, it was necessary to "constrain" two pairs of vertices to each other. First, we right clicked and went into Vertex mode. Then we Shift selected and chose a vertex from the top of the flag and a vertex next to it on the pole. The second set consisted

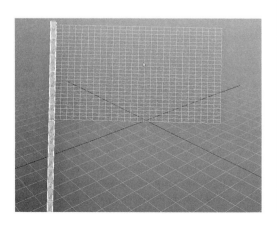

FIGURE 6.22   Flag and pole.

FIGURE 6.23   nDynamics.

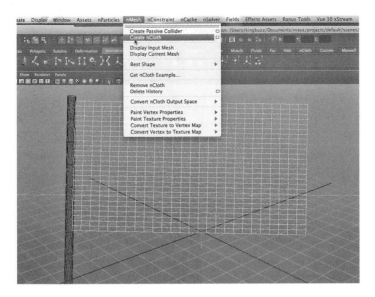

FIGURE 6.24   Create nCloth.

of a vertex at the bottom of the flag and a vertex on the pole next to it. After selecting each pair we chose:

nDynamics Main Menu → nConstraint → Component to Component

This sequence of actions can be seen in Figures 2.26, 2.27, and 2.28. Note that in Figure 6.27, we can see the top pair of vertices. They are white in the figure, but when seen in color, they are pink.

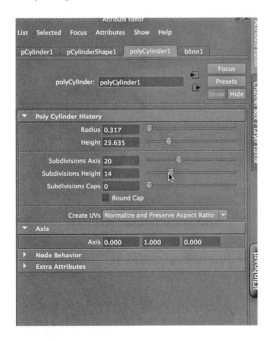

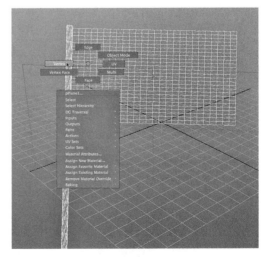

FIGURE 6.25   Adding vertices to the pole.   FIGURE 6.26   Vertex mode.

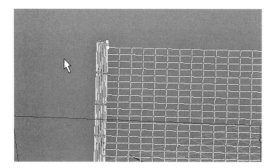

FIGURE 6.27 One vertex from each object selected.

FIGURE 6.28 nConstraint.

FIGURE 6.29 Colorado.

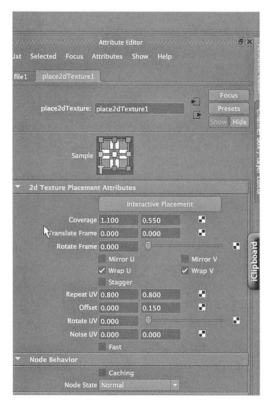

FIGURE 6.30 Texture settings.

Putting a Texture on the Flag

In Figure 6.29, we see the image of a Colorado flag that we are going to put on the model. It is imported into Maya as a file texture. Figure 6.30 shows the texture being adjusted to fit the flag.

Making the Flag Flap

Maya allows us to introduce "fields" that represent natural forces and assign them to objects. The flag was selected, and in Figure 6.31, a Turbulence field was created that only impacts the flag. The attributes of the Turbulence field are shown in Figure 6.32; the settings were cranked up so that the field would be strong. Figures 6.33 and 6.34 show two frames (a number of frames apart) as the flag flaps gracefully in the wind. In general, the air field is milder than the turbulence field. In a scene like this, a gravity field should also be attached to the flag, so that it droops a tiny bit as it flaps.

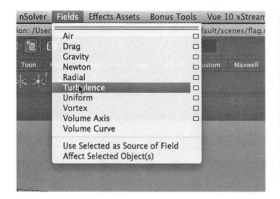

FIGURE 6.31   Turbulence.

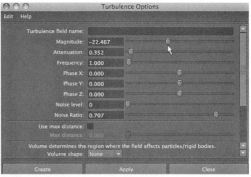

FIGURE 6.32   Turbulence settings.

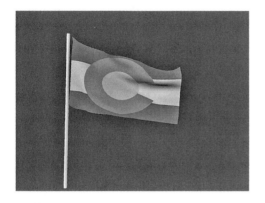

FIGURE 6.33   **(See p. CI-8 of Color Insert)**
Rendered earlier frame.

FIGURE 6.34   Rendered later frame.

CREATING RAIN WITH nDYNAMICS

We turn now to another dynamics example, one that uses hardware rendered particles that interact with physical surfaces in a scene.

Downward Gravity versus the Upward Bounce of a Collider

One of the easiest things to build with nDynamics (or with most particle dynamics engines) is rain. We will make use of a passive collider again, and we will look at adjusting a critical attribute of a collider: bounce. We will look at the use of natural fields, in particular gravity, and how bounce and gravity can be used together to create realistic movement.

Two Planes: Rain Clouds and the Ground

In Figure 6.35, we see two polygon planes. We have not increased the density of the geometry of either plane, as this is not necessary for our purposes right now. As in Figure 6.36, we are selecting nDynamics in the Main Menu Selector. Then, in Figure 6.37, with the top plane selected, we are creating an emitter that will be assigned

FIGURE 6.35   Two planes.

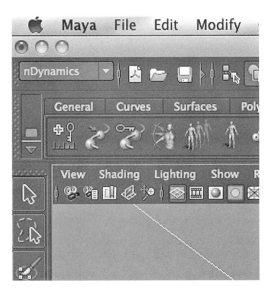

FIGURE 6.36   nDynamics.

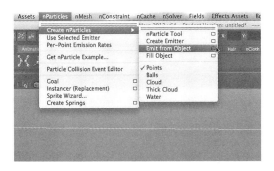

FIGURE 6.37   Create emitter.

to the plane; by choosing Emit from Object, we will make rain come down from the entire surface of the plane. The bottom plane will serve as the ground.

Rain Particles

In Figure 6.38, we are adjusting some of the attributes of the emitter. The rate of emission has been set to a fairly high number. Since we are using the hardware renderer, a high particle count will not be that burdensome at render time. The speed has been set to 10.

The Ground

In Figure 6.39, we turn the bottom plane into a passive collider. In Figure 6.40, we have cranked up the Bounce attribute so that when the rain hits the ground, it will bounce back up a bit. Then we run the animation using the Playback controls and create some particles.

Making It Rain

We select these particles, and in Figure 6.41, we attach a gravity field to those particles so they will move downward. In Figure 6.42,

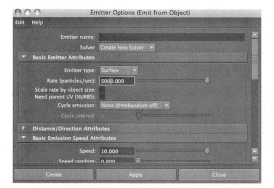

FIGURE 6.38   Emitter attributes.

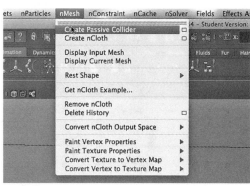

FIGURE 6.39   Passive collider.

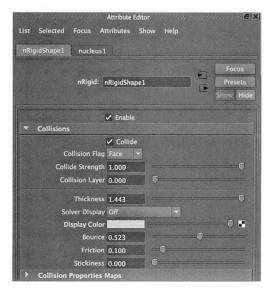

FIGURE 6.40   Bounce attribute.

FIGURE 6.41   Gravity field.

we choose Streak as our particle shape. (This is a hardware particle.) Then, using a couple of hundred frames, we play the scene, as shown in Figure 6.43. In the rendered image (using the Hardware renderer) in Figure 6.44, we can see that the raindrops are indeed bouncing back up a bit when they hit the ground.

By the way, when you attach an emitter to an object like the plane; the plane has a top and a bottom. We could have turned the plane 180 degrees and reversed the y direction of gravity, and the particles would have been emitted upward.

Instancing

There is another capability that can significantly extend the power of dynamics in Maya. We can use an emitter to generate many copies of an object that has been modeled by hand, such as a plague of locusts or the ships of alien invaders. First, we create a Dynamics or an nDynamics emitter that emits software particles. We let the emitter create some particles. We select them, and then we go to:

Dynamics Main Menu → Particles → Instancer

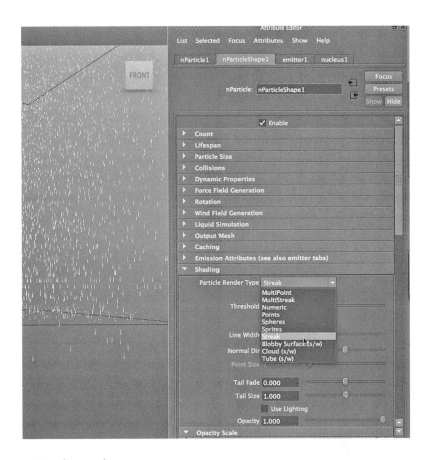

FIGURE 6.42   Streak particles.

FIGURE 6.43   Streak particle rain.

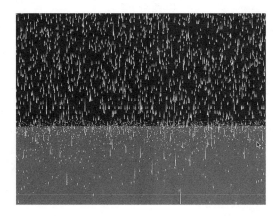

FIGURE 6.44   Rain rendered.

or

nDynamics Main Menu → nParticles → Instancer

We can replace the emitted particles with an object we have created.

In general, the term *instance* refers to any technique that creates copies of a model and not necessarily the particles generated by an emitter. Often, an instanced object automatically inherits its properties (such as materials) from the original object.

An example of a more general use of the word *instance* can be found by selecting:

any Main Menu → Edit → Special

If we check the Instance checkbox in the tool's settings, we find a tool that can be used to create a mirrored version of an object that will be automatically updated as we morph the original. It can be used to make a symmetric copy of half of a human face, saving us a lot of modeling time.

SPECIALIZED DYNAMICS APPLICATIONS

There are other applications besides Maya that animators often use for creating dynamics effects. One of them is RealFlow, a powerful stand-alone dynamics application that can work as a plug-in to Maya. Another is Houdini, which is actually a general-purpose 3D modeler and animator like Maya, but has particularly powerful dynamics capabilities.

CHAPTER 7

A First Look at Adding Animation

V IDEO MUST CONTAIN A minimum of about twenty frames per second for the motion to appear continuous. And in every frame, the models in your scene are potentially changing their position, shape, color, and other properties.

But digital animation does an almost astonishing amount of work for us. A model can change in many ways over a series of frames. Recall the three basic primitives: Translate (move in 3-space), Scale (in three dimensions), and Rotate (in 3-space). When a model is animated in Maya, these are the three core properties that define the animation of a model from frame to frame. We can also animate other properties of an object, like color and transparency. And yet, we don't have to tell Maya how to change our scene for every frame.

How does Maya make the task easier? The workhorse of movement in a 3D scene is interpolation. We can set what are called "keyframes." Periodically we change the properties of a model, place it in a frame somewhere on the Maya timeline, and then set a keyframe. Maya does the rest. It interpolates between keyframes so that models smoothly change their properties. Maya contains knowledge of how objects interact with each other in a 3D world, and so we can also program models to be propelled through space and collide with each other. We have already looked at particles colliding with objects, and later in this book we will look at multiple solid objects colliding. But right now, we are only concerned with the process of animating a single model, and we will do this via keyframing.

Before we look at keyframing we will start with a limited but easy form of animation.

MOVING AN OBJECT ALONG A MOTION PATH

One of the easiest ways to set up movement in a Maya scene is with what is known as "path" animation. A model can follow a curve drawn through a scene. We can make an aircraft fly by overhead and we can even make it bank while doing so. One variation on this is to animate a camera and to render the scene from the perspective of a camera moving along a path. This can be breathtaking and even dizzying.

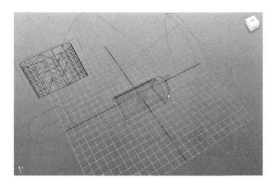

FIGURE 7.1　Can of Spam.　　　　FIGURE 7.2　Spam scene.

We will move a can of Spam along a path and into the mailbox we built earlier in Chapter 4. In Figure 7.1, we see a photo of a can of Spam, which will be used as a texture. Figure 7.2 shows the scene in wireframe. The mailbox is in the middle. The can of Spam is in the upper left and close to us, so it looks big. Figure 7.3 shows a render of the scene at the beginning, with the Spam high up and far away.

Creating a Path

In Figure 7.4, we select the CV curve tool. We lay down a curve in 3-space in Figure 7.5. The can of Spam is actually that short tubular object above the mailbox; it does not have its texture or its top and bottom in this image. At this point, we need to decide how many frames we want to use for the Spam flying into the box. The Timeline is set to 100 frames.

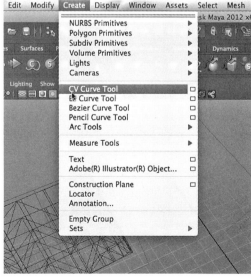

FIGURE 7.3　The Spam on its way—rendered.　　FIGURE 7.4　NURBS curve tool.

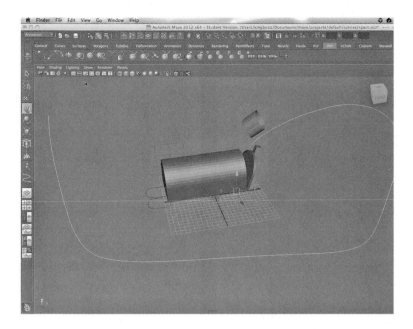

FIGURE 7.5   Curve for motion path.

Putting an Object on a Path

Now we go to the Animation Main Menu, as seen in Figure 7.6. We Shift-select the CV line and the Spam, then, as seen in Figure 7.7, we choose:

Animation Main Menu → Animate → Motion Paths → Attach to Motion Path

FIGURE 7.6   Selecting the Animation Main Menu.

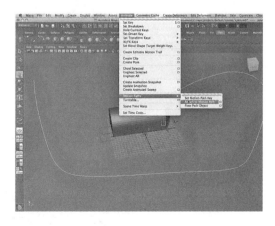

FIGURE 7.7   Attach to motion path.

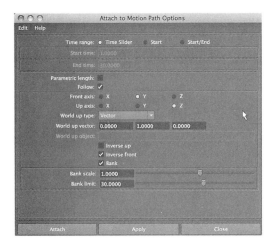

FIGURE 7.8   Path settings.

FIGURE 7.9   Rendered Spam in the box.

For an added effect, as shown in Figure 7.8, we go to the attributes of the motion path and set the banking to 30, the Front axis to y, and the Up axis to z.

We run the scene. At the end of its path, we see that the Spam has safely made it into your mailbox (see Figure 7.9).

From the Camera's Perspective: A River Ride

Let's look at a second example. Figure 7.10 shows a stunning scene built by D&D Creations. A motion path has been placed along the canyon, staying just above the waterline. A camera, called Camera_6, was created.

This scene was built to run in Vue, an amazing application for creating and animating natural scenery and environments. There is a Maya plug-in that Vue supplies that allows scenes from one version of their product, called Vue xStream, to be imported into Maya. This was done with D&D's scene, and only minor changes were made.

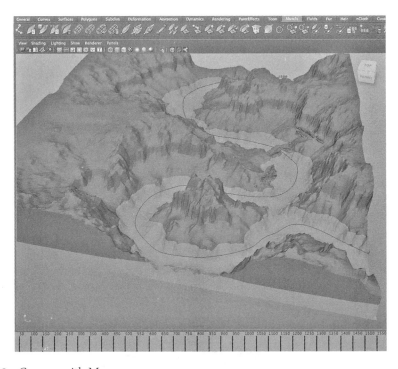

FIGURE 7.10   Canyon with Maya ocean.

Primarily, the water level has been raised to give the scene a powerful effect as we fly along just above the rushing water. (Raising the water level does, however, result in the canyon appearing to sit in the middle of the ocean.) A rendering of the scene is shown in Figure 7.11.

(Incidentally, e-on, which sells Vue, now has an application for generating very realistic plant life. It is called Plant Factory.)

FIGURE 7.11   Canyon and water rendered.

In Figure 7.12, we go to the menus in the top of the lower left part of the Main Window, which holds the bluish main design area, and we choose:

Panels → Perspective → Camera_6

This perspective is seen in Figure 7.13; this is the perspective from which the video was rendered, but this setting only controls our view inside the Maya Main window.

The lighter area along the CV curve is the water; above that, the terrain is dry. The resulting rendering is shown in Figure 7.14; the camera is approaching the mouth of the canyon, which is in the lower right in Figure 7.11.

Now, with the water rushing, we fly along the water, with the camera banking at each turn. A soundtrack of rushing water was added in a video editor after rendering the frames.

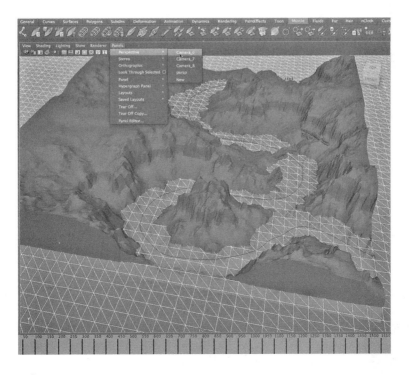

FIGURE 7.12   Choosing a perspective.

FIGURE 7.13   A perspective from the ground plane.

In Figures 7.15 and 7.16, we are in the middle of the animation path and about to fly under an arch. In Figures 7.17 and 7.18, we are banking back and forth as we follow the turns in the canyon. Finally, in Figure 7.19, we are in open water again.

The water in this scene was created quite easily by selecting:

Dynamics Main Menu → Fluid Effects → Ocean → Create Ocean

This created a particle effect that covered the entire x-z plane with a layer of particles. This is one of Maya's best prefab effects and can be easily tailored to look like a wide variety of water bodies. In Chapter 11, we will look at making our own ocean and create a swell.

FIGURE 7.14   **(See p. CI-8 of Color Insert)**
Approaching the canyon.

FIGURE 7.15   Under an arch.

FIGURE 7.16   Emerging from the arch.

FIGURE 7.17   Banking.

FIGURE 7.18   Banking again.

FIGURE 7.19   Back in open water.

KEYFRAMING AN OBJECT

Now, we get back to keyframing, the most general-purpose form of animation provided by 3D applications.

The Timeline

Along the bottom of the Main Window is a series of frames in the Time Slider. Look back to Figure 2.1. Notice that the number of frames that are showing is 24, probably less than a second's worth of animation. Below the right-hand side of the Time Slider you will see two numbers: 24 and 48. The number to the left, 24, is the number of frames that is displayed in the Time Slider. The number to the right, 48, is the total number of frames involved in the animation being keyframed.

Creating Keyframes

In Figure 7.20, we see a polygon cube primitive (from *Create → Polygon Primitives → Cube*). It is centered in the scene and sitting on the x-y plane. Now look down at the Time Slider. We cannot easily see this in Figure 7.20, but there is a red mark at frame 1 and a red mark at frame 47. These marks on the Time Slider were created by choosing:

LMB on the frame 1 in the Time Slider → LMB the cube → S

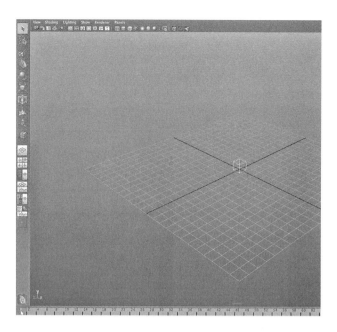

FIGURE 7.20 Cube centered.

You must select the frame first, then move/translate/scale your object, and then hit S, all in that precise order.

There are a large number of shortcut keys in Maya, and in the Preferences, you can tailor them. Hitting the S key to set a keyframe is one of the few shortcuts we will use in this book.

Next, we follow these steps:

LMB on frame 47 in the Time Slider → LMB the cube → S

There are two keyframes, which tells Maya that from frames 1 to 47, the cube should remain in the center of the scene.

Now, look at Figure 7.21. The keyframe at 47 was deleted by selecting the keyframe on the timeline, right clicking, and choosing Delete. Then, with frame 47 still selected, the cube was moved (translated) in 3-space. It was also rotated and scaled upward. This was done with the Move, Scale, and Rotate tools in the Toolbox. Then, the S key was hit.

To put it precisely, we follow these steps:

RMB frame 47 on the Time Slider → Delete → move/rotate/scale the cube → S

This now tells Maya that between frames 1 and 47, the cube should rotate, scale upward in size, and change its location in 3-space.

USING THE GRAPH EDITOR TO REUSE ANIMATION

Maya gives us a fine-grained way of visualizing, adjusting, and reusing keyframed animation. It is supported by a window called the Graph Editor.

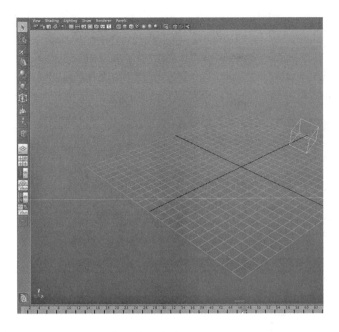

FIGURE 7.21   Cube translated, rotated, and scaled.

The Graph Editor

In Figure 7.22, we go to:

Window → Animation Editors → Graph Editor

The window shown in Figure 7.23 is the Graph Editor. The View menu item from the top of the Graph Editor is chosen and Select All is picked. This tells the Graph Editor to show the animation in all animated frames. The result is shown in Figure 7.24, which gives us a full view of the Graph Editor. (The cube in the Main Window has to be selected to see this.)

Notice that there are three sets of colored lines. Red tells us how the object was translated, rotated, and scaled in the x dimension. Green is for the y dimension. Blue is for the z dimension. Notice also how smoothly Maya interpolates for us. The Graph Editor can be used to carefully manipulate the way Maya interpolates.

There is something powerful that can be done with the Graph Editor; it gives us a way to take a small movement of an object in a scene and cycle through it many times.

Motion Cycles

One of the classic forms of motion reuse is to create what is called a "walk cycle," where a creature takes a couple of steps.

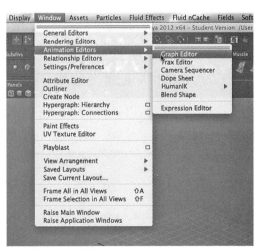

FIGURE 7.22   Graph Editor selection.

This movement is carefully keyframed and then any time we want the creature to walk again, we can reuse the motion. We can have a character walk across the Sahara, and all we have to do is teach him how to take two steps.

When creating this walk cycle, we want to make sure that at the end of the second step, the foot does not quite hit the ground, so that it does not appear that the foot sticks in place for two frames at the end of each cycle.

Our example is much simpler. In Figure 7.25, we take the following steps:

Swipe all the colored graphs → Graph Editor Main Menu → Edit → Copy → Paste

This gives the result shown in Figure 7.26. To see what effect it has in the Main Window, see Figure 7.27.

If we set the number of visible frames in the Time Slider to 95 and play the animation from frame 1, we see the box continue to translate, rotate, and scale through all of the frames.

FIGURE 7.23   Selecting Frame All.

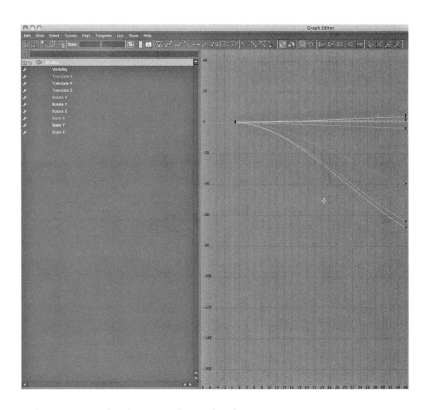

FIGURE 7.24   **(See p. CI-8 of Color Insert)** Graph Editor.

In the Graph Editor, we can adjust the rate of acceleration or deceleration of an object. A straight line represents motion at a constant speed, but few things in the real world move this way unless they are artificially powered, like a car. Imagine a bouncing ball. Its movement along the y-axis shows up as a curve going upward, and then the curve turns back and comes down. As it goes upward, it slows. Then as it falls, it accelerates. We can tune movement to simulate this by using tools in the Graph Editor that let us manipulate the

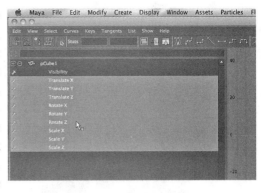

FIGURE 7.25   Selecting and copying graphs.

tangents on the curves in the Graph Editor. When it is time for our ball to fall back to Earth, we manipulate the tangent at the peak of the curve, making it completely horizontal. This gives us a gradual hump at the top, making the ball decelerate and then accelerate. (In a similar way, living creatures tend to "ease in" and "ease out" of motion, as animators put it, by accelerating and decelerating.)

The Graph Editor gives us a convenient way to track the rotation, translation, and scaling of an object in 3-space so that we can carefully tailor motion and reuse motion.

Driven Keys

Maya has a concept called "driven keys," which makes an attribute of an object controlled by the value of another attribute. This is as opposed to using the timeline to control when keyframes are used to animate an object. With driven keys, we can pop the hood of a car when a latch inside the car is pulled. The Graph Editor can be used to track the changes

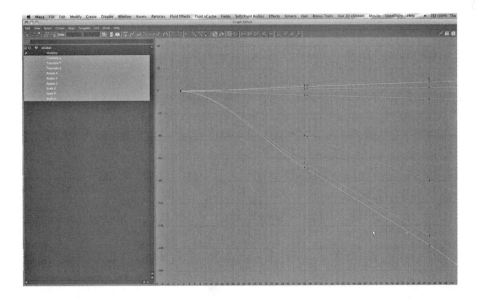

FIGURE 7.26   After paste.

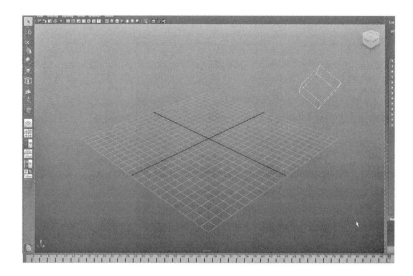

FIGURE 7.27   Final rotated, translated, scaled cube.

of the driven attribute based on the values of the driving attribute. A driven key can be created and set by going to:

Animation Main Menu → Animate → Set Driven Key

USING SKELETONS TO SIMULATE NATURAL MOVEMENT

One of the most difficult and tedious jobs is making a living creature move in a realistic fashion. We all have a deep intuitive feel for how a person moves, and we can easily (if perhaps subconsciously) detect unnatural movements, even when they are relatively minor.

One of the key reasons that animating a character that is walking or running, reaching for a book on a high shelf, or sitting down in a chair is difficult is that the entire body is involved. Even when the movement is largely isolated to one part of the body, such as a seated character reaching for the saltshaker, there is still movement of the eyes, the head, and the upper torso.

The complexity is not limited to humans and other bipeds. Most of us don't really know how a horse moves its legs when it runs and how that movement might involve its head, neck and tail; but again, unnatural movement is often detected, if only subconsciously. It is also true that animators typically strive for realism, and given that horses move differently than dogs or giraffes, quadrupeds can be particularly hard to animate.

Maya and other animation applications provide tools for creating skeletons, "binding" the skeleton to the surface of the creature, and then moving the various parts of the creature by moving the skeleton.

There are two main ways in which skeletons can be used to simulate natural body movement. The first is called "forward kinematics" (or FK) and the second is called "inverse kinematics" (or IK). Both are frequently used in animated projects with inverse kinematics being particularly powerful. (The word *kinematics* comes from the study of the motion of moving bodies in mechanics and physics.)

Inverse Kinematics versus Forward Kinematics

A Maya skeleton is made up of bones connected by joints. The skeleton does not render, and bones and joints have no geometry; they exist only to drive the motion of a character, critter, machine, or potentially anything else with complex internal motion.

In both IK and FK, the bones of a skeleton are put into a hierarchy, with the root being the center of movement. For a human, this is the hip region. From that root, the hierarchy branches off in three ways: the two legs and the upper torso. At the top of the spine, there are typically again three branches: the arms and the neck. The skeleton might involve bones for moving the jaw as well.

Bones can be used to simulate movement in many circumstances other than the limbs of a creature. We sometimes use bones to model the movement of eyes, or the movement of an attacking robot, or the motions of a coupling rod on a train.

The key distinction between IK and FK is that in FK, if a bone higher in the hierarchy is moved, the bones below it move along with it, and bones lower in the hierarchy can be moved without moving the bones higher up. Movement in an IK skeleton is more complex. If a bone lower in the hierarchy is moved, it might pull other bones higher up along with it. So, moving a foot might pull on the entire leg, the hips, the other leg, and upper torso.

Inverse Kinematics in a Leg

In Figures 7.28 and 7.29, we select:

Animation Main Menu → Skeleton → Joint Tool

FIGURE 7.28 Animation Main Menu.

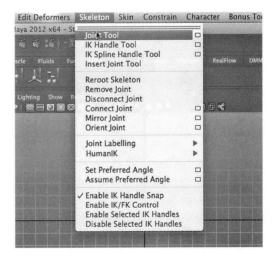

FIGURE 7.29 Joint tool.

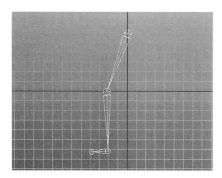

FIGURE 7.30   Leg from side.

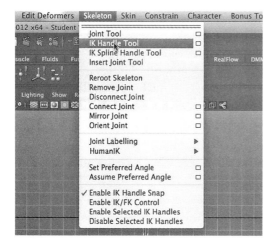

FIGURE 7.31   IK Handle tool.

FIGURE 7.32   IKRPsolver.

This tool lays down bones connected by joints. With four clicks, we can lay down the top joint of a leg, as seen in Figure 7.30, then the knee, the ankle, and then tip of the foot, creating four bones.

Notice that the leg has been laid down in the flattened front perspective, with the knee and lower part of the leg pulled outward in the negative y direction. This is not necessary, but many joints in a human are largely (but not totally) restricted to movement in a single plane; the knee is like this. Looking flat against the x-y axis (with z always at zero) when creating such bones makes it easier to model the movement of joints. It is also easier to create bones that are sized the way you want them if you work on a flattened perspective.

Here comes the IK part of the story. In Figure 7.31, we select the IK Handle tool. This will give us a way to interrelate the movement of bones up and down the hierarchy. In Figure 7.32, we see that there are solvers involved in skeletal movement, just like there are solvers involved in dynamics. Maya has multiple skeleton solvers, including the one we are using: the "rotate plane" solver. The solver knows how to move joints and bones in concert with each other.

With the IK Handle tool, we click on the top joint, then the ankle joint, creating a handle. Then we go back to the hip joint, click there, click on the knee, and then click on the ankle. This creates a second handle.

It is by placing these handles in a skeleton that we transform an FK skeleton into an IK skeleton. Rigging in Maya is the process of generating IK handles, and at the end of every handle is something called an "effector." When we manipulate effectors we engage the IK capabilities of the skeleton.

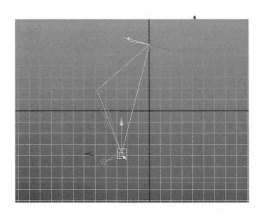

FIGURE 7.33   Lifting the ankle.

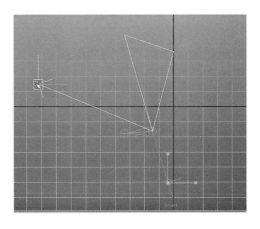

FIGURE 7.34   Pulling the effector too far.

The Power of Inverse Kinematics Skeletons

Consider Figure 7.33. We have grabbed the effector of the IK handle that ends at the ankle and we have moved it. When we do this, the solver is engaged and calculates how it must rotate joints upstream from the end of the handle in order to place the ankle where we want it. Consider Figure 7.34. On the left side of the figure, we see that the effector has been moved farther than the solver's calculations allow the ankle to be moved, so the IK handle has refused to follow the effector. (The location of the effector is called the "goal" because this is where we are trying to move the associated IK handle.) When we let go of the left mouse button, the effector will fly back to the end of the IK handle where it belongs, and we can try again to move the ankle.

In Figure 7.35, we have a leg with no IK handles and we will move its ankle as well, as shown in Figure 7.36. In Figure 7.37, we have gone back to the 3D perspective. We

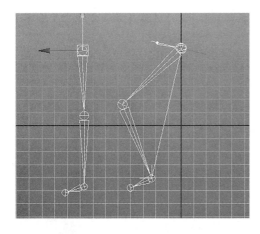

FIGURE 7.35   An FK leg and an IK leg.

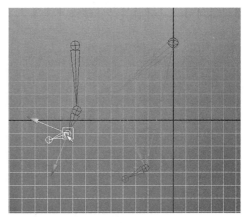

FIGURE 7.36   Manipulating the FK leg.

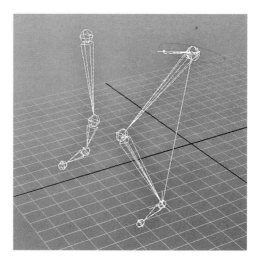

FIGURE 7.37 The result—one FK leg and one IK leg manipulated.

see that with the IK leg, when we move the ankle up and down, the flexing of the knee changes and this moves the upper leg. But in the other skeleton, we only affect the bone immediately above the ankle; the knee itself remains fixed.

Later, we will look at creating an entire skeleton with Maya.

CHAPTER 8

The Fuzzy Border between Modeling and Animating

THERE IS A FUZZY border between techniques used to model and techniques used to animate models. This makes sense, as part of animating a model often calls for altering its geometry. In this chapter, we are going to look at a few examples that underscore this duality. Along the way, we will also take a look at Maya Fur and Hair (nHair, actually), as well as Maya's Ocean dynamics effect.

USING NURBS, SHATTER, AND FUR TO MAKE AN EGG AND CRACK IT

Let's look at the Shatter tool in Maya. It breaks a surface into pieces in a controlled, yet semirandom fashion to create the look of something breaking. First, we set up the scene using NURBS.

Smooth Modeling for an Egg

In Figure 8.1, we see a NURBS egg. It was made by first creating a NURBS sphere, then going into Control Vertex mode (with a right click), as seen in Figure 8.2, and then selecting some of the control vertices (CVs) and pulling on them, as shown in Figure 8.3. This is an intermediate state created while pulling on a number of CVs. Then, with each successive pull, fewer CVs were pulled, until it formed a smooth egg shape.

Cracking the Egg with the Shatter Tool

Now, we go to the Dynamics menu, as shown in Figure 8.4. In Figure 8.5, we go into Surface Patch mode in NURBS modeling (with a right click). In Figure 8.6, we select a patch. Then, as seen in Figure 8.7, we choose:

Dynamics Main Menu → Effects → Create Shatter

The result is shown in Figure 8.8. The tool has taken that patch of egg and broken it into smaller NURBS patches. The settings for the shatter tool (which you can access by

clicking the box to the right of the Create Shatter menu item) can be seen in Figure 8.9, and, in particular, they control the shard count. The shards are clumped into semirandom chunks—just what we need for our cracked egg.

In Figure 8.10, we move some of our chunks away from the egg surface. Finally, we apply a white Blinn. Thus, we can take a modeling technique—the shatter tool—and use it to animate a cracking egg. All we need to add is the keyframing of the fragments in different directions.

FIGURE 8.1   A rendered egg.

A Chick and Fur

Next, we create a NURBS sphere and change the tab selector to Fur; this pulls up the Fur shelf. The Fur shelf provides a set of prefab shortcuts that can be used to quickly put fur on a character or creature.

With the new sphere selected, we choose the yellow fur, and see the result in Figure 8.11. But keep in mind that the view in the design window in the Main Window is always an inexact rendering of what is actually a 3D vector model. It is particularly difficult to quickly render fur, and so what we see in Figure 8.11 is actually quite different from what we will render.

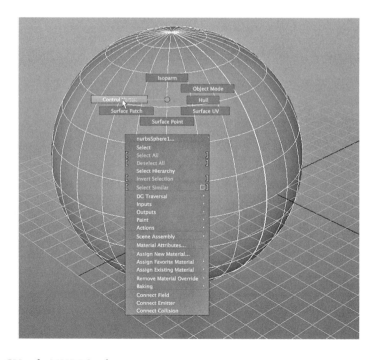

FIGURE 8.2   CVs of a NURBS sphere.

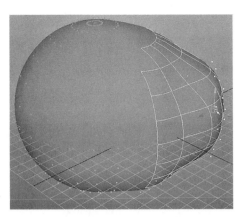

FIGURE 8.3   Pulling on NURBS CVs.

FIGURE 8.4   Dynamics menu.tiff.

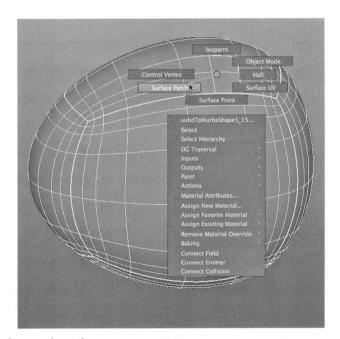

FIGURE 8.5   Surface patch mode.

In Figure 8.12, we have tucked the chick into the egg. In Figure 8.13, we adjust some of the attributes of the fur, in particular, its length.

The final render is shown in Figure 8.14. To apply fur to a model, you can use either polygon or NURBS modeling. In Chapter 13, we will look at the UV Texture Editor as a tool for carefully engineering the way a material is applied to a model. Cleaning up the (u, v) texture grid of a polygon model can also make fur look a lot better.

Maya Fur and nHair: An nDynamics Effect

Now we look at a more sophisticated example. This involves the use of both fur and hair.

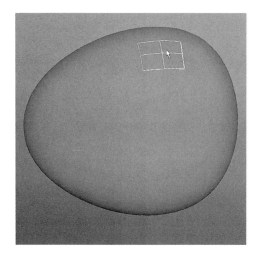

FIGURE 8.6   Select a patch.

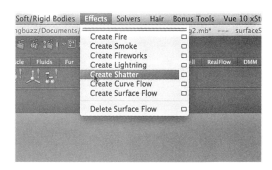

FIGURE 8.7   Create shatter tool.

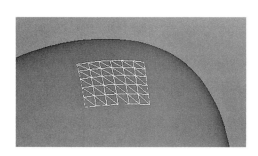

FIGURE 8.8   Shatter result.

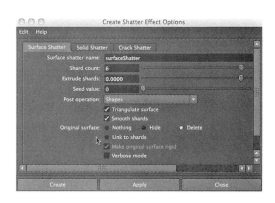

FIGURE 8.9   Shatter settings.

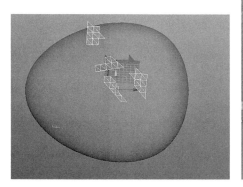

FIGURE 8.10   After moving shards.

FIGURE 8.11   Sphere with fur.

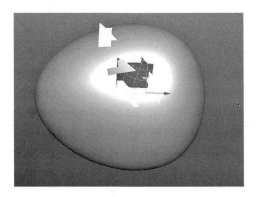

FIGURE 8.12 Chick inside.

There is a tool in Maya that can be used to create hair, and you will find a Shelf tab called nHair. Unlike the Fur shelf, the nHair shelf is abstract and takes some getting used to. As nHair is an nDynamics effect, it can be painted onto a piece of geometry; it uses the Artisan paint facility and Maya's painting metaphor. You can create hair by selecting an object in the scene and then clicking on the leftmost icon on the nHair shelf. You can also get to this tool by going to:

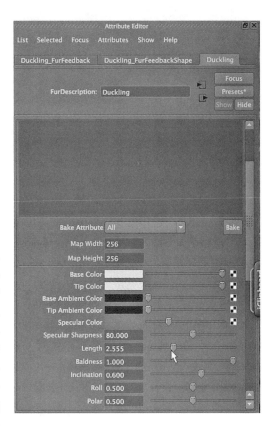

FIGURE 8.13 Fur settings.

nDynamics Main Menu → nHair

Both Fur and nHair are software effects and so they will not render with the Hardware renderer.

Using Fur is best when you want to give a creature an even, not too long coat of animal hair. You are likely to want to apply Fur in different shades, lengths, and perhaps curliness on different parts of an animal. For example, dogs have very short hair on their snouts, but longer hair on their bodies. Fur can also be used to put short, thick hair on a character, and this is what we will do next.

When putting fur or hair on a human or critter, you can often get much the same effect by using either Fur or nHair. Fur is easier to use but does not lend itself to organic and smooth animation. On the other hand, as nHair is an nDynamics effect, it animates quite nicely, and in particular, it interacts with fields like turbulence. nHair is, however, much more complex to use than Fur.

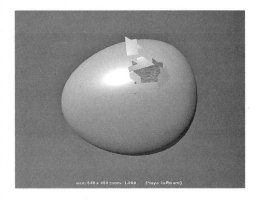

FIGURE 8.14 Final render of cracked egg.

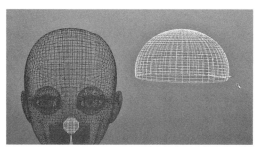

FIGURE 8.15   A fur cap.

What we will look at in the following example is an intriguing blend of fur and nHair technology. We will leverage the ease of use of fur, while taking advantage of nHair's far superior animation capabilities.

In Figure 8.15, we see the head of a character and a hemisphere. The character is from Daz Studio, and we will look more closely at him in Chapter 11. The sphere is just slightly bigger than the top of the character's head and we will put our fur on this fur/hair "cap" instead of placing it directly on the head of the character. There are a few reasons for this. First, both nHair and Fur work best on polygon surfaces with uniform polygon geometry, that is, where the vertices are evenly spaced on the mesh. (Both can be used with NURBS as well, but they are a bit easier to work with on polygon geometry.) Another reason for the cap is so that we can easily reuse a fur/hair effect. Perhaps the biggest reason is that we often want to carefully edit the shape of the cap to match the precise geometry where we want to place fur/hair on a character's head, and this is much easier to do on a separate piece of geometry. (In our example, we will tailor its shape after we have created the fur/hair effect.)

In Figure 8.16, we have selected:

Rendering Main Menu → Fur → Attach Fur Description → New

The Attribute box that pops up is shown in Figure 8.17.

There are a number of attributes that can be manipulated on the Fur Description object. Base Color, Tip Color, and Length of the fur are key attributes. The result of adjusting these attributes can be seen in the rendering in Figure 8.18. Next, the Density, Inclination, and Roll were adjusted, as seen in Figure 8.19, to get the Fur standing upright. The Inclination was painted on by going to:

Rendering Main Menu → Fur → Paint Fur Attributes Tool (see Figure 8.20)

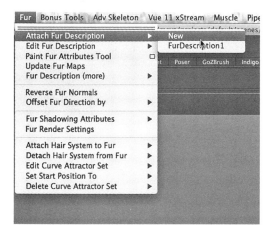

FIGURE 8.16   A fur description.

Next, with the fur cap selected, the nHair was created:

nDynamics Main Menu → nHair → Create Hair (see Figure 8.21)

This is where we introduced the nDynamics effect that will enable us to animate our Fur. Creating an nHair object creates a particle system.

A critical setting is the Output value, which must be set to Paint Effects and NURBS curves (see Figure 8.22). The created hair can be seen in Figure 8.23.

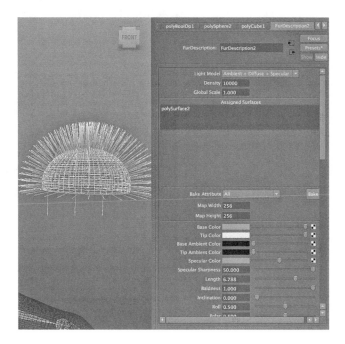

FIGURE 8.17   Setting density and length and color.

Now, the fur and the hair will be connected so that we can use the Fur object as the "hair" of our character and use nHair to control the animation of the Fur. This is done by going to:

any Main Menu → Window → Relationship Editors → Hair/Fur Linking (see Figure 8.24)

The hairSystemShape and FurDescription must both be selected to complete this linking.

Next, we look at animating the Fur object. First, we select:

nDynamics Main Menu → nHair → Display → Start Position (see Figure 8.25)

Next, with the hair spikes selected, as seen in Figure 8.26, we select:

nDynamics Main Menu → nHair → Convert Selection → To Start Curves

This initializes the animation.

Next, we choose:

nDynamics Main Menu → nHair → Classic Hair → Create Constraint → Collide Sphere (see Figure 8.27)

This tells Maya that we want the Fur and nHair to collide with a sphere so that we can keep it from going right through our fur/hair

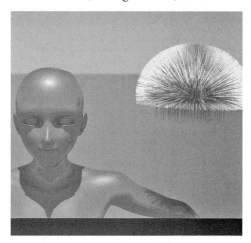

FIGURE 8.18   Pink man and fur rendered.

FIGURE 8.19   Density and inclination and roll.

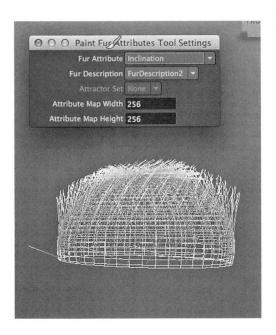

FIGURE 8.20   Painting inclination.

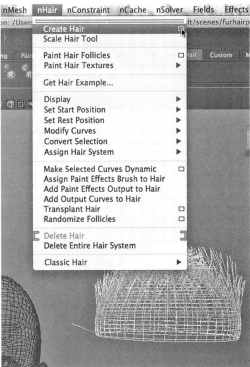

FIGURE 8.21   Creating nHair.

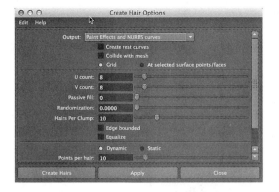

FIGURE 8.22 Paint effects and NURBS settings.

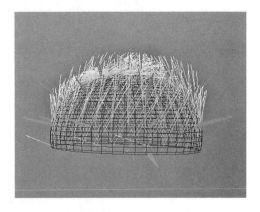

FIGURE 8.23 The hairs.

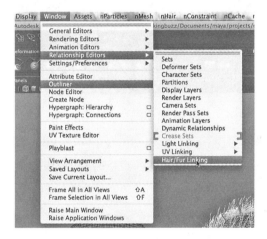

FIGURE 8.24 Hair fur linking.

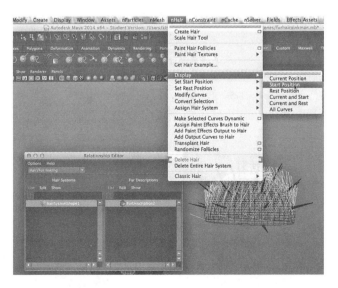

FIGURE 8.25 The start position.

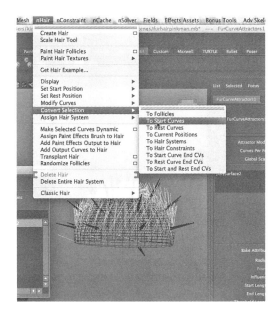

FIGURE 8.26 Start curves.

cap. Note that "Classic Hair" references an older version of the hair system that was used before nHair was introduced into Maya. A tiny sphere pops up in the middle of our Fur object. It must be resized with the Scale tool to match the diameter and shape of our fur/hair cap, as seen in Figure 8.28.

FIGURE 8.27 Collision constraint.

Next, the cap, hair, and fur are placed on the character's head. At this point, the cap was sculpted to fit the desired pattern of hair on our character. We make sure the timeline at the bottom of the Main Window is set to the first frame. With the reshaped sphere and the nHair selected, we choose:

nDynamics Main Menu → nHair → Display → Current Position

This is seen in Figure 8.29.

Our character, which has a pink Blinn surface, has yellow hair. The hair can be seen in the rendering in Figure 8.30, taken at frame 1. Figure 8.31 shows us the corresponding top view of the hair. The hair system is a dynamics effect, and to activate it, we hit the play button on the bottom right of the Main Window. We saw in the Trix example that when we created the nDynamics effect, a nucleus tab appeared in the attribute box; similarly, the nHair dynamics effect has a nucleus tab in its attribute box, where we find fields that animate the hair over a series of frames. So, the hair moves, and it pulls the fur along with it, as seen in

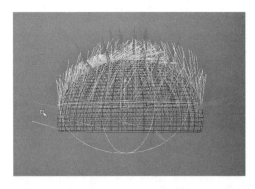

FIGURE 8.28 **(See p. CI-14 of Color Insert)** Resized sphere.

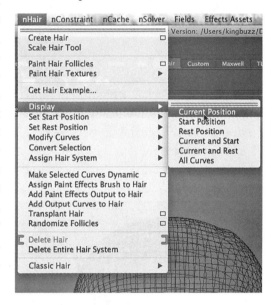

FIGURE 8.29 Current position.

FIGURE 8.30 **(See p. CI-14 of Color Insert)** Pink man with punk yellow hair.

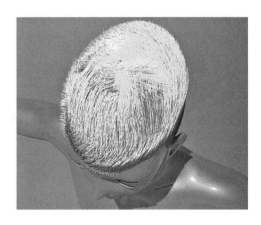

FIGURE 8.31 Top of head before.

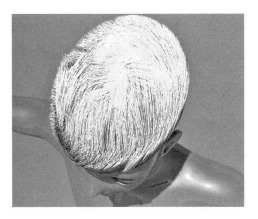

FIGURE 8.32   Top after turbulence.

Figure 8.32. The hair/fur combination will move every time we run the animation.

This example illustrates a common technique seen in animation applications. One object that is easy to animate is used to animate another object. The nHair, which is a dynamics effect and will react to the timeline being played, is bound to the Fur object, so that it will move in turn.

Finally, we need to prevent the hair cap from rendering. We can do that by going to its attribute box, finding the Render Stats tab, and unclicking Primary Visibility. We should also uncheck Visible in Reflections and Visible in Refractions (see Figure 8.33).

USING BLEND SHAPE TO ANIMATE THE LEG OF THE CHICK BEING BORN

We are going to look at a handful of tools that are called "deformers." They can be used to craft the surface of a model. They can also be used to animate a model, as deformers can be keyframed to change the shape of an object over a series of frames.

The deformers are found in Maya under the Animation Main Menu. There is a cluster of deformers listed under Nonlinear, and we will look at one of them. But we will start out with the one that is not on the nonlinear deformer menu dropdown.

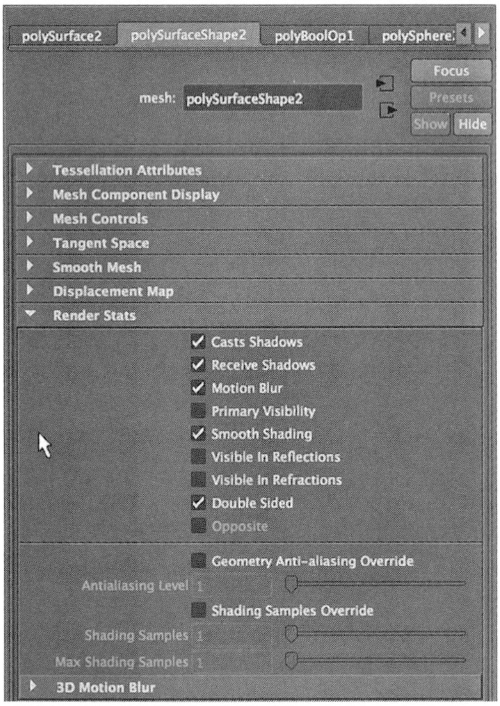

Animating a Chick Leg with a Blend Shape

We will focus on Blend Shape now, a particularly powerful deformer that is frequently used to simulate repetitive, organic motion, such as mouths that break into a smile and then lose that smile, eyes that blink, or a heart beating.

Here is the simplest way to use a Blend Shape. We create a model and make two or more copies of it. We then alter the shape of the copies to make them look different. Then we use Blend Shape to morph the original model using the altered copies as templates for the morphing process. Thus, the outer shape of the original model is animated by transforming the geometry through various stages based on the deformed shapes of the copies.

FIGURE 8.33   Making the cap invisible.

Let's add a leg to our cracked egg. The foot will have four toes, and we will animate the leg and the toes using a Blend Shape. In Figure 8.34, we see the polygon leg in the egg, kicking its way out. There are also two copies of it sitting outside the egg. These two will be removed from the scene later. They have been manipulated to change their shape and will serve as two morph points; we will use these to animate the chick's leg.

Now, we Shift-select, in this order: the first copy, the second copy, and the original. It is important to choose the original last.

Then we choose:

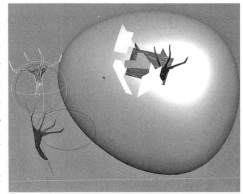

FIGURE 8.34   Chick leg and two copies.

Animation Main Menu → Create Deformers → Blend Shape (see Figure 8.35)

Now, as shown in Figure 8.36, we choose:

any Main Menu → Window → Animation Editors → Blend Shape

This pulls up the window we will use to control the Blend Shape animation. In Figure 8.37, we see three different images taken of the Blend Shape Editor. The way we use this window is as follows: First, we select frame 1 on the Timeline. We then move the sliders and we see that the leg in the egg moves. Then we hit Key All. Then we select frame 20. We move the sliders to different positions and hit Key All. We do this one more time, choosing frame 40, moving the sliders, and hitting Key All. (We see that when using Blend Shape to create an animation, we set our keyframes in the Blend Shape Editor, not on the Timeline.)

The renders that we get at frames 1, 20, and 40 are shown in Figure 8.38. We see that the two sliders have been used to move the leg inside the egg from its original shape into some

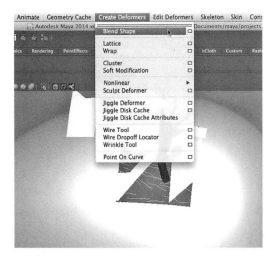

FIGURE 8.35 Creating a nonlinear Blend Shape deformer.

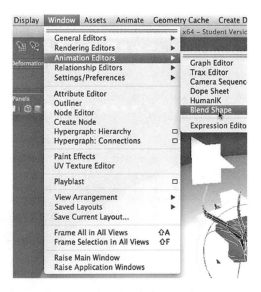

FIGURE 8.36   The Blend Shape Editor.

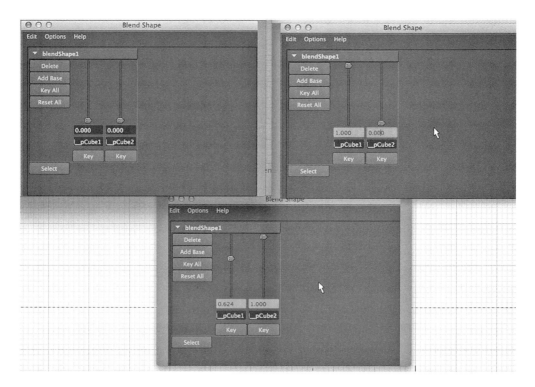

FIGURE 8.37   Keyframes for Blend Shape.

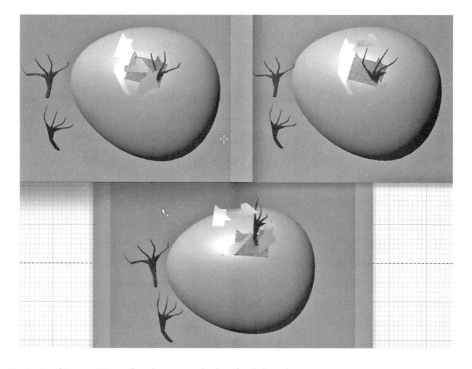

FIGURE 8.38   **(See p. CI-3 of Color Insert)** The chick breakout.

combination of the two copies, and by moving the sliders differently, we get different final forms of the leg.

There are two other sets of keyframes used in this rendering. One was used to animate the pieces of shell as they break off and fly away. The other was used to push the leg outward a bit as he escapes.

We can remove the two copies of the leg, and then render the scene as video. Maya will interpolate, giving us an animated chick leg trying to kick its way out of the shell.

USING A BEND DEFORMER TO ANIMATE ROLLING UP A POOL COVER

Now, we move into a set of deformers that are called "nonlinear." These are deformers that, unlike blend shape, do not intrinsically change an object over time. Nonlinear deformers can be used effectively to craft the surface of a model. By adjusting the settings of a deformer tool over a series of keyframes, we can also use it to animate the morphing of an object. Since each nonlinear deformer uses a different, but specific mathematical algorithm, they can be used to alter the appearance of models in mathematically elegant ways.

Here, we will look at Bend. The various nonlinear deformers have very different behavior—and all of them are easy to use. Try experimenting with them.

The Bend Deformer

We find the set of deformers under the listing "nonlinear" on the Create Deformers drop-down (on the Animate Main Menu). Like many of the tools in Maya, their settings can be controlled with either an iconic handle or by using a Settings box.

The Bend deformer can be used to put a bend in a piece of plumbing or ductwork or to create a wound-up garden hose.

We animate with the nonlinear deformers differently than we animate with Blend Shape. We use a deformer to incrementally alter the form of an object, and then create a series of varying keyframes (using the S key) with the object deformed differently at each keyframe. We could, for example, animate the backward bend and forward snap of a catapult.

We are going to use it to roll up a pool cover. Essentially, the bend deformer can warp an object into a smooth arc, and the degree of the arc can be precisely controlled.

Animating a Swimming Pool Cover

To make a pool cover, we will need a pool, at least a simple one. Figure 8.39 is a basic wireframe model of a pool with a cover over it. Notice that the pool cover is a flattened cube, only one polygon thick, with a significant amount of geometric detail running parallel to the edge of the pool—something we will need to get the cover to roll up smoothly.

With the pool cover selected, we choose:

Animation Main Menu → Create Deformers → Nonlinear → Bend (see Figure 8.40)

If we pull up the settings for the deformer, as shown in Figure 8.41, we see that the curvature has been set to a high negative number. We have set the high bound to 5.

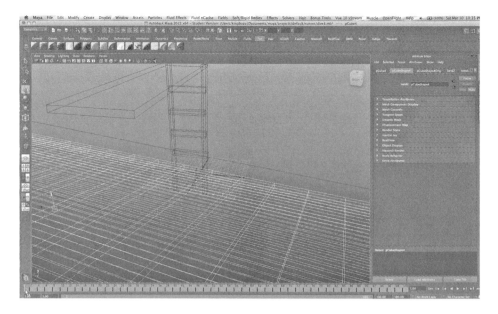

FIGURE 8.39   Pool cover.

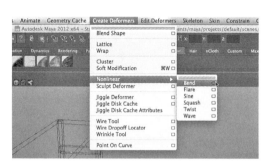

FIGURE 8.40   Bend deformer.

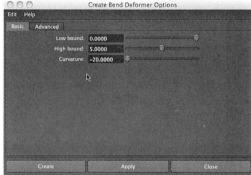

FIGURE 8.41   Bend deformer settings.

In Figure 8.42, we see the manipulator for the deformer. We select the manipulator (or handle), and by using the move tool to push it toward the edge of the pool along a single axis, the cover neatly rolls up (see Figure 8.43). If we then pull away, the cover pulls open. By the way, if we turn the manipulator upside down, the pool cover will roll up upside down. The orientation of the manipulator in 3-space is critical to its behavior.

It is the –20 value for the curvature that causes the cover to roll up in a tight roll and not just into a single, large loop. In Figure 8.44, we see the pool cover almost entirely rolled up.

Again, Maya nicely interpolates between the keyframes, so that the cover can roll open and close smoothly.

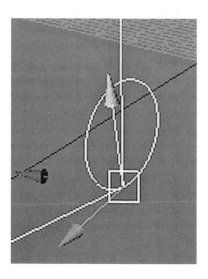

FIGURE 8.42   Deformer manipulator.

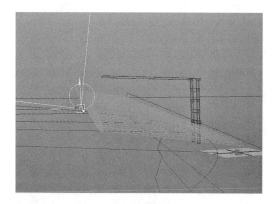

FIGURE 8.43   Rolling cover.

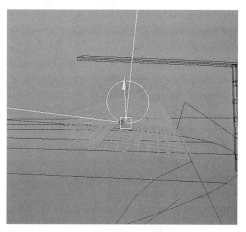

FIGURE 8.44   Cover almost rolled up.

BOUNCING A SQUISHY BALL WITH A SQUASH DEFORMER

We will use a deformer, the scale tool, and keyframing to bounce a ball so that it squashes on the ground and then stretches as it bounces up.

First we create a NURBS ball. Then we select the ball and choose:

Animation Main Menu → Create Deformers → Nonlinear → Squash (see Figure 8.45)

We place the ball on the lower plane and then select the deformer. We use the move tool to lower the pink deformer handle inside the ball to squash the ball (see Figure 8.46).

Keyframing the Ball

We then keyframe the ball to go up and down over a series of at least 75 frames (so we can easily see it move and deform). This is how we set the keyframes:

We start at the top and set the first keyframe there (with the s key).

But before we set the keyframe, we use the scale tool to stretch the ball out top to bottom.

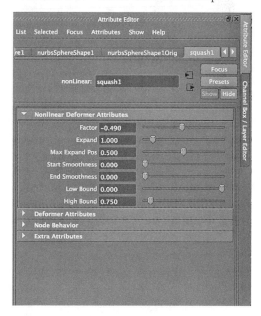

FIGURE 8.45   Squash deformer.

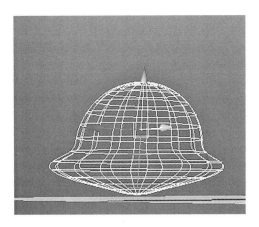

FIGURE 8.46   Squashed ball.

Then we go to frame 30 or so, move the ball to the ground (and the deformer will automatically squash it for us). We set the second keyframe there.

Then we keyframe it at the top again, at about keyframe 75.

But again, before we set the keyframe, we use the scale tool to stretch it out top to bottom again.

Running and Rendering the Scene

In Figures 8.47 and 8.48, we see it fall and squash, then bounce and stretch. Maya even makes it stretch gradually as it moves upward.

FIGURE 8.47   Stretched ball.

FIGURE 8.48   Ball hitting the bottom.

USING THE LATTICE DEFORMER TO DAMAGE OUR MAILBOX

The Lattice Deformer is good for pushing and pulling on an object in a top-down way. We will use it to age the mailbox built earlier in this book. We begin by selecting the mailbox and choosing:

Animation Main Menu → Create Deformers → Nonlinear → Lattice Deformer (see Figure 8.49)

Morphing the Mailbox

The settings for the tool, which we get if we click on the little square box to the right of the Lattice entry on the Create Deformers dropdown, are shown in Figure 8.50.

There is an advantage to manipulating the mailbox via a lattice deformer instead

FIGURE 8.49   Lattice deformer.

of by manipulating the wireframe of the object itself: We can control the area of the surface of our mailbox that is deformed by adjusting the divisions and other settings of the deformer, and not by actually altering the density of geometry of the object (see Figure 8.51).

Now, we select vertices, called Lattice Points, on the deformer and move them (see Figure 8.52).

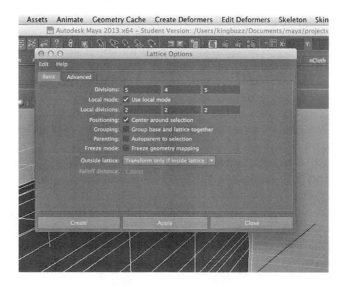

FIGURE 8.50   Lattice deformer settings.

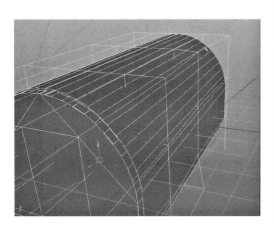

FIGURE 8.51   The deformer in place.

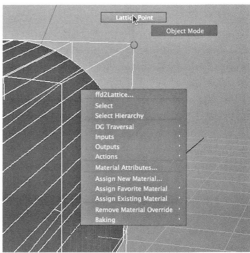

FIGURE 8.52   Lattice point mode.

The Rendered Result

After we move the lattice points, we get the result shown in Figure 8.53.

A Note on Using the Lattice Deformer

Figure 8.54 shows the tabs that appear when we create the lattice deformer. Note that there is a tab named ffd2Lattice. (The 2 denotes the second lattice deformer created in the scene.)

When you change the shape of the lattice by moving lattice points around, you change the values under the ffd2Lattice tab, and this in turn alters the shape of the model. You can update the values under the tab (instead of moving points around) and this will alter the model.

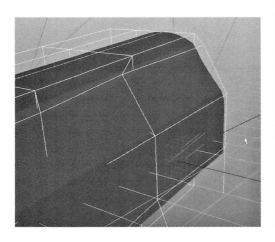

FIGURE 8.53   The deformed mailbox.

FIGURE 8.54   Attributes of the lattice.

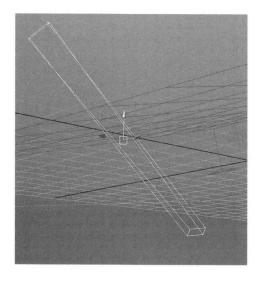

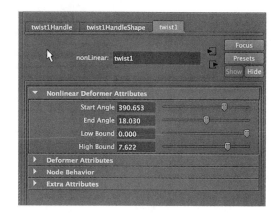

FIGURE 8.55   A board and a twist deformer.   FIGURE 8.56   Twist deformer settings.

USING DEFORMERS FOR MODELING: AN IMPORTANT DETAIL

One thing to keep in mind is that the nonlinear deformers can be used to construct a model or to animate a scene. In the case of creating a static model, there is one little thing that must be done. In Figure 8.55, we see a board with a deformer assigned to it. The attribute box was used to manipulate the settings of the deformer (see Figure 8.56). Then, with the deformer and the board Shift-selected, history was deleted, by choosing:

any Main Menu → Delete by Type → History (see Figure 8.57)

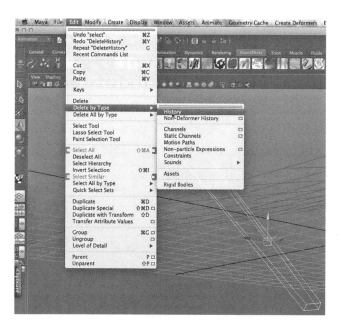

FIGURE 8.57   Deleting history.

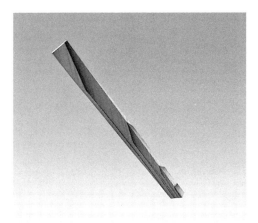

FIGURE 8.58   Twisted board.

The result is a twisted board that will not twist or untwist any more (see Figure 8.58).

Maya keeps a history of the manipulations that have been performed on each object. When we delete the history of the deformer and the board, we cause Maya to forget that there was a deformer attached to the board. This prevents us from using the deformer to manipulate the object further. But, importantly, if we try to simply delete the deformer, we will put the board back to the state it was in before we applied the deformer to it.

CHAPTER 9

Light Fog, Fluids, and Another Look at Materials

W E ARE GOING TO take another look at materials. We will tile a texture to cover a large area, experiment with a few different ways to make glass, render with the mental ray renderer, and make a material look like a light source. Along the way, we will slip in a light effect called fog and we will use a fluid particle effect.

FIXING A TILED TEXTURE WITH OVERLAYS

A common task when creating 3D models is prepping a file texture that looks great on its own but needs to be repeated in order to cover a large area. Most of the time you cannot simply enlarge the texture. Even if you have a photo-enlarging application that will allow you to add pixels so that the image does not become pixelated as you enlarge it, it is usually true that there is some natural granularity of the texture that needs to be preserved when applying it to your model. If you have a brick wall, you do not want a twenty-foot expanse of it covered with a single giant brick; what you need to do is take the texture you have on hand and tile it.

We are going to look at the key problem of concealing what are often obvious borders between the individual tiles. With a brick wall, one way to do this is to use interlocking sections of brick texture. This makes the job of tiling it very easy. Later, we will look at the tougher problem of tiling a texture that does not have this interlocking property. Once a texture has been prepped to be tiled without the edges of the tiles showing, we call it a "seamless" texture.

If you do need a photo-enlarging application, a good product for enlarging images without having to stretch the pixels is the onOne Perfect suite. It works as a stand-alone application and as a Photoshop/Aperture/Lightroom plug-in.

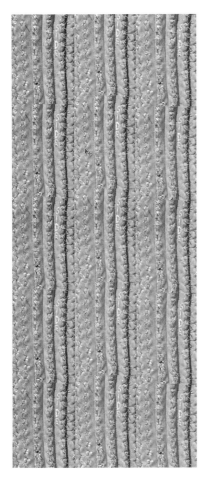

FIGURE 9.1   Original cactus patches.

Experimenting with Textures

Right now, we will look at a simple way to make those seams between tiles less obvious. The goal is to get the tiled texture to a point where the seams will not be easily visible from whatever perspective and distance, and under whatever lighting we plan to render it.

Adding Noise to the Tiling Lines

Remember our cactus texture? The tiled version of it is shown in Figure 9.1. We can clearly see the horizontal lines in it, because they cut against the grain of the texture. What we want to do is soften those lines. One way to do this is to use another texture to add some noise to that tiled grain. We will do some experimentation to see just what sort of texture, if added as a layer to our tiled cactus texture, will get the job done.

Consider Figures 9.2 and 9.3, these are the rust textures we looked at earlier. Now look at Figures 9.4 and 9.5, these are organic textures, both of bushes. All four of these textures offer a more irregular grain.

First, though, we need to decide just how to add this layer to the tiled cactus texture. What we will use is a "saturation" layer. Saturation refers to the brightness of colors. Another way to look at it is that low saturation tends to wash out a color. High saturation means the color is more vibrant. Our goal will be to use the colors of the new texture layer to influence the colors of the

FIGURE 9.2   Rusty metal 1.

FIGURE 9.3   Rusty metal 2.

FIGURE 9.4 **(See p. CI-9 of Color Insert)** Bush texture number 1.

FIGURE 9.5 **(See p. CI-9 of Color Insert)** Bush texture number 2.

tiled cactus texture. Our hope is that the irregular color pattern of the saturation layer will conceal the sharp boundaries we see between the separate tiles in Figure 9.1.

Figures 9.6, 9.7, 9.8, and 9.9 show us the settings for each saturation layer. Figures 9.10, 9.11, 9.12, and 9.13 (see Color Insert for these figures) give us the one-to-one comparisons between the original tiled texture and the tiled texture with each of the four saturation layers added. All four of them do indeed improve the appearance of our tiled texture. The first two, the ones with the rust layers, are probably too patchy, with obvious dark and light areas. The first bush has too much yellow in it. But the fourth one is pretty good. We can use that on the cactus and the lines between the tiles will not be so obvious.

Two Final Notes on Tiling

Even if the borders between tiles are eradicated, the tiling can still be detected if the texture has significantly varying color patterns inside each tile. If you look carefully at the brick wall behind our cabana, you will see the pattern repeating.

And a place to go for nice textures is www.subtlepatterns.com.

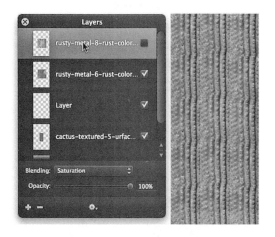

FIGURE 9.6 Rusty metal 1 settings.

FIGURE 9.7 Rusty metal 2 settings.

FIGURE 9.8   Bush 1 settings.

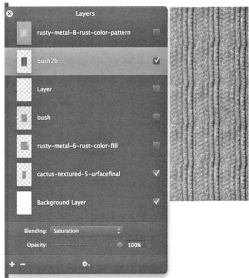

FIGURE 9.9   Bush 2 settings.

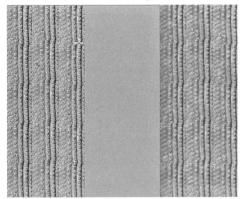

FIGURE 9.10   **(See p. CI-9 of Color Insert)**
Rusty metal 1—compare.

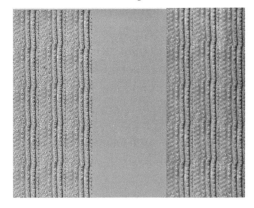

FIGURE 9.11   **(See p. CI-9 of Color Insert)**
Rusty metal 2—compare.

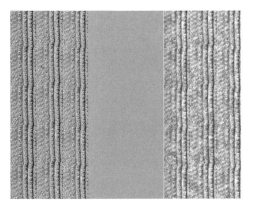

FIGURE 9.12   **(See p. CI-9 of Color Insert)**
Bush 1—compare.

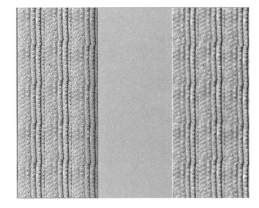

FIGURE 9.13   **(See p. CI-9 of Color Insert)**
Bush 2—compare.

MAKING A SEAMLESS TEXTURE WITH MAYA PAINT

We will look at one interesting alternative to doctoring a texture to make it tile seamlessly: using the painting canvas in Maya to create a texture from scratch.

Painting a Seamless Tiled Texture

By going to Windows (on the Main Menu) and then choosing Paint Effects, you will reveal the Maya painting canvas. On the Canvas window, you can select Canvas and then choose New Image. A window will pop up that will allow you to give your image a name, choose a background color, and select an image size.

In the middle of the top menu on the canvas window, Figure 9.14, are two icons that need to be selected so that the texture we are making will wrap in both dimensions. They are white icons with blue paint strokes on them. There are red arrows on the top of the x-wrap icon and on the left side of the y-wrap icon.

Next you paint your texture image, while making sure you use both the top/bottom wrapping and the left/right wrapping. You will have to play around with it. You should paint strokes that go off the canvas in both dimensions.

When you save your image, it will end up in:

Documents → Maya → projects → sourceimages

Creating and Tiling a File Texture

Go to the Hypershade and create a file texture; make sure it is a Normal (not Projection) texture. Use the painting you just made and saved in sourceimages as the file for this texture. Go to the attributes of the file texture and select the place2dTexture1 tab. (This should be the default name for the first texture you create in your scene.) Set the two Repeat UV numbers to 3 and 3. (Or whatever nonzero numbers you want.)

Notice that because the paint tool will continue a line that goes off the Canvas by drawing it on the other side of the image, the creator of the image in Figure 9.15 did not have to manually line up the four lines that go off the Canvas in both directions. Our wrapable texture looks like Figure 9.16 on a polygon plane.

FIGURE 9.14   Maya's canvas.

FIGURE 9.15   A seamless texture.

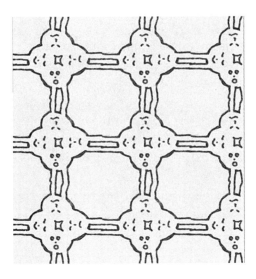

FIGURE 9.16   Tiled texture.

MAKING GLASS BOTTLES WITH NURBS AND MENTAL RAY

We return to glass now and consider three variations on making glass. We will use the same material for the three bottles we are going to make and all three will have the same outward geometry, but we will be trying out some variations in the density of the geometry of the bottles.

All three will be made from NURBS geometry, but one will have very little density in its geometry, another will have extremely dense geometry, and the third will have the same internal geometry as the first, but we will tuck one copy of the bottle inside another.

The Three Bottles

In Figure 9.17, we see two bottles. The one to the right is a NURBS curve that has been revolved in 3-space. The one to the left started out as the same bottle, but it was selected and we chose:

any Main Menu → Modify → Convert → NURBS to Polygons

The model has been turned into a polygon model, which increased its geometric detail.

Next, we selected the bottle again and chose:

FIGURE 9.17   Two NURBS bottles.

any Main Menu → Modify → Convert → Polygons to Subdiv

This turned it into a subdivision object, which further increased its geometric detail, and the result is the bottle in the image. It was converted one more time:

any Main Menu → Modify → Convert → Subdiv to NURBS

This was done so that both bottles would be NURBS models; but this last conversion did not alter its geometric detail. Also, we cannot continue to work with a model that is in subdivision format.

Notice that the bottle on the left not only has dense geometry; it also has a homogeneous swirly pattern, something that we hope will result in interesting rendering effects. We have already made use of the mia_material and its glass presets and we will make use of it again. Accordingly, we will be rendering with mental ray. In Figure 9.18, we have made an instance of this material. In Figure 9.19, the reflection color is set to a Caribbean blue so the bottles will have a little color in them. This will help separate the bottles from their backgrounds.

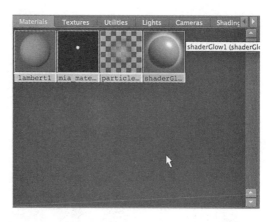

FIGURE 9.18   Mia glass material.

mental ray Settings

In Figure 9.20, the mental ray renderer's Quality settings have been ramped up. In particular, Max Sample Level is set to 2. The raytracing Reflections and Refractions have been increased dramatically. In Figure 9.21, Global Illumination and Final Gathering have both been selected. All of this might increase rendering time significantly.

A Bottle inside a Bottle

In Figure 9.22, we have made a copy of the bottle with the not-very-dense geometry. We moved it over to the right, selected the new bottle, did a Copy operation from the Edit dropdown, and then did a Paste operation from the Edit dropdown. When we did these copy and paste operations, the two bottles ended up in the exact same place in World space. We selected one of the copies and scaled its x, y, and z dimensions down to .95 of the original. There are now two bottles, one inside the other, and together they form the third bottle from the left in Figure 9.23. Now, light will move through the first bottle, refracting, and then will hit the second bottle and refract again.

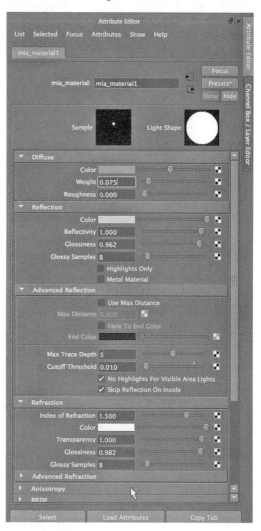

FIGURE 9.19   Mia material attributes.

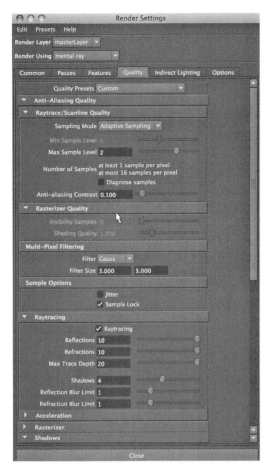

FIGURE 9.20   This shows mental ray settings.

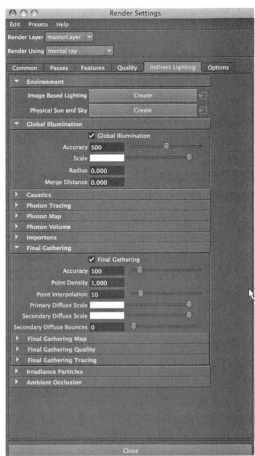

FIGURE 9.21   More mental ray settings.

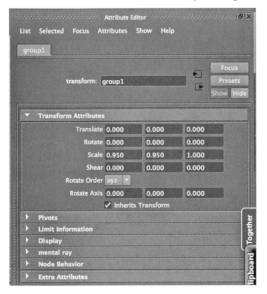

FIGURE 9.22   Inner bottle.

The Render

In Figure 9.23, we see the three bottles. Figure 9.24 shows the render. The black and white stripes behind the bottles will help us compare the differing ways these bottles reflect and refract light.

Compare the simplest bottle, on the left, with the bottle-in-a-bottle on the right. The one on the right, as we might have expected, seems to be made out of thicker glass. The bottle has thick, black sides.

The bottle in the middle looks a lot like the bottle on the left, except that the reflected and refracted light is jagged. This

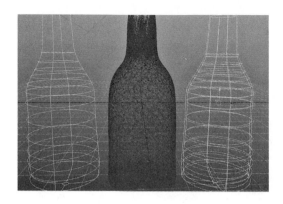
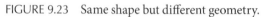

FIGURE 9.23   Same shape but different geometry.

FIGURE 9.24   **(See p. CI-10 of Color Insert)** Three glass bottles rendered.

phenomenon is caused by the complex swirling geometry that was a result of the conversions to polygons and then to subdivision.

GLASS AND PARTICLES FOR A SINGLE-FRAME IMAGE

Maya can be used to make stunning single-frame images. 3D modeling programs are frequently used to make lifelike images for magazine articles and ads, and for commercial, governmental, and academic Web sites. We can also create more abstract art, images that are not meant to be realistic but are meant to be eye-catching. We will try it with NURBS and polygon modeling, along with glass and particle dynamics.

The Scene

Figure 9.25 shows us the scene. We have taken the simple NURBS bottle we made previously, along with a glass made from revolving a curve. The glass has been converted into a polygon model so that it can more easily be used to capture particles.

There are two particle effects in the scene. Both were made by choosing:

Dynamics Main Menu → Fluid Effects → Fluid Containers

See Figure 9.26, and note that this is a Dynamics effect, not nDynamics.

Fluid Containers

Maya has a capability for creating containers that will hold a volume of particles. It is an easy way to fill a container with fluid, as well as to create a flow of fluid into or out a container. We will use one emitter to create a fluid stream from the bottle and another to create particles that will fill the glass.

In Figure 9.26, we are creating an emitter and a particle container at the same time:

Dynamics Main Menu → Fluid Effects → Create 3D Container with Emitter

Looking back at Figure 9.25, we see the container that holds the particles that are coming out of the bottle. Maya defaults to putting the emitter in the center of the container. But

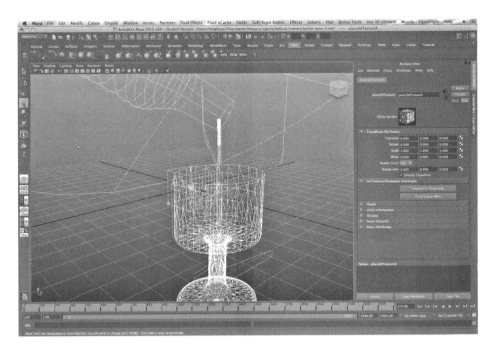

FIGURE 9.25 Glass for particles.

we have pulled the emitter upward and tucked it just inside the mouth of the bottle, which is just at the top of the container assigned to that emitter.

Figure 9.27 shows the attributes of that emitter. Notice the –1 Buoyancy. That is the way we will be able to make the particles go downward. We have also reshaped the container to make it very tall along the y-axis, but very narrow along the x-axis and the z-axis. This is to simulate a stream of fluid.

Again, looking back at Figure 9.25, there is a container inside the glass and it fills up most of the space in the glass. Figure 9.28 shows the attributes of that container. It will trap particles generated from its assigned emitter. We have also given it a –1 buoyancy value. We have left its emitter in the center of the container inside the glass.

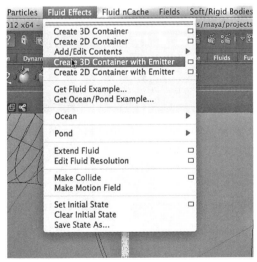

FIGURE 9.26 Create container.

mental ray Glass

In Figure 9.29, we have made a glass material for both the bottle and the glass. We have two instances of it: one for the glass and one for the bottle. The attributes of the material for the glass bottle are shown in Figure 9.30. Notice that the Refraction Color has been set to a very light blue. In Figure 9.31, we see the attributes of the glass material assigned to

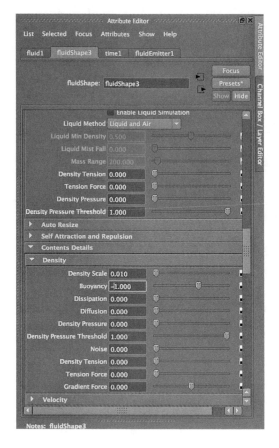

FIGURE 9.27   Emitter attributes.

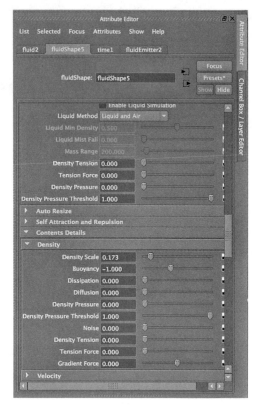

FIGURE 9.28   Container attributes.

the glass cup. The attribute to note is the Reflection Color, which has been set to a darker but soft blue.

The Background

As we have seen earlier, we need a background to properly render glass. In this scene we are using a granite from the Maya materials in the Hypershade, shown in Figure 9.32. The attributes of the granite have been changed. The Color has been changed to a yellow. The Cell Size of the granite has also been increased to remove the speckled look we get from the default granite. (This attribute is not shown in the figure, but is available on the granite1 tab of the attributes for the granite material.) Also, notice that when the granite texture was created, there was no corresponding material made. This does not happen until the texture is assigned to an object. Only then does the granite material appear in the Hypershade.

Rendering Settings

In the mental ray settings, the Reflections, Refractions, and Max Trace Depth values have been cranked up (see Figure 9.33). Global Illumination and Final Gathering are also turned on (see Figure 9.34).

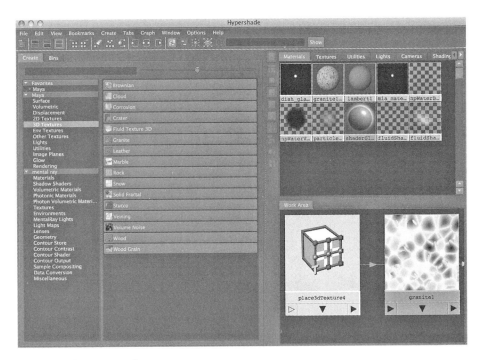

FIGURE 9.29   Glass material.

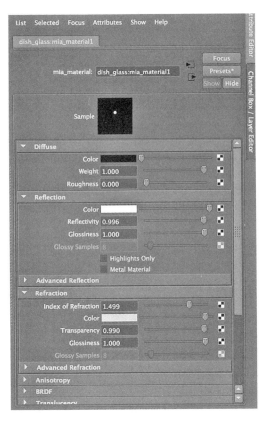

FIGURE 9.30   Glass material attributes.

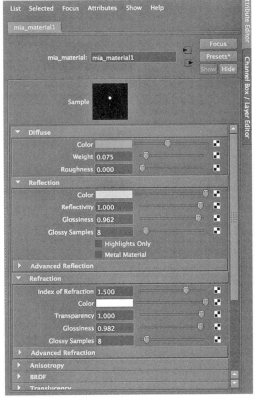

FIGURE 9.31   Attributes assigned to the glass.

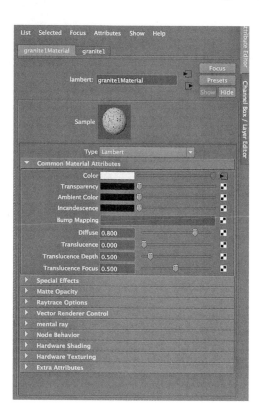

FIGURE 9.32   Granite material.

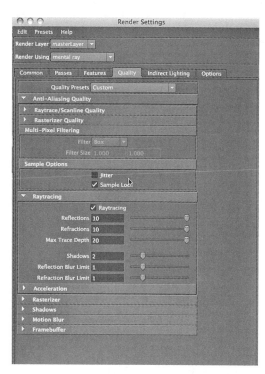

FIGURE 9.33   This shows mental ray settings.

The scene was run for a couple of hundred frames to generate the two particle effects. On my 17-inch MacBook Pro with a quad-core i7 in it, the rendering of one frame took about three minutes. We see the result shown in Figure 9.35.

USING LIGHT FOG AND GLOW TO CREATE A NIGHT SCENE

Maya provides several canned effects. We are going to look at two of them. One is fog, an effect that can be assigned to a light. The other is glow, an effect that can turn the surface of an object into a light source. This is an important concept in 3D modeling and rendering, and one that has grown in popularity recently. As we have discussed, materials, lights, and rendering are all closely bound together, and if you

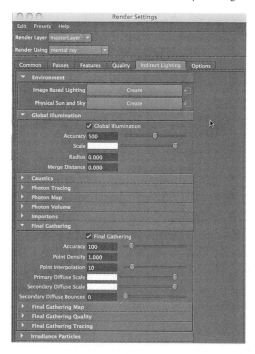

FIGURE 9.34   With global illumination and final gathering.

use an outside renderer, you often want to make use of the materials and lights supplied by that renderer. And it is becoming more common to find materials that are self-illuminating and therefore do not require the introduction of explicit lights into a scene.

Also, if you ever want to experiment with different materials/lights/rendering packages, there is a thriving market for plug-ins to SketchUp, a popular vector drawing program that can be used to create 3D models. It has its own materials and lights, but it does not come with a native renderer. I have used Maxwell, LightUp, Renditioner, V-Ray,

FIGURE 9.35 **(See p. CI-3 of Color Insert)** Stylized glass and bottle render.

Shaderlight, Indigo, and Twilight. Some of these are Mac only or Windows only. They tend to come with their own lights and materials and add dramatically to the visual impact of SketchUp models.

Fog

Maya has an effect that allows us to attach fog to a light. To do this, Maya takes a standard light (but not ambient or directional light) and adds a volumetric (i.e., volume-based) material to the area lit up by the light. We can then adjust the properties of that volume to simulate fog. This effect is computationally intensive and although Maya does not implement this with a particle emitter, the visual effects and the rendering time are similar. The difference is that the fog is static while a particle effect is dynamic, with the particles moving and changing their light properties from frame to frame.

A Sidewalk and Street Scene with Fog

In Figure 9.36, we see the street scene built in Chapter 5. In Figure 9.37, we are in the Hypershade window and have chosen:

Create → Volumetric Materials → Light Fog

In Figure 9.38, we middle mouse button click and hold on the light fog material in the Hypershade, and then drag it to the Light Fog attribute inside the Light Effects tab of the point light's Attribute Editor. This is the light that sits inside the street light orb on the left side of the scene. We drop the light fog in the black box and hit the Return key. Figure 9.39 shows the adjustments made to the other attributes under the Light Effects tab; in particular we have cranked the Radius way up and have assigned a small value for Fog Intensity.

We then go to the Hypershade and select the light fog material. As in Figure 9.40, its attributes appear in the Main Window. The color is set to white and the density of the fog is set to a very low value.

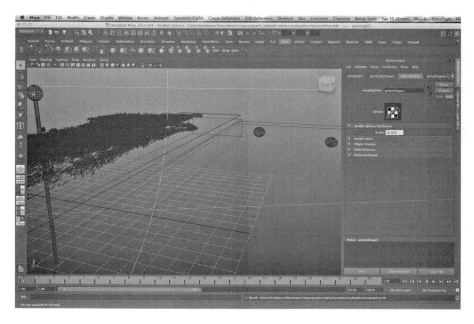

FIGURE 9.36   Street scene.

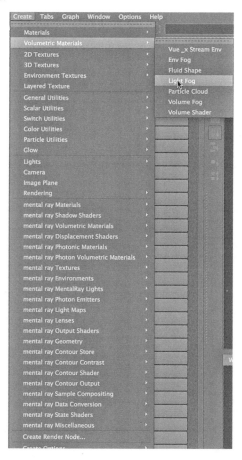

FIGURE 9.37   Light fog creation.

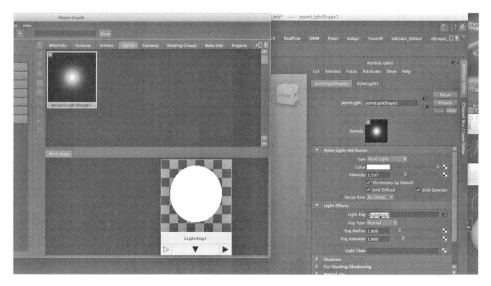

FIGURE 9.38   Dragging light fog to the light.

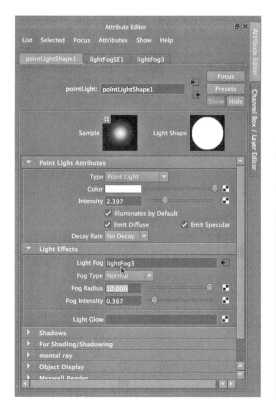

FIGURE 9.39   Light effect attributes.

FIGURE 9.40   Light fog attributes.

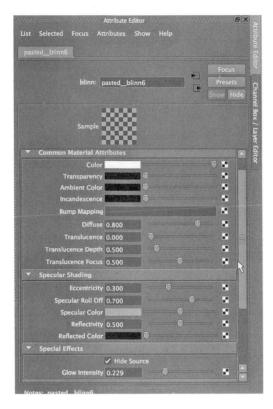

FIGURE 9.41   Headlight attributes.

FIGURE 9.42   Streetlight point light.

FIGURE 9.43   Fog and headlights.

Making a Material Behave Like a Light

We have been explicitly placing lights in scenes. There is an alternative way of introducing light into a scene, and this is by giving materials on objects the ability to generate light. There are several ways to do this sort of thing in Maya, and here, we look at one of the most widely used: Glow Intensity.

In Figure 9.36, two objects have been added to the scene. They are spheres sitting in the upper-right part of the scene. They have had a Blinn material assigned to them, and its attributes are seen in Figure 9.41. Notice the bottom slider. We have assigned the material a nonzero value in the Glow Intensity box. We have also selected Hide Source because we do not actually want to see the spheres themselves, just their glow effect.

The Render

As a reminder, in Figure 9.42, we see that there is only one light in the scene: the point light in the streetlight. But in Figure 9.43, we see two new lights: the headlights. We see the fog as well.

CHAPTER 10

An Example Model: A Closet

W E WILL CONSTRUCT THE glass doors of a closet, create a shirt out of nCloth, and then hang it on a hanger in the closet. Along the way, we will look at animating an object from the perspective of its Object Space, and not World Space. We will also look at rendering a scene from the perspective of an animated camera, making specific lights shine only on specific objects, surgically adding edges to a polygon model, and timing an audio soundtrack to the movement in a scene. Just as we do not use the default lighting in a scene, we typically do not use the default camera either. Default lighting and the default camera, along with the default Lambert that Maya puts on new objects, are only there to get us going quickly when we are beginning to build a scene.

MULTIPLE COORDINATE SYSTEMS IN MAYA

We are going to look at the movement of a door of a closet in this example. Recall that there are actually four coordinate systems in Maya:

1. *World Space* is the (x, y, z) coordinate system of the entire scene.

2. *Object Space* is the (x, y, z) coordinate system of a given object. The center of this grid (0, 0, 0) is centered on the object, not the scene.

3. The *Local Space* (x, y, z) of a given object is the Object Space of its parent. This relationship holds for every nonroot node in the hierarchy. This ensures that although an object in the hierarchy might have its own independent movement in the scene, it will be constrained by every other object all the way up to the root of the hierarchy.

4. The *Surface Space* (u, v) of an object corresponds to the surface of a given object.

This means that as we construct a model, we must put objects into hierarchies in the Outliner, and as we do this, we must keep in mind the way we plan on animating these objects.

As an experiment, create a polygon cube; you might want to stretch it out and make a rectangular prism. Next, go into object mode and rotate the model randomly; just don't put it back the way it was. Now select the object and go to:

any Main Window → Modify → Transformation Tools → Scale

Select the little box to the right of the word Scale, so you can see the settings of the tool. There are some choices labeled Scale Axis. Try selecting World, then look at the green, blue, and red boxes of the icon for the Scale tool. They stand for the x-axis (red), the y-axis (green), and the z-axis (blue). Now change the Scale Axis to Object.

Did you notice that the Scale tool changed its orientation? This underscores the fact that each object in the scene has its own coordinate system. We will rely on this as we animate the doors of a closet.

OPENING AND CLOSING DOORS WITH THE ROTATE TOOL, AND BOUNDING BOXES

In Figure 10.1, we see a closet with two doors. In Figure 10.2, we have gone into Object mode and selected the right door. Then while holding down the D key, we used the Move tool to slide the rotation point (as shown by a yellow box with a circular icon in the center) to the far right side of the door. The result is shown in Figure 10.3. Now, in Figure 10.4, we are using the Rotate tool to open the door. The result is shown in Figure 10.5.

The yellow box started out in the center of the door. If we had rotated the door then, it would have rotated on its middle. This is another aspect of the local nature of objects in Maya. An object always has a center of rotation. It is called the Pivot. With the closet selected, the Pivot of the door will not change its placement with respect to the door or with respect to the closet as a whole if we go between Local and World in the Rotate mode settings, but the naming of the x, y, and z axes might change. When this is done, the colors of the circles on the Rotate tool do change.

There is a concept that is often confused with the notion of a pivot point. It is not shown in the figures, but if we select one of the doors, then go to Shading (in the blue work area)

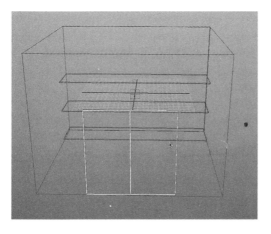

FIGURE 10.1   Closet and doors.

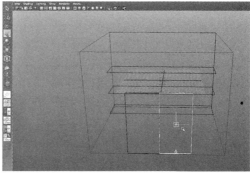

FIGURE 10.2   Right door rotation point.

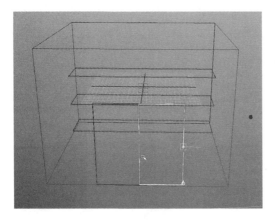

FIGURE 10.3   Rotation point moved.

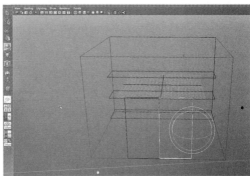

FIGURE 10.4   Rotate tool.

and change Shading to Bounding Box, we will see a flattened cube that has the door in the center of it. This is the bounding box; every object has a bounding box that encloses the object. The pivot point and the center of the bounding box can indeed be the same, but the pivot point can be moved freely—and indeed, we just did that.

After moving the pivot of both doors and then rotating them, we get the image in Figure 10.6.

Also, if we select the closet as a whole, we can change its pivot. But we will leave it in the center of the closet.

Adding Detail to the Doors with the Interactive Split Tool

The closet was made from a polygon cube, and each door was constructed from a single, flattened polygon cube, with the door panels made by extruding faces. The glass panes in the center of the doors are simply rectangles that were not extruded; they are on the same plane as the original cube, and all we had to do was assign both sides of each pane (at the front and the back of the door) a mia_material glass material.

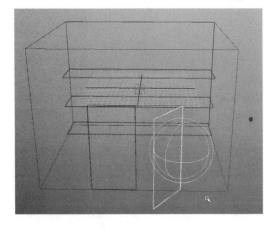

FIGURE 10.5   Door open.

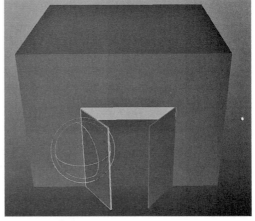

FIGURE 10.6   Both doors open.

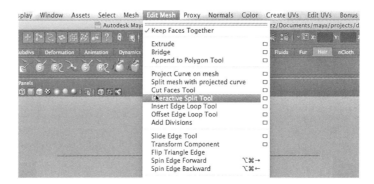

FIGURE 10.7   Choose Interactive Split tool.

For example, in Figure 10.7, we are about to add some detail to one of the flat doors. We are selecting:

Polygons Main Menu → Edit Mesh → Interactive Split Tool

(Note that in Maya 2015, the Interactive Split tool has been absorbed into a new tool called the Multi-Cut tool.)

We get an arrow-shaped tool, as shown in Figure 10.8. We click on the left side of the door, then on the right side, then hit Enter. We have added an edge. In Figure 10.8, there are already a number of splits that have been made, adding a lot of faces to our model. We then selectively extrude some of these faces, and the resulting panels can be seen in Figure 10.9.

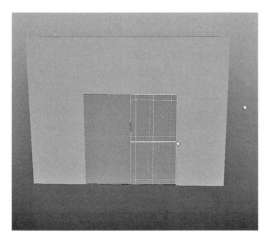

FIGURE 10.8   The Interactive Split tool.

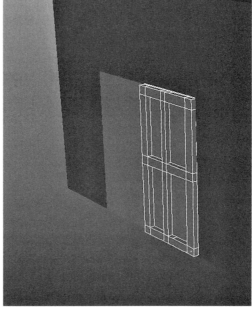

FIGURE 10.9   After extruding faces.

In the Outliner (Figure 10.10), the doors have been made children of the closet itself.

The Render

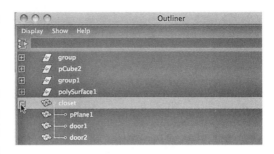

FIGURE 10.10   The Outliner.

We have done a few more things to the doors. In particular, the door panels have a white Blinn on them. The knobs have a gold Blinn on them, and for the glass panes we are using the mental ray mia_material and have chosen the Frosted Glass preset. The final result is shown in Figure 10.11.

One More Look at World Space versus Object Space

The closet as a whole has its own bounding box, its own pivot point, and its own orientation in World Space. Each door has its own bounding box, its own pivot point, and its own orientation—but the location of a door's bounding box and its pivot point in 3-space, as well as its orientation in 3-space, will change if the closet moves or rotates in 3-space.

MAKING A SHIRT OUT OF nCLOTH AND RENDERING FROM A CAMERA'S PERSPECTIVE

We will now hang a shirt in the closet and view the scene from the perspective of a camera that we create.

A Shirt Made of nCloth: Starting with a Basic Shape

To create nCloth, we need to be using polygon modeling. In Figure 10.12, we see a cube. We make the cube similar to the dimensions of a T-shirt, and create it with Subdivisions Width 1,

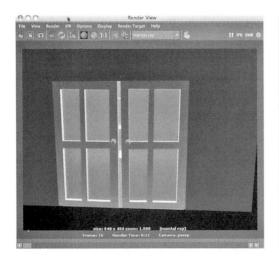

FIGURE 10.11   Doors rendered.

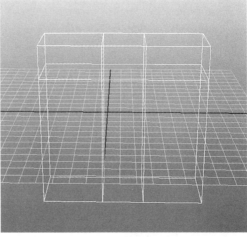

FIGURE 10.12   Cube with edge loops.

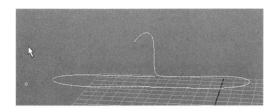

FIGURE 10.13 Hanger shape with CV Curve tool.

Subdivisions Height 1, and Subdivisions Depth 1, found in the Poly Cube History tab of the Attribute Editor. Then we go into face mode with a right click for the Marking Menu and choose:

Polygons Main Menu → Edit Mesh → Insert Edge Loop

This is used to create the necessary geometric detail, including faces on each of the two sides of the cube, at the top of the sides. These will turn into the two sleeves of the T-shirt. We also need a face at the top of the cube, in the center, to make a neck hole.

A NURBS Hanger

To make the hanger, we will use the CV Curve tool, which can be found at:

any Main Menu → Create → CV Curve Tool

First, we make a line in the shape of a hanger, as in Figure 10.13. Then a small NURBS circle is extruded along this line. This creates a hanger, which is turned into polygon geometry by selecting the hanger, going into Object mode, and choosing:

any Main Menu → Modify → Convert NURBS to Polygons

Extruding Sleeves, Making Arm and Neck Holes, and Refining the Shape of the Shirt

As shown in Figure 10.14, we go into face mode and choose:

Polygons Main Menu → Edit Mesh → Extrude

We use this tool to make the two arms. Then, again in face mode, we delete faces, thereby making room for a neck hole, two armholes, and a wide hole at the bottom for the torso of our wearer.

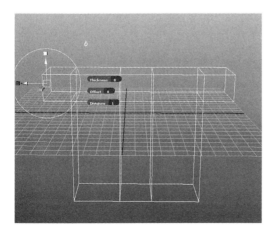

FIGURE 10.14 Arms extruded.

Then we go into object mode, select the shirt, and choose:

Polygons Main Menu → Mesh → Smooth

This smooths the shirt.

Then the Rotate and Move tools are used to angle the two sleeves downward, and the Scale tool is used to make the shirt a little wider at the bottom than the top. The hanger is placed inside the shirt. The result is seen in Figure 10.15.

Then, as seen in Figure 10.16, we select:

nDynamics Main Menu → nMesh → Create nCloth

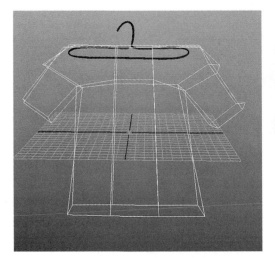

FIGURE 10.15   Smoothed and sleeves angled.

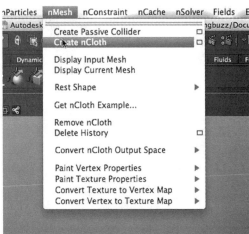

FIGURE 10.16   Create nCloth.

We create a Lambert, give it a green color and assign it to the shirt. Next, as shown in Figures 10.17, 10.18, and 10.19, we iteratively smooth the shirt by using:

Polygons Main Menu → Mesh → Smooth

When we look at Figure 10.17, in particular at the armpit area of our shirt, we see that the Smooth tool has made angled edges at about 45 degrees from the y-axis. Over the next two smoothing passes, we see that this geometry gradually turns into fairly smooth curves. This is a powerful aspect of the Smooth tool: it creates angled faces where we need to bridge faces that are horizontal with faces that are vertical.

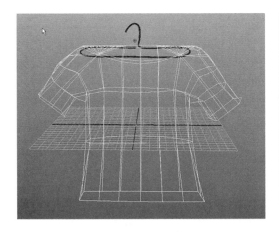

FIGURE 10.17   Smoothing the shirt—pass 1.

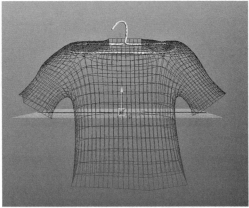

FIGURE 10.18   Constrained edges and more smoothing.

FIGURE 10.19 After several more smooth passes.

A Passive Collider Hanger and Fields

We want the shirt to hang on the hanger, so we do two things. First, we turn the hanger into a passive collider by selecting it and then choosing:

nDynamics Main Menu → nMesh → Create Passive Collider

Second, we select the shirt and go into Vertex Mode, and then we do the same with the hanger. We choose a vertex on the hanger and we Shift-select a vertex on the top of the shirt, and we choose:

nDynamics Main Menu → nConstraint → Component to Component

We do this for a series of paired vertices along the top of the shirt and the top of the hanger.

As seen in Figure 10.20, we discover that the operation that created the nCloth has also created a tab in the Attribute Editor of the shirt. This tab is called nucleus1, and this makes sense, since the shirt has been turned into a particle effect. The attributes under this tab let us set parameters for the solver that computes the movements of nParticles. In particular we see that we can influence this solver by creating gravity and wind.

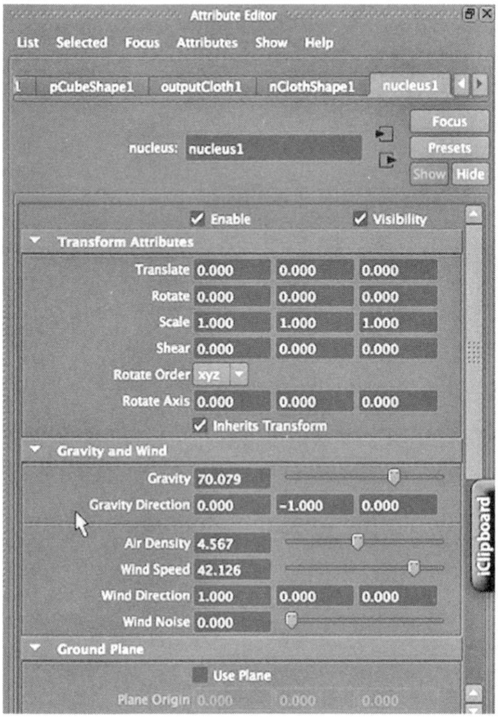

Letting the Cloth Drape on the Hanger and Creating a Camera

We run a hundred frames and watch the shirt drape on the hanger. The result is shown in Figure 10.21.

In Figure 10.22, we are outside the closet. We can see the shirt through the glazed closet doors, hanging on a rod.

In Figure 10.23, we choose:

any Main Menu → Create → Cameras → Camera and Aim

The Aim can be attached to an object so that the camera, no matter where it is moved or how it is rotated, will always point at that object. We place the Aim on the shirt. This will allow us to keep the camera focused on the shirt.

FIGURE 10.20 Nucleus settings.

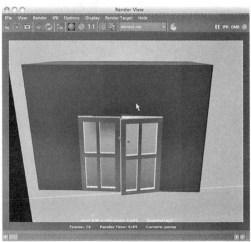

FIGURE 10.21 **(See p. CI-8 of Color Insert)** FIGURE 10.22 Out of the closet.
The cloth T-shirt rendered.

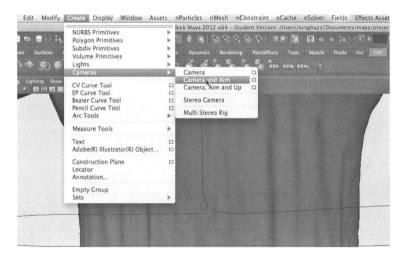

FIGURE 10.23 Create camera.

With the aim on the shirt, we use the Move tool to push the camera forward. We rotate the scene 90 degrees and look at our camera and aim, along with the side of the shirt (see Figure 10.24). Then we pull the camera out of the closet and move away from the scene to see our overall scene (see Figure 10.25).

The Camera's Perspective and Rendering

Until now, we have been looking through the default camera. In the blue design area on the right part of the screen, we choose:

Panels → Perspective → Camera1

This changes our perspective to that of the camera. The result is seen in Figure 10.26.

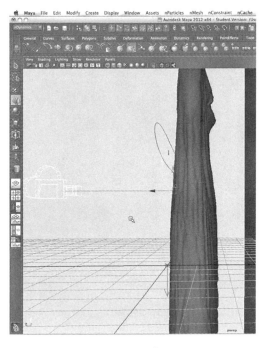

FIGURE 10.24   Camera in closet.

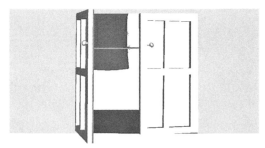

FIGURE 10.25   Camera pointed at closet.

FIGURE 10.26   The camera perspective.

Now, we select:

any Main Menu → Window → Rendering Editors → Render View

As in Figure 10.27, we go to the menu at the top of the Render View and choose:

Render → Render → Camera1

Now, not only are we are seeing what our camera sees, but the renderer will render from that same perspective. We click on the little "camera action" icon just underneath the word File on the Render View top menu. Finally, we render the scene, as seen in Figure 10.28.

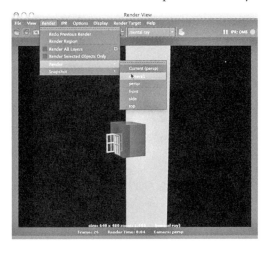

FIGURE 10.27   Render perspective.

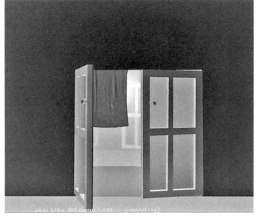

FIGURE 10.28   Shirt in closet—rendered.

TIMING ANIMATION TO A SOUNDTRACK AND RENDERING MULTIPLE FRAMES

Maya provides us with a powerful tool for making sure that the images and the audio of a scene are in sync.

Opening up the Time Slider: Making Room for Audio

Although 3D modeling and animation applications like Maya are not audio editors, there is one particular task that is best done inside the animation application, and that is the timing of movement to a soundtrack. Maya's capability for this is a bit hidden. If you go to the lower right-hand part of the Main Window, you will find a small square box with a red icon in it. See Figure 10.29; it shows the Main Window, with the curser on the icon and the resulting window that pops up when you click on it.

Note the Height setting in the figure. Normally, it is set to 1×. If you change it to 2× or 4×, the Timeline will open. That is where we will find the wave for our soundtrack when we import it.

Sound in Maya

You must use either .wav or .aif with Maya. These are relatively uncompressed, high-quality sound formats. If you have sound in some other format, such as .mp3, you will need

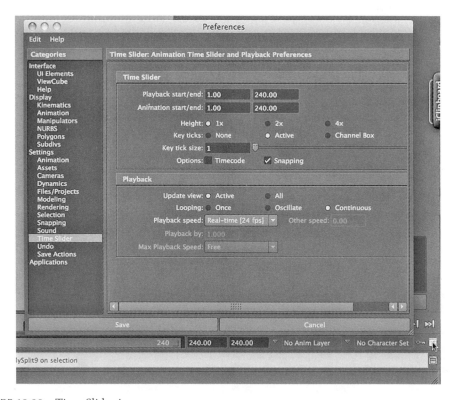

FIGURE 10.29   Time Slider icon.

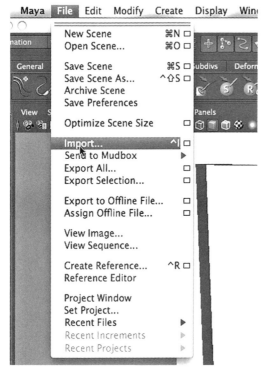

to convert it before trying to import it into Maya.

In Figure 10.30, we see the import tool. With the Timeline open and a sound file imported, your Timeline will look like Figure 10.31.

You can import a number of sound files into a scene. This is a common thing to do, as it is unlikely that you would have your sound all in one file before you import it into your video editor to serve as the audio track for your final video. So if you have more than one sound file in Maya, you can click on the Timeline, choose Sound, and then pick the file you want. In Figure 10.32, "doorclosing" is being selected.

FIGURE 10.30   Import tool.

Guiding the Keyframing of a Scene with the Sound Wave

For introductory students in 3D animation, I generally advise keeping the soundtrack simple and letting it guide the animation, rather than setting up the action first and creating a soundtrack to fit. The reason is simple: We are here to learn to animate, not to edit sound. You might use a piece of music or some simple sound effects. It is a good idea to use a soundtrack that has some sharp peaks in the sound wave; you can leverage these peaks to accentuate motion in your scene. Consider recording sounds with a microphone, making a soundtrack out of these, and then creating your animation to suit the soundtrack.

In the scene we examine for this example, the soundtrack was produced first and the keyframing was then driven by the sound, which Maya can play for us as we run the scene. In Figure 10.29, we have selected "Real-time"; we must do this if we want Maya to play the sound. This way, we can listen to the sound and watch the sound wave, and then keyframe accordingly.

In Figure 10.33, we see the animation of the closet doors; in it we have keyframed them closing. I recorded double doors closing and used this as the soundtrack. You can see that at

FIGURE 10.31   Sound in Timeline.

around frame 18, the right-hand door closes. At frame 37, the left-hand door closes. This is a louder sound, because the striker plate is hit with the bolt in the left-hand door. The keyframes shown in Figure 10.33 are for the right door. It closes first and finishes just as the first sound peak hits. The left-hand door's keyframes are shown in Figure 10.34. Its final motion, that of closing, happens just at the beginning of the second, larger peak in the sound wave.

FIGURE 10.32   Selecting Sound.

Rendering with the Batch Renderer

For the most part, we have only been rendering single frames in the Render View window. Remember that to render a series of frames (so that we can turn this into video), we open the Render View window and choose:

Options → Render Settings

We need to change some settings in this window, seen in Figure 10.35. There is a dropdown near the top of the Render Settings window wherein we choose the renderer; for our purposes, there are two choices, Maya Software and mental ray. In this example, we choose mental ray.

In the Common tab, the Frame/Animation ext setting is name#.ext. Maya will default to assigning the value of "name" to be the same as the scene name. Each frame needs

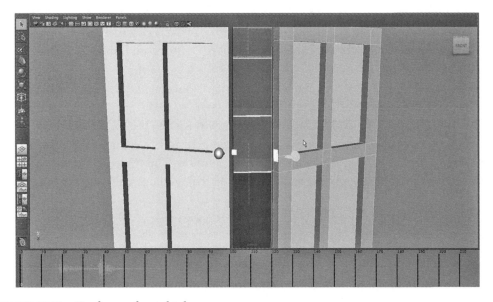

FIGURE 10.33   Keyframes for right door.

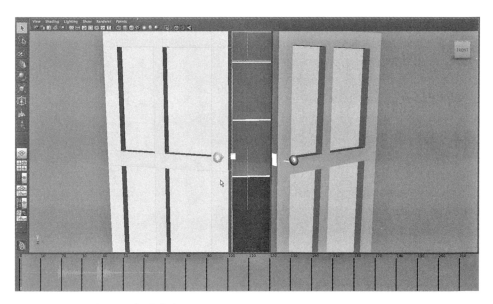

FIGURE 10.34   Keyframes for left door.

a unique name, and so Maya will embed the frame number in each name. The setting in Figure 10.35 means that the name of each frame will consist of the scene name concatenated with the frame number. So, if we are working on myproject.mb, and if we are rendering .jpg images, our series of frames will be named myproject1.jpg, myproject2.jpg, and so on.

We are also choosing to render fifty frames, starting at frame one and not skipping any frames. (We might choose to skip frames if we are doing a test render.) This covers the period of time from the beginning of the animation until just after the second door has closed. We must also choose a camera to render from, and in this case, we are using the default camera called "persp," the default camera that is created by Maya. (In truth, when creating frames that will be used in our final video, we would almost always choose a camera we have created, and not the camera called persp.) The resolution is set to 640 by 480, which is very low def.

We must use the Batch renderer, not the camera action icon in the Render View, to make a series of frames. This is seen in Figure 10.36.

This will produce a series of images. Later, we will import these frames into our video editor and place them on a video track. The sound will be imported into a soundtrack in the video editor. Then, when we export the video, the sound will be synced to the video, and the editor will create a video container such as .mov or .avi, with our video and sound inside.

USING THE GRAPH EDITOR IN MAYA TO FINE-TUNE ANIMATION

We looked at the Graph Editor and how it can be used to reuse motion cycles in Chapter 7. Here, we look at one specific feature of the Graph Editor and how it can be used to fine-tune the keyframing of objects in your scene. Figure 10.37 shows the top of the Graph Editor.

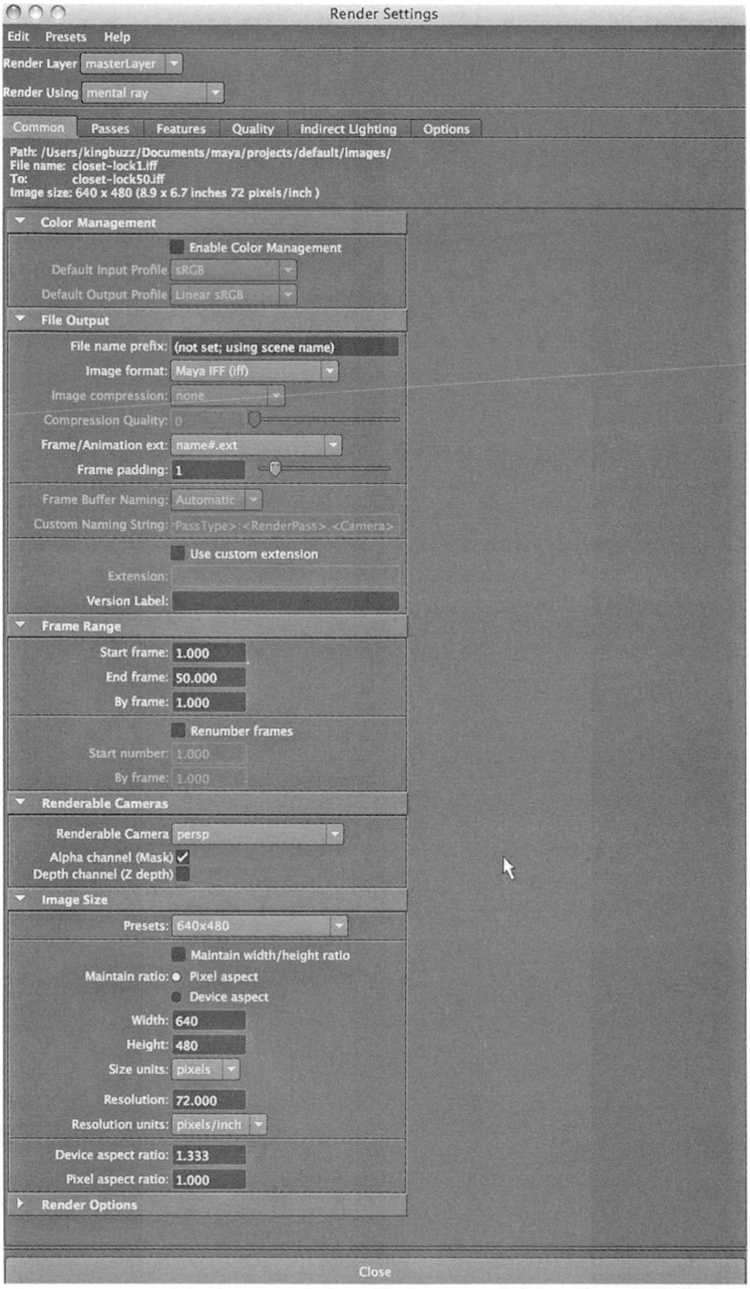

FIGURE 10.35   Render settings.

Frame and Value

Notice the two boxes in the upper-right corner. When they have values in them, they are pinkish-purple. Values appear there whenever some curve in the Graph Editor is selected. Remember that the Graph Editor shows the Translation (movement), Rotation, and Scaling of objects in your scene as the frames go by. The Frame box shows a frame number and the

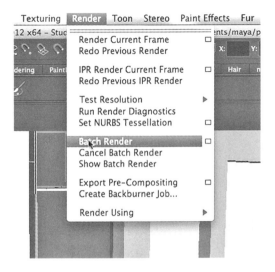

FIGURE 10.36   Batch Render.

Value box shows the y value of a given point on the selected graph at the frame number in the Frame box.

Figure 10.38 shows our closet with the doors partly open. Notice that the left door has been selected in the Maya Main Window. This causes the keyframes for the left door to be marked in red on the Timeline at the bottom of the Main Window; there are two keyframes showing. The first is when the left door starts to move and the second is when it shuts.

The Rotation Curve

In Figure 10.39, we see that the Rotate x curve is visible. This tells us how the door rotates over a series of frames. In the image, it is moving between frame 11 and frame 36, just as our keyframes in Figure 10.38 suggest. Figure 10.40 is a closeup of that curve.

The curve looks like the image in Figure 10.41 if we click on Frame 36 on the Timeline and then select the curve in the Graph Editor. Notice that the frame number is showing in the Frame box. The scene at Frame 36 appears in Figure 10.42; the doors are closed.

We change the keyframing by putting a mathematical expression in the Value box. See Figure 10.43; we are still at frame 36, but now the left door is only half closed, as shown in Figure 10.44.

In general we can add, subtract, multiply, and divide values by inserting expressions in the Value box.

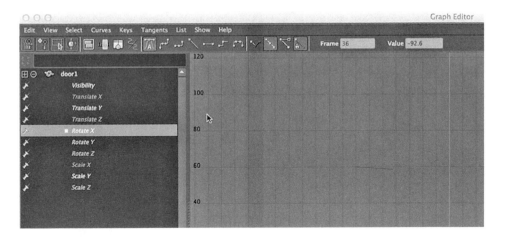

FIGURE 10.37   The Graph Editor.

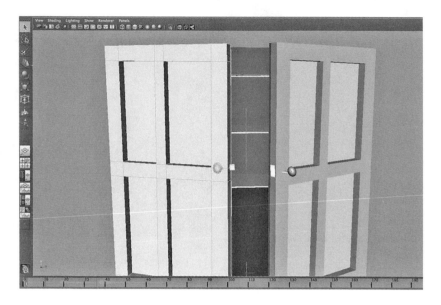

FIGURE 10.38   Selecting left door.

A USEFUL TOOL: FCHECK

One tip: When Maya is installed, a program called fcheck is installed with it. You can use this application to make a quick video to check out your animation. It is not intended for production time renderings. Its name comes from the term "frame sequence check" and can be found by going to:

any Main Menu → Window → Playblast

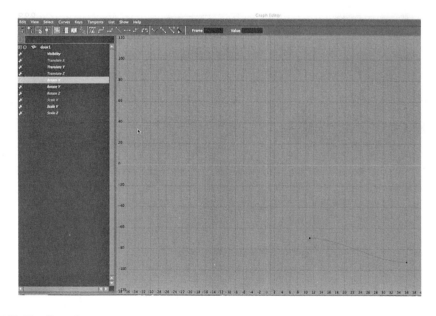

FIGURE 10.39   Rotation curve.

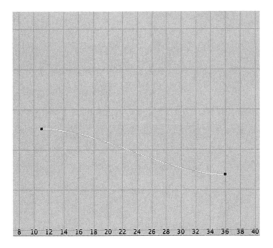

FIGURE 10.40 The rotation curve closeup.

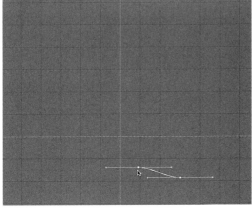

FIGURE 10.41 Frame 36 on curve.

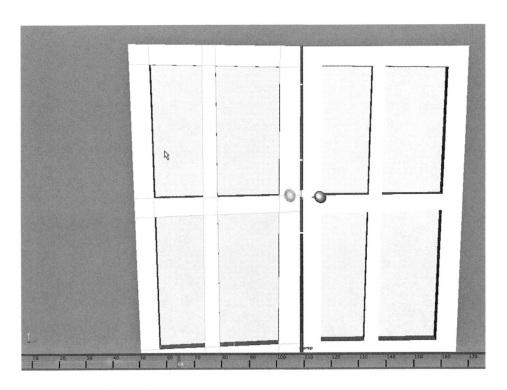

FIGURE 10.42 The door at that frame.

FIGURE 10.43 Changing the number of frames.

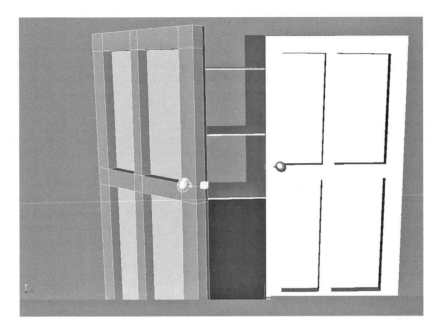

FIGURE 10.44 The door closes partially.

When it comes time, however, to create the actual video for your animated project, you will use a full video editor. You might find that your video editor does not facilitate the transformation of single frames into continuous video segments that you can then edit in your video editor. Try using MPEG Streamclip (free), Quicktime 7 Pro (not free), or Compressor, which installs with Apple Final Cut.

LIGHT LINKING TO ACCENTUATE THE CLOSET DOORS

It is always good to remember that the best lights are often the lights that are most naturally a part of a given scene. But sometimes, the artificial nature of a scene requires us to introduce lights in an artificial fashion.

Controlling Lights

We have seen that we can control what lights are turned on in a scene, as well as whether a given object can cast or receive shadows. There is another tool in the light-controlling arsenal, and it is called "light linking." The idea is to surgically assign lights to specific objects.

There is a separate window for doing this. Choose:

any Main Menu → Window → Relationship Editors → Light Linking

Here, we find a choice between using the perspective of the lights and using the perspective of objects in the scene to control the relationship between lights and the models in a scene. We will accomplish the same task of linking lights to objects in a way that is quicker and simpler. We will do this by working inside the Hypershade, not the Light Linking window.

First, though, we need some background concepts.

Why Control Lights Artificially?

A good heuristic to consider when designing a scene is to start out with lights that correspond to objects in the real world that would naturally be generating light. For indoor scenes, this would include nightstand lights, overhead kitchen lights, light coming in from windows, and television and computer screens. Point lights, spotlights, and area lights, in particular, are used to create sources of light indoors. Outdoors, we might use directional light to simulate the effects of the sun. Both indoors and outdoors, ambient light might naturally model the effects of evenly spread light.

But there are problems with this approach. Directional and ambient light in particular can wash out shadows, which are necessary for rooting objects to the ground and to other surfaces, like tabletops and cliffs. Other parts of a scene might render too darkly.

More subtly, there is something inherently unnatural about a 3D Maya scene. We are working within a confined space.

Three-Point Lighting

Before we look at light linking, there is a lighting paradigm that comes from filmmaking and is sometimes useful as a guide to placing lights in an animated scene. This says that there are three critical light sources.

First, there is the Key light. This is the main source of light and is likely to include the sun outdoors or ceiling lights indoors. Either way, we can control the angle of this light and use it to illuminate the aspects of our scenes that we want our viewers to be drawn to.

The Key light might cast harsh shadows that black out some of the objects in a scene. So, the second sort of light is a Fill light; it comes from the sidelines and it can serve to soften shadows and light up otherwise hidden objects. Its source is not obvious.

Third, there is a Back light, which comes from the back of the scene. It creates a silhouette effect, and is used to draw out the objects that are the focus of action from the background.

Keep in mind that even if you closely follow this paradigm, it does not at all mean that you should have exactly three lights in your scene.

This approach to lighting is in keeping with Maya's live action metaphor.

Fill Lights in Maya

Remember that we create lights by choosing:

any Main Menu → Create → Lights

Earlier, we looked at creating the various kinds of light that are available in Maya. One thing we have not looked at is using lights as precise, local fill lights. Figure 10.45 is a rendering of our Moai statue. The only light is a directional light.

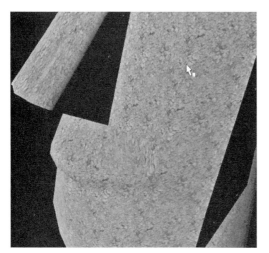

FIGURE 10.45　A dark spot on the Moai.

FIGURE 10.47 With extra light on the nose and cheek.

FIGURE 10.46 Point light settings.

Now, in Figure 10.46, we create a point light and locate it near the left bridge of the nose. We have softened the shadow (see Figure 10.47).

Another way that we might try to create a fill light would be to use a Volume light. This is a light that is set to shine inward from the shell of some geometric object. See Figure 10.48 for the settings of a Volume light. We have chosen to use a sphere; the light should shine inward from the inside surface of that sphere. The problem is that Maya seems to have a lot of trouble rendering volume lights with either the Maya software renderer or mental ray. Volume lights seem to be permanently disabled in Maya, unless we use the Hardware renderer, as seen in Figure 10.49.

Placing and Positioning Models in a Scene

There is a related consideration, and this is the placement of models in your scene. We tend to see more depth if we are looking at a model from an angle, rather than flat on. Therefore, having a person turned slightly to the side helps. Viewing a house from a slight angle is also a good idea. We can control this by carefully managing the angle at which we render a scene. Setting up lights to accommodate this is important.

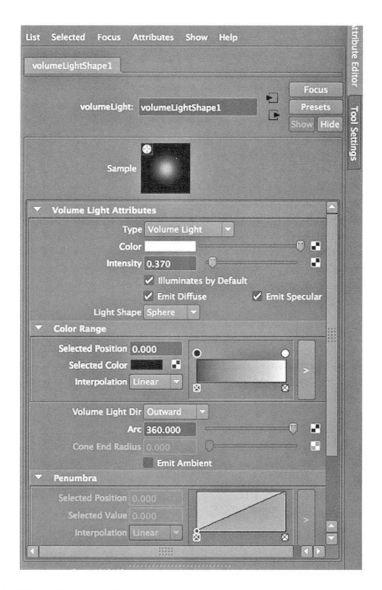

FIGURE 10.48   Using a Volume light.

Controlling Lights from the Hypershade

All this means that we want to carefully control what lights illuminate what objects.

Now, we get back to light linking. We will use our double-door closet model. In our original scene, the only light comes from a single source inside the closet. Now, however, we have added an ambient light. In Figure 10.50, we are in the Hypershade and are inside the Lights tab. We have selected an object or Shift-selected a set of objects in the Main Window. We right click on our light and choose Make Links with Selected Objects.

FIGURE 10.49   Using the hardware renderer.

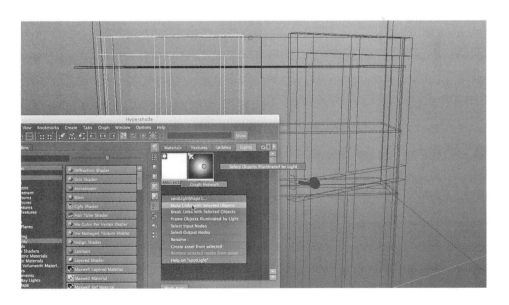

FIGURE 10.50   Make links.

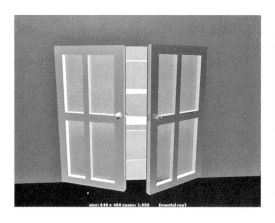

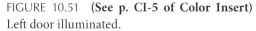

FIGURE 10.51 **(See p. CI-5 of Color Insert)**
Left door illuminated.

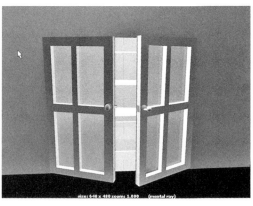

FIGURE 10.52   Right door illuminated.

There is also a Break Links choice. In the figure, we can see that the left door is chosen in the scene. We have also broken links with the right door.

The result is shown in Figure 10.51. If we switch everything, and make the left door not illuminated by the light and the right door illuminated by it, we get what we see in Figure 10.52. There is a significant difference.

CHAPTER 11

Specialized Animation Techniques

W E HAVE LOOKED AT a number of objects and tools that can be used to animate a scene, including motion paths, nonlinear deformers, skeletons, and blend shape. We have also looked at the process of keyframing within the Timeline and within the Blend Shape Window. We have used the Graph Editor to refine and to reuse motion.

In this chapter, we are going to look at creating an entire skeleton and using it to animate a model. We will also look at active bodies and their collisions, natural fields, animating the transparency of an object, and using scripts to animate a model with an expression.

SKELETONS, INVERSE KINEMATICS HANDLES, RIGGING, AND SKINNING A SIMPLE HUMANOID

Models of humans are typically animated by using a skeleton. But because people's movements are so complex, and because we instantly recognize unnatural movements, building and animating a human skeleton is a daunting task. Luckily, Maya has something powerful to help us: a skeleton generator.

HIK: The Skeleton Maker in Maya

In Chapter 7, we looked at a simple skeleton: a human leg. We noted the key difference between forward kinematics (FK) and inverse kinematics (IK). With FK, if a joint higher in the hierarchy is moved, all joints below follow along, and if we move a lower joint, and other joints need to move as well, we generally have to manually move those joints. With IK, we can move a joint lower in the hierarchy, and the joints above it will move accordingly. If a human wants to grab an object that is beyond his reach, the hips and the legs will move, too. This lets us naturally model the coordinated, skeleton-wide movement that real-world humans and creatures exhibit. Now we look at the tool within Maya that will generate IK skeletons for us.

The skeleton generator lets us build a tailored skeleton for a biped. It creates a complete, integrated set of IK controls. Autodesk calls this feature "HIK," for human inverse kinematics.

In Figure 11.1, we see one of the generic characters that can be purchased from the Daz site. He is an anime guy named Hiro: we have seen him already, when we gave him a nice

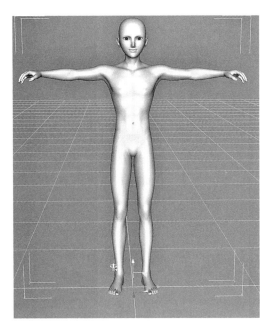

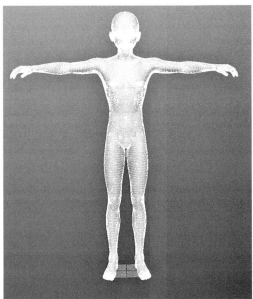

FIGURE 11.1　Hiro—a Daz3D anime character.　　FIGURE 11.2　Daz3D anime object in Maya.

hairstyle in Chapter 8. In Figure 11.2, he has been exported out of Daz Studio as a wireframe (.obj format) and then imported into Maya. (The Daz characters come with fully rigged skeletons, but we want to build our own here.)

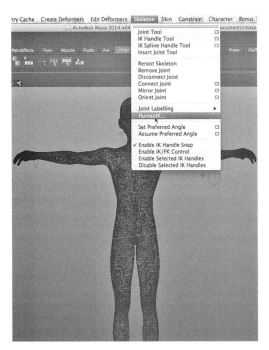

FIGURE 11.3　The IK skeleton generator.

A skeleton consists of joints and bones. But if we want to manipulate the skeleton with inverse kinematics, we need to add a system of controls. Previously, we created IK handles to do this job. We were only animating a single leg, and rigging an entire skeleton is of course a lot more work. Luckily, the HIK skeleton generator creates a skeleton, as well as all the necessary IK handles, thus giving us a fully rigged skeleton.

But there is still one more task to perform. We need to attach the skeleton to the surface of our character. We call this process "skinning" or "binding" the character's surface to the rigged skeleton.

Maya's Skeleton Generator

In Figure 11.3, we choose:

Animation Main Menu → Skeleton → Human IK

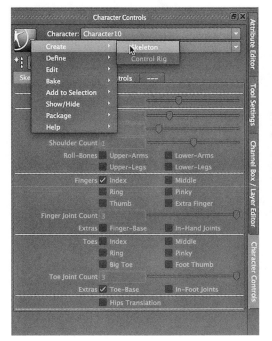

FIGURE 11.4   Making a skeleton.

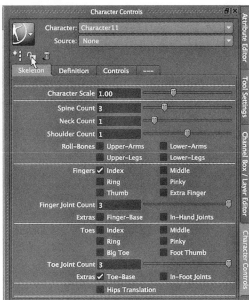

FIGURE 11.5   Locking the skeleton.

A new window pops up. Figure 11.4 shows us creating a skeleton, which had to be rescaled a bit in the y-axis; the bones in his spine were stretched a bit to accomplish this.

In Figure 11.5, we are locking the skeleton. We do this before creating the rig.

Skinning

Next, we must attach Hiro to his new skeleton. In Figure 11.6, we are performing a "smooth binding" of the character's surface to the rigged skeleton by Shift-selecting the skeleton and Hiro, and then choosing:

Animation Main Menu → Skin → Smooth Bind

In Figure 11.7, our skeleton is flat along the x-y plane and its arms are outstretched at 90 degrees, with the legs straight down and just a little space between them. This is called a "bind pose." This is the best way to rig and skin a character, so that we can return to an eas-ily recognizable, neutral posing of the skel-eton and the skin if we want to refine the binding or the rigging. The skeleton needs to be placed carefully inside the skin, with each joint in the skeleton properly centered.

The reason we chose smooth instead of "rigid" is that we want the surface of our character to deform smoothly when a joint is flexed. A rigid bind is a binding

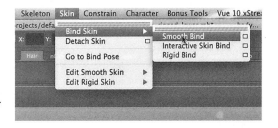

FIGURE 11.6   Smooth bind.

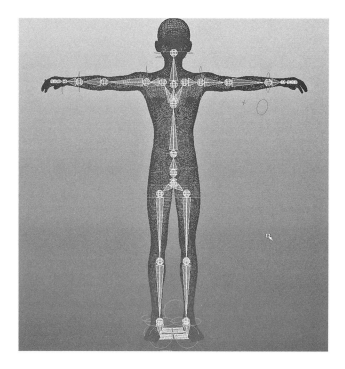

FIGURE 11.7 The rig.

where each vertex on the surface "skin" is bound to only one joint. A "smooth" bind is a bind where vertices on the skin are controlled by multiple joints. As we move away from the bind point, the joints exhibit less control. This more naturally emulates the way the skin on a real human responds when a joint is flexed.

It is common to have to reskin characters because the character or the skeleton has to be changed, or because the existing binding is imperfect. Our binding is not at all perfect, and it can be redone by first choosing:

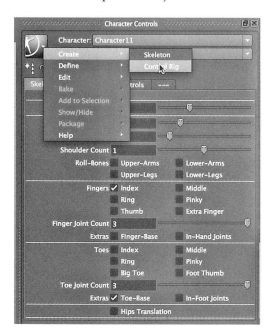

FIGURE 11.8 Making the rig.

Animation Main Menu → Skin → Detach Skin

The Rig

In Figure 11.8, we are generating the rig, which we saw in Figure 11.7. There are red loops along the character and a red rectangle at the root of the skeleton. In Figure 11.7, the hoops appear in gray, and the rectangle is also gray. Remember that these are called "effectors," and when we manipulate them, we engage the IK capabilities of the skeleton. Rigging in Maya is the process of generating IK handles, and at the end of every handle is an effector.

A pink Blinn material has been placed on Hiro. In Figure 11.9, we are pulling upward on the left ankle effector. In Figure 11.10, we are pulling down on the hip effector. We see that when we pull on an effector, the skeleton moves, and in particular, pulling on the root effector—the hips—can move the entire skeleton.

(It is critical that we perform these tasks in exactly this order: generate the skeleton, bind the skin to the skeleton, generate the rig. If we try, for instance, to generate the rig before performing the binding, Hiro will not animate.)

Solvers

In Figure 11.11, we see the attributes of an IK Handle. We see that there are three

FIGURE 11.9   Moving the ankle effector.

IK solvers available in Maya. The one we often choose for building human skeletons is the Rotate Plane Solver, as seen in Figure 11.12. This solver allows us to carefully control bones and joints that should be restricted to motion in a single plane, with a small amount of movement allowed at right angles to that plane. However, when we generate an entire skeleton, Maya uses the Human IK solver.

Making Your Character's Body More Organic

Real people have muscles that stretch and contract as joints are moved. We also have immobile bones, such as the collarbone, that deform skin as we move. And, our joints consist of bone—unlike the joints we create with the Joint tool, which have no geometry and do not affect the shape of the rendered area around the joints. There are three kinds of tools in the "muscle system" that help us compensate for

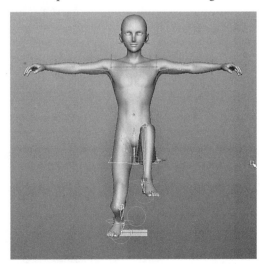

FIGURE 11.10   Moving the hip effector.

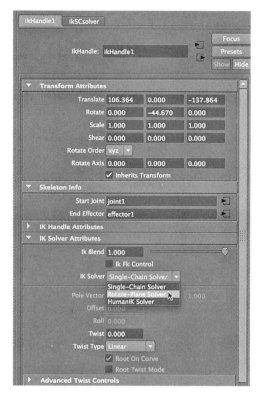

FIGURE 11.11   Maya's three solvers.

these differences. They are all accessible by choosing:

Animation Main Menu → Muscle

Maya supports "capsules," which are rigid and can be used to make joints appear solid. We can convert joints into capsules so that the joints have geometry that will deform the skin that moves over them. Maya also supports "bones," which are similar to capsules, except that we can control their geometry. (These bones have nothing to do with the bones that get laid down between joints as we build a skeleton.)

Maya also supports "muscles," which are attached beneath the surface of your character's skin. They will cause the skin to deform. Each muscle is connected in two places, and when the limb is extended, the two connection points will move apart and the muscle will extend itself. As the limb is closed, the

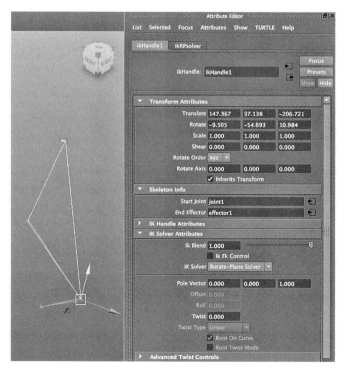

FIGURE 11.12   The Rotate Plane solver.

two connection points will move closer and the muscle will bulge outward.

Making a smooth binding look realistic by inserting these three sorts of constructs is a complex task. For the new user, this typically involves much experimentation and iteration.

There is actually a simpler, although less powerful, alterative to the muscle system in Maya. It can be used to significantly improve the naturalness of joint movement in Maya, and it gives us a feel for the importance of placing hard objects underneath the skin of a character. This technique involves the creation of "influencers" below the skin of a character.

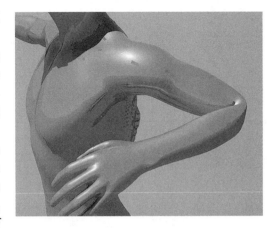

FIGURE 11.13 **(See p. CI-14 of Color Insert)** A folded elbow.

We are going to do some careful analysis of how Hiro bends. In Figure 11.13, the wrist effector has been moved, causing the shoulder and elbow joints to move. Notice the unnatural folding of the elbow. It is almost like it is made of paper.

Now, in Figure 11.14, an egg-shaped polygon sphere has been placed just under the skin, and overlapping the boundary of the joint and the lower arm bone. In Figure 11.15, the sphere and the elbow joint have been Shift-selected. In Figure 11.16, we have chosen:

Animation Main Menu → Skin → Add Influence

This allows the sphere to affect the geometry of the elbow as it flexes. (The default settings for this tool have been used; they appear in Figure 11.17.)

Then we move the wrist again, and the improvement is obvious (see Figure 11.18).

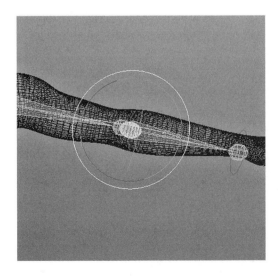

FIGURE 11.14 Inserted egg.

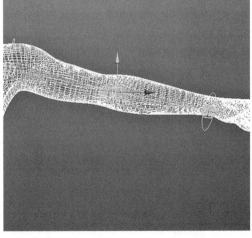

FIGURE 11.15 Egg and skin selected.

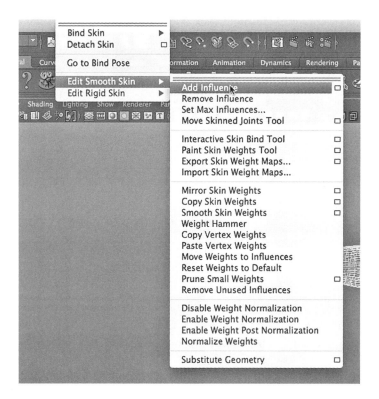

FIGURE 11.16 Adding an influence.

Controlling the Movement of a Skeleton: Pinning and Constraining, and the Sticky Checkbox

We have seen that IK handles control the overall movement of the skeleton, and that the thing we actually use to move the skeleton is called an effector; the left wrist effector is a green loop in the Maya Main Window, and because of the view perspective, appears as a

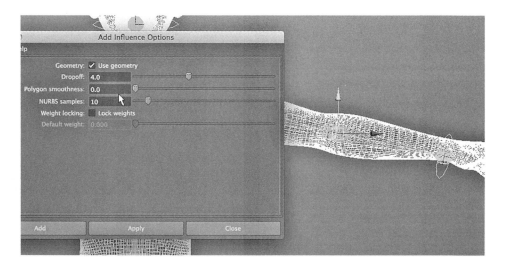

FIGURE 11.17 Default influence settings.

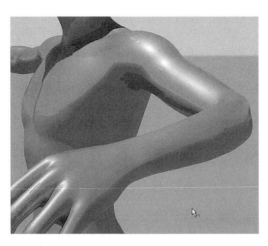

FIGURE 11.18 **(See p. CI-14 of Color Insert)**
An improved elbow.

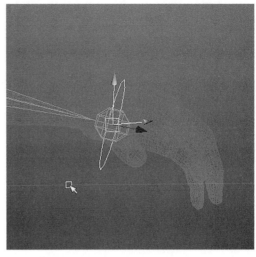

FIGURE 11.19 The wrist effector.

narrow ellipse in Figure 11.19. In Figure 11.20, we see the hip effector; this is an important one, as the root of the skeleton is at the hips.

In Figure 11.21, we have used the Move tool to push the hips toward the ground (i.e., the x-z plane). Notice that the feet stay put, and as a result, the knees and ankles bend. In Figure 11.22, we are "unpinning" the left foot. Now, when we push down on the hips, we get the result seen in Figure 11.23.

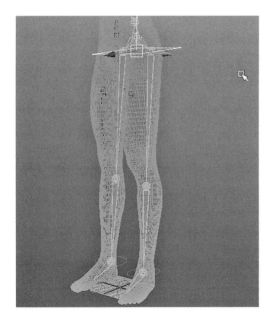

FIGURE 11.20 The hip effector.

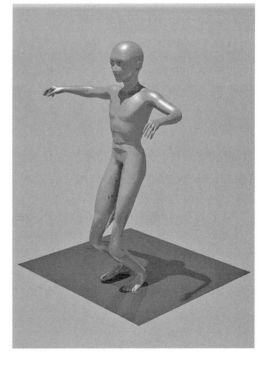

FIGURE 11.21 IK pink man squatting.

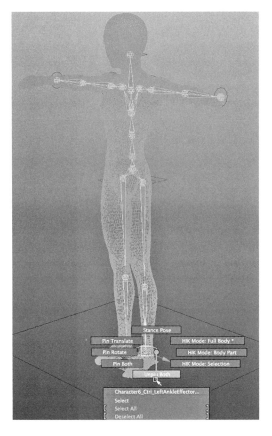

FIGURE 11.22   Unpinning the left foot.

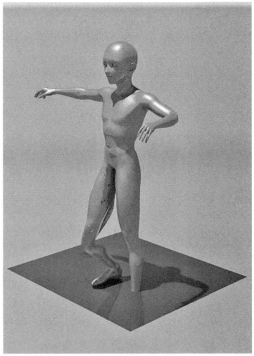

FIGURE 11.23   The result—foot breaks through.

A common technique to use while animating a human is to cause part of the skeleton to be aimed at an object. In Figure 11.24, we see our pink man kicking a ball. In Figure 11.25, we Shift-select the ankle effector of the left leg and the ball, then we choose:

Animation Main Menu → Constrain → Aim

Now, we move the ball forward, and the pink man's foot follows it, apparently kicking the ball (see Figure 11.26).

There is another setting that can be used to enhance the richness of a character's movement. In Figure 11.27, we have generated another skeleton. Instead of generating the corresponding rig with Maya's skeleton building tool, we are putting in two shoulder-to-wrist IK handles manually using the IK Handle tool. In Figure 11.28, we see the settings for the IK Handle Tool; for the left hand we did not check off Sticky, but for the right hand we did check it off. Then, when we pull down on the hip, the right wrist is stuck where it is in the scene, seemingly (but not really) stopping when it comes into contact with the plane (see Figure 11.29).

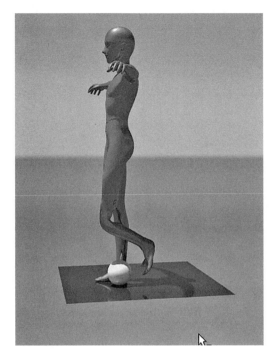

FIGURE 11.24 Pink man kicking ball with left foot.

A Last Remark

Skeletons are not the only way to provide a level of authenticity to the movement of the skin of a character. Particularly with facial animation, blend shape deformers are frequently used to help animate the movement of facial muscles.

ACTIVE RIGID OBJECTS AND GRAVITY: A BOWLING BALL AND PINS

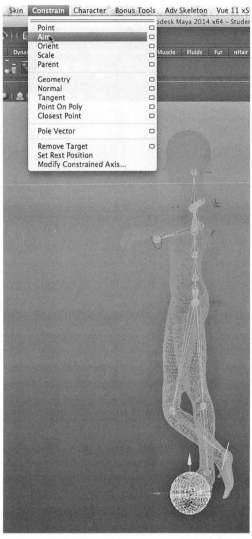

FIGURE 11.25 Using an aim constraint between foot and ball.

In the real world, when objects collide two things can happen. One or both of the objects might deform, thereby absorbing some or all of the energy. Or both objects might remain rigid and one of them, or perhaps both of them, would rebound. Maya has a physics engine that can model the collisions of "rigid" objects and "soft" objects. The first kind will maintain their geometric shape during a collision; the second kind will deform.

There are a number of factors that an animation application like Maya might take into account when it calculates the result of a collision. Speed, acceleration (or deceleration),

FIGURE 11.26   The left foot following the ball.

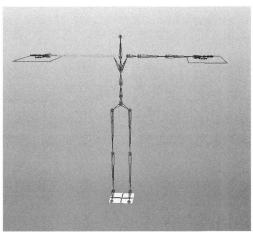

FIGURE 11.27   Two hands and two planes.

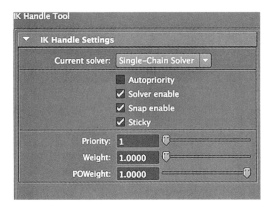

FIGURE 11.28   Right wrist effector Sticky.

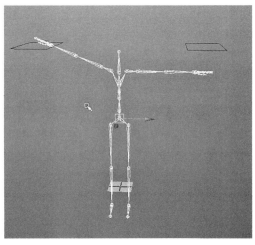

FIGURE 11.29   The right hand sticks.

fields (like gravity), friction, the bounce characteristics of a rigid body, the deformation characteristics of a soft body, and the shape of the two objects are all factors. This last factor can be particularly complex to take into account, and Maya can only approximate what would happen in the real world. Two geometrically complex objects might rebound in a wide variety of ways, depending on their orientation in 3-space at the moment they contact each other.

The Bowling Ball and Pins: Collisions

We have already made use of Maya's ability to let particles collide with rigid bodies (see the examples we have done with nCloth and rain). Here, we look at multiple objects colliding with each other. We will use a classic example: a bowling ball hitting pins.

The pins were made by using the CV Curve tool to create a curved line:

any Main Menu → CV Curve Tool

Then, the curve was revolved in 3-space:

Surfaces Main Menu → Surfaces → Revolve

In Figure 11.30, we see three pins as they are being hit by a bowling ball. There has been a chain reaction, wherein one pin has been struck by the ball, and it has knocked another backward.

How did this all happen?

Four Rigid Bodies

The ball has been transformed into an active rigid body by selecting it and choosing:

Dynamics Main Menu → Soft/Rigid Bodies → Create Active Rigid Body

The three pins were turned into active rigid bodies by selecting them and choosing:

Dynamics Main Menu → Soft/Rigid Bodies → Create Active Rigid Body

FIGURE 11.30   A chain reaction.

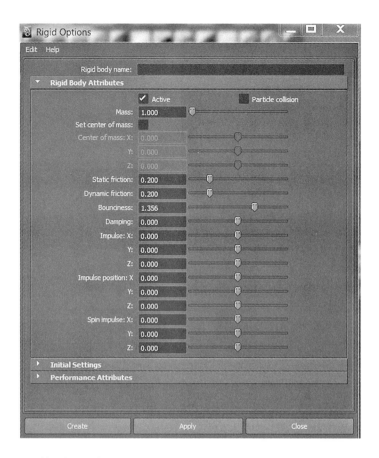

FIGURE 11.31   Rigid body attributes.

The ball and the set of pins were given differing Bounciness attribute values (see Figure 11.31).

Making the Ball Move: Gravity!

As for making the ball move, in Figure 11.32, the ball has been selected and a strong gravity field has been applied to it, with its value being negative along the y-axis. (See Fields on the Dynamics Main Menu.)

This is a reminder that we should not be overly influenced by the way Maya names things. We have seen that materials and textures can be used very creatively, in ways that would not be suggested by their names. The same is true with fields.

That's it. All we have to do from there is play some frames. (Frames of bowling, get it?)

Calculating Collisions

Consider the calculations that Maya must perform while animating the movement of objects that eventually come into contact with each other. Detecting collisions is complex if the objects have complex shapes or are coming at each other at an angle (not head-on).

We have seen that every polygon or NURBS object has a "bounding box." This is the smallest rescaled cube that encloses the entire object. One simplification that is often used is to track the position of the bounding boxes of two objects that are moving toward each other and to use this information to decide when there might be a pending collision. If the bounding boxes of two moving objects do not collide—something the application can calculate very quickly—there is no need to perform more complex calculations that will determine if the two objects really do collide.

USING SOFT BODY DYNAMICS TO AGE A MOAI STATUE

Collisions become more complicated to compute if there are soft objects involved. Soft objects can be created in the same way we create hard objects: in the Soft/Rigid Bodies dropdown. Soft objects will deform if they collide with rigid objects. They can also be deformed by fields like gravity.

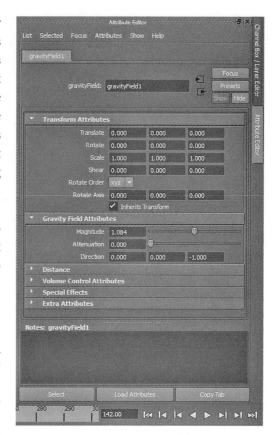

FIGURE 11.32   Gravity field.

We will look at using soft body dynamics to age a Moai statue.

Turning the Moai into a Soft Body

The Moai statue that we built in Chapter 4 is shown in Figure 11.33. It was made out of stone a long time ago. It has sat in the open on a windswept, treeless island for many hundreds of years.

In Figure 11.34, we have chosen:

Dynamics Main Menu → Dynamics → Soft/Rigid Bodies → Create Soft Body

In Figure 11.35, with the Moai selected, we go to:

Dynamics Main Menu → Fields → Turbulence

It is not shown in the figure, but the Magnitude of the field is about 40—not too strong. We do not want to blast our Moai away. Also, the Phase x and Phase y settings of the Turbulence tool are set to –1.

FIGURE 11.33   The Moai wireframe.

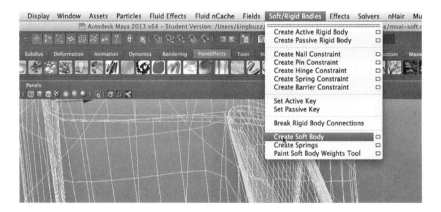

FIGURE 11.34   Creating a soft body.

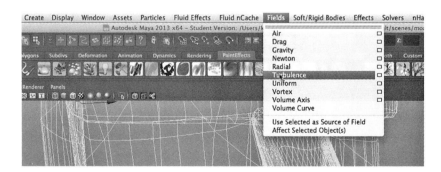

FIGURE 11.35   The turbulence field.

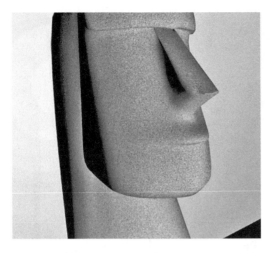

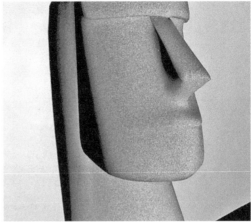

FIGURE 11.36   The Moai before turbulence.   FIGURE 11.37   The Moai after turbulence.

Before and After

Figure 11.36 shows the Moai before running the scene, and Figure 11.37 shows it after running about a hundred frames. The turbulence has gently eroded the nose and the mouth and the jaw. If we want to, we can move the turbulence field around and age more of the Moai's face.

USING THE CHANNEL BOX FOR KEYFRAMING THE TRANSPARENCY OF A MOAI

The geometry and location of an object are not the only things we can animate. Another way is to vary the attributes of a material belonging to that object over a series of keyframes—and there are a lot of attributes of a material that can be animated.

Remember that we can move between the Attribute Box and the Channel box with Control+A. By going to the Channel box we can unveil a set of attributes belonging to the selected object and use them to keyframe an animation. We will look at animating a material, as opposed to an object or model, by manipulating its transparency settings.

Making Our Moai Disappear

In Figure 11.38, we see the steel version of our Moai. In Figure 11.39, we see the Channel box. There are three transparency settings, one for each of the three colors in the color spectrum: Red, Green, and Blue. In Figure 11.39, they are all set to zero, meaning there is no transparency.

We have moved along the timeline, jumping ahead ten frames at a time, for a total of about a hundred frames, increasing the amount of transparency in each channel by ten with each keyframe. Figure 11.40 shows the value of the transparency channel for the Moai on the first frame, which is also our first keyframe.

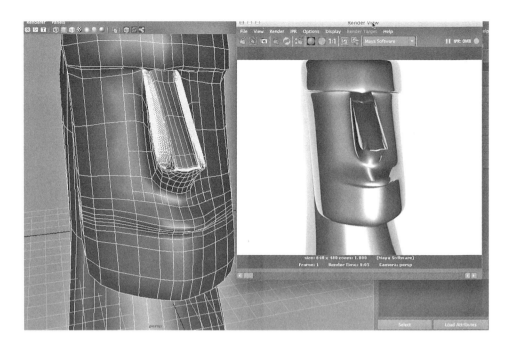

FIGURE 11.38   Steel Moai.

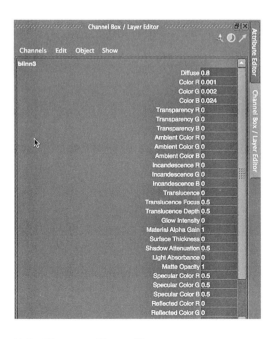

FIGURE 11.39   Channel box.

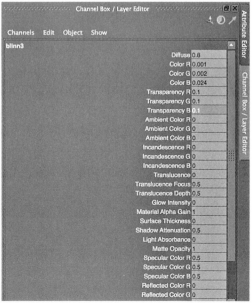

FIGURE 11.40   The transparency channel.

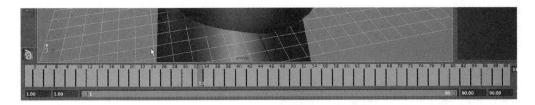

FIGURE 11.41   Keyframes for transparency animation.

Figure 11.41 shows us the positions of these keyframes. Remember that we make them with the S key. To create an animation where the Moai disappears over the course of a hundred frames, we would need to use the batch renderer, as seen in Figure 11.42. (Inside the Render Options, we have gone to the Common tab, and have set the Start, End, and By frame parameters to 1, 100, and 1.) In Figure 11.43, we see a rendering of our fading Moai at about fifty frames.

USING AN EXPRESSION TO ROTATE A DOORKNOB

A topic that is out of the scope of this book is a comprehensive coverage of Maya's scripting language (Maya Embedded Language, or MEL).

You can build an entire animated project simply using MEL, and not the huge Maya GUI (graphical user interface). There are things that are not at all straightforward to do with the GUI that can be accomplished with MEL.

There are primitives that can be used to create and assign variables, and create basic shapes like spheres and cubes, in both modeling techniques. We can also translate (move), scale, and revolve. MEL operations can be used to rig skeletons, create dynamics effects (including cloth), create "crowd" effects, and perform renderings.

FIGURE 11.42   Batch render.

FIGURE 11.43   Moai half faded.

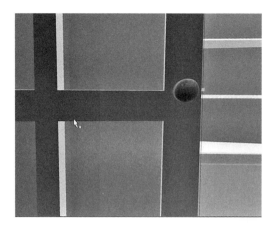

FIGURE 11.44   Left door.

There are many MEL scripts available online (a lot of them are free) that can be used to extend the capabilities of Maya. MEL can be used to extend the user interface with user-created procedures. One simple way of doing this is to create a new tab in the interface and then drag MEL code to the shelf of this tab. MEL has been used to provide powerful third-party plug-ins to Maya, something that will be discussed in Chapter 14.

MEL has a number of operations for performing program logic decisions and performing mathematics. It is not, however, meant to be used as a general purpose scripting language.

There are many cases in which keyframing the motion of an object is very difficult, in particular, in situations that require precise, cyclic changes in the attribute of an object, or in the relationship between two or more attributes. One of the easiest ways to use MEL is to create expressions that can be assigned to attributes of objects in a scene.

In Figure 11.44, we see the left door of our closet. Note the position of the knob and that the bolt is all the way out. The door is closed and we have removed the right door so we can more easily see what is going on.

In Figure 11.45, we have chosen:

any Main Menu → Window → Animation Editors → Expression Editor

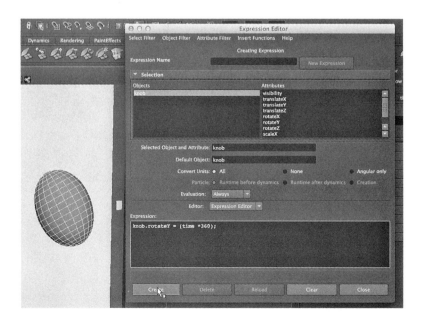

FIGURE 11.45   Expression Editor.

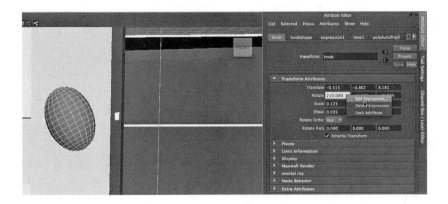

FIGURE 11.46   Knob expression.

Then we have written a simple MEL code fragment. It is: Knob.rotateY = (time *360).

Knob is the name given to the left knob. RotateY is the y-rotation attribute of the knob. Time is a MEL keyword that represents the frame number divided by the frame rate. All we have to do is hit Create in the lower left of the Expression Editor and then run our scene.

(Another way to apply the expression to the knob is to right click on its Rotate attribute, as seen in Figure 11.46.)

Maya now provides some support for scripting using Python, a language that many other animation applications, including Vue, Rhino3D, Poser, Blender, and Houdini, use.

The Rendering

We have manually keyframed the movement of the bolt into the door as it opens, as well as the opening of the door itself. The final frame is shown in Figure 11.47. Note the position of the knob.

A Note on Using the Outliner Window

Carefully building the scene hierarchy is what facilitated the rotation of the knob. The Outliner window has been used to make the bolt and the knob children of the door, thus allowing the bolt and knob to have their own independent motion, but to also be constrained by the motion of the door.

USING MAYA EXPRESSIONS AND VARIABLES TO ANIMATE MODELS

We will look at a couple of examples where expressions can be used to animate an object. Then, we will look at a few useful MEL system variables and at defining user variables.

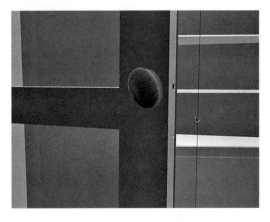

FIGURE 11.47   Moved door and rotated knob.

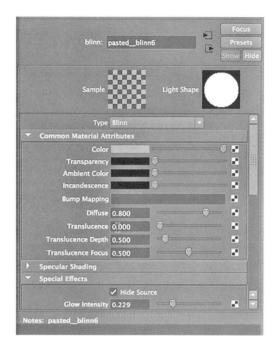

FIGURE 11.48   Blinn material.

Example 1: Applying an Expression to the Visibility Attribute of an Object That Has a Material with a Glow Intensity

We will start with our street scene, with the fog and the car headlights. What we will do now is color those lights—one red and one blue—and have them flash on and off randomly.

The "lights" are actually spheres with Blinn materials that have a glow intensity. They are not Maya lights. Figure 11.48 shows the attribute editor after we have selected the Blinn material for one of them. We will apply our expression to the visibility of the two spheres, not to the material on the spheres.

In Figure 11.49, one of the spheres has been selected in the Main Window, and we have opened up the Expression Editor by going to Window at the top of the Main Menu, selecting Animation Editors, and then choosing Expression Editor. Then we clicked on the visibility attribute in the second column from the left.

The expression, after we have typed it in and hit Create, is at the bottom of the image.

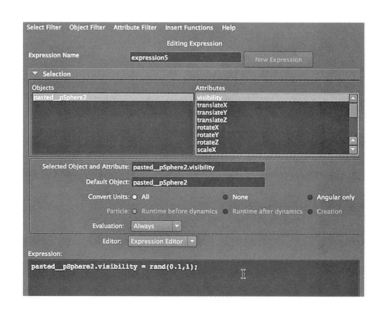

FIGURE 11.49   Visibility attribute.

FIGURE 11.50   Random render 1.

FIGURE 11.51   Random render 2.

The expression makes use of a random function that reevaluates the visibility of the sphere for every frame. This is a great function to have, because one of the most difficult things to do is to create what appears to be partly random movement. We then must do the same thing to the other sphere.

Finally, Figures 11.50, 11.51, and 11.52 show a sequence of three frames spread across thirty frames of animation. We have flashing emergency lights, perhaps from an approaching police car.

Example 2: Our Squashing Ball

Earlier, we looked at using a Squash deformer to flatten a ball when it hits the ground. You might remember that we used the scale tool and keyframing to make the ball stretch out as it went up.

We will do this again but in reverse, and not by using the scale tool. We will use a squash deformer when the ball hits the floor, as we did before. But we will use an expression to stretch the ball out as it comes down. The stretch expression is shown in Figure 11.53.

The results are shown in Figures 11.54, 11.55, and 11.56.

More Maya Embedded Language (MEL)

Let's take a quick look at some other aspects of MEL.

Useful MEL Variables

currentTime is a system variable that contains the current timestamp.

frame is a system variable that holds the current frame number. This is very useful, since expressions get evaluated on every frame.

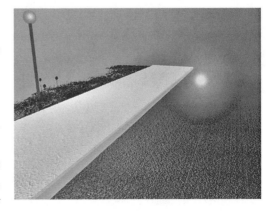

FIGURE 11.52   Random render 3.

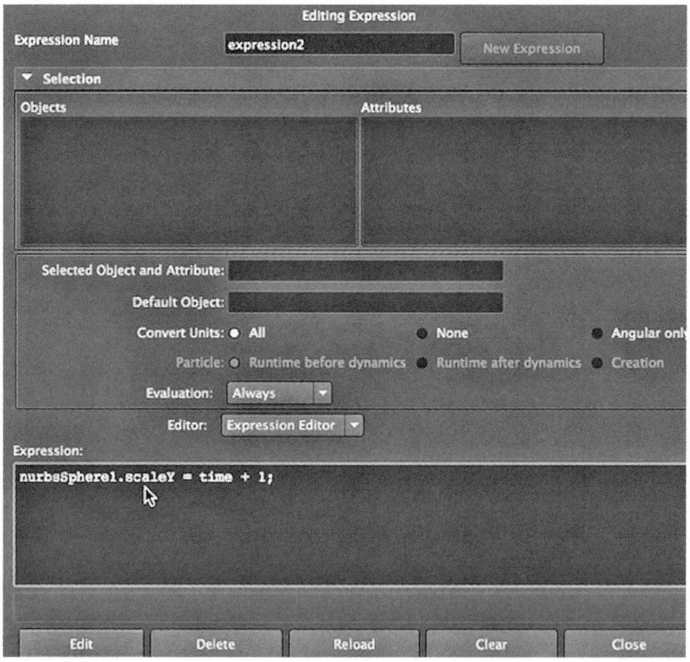

FIGURE 11.53   Scale attribute expression.

User-Defined Variables

Variables created by the programmer always have a dollar sign ($) in the front, for example, int *$buzzint;*.

After the $ there has to be a character, and not a number.

Another example of a user-defined variable: *float $buzzarray[] = {1.1, 32.2, 23.3, 14.4, 45.6};*

One more example: *matrix $buzzmatrix[9] [2] ;*

Local Variables

Here are two local variables:

   {int $kingint = 1; int $buzzint = 0; if ($kingint = 1) print ($buzzint);};

The curly brackets mark the scoping of the two variables.

Global Variables

This program will print the same result as the one above, but it contains a global and a local variable:

   global int $kingint = 1; proc buzzproc() {int $buzzint = 0; if ($kingint = 1) print
      $buzzint;} buzzproc();

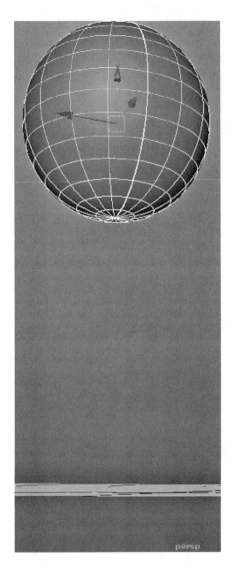

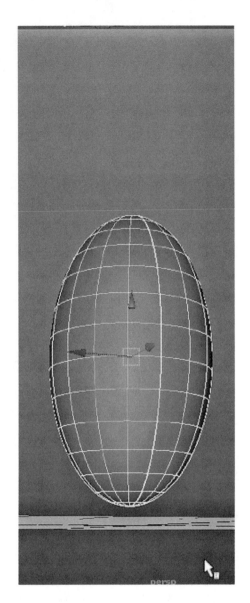

FIGURE 11.54   The first ball dropping render.   FIGURE 11.55   The second ball dropping render.

Control Structures

Last, we note that MEL has a handful of control structures. Here is an example:

```
global int $kingint = 1; proc buzzproc() {int $buzzint = 0; while ($buzzint < 3) {print
    $buzzint; $buzzint = $buzzint – 1;};} buzzproc();
```

Note that this program will run forever.

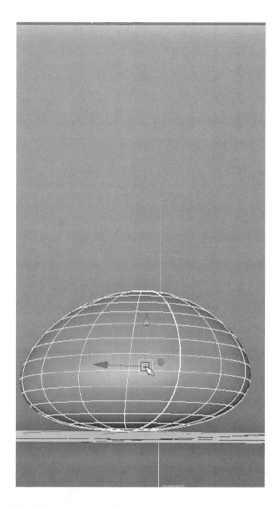

FIGURE 11.56 The third ball dropping render.

CREATING AN OCEAN WATER SWELL

We end with another brief example of using a gravity field to add motion to a scene; in this case we will also use a dynamics effect: nCloth.

Using nCloth as Water and Applying Gravity

In Figure 11.57, a polygon plane that has a high vertex count can be seen. Above it is a polygon sphere. Figure 11.58 shows the attribute editor of the plane. This is after selecting the plane, and choosing:

> *nDynamics Main Menu → nMesh → Create nCloth*

Next, we place the ball above the plane, select the ball, and then select:

> *nDynamics → Fields → Gravity*

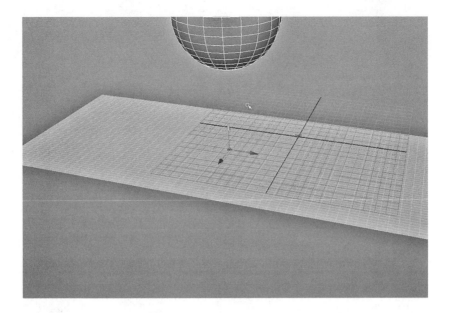

FIGURE 11.57   High vertex count plane.

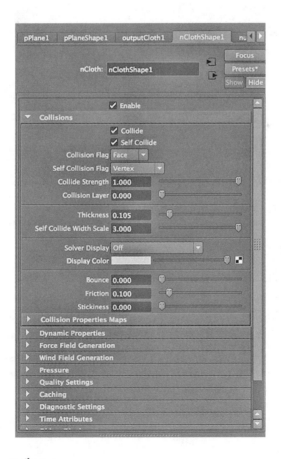

FIGURE 11.58   nCloth attributes.

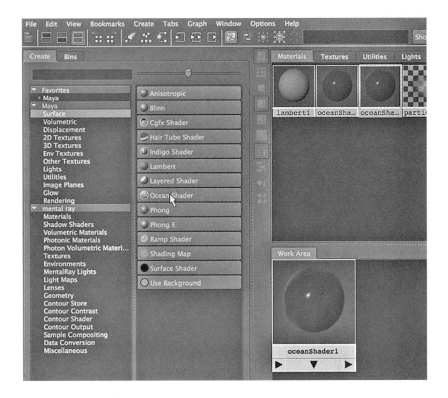

FIGURE 11.59   The ocean shader.

(You might want to check the attributes of the gravity field to make sure it is going downward in the y dimension.)

Then, in Figure 11.59, we go to:

any Main Menu → Window → Rendering Editors → Hypershade

We make an instance of the Ocean Shader. Next, we select the plane in the Main Window. Then we select the Ocean Shader we just made in the Hypershade, right click, and choose Assign Material to Selection.

The Ball Falls through the Water and Creates a Rippling Swell

We set the scene up with about 200 frames and play the scene, with the ball starting up in the air and falling through the plane. Figure 11.60 shows the plane after the ball passes through.

As the scene continues, the water develops a deep swell that ripples. Figures 11.61, 11.62, and 11.63 show three frames. The first is before the ball falls. The second is after the ball has just passed through, and the third is a number of frames later.

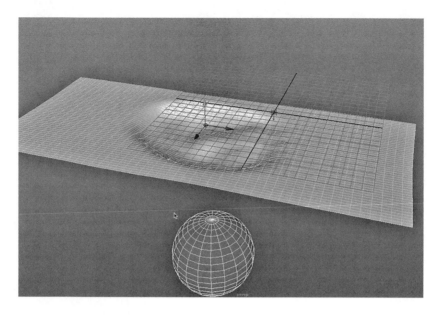

FIGURE 11.60   Ball creating a splash.

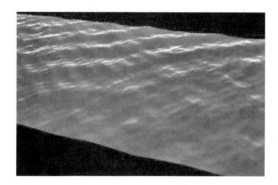

FIGURE 11.61   The swell rendered.

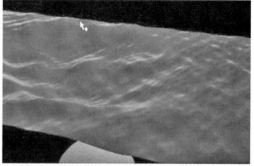

FIGURE 11.62   The swell deepens.

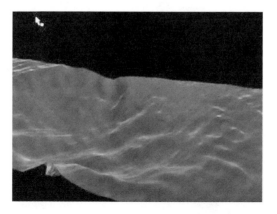

FIGURE 11.63   The swell bottoms out.

CHAPTER 12

Specialized Materials and Material Effects

T HERE ARE A HANDFUL of specialized effects that come with Maya, and we look at three of them in this chapter. First, we look at creating what appears to be 2D animation with Maya. Then we look at painting in Maya, a powerful paradigm that is used in multiple contexts. Finally, we address a common problem when creating an outdoor scene: providing lighting that naturally resembles daylight.

MAKING A TOON COW

Since this book is about 3D animation, it might seem that 2D animation is outside our scope. But it's not. That is because there are actually two ways to make 2D animation with Maya. Well, to be precise, two ways to make our 3D animation look 2D.

Why would you want to do this? 2D animation has a completely different look than 3D. 2D animation is based on vector graphics, along with the distinct assignment of colors to areas enclosed or partly enclosed by lines. This means that we do not gradually fade one color into another and we leave the borders between colors sharp. This is how we obtain the flat 2D cartoon look. Often this is the best way to create a model that looks funny. The problem with 2D animation is that we have to draw our models from multiple perspectives. This is time consuming and more significantly, some of us are not the best drawing artists.

Maya can render a 3D scene as if it was 2D, and we can simulate 2D by making use of special shaders.

The Vector Renderer

Until now, we have only looked at using three renderers: Maya Software, mental ray, and Maya Hardware. But there is another one, called Maya Vector. If you go to the Render Settings and select Render Using, you will find the Maya Vector renderer. If you go to the

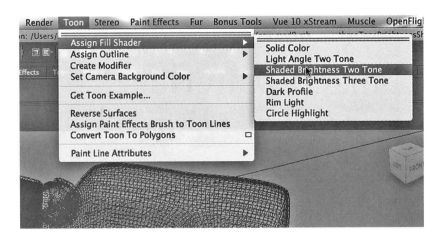

FIGURE 12.1   Shaded brightness two tone.

Common tab, you will also find that one of the choices for Image format is SWF, which is Flash animation, the most widely used vector animation format. The vector renderer can also produce vector images in Adobe Illustrator (AI) format.

The problem is that it is up to us to create a 3D scene that will look good when it is vector rendered. This can be quite tedious to do. If you are, for example, using polygon modeling, you have to carefully control the number of faces on your object and the colors you put on those faces if you want the vector renderer to produce that flat 2D cartoon look.

But Maya has another way to get the job done.

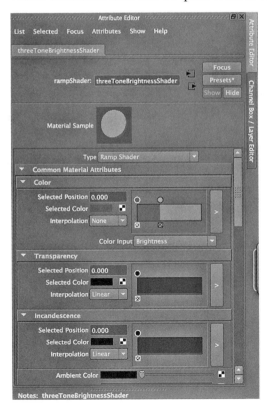

The Toon Shader

The second way to get a 2D vector look is by using the Toon shader in Maya. We select the model and then choose:

Rendering Main Menu → Toon → Shaded Brightness Two Tone (see Figure 12.1)

What Maya does is create a ramp shader with two colors. If you look at Figure 12.2, you can see that the two colors have been set to a dark and a light brown.

Next, we choose:

Rendering Main Menu → Toon → Assign Outline (see Figure 12.3)

FIGURE 12.2   Two colors selected.

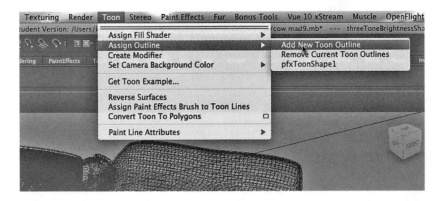

FIGURE 12.3   Assign Outline.

FIGURE 12.4   Background color.

This tells Maya to add an outline around areas of a given color, in order to simulate the lines that might be drawn by a 2D vector artist.

Finally, as seen in Figure 12.4, we choose a background color and have Maya place it on a plane that is perpendicular to the default camera perspective:

> *Rendering Main Menu → Toon → Set Camera Background Color*

The resulting render is shown in Figure 12.5. Maya has taken care of the task of deciding where each of the two colors will be placed on the cow, as well as where to draw the black outlines.

MAKING A GRAFFITI-COVERED WALL WITH PAINT EFFECTS

The paint metaphor is used widely in Maya, and the Artisan engine inside Maya supports a number of tools, in particular, the

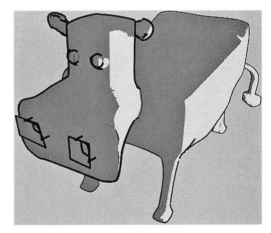

FIGURE 12.5   Toon cow render.

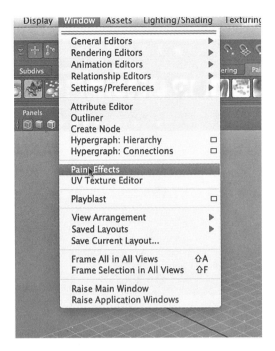

FIGURE 12.6   Paint Effects.

painting tools. We have already looked a bit at 3D painting when we created the grass in our nighttime street scene.

The Paint Effects Canvas

Now, we will look at 2D painting and at Maya's Canvas window. In Figure 12.6, we have chosen:

any Main Menu → Window → Paint Effects

In Figure 12.7, we see the Canvas.

Painting on an Image

With the Canvas, we can import an image and then paint on it; see Figure 12.8. We will create some graffiti using the canvas. As seen in Figure 12.9, we have imported an image of a brick wall. In Figure 12.10, we are selecting:

Paint Effects Window → Brush → Get Brush

This opens the Visor, as shown in Figure 12.11. There is a large library of canned paint effects. We chose the black airbrush effect, as seen in the upper right of Figure 12.11.

In Figure 12.12, we have painted on the wall and are saving it as an image. Then in Figure 12.13, we have created a file texture out of the image and it has been applied to a surface in a Maya scene.

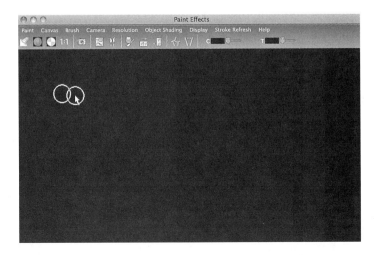

FIGURE 12.7   The canvas.

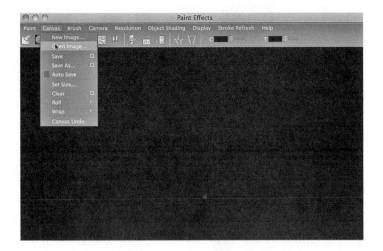

FIGURE 12.8   Open image.

FIGURE 12.9   Brick wall.

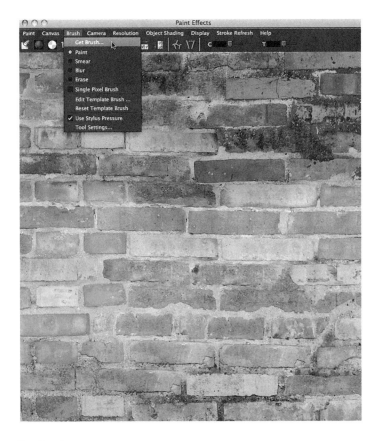

FIGURE 12.10 Get Brush.

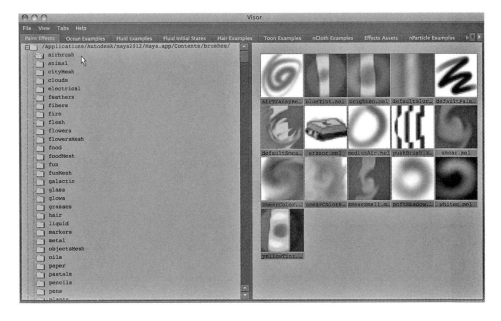

FIGURE 12.11 Visor window.

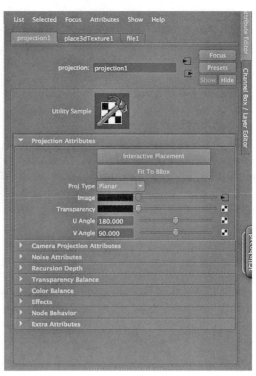

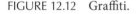

FIGURE 12.12   Graffiti.

FIGURE 12.13   The canvas image as a file texture.

To provide a comparison between 2D and 3D paint effects, in Figure 12.14 a polygon geometry tree is being added to the scene. The final result is shown in Figure 12.15; we have rendered a plane in Maya that has our brick as a texture. The tree is standing in front of the wall and is planted in the ground plane.

Choosing a More Realistic Effect

The problem with the result in Figure 12.12 is that the paint is very dark, and there is no transparency in it, and so it does not look like it has soaked into the bricks. It seems to float over them.

So we have made two changes to Figure 12.12. We went back to the Visor and chose a narrower brush and gave the color some transparency. In Figure 12.16, it looks a little more like the writing is actually on the wall. Another alternative would have been to choose a lighter canned airbrush, such as the one in the center of Figure 12.17.

THE MENTAL RAY SKY DOME

The mental ray renderer comes with a beautiful light and color effect, something that is often called a "sky dome," which simulates the natural diffuse light of an outdoor scene. It looks dramatically better than simply putting a light blue on a background plane. In

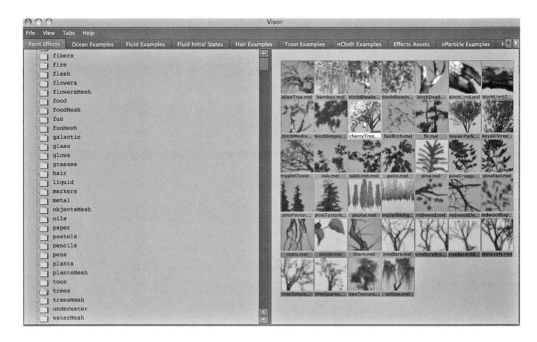

FIGURE 12.14 Paint Effects—trees.

general, we are looking for that gradual increase in color intensity that we see when we look upward from the horizon, and that is what mental ray gives us.

Figure 12.18 shows our pavement, sidewalk, and light pole scene. The fog is gone, we have added some more light poles, and we have moved everything off to the horizon.

In Figure 12.19, we have chosen:

any Main Menu → Render View → Options → Render Settings → Indirect Lighting tab

FIGURE 12.15 Graffiti with tree rendered.

FIGURE 12.16 Transparent graffiti.

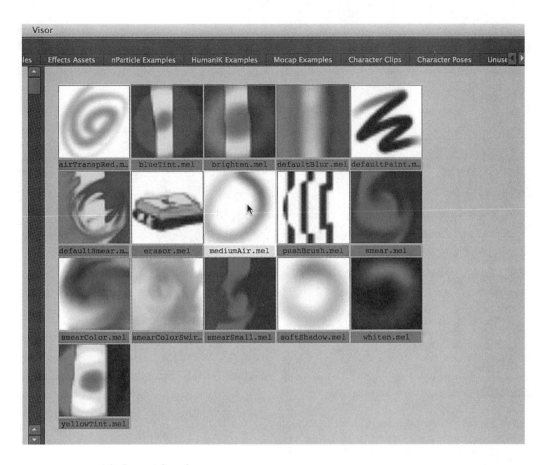

FIGURE 12.17 A lighter airbrush.

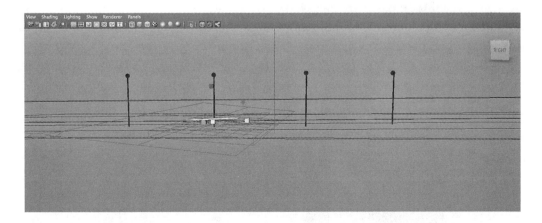

FIGURE 12.18 Pavement and sidewalk scene.

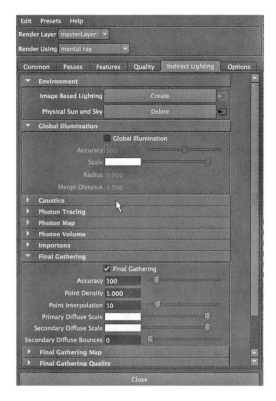

FIGURE 12.19 This shows mental ray settings.

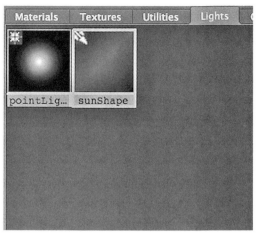

FIGURE 12.20 A directional light.

Then we clicked on Create next to the words Physical Sun and Sky. The sun and sky is created with code and so no matter what direction the rendering camera turns, the sky is still there. We have also checked Final Gathering in the Render Settings, because Autodesk advises that it be used with the Sun and Sky, although in our example, it had no noticeable impact.

Maya has generated a number of objects we can see in the Hypershade. Figure 12.20 shows us a sunShape directional light. (The point light was already in our scene and it has been turned off.) In Figure 12.21, we see what is under the Utilities tab. The bump maps and placeTexture nodes were already present on our scene, but there are three new items. The mia_exposure node throttles the wide spectrum of brightness we would normally get in an outdoor scene, so that it can be displayed effectively on a raster display. The mia_physicalsky and mia_physicalsun nodes give us natural daylight.

Procedural environments are quite powerful. The Sun and Sky shader will carefully mimic the appearance of a sunny sky, with an almost white on the horizon (and sometimes

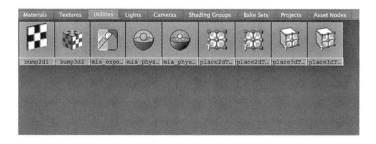

FIGURE 12.21 The Utilities tab.

also a bit brownish), then gradually turning to a cool blue above. The orange and yellow "sunset" sky in Figure 1.2 (see p. CI-2 of Color Insert) was created with software and is another typical sky dome.

The Rendering

Figure 12.22 shows the final result. The foreground is textured with an image of dried dirt. Behind it are the sidewalk and the road. Notice how the sky looks warmer closer to the horizon.

FIGURE 12.22 **(See p. CI-13 of Color Insert)** The street on the horizon.

BAKING A MATERIAL

It can take a lot of render time to calculate the appearance of a material on an object in a Maya scene. But we can have Maya calculate the complex interaction between lights in a scene and a material that has been placed on an object. Then we have Maya "bake" the result into a file texture. This texture will render far more quickly, and so the process of rendering many frames can be reduced to a small fraction of the time that would have been otherwise required.

In Figure 12.23 we see a version of our Moai model. It is an orange color that is partly transparent. It is being rendered with the Maya Software renderer, and the raytracing sliders in the Render Settings have been set to Reflections = 1, Refractions = 6, and Shadows = 2.

Rendering this single-frame image took just over 15 seconds on an iMac with 16 gigabytes of memory, a quad-core i7, and an NVIDIA graphics card with two gigabytes of dedicated memory.

Then, the Moai model in the Main Window and the transparent material in the Hypershade were Shift-selected. As seen in Figure 12.24, we chose:

Hypershade Main Menu → Edit → Convert to File Texture (Maya Software)

The render shown in Figure 2.25 was instantaneous, even with the Moai copied and pasted to make a duplicate.

The downside of this is that the way the material and light on the Moai interact with each other is now frozen. And this specific technique does not work with mental ray.

FIGURE 12.23 **(See p. CI-4 of Color Insert)** A complex material and light effect.

FIGURE 12.24   Baking to a file texture.

A HOMEMADE SKY DOME

The background in the render seen in Figures 12.23 and 12.25 shows a homemade sky dome. The Moai was placed inside a huge polygon sphere, and then a ramp texture was applied to the sphere. The ramp texture is shown in Figure 12.26. By using multiple shades of blue, along with white and tan, we were able to approximate the appearance we would have gotten by using the mental ray Sun and Sky.

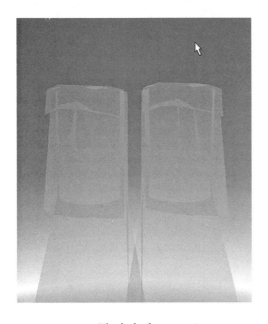

FIGURE 12.25   The baked texture in use.

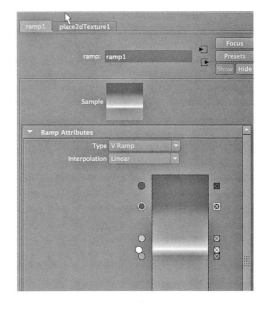

FIGURE 12.26   The sky dome texture.

CHAPTER 13

The UV Texture Editor

W E NOTED IN CHAPTER 5 that before we create a 2D texture we must choose between the settings Normal and Projection. For the examples in this chapter, we focus on textures made by first clicking the Normal radio button on the Create 2D Textures tool in the Hypershade.

THE (U, V) SURFACING PROBLEM

One of the more tedious problems facing the 3D animator consists of putting textures on irregularly shaped surfaces. The crux of the problem is that the (u, v) grid on the surface of a model can stretch over geometry that varies significantly in its relief and, as a result, the density of vertices can also vary dramatically.

Consider the Moai wireframe in Figure 4.66. The model was crafted out of a polygon cylinder by extruding and rotating faces, and by pulling on vertices, edges, and faces. Denser geometry was added to smooth various angles on the model, in particular, along the bridge of the nose.

A checkerboard texture has been made by going to the Hypershade and selecting:

Create → 2D Textures → 2D Projection

Rather than creating a texture immediately, we clicked on the 2D Projection radio button. Then we created a Checker 2D texture. Still in the Hypershade window, we selected the Textures tab on the top right of the window, and clicked on the square icon labeled "projection" that was created when we created the checkerboard texture. This pulls up the attribute editor of the Maya object that controls the laying down of the texture on an object.

We selected the projection tab in the attribute editor, and went to Proj Type and chose cylindrical. The result of applying this texture to the Moai is shown in Figure 13.1. You can see that the squares of white and black have been badly stretched out of shape, and as a result, the material is placed very irregularly.

To help manage the difficult job of laying down a texture, there is a special window in Maya called the UV Editor. To use this capability, however, we need to first select:

Create → 2D Textures → 2D Normal

FIGURE 13.1 Checkerboard Moai.   FIGURE 13.2 File texture on a plane.

A PLANAR PROJECTION OF A NORMAL FILE TEXTURE AND USING THE MOVE AND SCALE TOOLS TO ADJUST IT

Figure 13.2 shows the first cut at putting a file texture on a rectangular polygon plane. This texture was created with the Normal radio button selected. The image has a black background with lettering that has a ramp texture on it. What we see in Figure 13.3 is what appears if we select:

any Main Menu → Window → UV Texture Editor

The white horizontal line shows us where the file texture is being cut off.

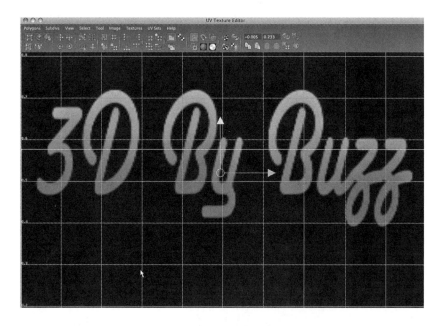

FIGURE 13.3 UV Texture Editor with plane selected.

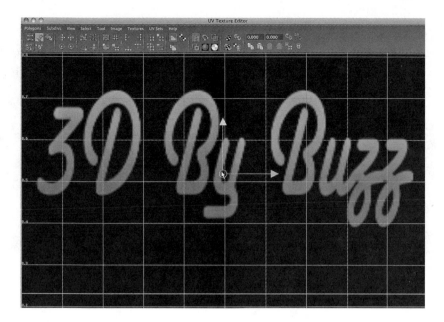

FIGURE 13.4   The UV Texture Editor move tool.

In Figure 13.3, we have chosen:

UV Texture Editor → Tool → Move UV Shell Tool

This is a 2D move tool that works on the (u, v) surface of the plane. In Figure 13.4, we have used this tool to shift the texture upward on the plane. The resulting render is shown in Figure 13.5.

Using the Scale Tool in the UV Editor

In Figure 13.6, we have added a second plane and applied the same texture to it. The resulting render is shown in Figure 13.7. On the top plane, the texture largely misses the mark. In Figure 13.8, we see why this is true: note the position of the white line. In Figure 13.9, we have hit the R key and this has changed the move tool to the scale tool, and again, we see that this tool is a 2D tool. Another way to get to this tool is to choose:

UV Texture Editor → Tool → Smooth UV Tool

(We can go back to the Move tool by hitting the W key.)

In the UV Texture Editor, we rescale the way in which the texture is laid down by using the Scale tool, as seen in Figure 13.9. Notice that we are adjusting the (u, v) grid and not the texture. So, scaling the grid

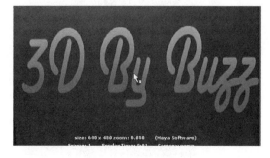

FIGURE 13.5   New render—after move.

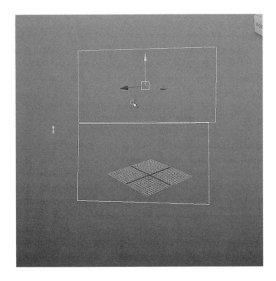

FIGURE 13.6   New plane.

FIGURE 13.7   Texture applied to both planes.

larger will make the texture smaller grained and scaling the grid smaller will make the texture larger grained.

The resulting render is shown in Figure 13.10. Now we see that the bottom plane looks normal, but the top one is compressed from top to bottom. That is a result of using the scale tool on the (u, v) grid and only scaling along the u-axis, and not both the u and the v axes.

Rotating and Flipping

In Figure 13.11, we are looking at the bottom plane. It shows us the result of choosing:

FIGURE 13.8   Top plane.

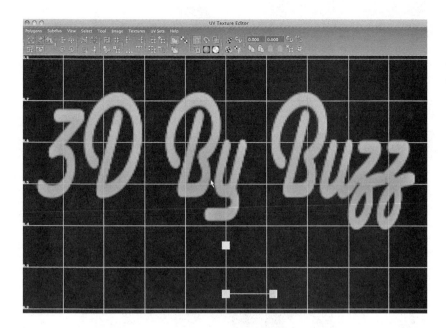

FIGURE 13.9   The UV Texture Editor scale tool.

UV Texture Editor → second row of icons → the red clockwise circular arrow at the left

Note that we have clicked on it twice, each time rotating the texture 45 degrees. It is not shown in the figure, but we have also used the Scale tool to widen the texture from left to right, so that the two horizontal lines in Figure 13.11 do not lie across the writing. The resulting render is shown in Figure 13.12. You can see that the lettering is rotated 90 degrees and it is compressed from top to bottom because we stretched the (u, v) grid.

In Figure 13.13, we have gone back to the scene as shown in Figure 13.11 and chosen:

UV Texture Editor → top row of icons → the fourth from the left

After using this "flip" tool, the resulting render is shown in Figure 13.14.

In Figure 13.15, we are manipulating the Stretch tool (it is selected in the upper left of the Window) and the result is seen in Figure 13.16.

A CLOSER LOOK AT THE UV EDITOR: CREATING AND MANIPULATING UV MAPS

Now, we will look at a tool that can be used to make small-scale changes to the layout of a texture.

A Doorknob's (u, v) Texture Mapping

Figure 13.17 is a composite image. The left part shows how we made a file texture for a doorknob. We used the 2D Normal setting. On the right of

FIGURE 13.10   Render—after scaling.

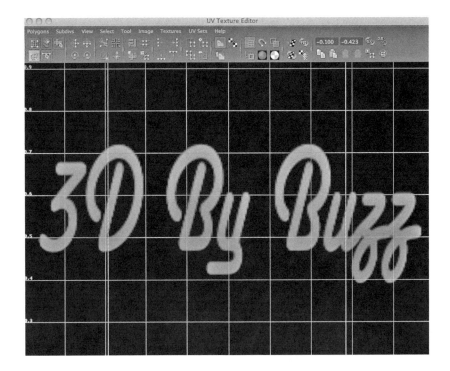

FIGURE 13.11   Two rotations.

FIGURE 13.12   Render—after rotating.

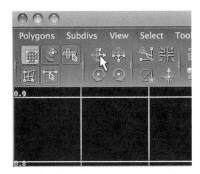

FIGURE 13.13   The UV Texture Editor flip tool.

FIGURE 13.14   Result of a flip.

FIGURE 13.15   UV Texture Editor stretch tool.

FIGURE 13.16   Render—after stretch.

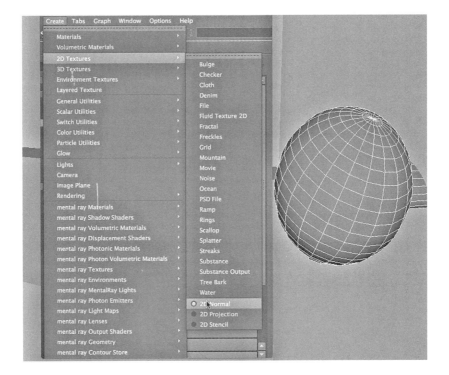

FIGURE 13.17   Doorknob.

Figure 13.17 is the knob of the left door from our closet model. Figure 13.18 shows us the image that is being used as a texture for our knob. Again, this is a 2D normal texture. Our goal is to use this texture to give the knob a faded, rusty look. (The coloring of the texture can be seen in Figure 13.27 in the Color Insert on p. CI-15.)

We go to:

Polygons Main Menu → Create UVs

We find a useful set of menu choices under the Create UVs dropdown. They are Planar, Cylindrical, Spherical, and Automatic. They can be used to quickly (and often dramatically) recast the layout of the (u, v) grid. We will not select any of them just yet. In Figure 13.19, we have selected the knob in the Main Window and opened the UV Editor. We can now see the default (u, v) layout that was created when we assigned the file texture to our knob. It is shown in Figure 13.20.

In Figures 13.21 and 13.22, we see what happens if we choose the Automatic setting. The (u, v) mapping has been radically changed.

We go to the Main Window, select the knob, and choose Face mode with a right click, and then swipe some faces of the knob. The part of the (u, v) layout that covers those faces is shown in the UV Texture Editor. We can also eyeball the relationship between the newly remapped (u, v) grid and the rendered model by comparing Figures 13.22 and 13.23. We see where the mostly solid blue parts of the texture are laid down on the knob. Likewise, we see where the mostly white parts of the texture are laid down.

FIGURE 13.18 Doorknob image.

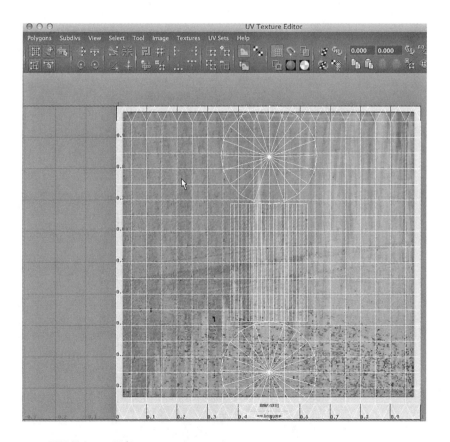

FIGURE 13.19 UV Texture Editor.

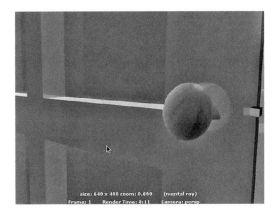

FIGURE 13.20 **(See p. CI-15 of Color Insert)** Doorknob render with blue and white texture.

In Figure 13.24, we try the cylindrical mapping. The renderings in Figures 13.23 and 13.25 do not look very good. Rather than the texture resembling worn blue paint, the knob looks more like someone has covered it with plastic and some of it has peeled off. There is too much of a sharp contrast between the solid blue of the knob and the solid white.

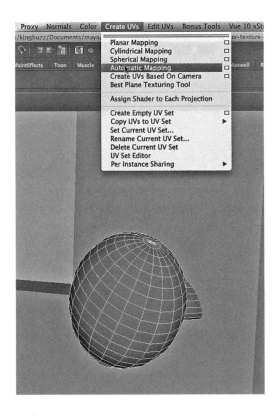

FIGURE 13.21 Automatic Mapping.

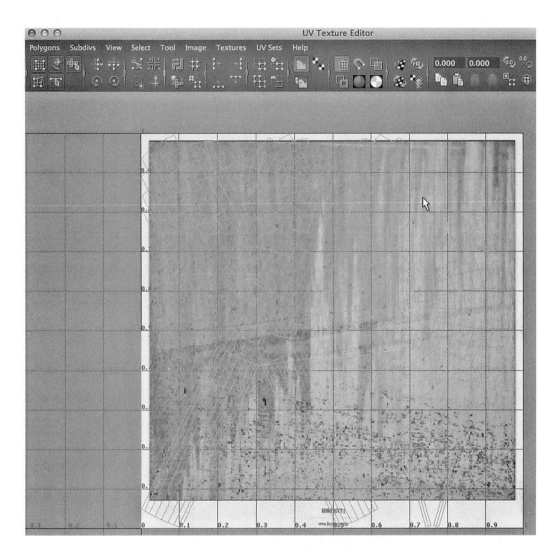

FIGURE 13.22   UV Texture Editor.

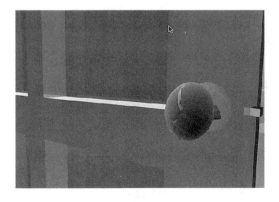

FIGURE 13.23   Render—after mapping.

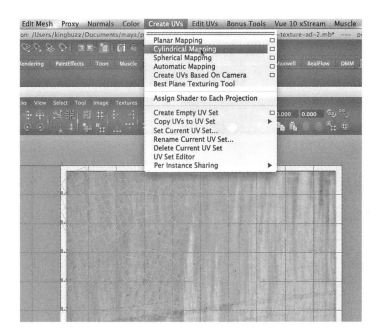

FIGURE 13.24   Cylindrical Mapping.

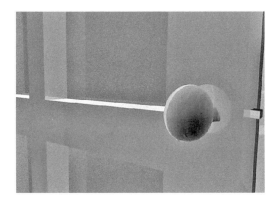

FIGURE 13.25   **(See p. CI-15 of Color Insert)** Doorknob render after Cylindrical Mapping.

The UV Smudge Tool

We will now go back to the default layout, as seen in Figure 13.26, and work from there. We will go to the UV Texture Editor and choose:

Tool → UV Smudge Tool

We want to remove some of the sharp lines that we see in the rendering in Figure 13.20 to give the effect of worn paint. We also want to put a little of the rust in the texture on the knob. We right click in the UV Editor, as seen in Figure 13.27, and use the Smudge Tool to move some vertices around, thereby breaking up those sharp lines. The fairly subtle result is shown in Figure 13.28. You be the judge.

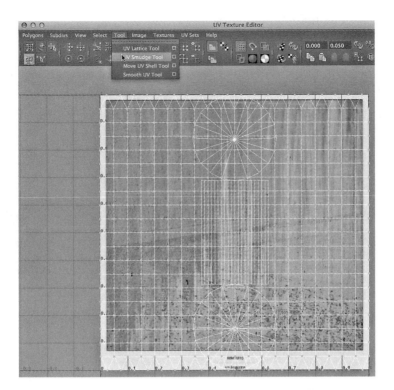

FIGURE 13.26   The UV Texture Editor smudge tool.

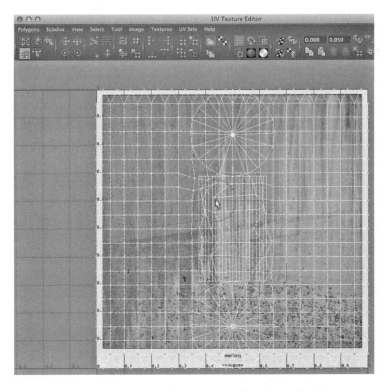

FIGURE 13.27   **(See p. CI-15 of Color Insert)** UV texture being smudged.

FIGURE 13.28 **(See p. CI-15 of Color Insert)** A final doorknob with new texture mapping.

FIGURE 13.29 Maya's checkerboard.

A COMPARISON OF DIFFERENT UV EDITOR MAPPINGS

We are going to take a look at two different textures and compare their appearance on the Moai after applying various mappings in the UV Texture Editor.

In Figure 13.29, we see the default mapping of the checkerboard on our Moai. This is what we get if we simply open the model with Maya and then open the UV Texture Editor. The resulting render is shown in Figure 13.30.

Compared to a Projection texture, the default layout of a Normal 2D texture has fewer repetitions of the given texture on the surface of the object. This is why the checkerboard in Figure 13.30 is so large. This might seem arbitrary, but it does serve to alert us in case we created a Normal texture, but intended it to be a Projection texture (or vice versa).

Figure 13.31 shows the result if we go to Create UVs and choose the automatic mapping, and the companion render is shown in Figure 13.32. We see in Figure 13.31 that we can recognize pieces of the Moai. In particular, the top to bottom length of the right side, and the top to bottom length of the left side of the Moai can be seen in the bottom half in the center of Figure 13.31.

Figures 13.33 and 13.34 show the cylindrical UV mapping, along with its rendering. The checkerboard squares are stretched out and they vary in size, with the ones on the nose bigger and the ones along the forehead smaller. If we look at the top left of Figure 13.33, we see why: the (u, v) grid for the nose is packed very tightly.

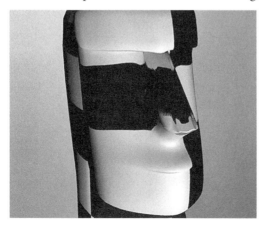

FIGURE 13.30 Moai with checkerboard.

FIGURE 13.31   The automatic mapping.   FIGURE 13.32   Render—after automatic mapping.

Figures 13.35 and 13.36 show the cylindrical mapping, but after using the UV Editor (and hitting R to get the Scale tool) and pulling the grid tighter. The resulting render, in Figure 13.36, has more even-sided checkerboard tiles.

There are still many problems in Figure 13.36. The nose has a black cube that is stretched out top to bottom, and on the right top of the face are some truncated squares. We should not be surprised at the uneven nature of the checkerboard, because if we look at Figure 13.35, we see that the (u, v) grid is far from being homogeneous in its granularity. But this second cylindrical mapping is the best. This makes sense, as our Moai started out as a cylinder. Figure 13.37 is a closeup of the neck of the Moai. We see the wraparound point, where the checkerboard does not line up properly.

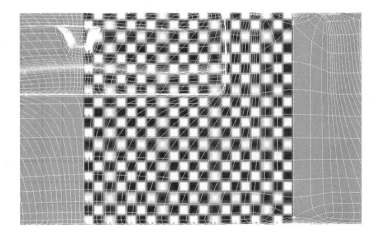

FIGURE 13.33   Cylindrical mapping.

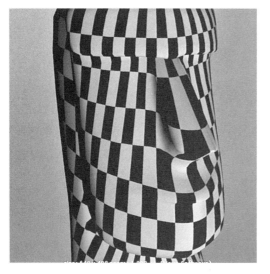

FIGURE 13.34 Render—after cylindrical mapping.

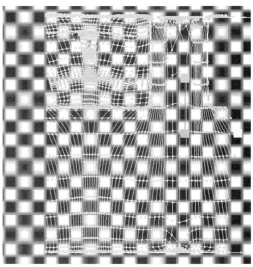

FIGURE 13.35 Rescaled cylindrical mapping.

Overall, we might want to apply our texture with a cylindrical mapping but to smaller pieces of the Moai, perhaps doing the neck, face, and torso separately. We also need to be careful about exposing the seam when we animate and render our model.

Next, we create a file texture and choose a photograph of a granite rock. We apply it to the Moai. We will look at two closeups of the left side of its face. Figure 13.38 shows the cylindrical mapping, and Figure 13.39 shows the automatic mapping. This time, the automatic mapping is better by far. The cylindrical mapping stretched out parts of the texture. The automatic mapping kept the granularity more uniform in size and shape.

FIGURE 13.36 Rescaled cylindrical render.

FIGURE 13.37 Neck closeup.

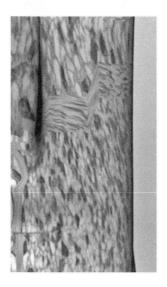 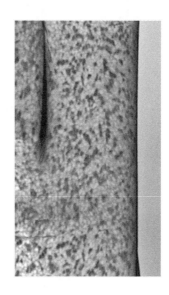

FIGURE 13.38 Rock texture after cylindrical mapping.

FIGURE 13.39 Rock texture after automatic mapping.

There is an overriding point here. If we start out with a geometric primitive, in this case a polygon cylinder, our job of cleaning up the (u, v) grid so that we get an even texture is going to be harder if the primitive has been dramatically altered during the modeling process. The original cylinder, especially on the face of the Moai, has been pushed and pulled so much that the (u, v) grid has been badly distorted, giving us a challenging texture job.

CHAPTER 14

Multi-App Maya Workflow, Managing Complex Scenes, and Sculpting Applications

THERE HAS BEEN A lot of criticism in recent years of "feature creep" in media applications, where more and more capabilities get shoved into an application, and at some point people begin to notice that the learning curve for the novice is extremely steep. This has led to a generation of minimalistic and specialized applications that provide standalone support for modeling (often only polygon modeling), dynamics, and materials/rendering.

While this may seem like a good idea, there can be significant complications, as it is often difficult to set up a functioning multi-app workflow because of the incompatibilities of data formats across applications. Import/export formats are numerous and highly problematic.

This is a strong argument in favor of using Maya exclusively, so we don't have to import models into other applications to put materials on them, and then animate and render them. As an alternative, a number of plug-ins have been crafted by various vendors of alternative applications. These plug-ins support connections between Maya and these applications. They do not provide generic, application-independent import/export formats. Clearly, this approach does not scale and leads to a complex world of one-to-one solutions.

In this chapter, we take a quick look at workflow between Maya and other applications, and at Maya plug-ins.

We are not talking about image, audio, or video editing applications, as they do not have to import or export models or scenes. These applications generally do not present complex inter-application workflow problems.

THE INTER-APP WORKFLOW DILEMMA

There are a small set of somewhat widely used data format standards. COLLADA, which stands for Collaborative Design Activity (and is an XML-based exchange format), and FBX, a proprietary format owned by Autodesk, provide some generic interoperability. Both of these standards focus on the goal of moving entire models or scenes, complete with geometry, materials, and animation. But using these formats in a workflow is tricky at best; often it is highly unpredictable. An older format that is good for moving polygon wireframes around is OBJ; because of its low level nature, it tends to work quite well, and so it is widely used.

Plug-Ins That Work Pretty Well

We are going to assume here that Maya is the "home" application, the place where the animator is putting together all the pieces of a scene. Outside applications will be used either as a source of input to Maya, or only used in the later stages of the animation process, notably for rendering. There are a handful of plug-ins that I have found to be very useful and reasonably stable.

There are two places where plug-ins generally get installed in the Maya interface. Most of them appear as new tabs on the Shelf. In Figure 14.1, we see several of these plug-in tabs. We'll take a quick look at a few of them. There is also a plug-in in Figure 14.1 that installs directly into the Main Menu; it is called Vue xStream and we'll look at it, too.

Regardless of how they appear in the Maya interface, you usually have to go to the Maya plug-ins window and activate them (go to Window, select Settings/Preferences, and then Plug-in Manager); they generally do not activate by default.

Specialized Modeling: Bipeds

One of the most common reasons for using a Maya plug-in is to leverage the specialized modeling capabilities of other applications. If what you want is a complete biped built reasonably quickly, Poser is an application you might consider. Figure 14.2 is a composite image showing the Maya interface on the right and part of the Poser interface on the left. You can import a Poser model into Maya, and then whenever you want, you can go back

FIGURE 14.1   Plug-ins in tabs.

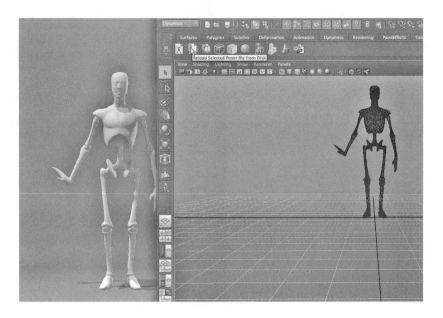

FIGURE 14.2   Poser plug-ins.

to Poser to change the model. Then you click on the second icon from the left on the Poser shelf in Maya—and bingo, the biped inside Maya is automatically updated.

The Poser plug-ins do not come with Poser unless you buy Poser "Pro," which includes plug-ins for several applications, including Maya. It is a shame that as of this writing, there is no Daz Studio plug-in for Maya, as their human figures are superior to those found in Poser. (I have tried using FBX as an export out of Daz Studio and an import into Maya, but my results have been at best very mixed.)

Exterior Environments: Vue and Terragen

Figure 14.3 is another composite image; it shows the Maya interface on the right and Vue xStream on the right. In the upper right, you can see the dropdowns installed by the

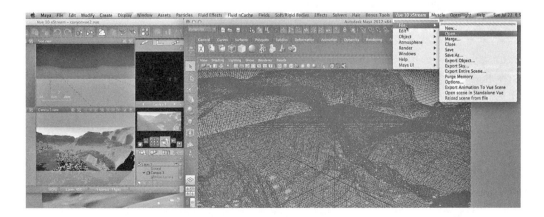

FIGURE 14.3   Vue plug-ins.

FIGURE 14.4   Terragen interface.

Vue plug-in. Vue installs the plug-in automatically if you happen to have Maya installed before you install Vue. Vue has been aggressive about building plug-ins for multiple modeling and animation applications, and so it is fairly easy to work into almost any workflow.

Vue can be used to make truly stunning environments. Figure 14.3 shows a Vue scene that we looked at previously; it was built by D&D Creations. One complication with Vue environments is that they are often extremely large in terms of polygon counts; this and the fact that outdoor lighting can be complex and can cause rendering times to skyrocket. (E-on software sells Vue.)

Terragen by Planetside can be used to generate very realistic terrain, atmospheres, and water effects. It is surprisingly easy to use. You can download a trial version from their site. The interface appears in Figure 14.4. Along the top are the items that can be created with this application and inserted into a 3D scene. They include terrain, shaders, water, atmosphere, lighting, and cameras. The left lower window, Figure 14.5, shows how terrain can be generated with Terragen.

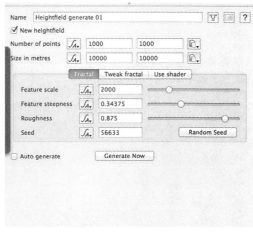

FIGURE 14.5   Generating a height field.

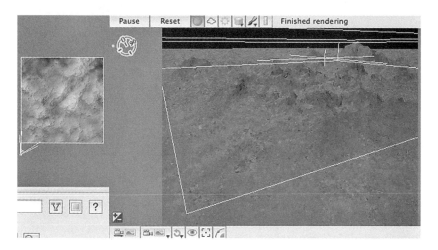

FIGURE 14.6   Previewing the terrain.

Hitting the Generate Now button will create, in a semirandom fashion, a polygon mesh terrain based on the parameters set in this window. Figure 14.6 is a closeup of the upper-right-hand section of the Main Window. This is where you can preview your generated terrain. The rendered scene with the atmosphere and water created but without the terrain being generated is shown in Figure 14.7. After hitting the Generate button and rerendering the scene, it appears as shown in Figure 14.8.

Terragen's native format is a form of "heightfield," a format used by various applications to specify rugged terrain. Usually, these are raster images (grids of pixels), where the color of the pixel controls the height of the terrain at a given point. Often these are grayscale images, where black is the largest depression that can be specified, and white is

FIGURE 14.7   Atmosphere and water.

FIGURE 14.8 **(See p. CI-13 of Color Insert)** Generated terrain from Terragen.

the highest elevation that can be specified; shades of gray represent heights between the high and low value.

As of this writing, there is no Terragen plug-in for Maya. But geometry can be exported from Terragen and then used in an application like Maya. The choices include exporting as FBX or OBJ. It is a bit convoluted to export FBX out of Terragen.

Specialized Modeling: Sculpting with ZBrush

Figure 14.9 is yet another composite image; this one shows ZBrush on the left and Maya on the right. It installs as a tabbed shelf, with only one icon called GoZ. The ZBrush team (the company is called Pixologic) has also been aggressive about making their application interoperate with other applications via their "GoZ" series of plug-ins.

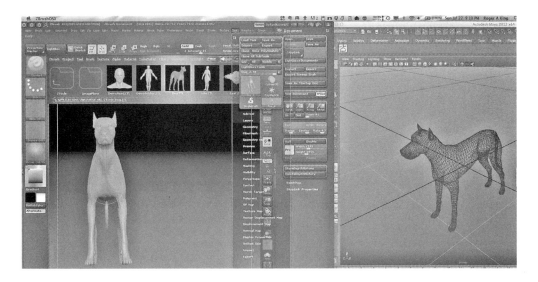

FIGURE 14.9 ZBrush plug-ins.

FIGURE 14.10   Maxwell plug-in.

ZBrush is a modeling application that uses a sculpting paradigm. Many artists find that ZBrush feels more intuitive and that it gives the modeler a tactile sense of fluidly forming a model. It does tend to create models with a lot of polygons, but this issue can be addressed when a model is imported into Maya. In Figure 14.9, we see one of the canned starter objects that comes with ZBrush, a dog.

Stand-Alone Renderers: Maxwell, Octane, and Indigo

The world of renderers has been growing quickly and two that I have used are Maxwell and Indigo. Both are quite powerful and they come with their own materials and lights capabilities. Figure 14.10 shows a quick-render capability that comes with the Maxwell renderer; it is very useful for testing purposes. (We are using the ZBrush dog in the figure.) The shelf that is installed with the Maxwell plug-in is extensive and tightly integrates Maxwell with Maya.

Octane, sold by Otoy, is a CUDA compliant renderer. If you have a compatible graphics card, Octane is quite fast and creates beautiful renderings.

Translating Materials: The Rendering Plug-In's Main Job

There is a tight interrelationship between the materials and textures provided by a program like Maya and the calculations that the renderer performs to see how a surface interacts with light at render time. Thus, second-party renderers typically depend on plug-ins whose main job is to translate one set of materials into a set of materials that are native to the renderer. There is a similar need to translate lights so that they are recognized by the renderer.

SCULPTING APPLICATIONS AND SCULPTING WITH MAYA

We have already looked at using the Sculpt Geometry tool in Maya. It is a key tool for animators who want to have that sense of crafting an object in a direct, hands-on fashion, almost like working with clay.

ZBrush and Mudbox

More animators are moving toward ZBrush by Pixologic and Mudbox by Autodesk, both of which offer an organic sculpting capability for crafting organic models. Many animators are creating their characters in one of these applications and then importing them into Maya for refining, applying materials, and then animating.

Autodesk has embedded in Mudbox and Maya a workflow that allows the modeler to move smoothly in both directions between the two applications, and no plug-ins are necessary.

Reducing Meshes in Maya

Figure 14.11 shows a stock model that comes with Mudbox. We have smoothed it to get a more dense mesh. In Figure 14.11, we see the horse being exported out of Mudbox and into Maya. Figure 14.12 shows the mesh after importing it.

Figure 14.13 shows the Reduce Mesh tool in Maya, found by choosing:

Polygons Main Menu → Mesh → Reduce

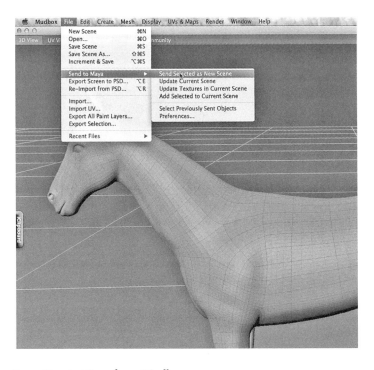

FIGURE 14.11 Exporting to Maya from Mudbox.

This is an important tool. The problem is that sculpting applications like Mudbox and ZBrush make it all too easy to create a beautiful and smooth—but highly dense—mesh. Thus, when we get the horse into Maya, we might find that it takes a lot of calculations for Maya to simulate the movement of light as it bounces off all those polygons, creating long render times.

In Figure 14.14, we see the settings of the Reduce tool. The result of applying the tool is shown in Figure 14.15. After another round of reducing, the result is shown in Figure 14.16. The corresponding rendering is seen in Figure 14.17. Notice that the Reduce tool does a good job of maintaining detail where it is needed and removing detail where fewer vertices/edges/ faces are needed. Figure 14.18 is another rendering, this one corresponding to the original Maya mesh shown in Figure 14.12. It is indeed smoother but perhaps not as smooth as we might have expected. The mesh of Figure 14.16 will be easier to manipulate by working with Maya's vertex/edge/face mesh tools. We can smooth the horse later, if we want.

A reduce polygons tool has to be used carefully, however. After using a reduce tool, it is a good idea to look at the areas of particularly dense geometry on the model to see if critical aspects of the model have been damaged. For example, in Figure 14.15, there are concentric circles around the eyes of the horse; they are used to gracefully create the detailed geometry surrounding the eyeballs. If you look at Figure 14.16, that geometry has been damaged. Most likely we do not want to reduce the model this aggressively.

FIGURE 14.12   Mudbox mesh in Maya.tif.

Maya's Soft Modification Tool

Although the Sculpt Geometry tool, which uses a painting metaphor and can be used with polygon and NURBS models, is very popular, there is another tool in Maya that can be used in a similar way. It shares something with the Sculpt Geometry tool and with another tool that we have looked at earlier, the Soft-Select setting on the Move tool. The Soft Modification tool can

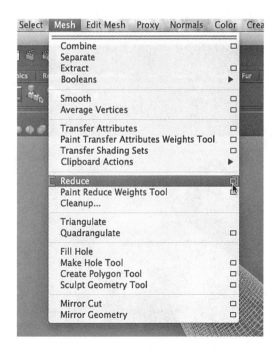

FIGURE 14.13   The Reduce mesh tool.

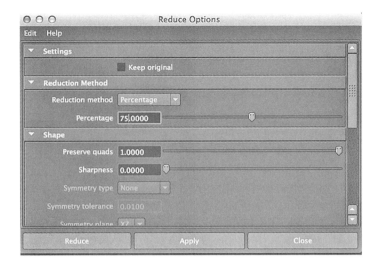

FIGURE 14.14   Reduce settings.

FIGURE 14.15   First reduction.

FIGURE 14.16   Second reduction.

FIGURE 14.17   Reduced horse.

FIGURE 14.18   Dense mesh rendered.

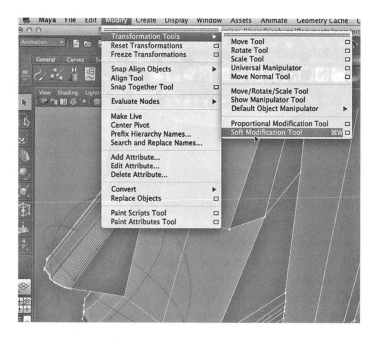

FIGURE 14.19   The Soft Modification tool.

be carefully tuned to have a dropoff effect on geometry surrounding the point of application of the tool.

Figure 14.19 shows how the Soft Modification Tool can be selected:

any Main Menu → Modify → Transformation Tools → Soft Modification Tool

Its settings are shown in Figure 14.20. Note that the top slider controls the falloff radius.

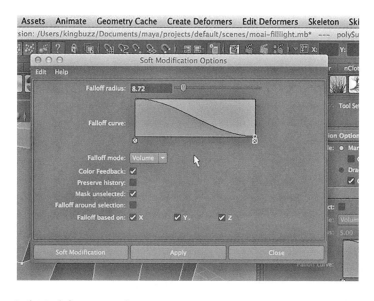

FIGURE 14.20   Soft Modification tool settings.

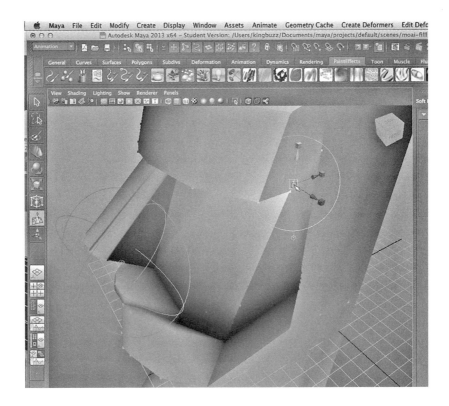

FIGURE 14.21   Using the Soft Modification tool.

In Figure 14.21, we see what happens when we right click, go into Object mode, and select our Moai model. It does the same thing that the Soft Select tool does; it uses a rainbow of colors to tell us how far outward the tool will have an effect. The tool needs to have a very low setting on the slider in order to make modifications localized.

CHAPTER 15

Advanced Light and Materials Properties and Effects

I**N THIS CHAPTER WE** look at some advanced topics involving light and materials.

AMBIENT OCCLUSION

Ambient occlusion refers to the ability to control the spread of ambient light. In English, to occlude something is to block it. So, by controlling ambient occlusion we can increase or decrease the spread of ambient light. If we block it more, small areas in a render will turn dark. If we let ambient light spread, we will wash out areas that otherwise might have been in shadow.

Ambient occlusion in Maya is used to keep ambient (widely dispersed) light from washing out small areas. We might use ambient occlusion to add shadows to small areas in order to draw out the small-grained relief on the surface of a model.

Figure 15.1 contains two copies of the Mudbox default horse. They have a reflective mia_material on them, as seen in Figure 15.2. A background plane with a light Blinn on it has been added. There are three lights in the scene, two ambient lights and a spotlight; see Figure 15.3. Note that we have not checked off the Use Ambient Occlusion option in the attribute box of the material; see Figure 15.4. See the render in Figure 15.5, or, for a better view of the horse renderings, see the color figures on: http://3DbyBuzz.com.

Now, we want to start controlling the effects of ambient light. There is a group of attributes of the mental ray mia_material that we can set by checking the Use Ambient Occlusion box.

In Figure 15.6, we have checked this box. We are going to focus on two attributes as we strive to gain control of ambient light. First, we change the color of the light to white, as seen in Figure 15.6. The result is seen in the render in Figure 15.7.

FIGURE 15.1   Horses.

FIGURE 15.2   Mia_material blue.

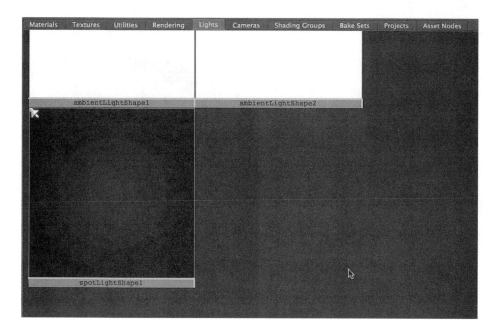

FIGURE 15.3   Two ambient lights and a spotlight.

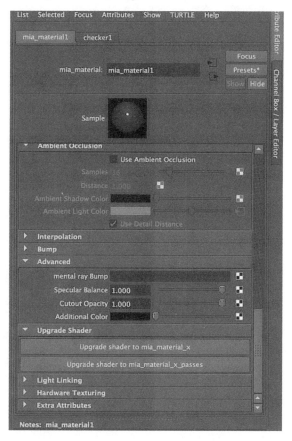

FIGURE 15.4   Ambient occlusion not checked.

FIGURE 15.5   Default render of horses.

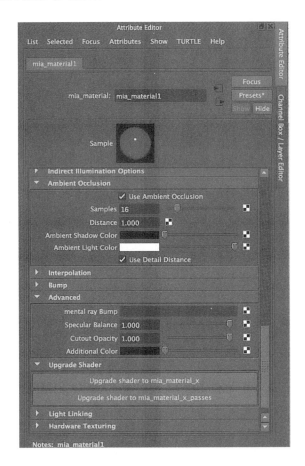

FIGURE 15.6   Ambient occlusion and white light.

FIGURE 15.7   Render of AO and white light.

Now, in Figure 15.8, we have changed the light color to a gray. We get the render seen in Figure 15.9. This is a better balance, as we can now more easily see the variations in the color of the horses; they have a deeper 3D appearance.

Then we change the Distance to 100 and get the render in Figure 15.10. This is probably the best render yet, as it draws out the more shadowed parts of the horses while maintaining the overall contrast.

So, what have we done?

First, we probably want a gray light, so we don't get a stark, washed out look.

What about the Distance attribute? It controls how far the effects of ambient occlusion spread from a given point. A larger number makes things darker and a smaller number makes them brighter. Why? Because as we increase the Distance, we are increasing the distance over which we limit the movement of ambient light.

Just to point out the importance of choosing a color for the light in the scene, in Figure 15.11, we have replaced the Ambient Light Color by clicking on the small checkerboard at the right of the slider and then choosing the checkerboard texture in the Hypershade. So, parts of the ambient light have been turned to black, while others are as bright as the horses in Figure 15.7.

GLOBAL ILLUMINATION AND FINAL GATHERING

We have looked at depth map versus raytraced shadows as well. We will review Global Illumination and Global Illumination and Final Gathering and then introduce a couple of new things: Caustics and Irradiance. Our goal is to consider a few different ways of adding light effects to a scene. We will be using the mental ray renderer.

As a reminder, Final Gathering, which is an option you can set in the mental ray renderer, adds some extra computations to the raytracer, and in doing so, fills in small dark

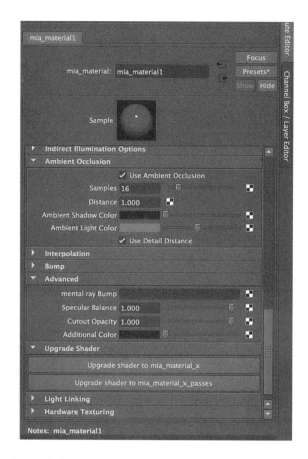

FIGURE 15.8 AO with gray light.

FIGURE 15.9 Using a small Distance setting.

FIGURE 15.10   Using a larger Distance value.

FIGURE 15.11   Render of AO and checkerboard light.

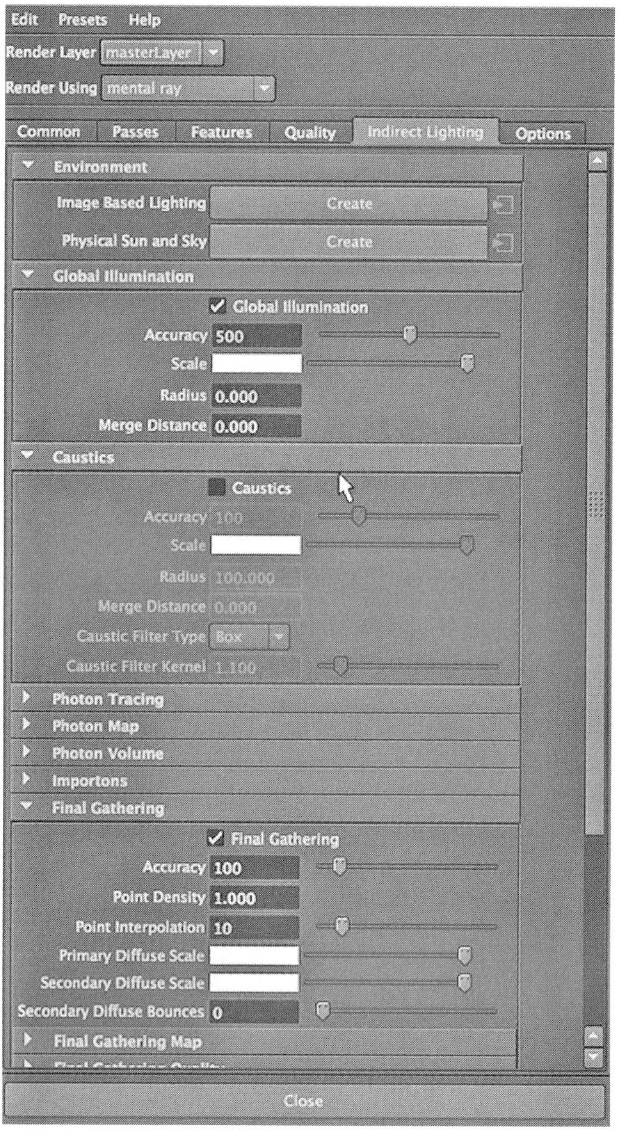

FIGURE 15.12   Global Illumination and Final Gathering.

areas. These often occur when one part of a model is casting a shadow on itself. By using Final Gathering, we put some extra rays in those little spots.

We go to:

any Main Menu → Window → Rendering Editors → Render View

We select mental ray, and then go to the Indirect Lighting tab and choose Global Illumination (see Figure 15.12). We will also turn on Final Gathering, which does a similar job but is less effective.

Figure 15.13 shows the scene without Global Illumination and Final Gathering. Notice the area around the brass bolt. Look at the same area in Figure 15.14, rendered with Global Illumination and Final Gathering.

CAUSTICS

Caustics are used to create the harsh light reflections and refractions we often get when light hits a glass object. We will manipulate both the lights in a scene and the mental ray settings to create Caustics.

FIGURE 15.13   Render without GI and FG.

We have a NURBS curve that has been revolved to make a dish. A mental ray mia_material with a GlassThin preset has been created (see Figure 15.15) and applied to the dish (see Figure 15.16).

The scene without Caustics is shown in Figure 15.17. Figure 15.18 shows turning on Caustics in the mental ray Render Settings. In Figure 15.19, we turn on photon emitting in the attributes of the dominant light in the scene, which happens to be a spotlight with a wide cone. The other light in the scene is also a spotlight with a wide cone, but its intensity is much lower.

FIGURE 15.14   Render with GI and FG.

We render the scene again, and the result is shown in Figure 15.20.

LIGHT EMITTING MATERIALS: IRRADIANCE

First, we choose a highly reflective material from the mental ray list of materials (see Figure 15.21). We apply this material to the dish, as seen in Figure 15.22.

Now, we turn down the Intensity attributes of our two spotlights and render. The result is shown in Figure 15.23. There is very little light in the scene. Now, we turn up the irradiance of the material, as shown in Figure 15.24. The result can be seen in Figure 15.25. We have an otherworldly goblet.

COLORING MENTAL RAY'S GLASS MATERIAL

One way to color a surface with a transparent material on it is by adding color to the light that refracts through that material. First, we go to:

any Main menu → Window → Rendering Editors → Hypershade

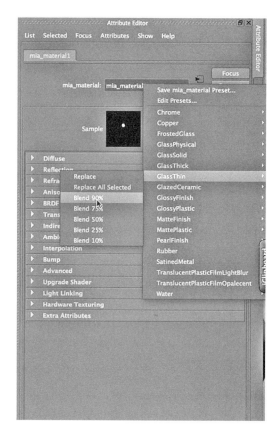

FIGURE 15.15 The glass mia_material.

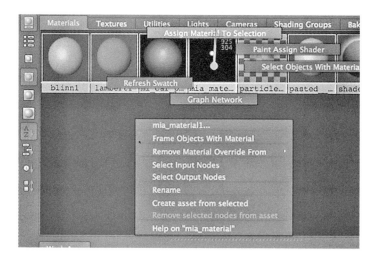

FIGURE 15.16 Assigning glass material.

FIGURE 15.17 **(See p. CI-16 of Color Insert)** Render without Caustics.

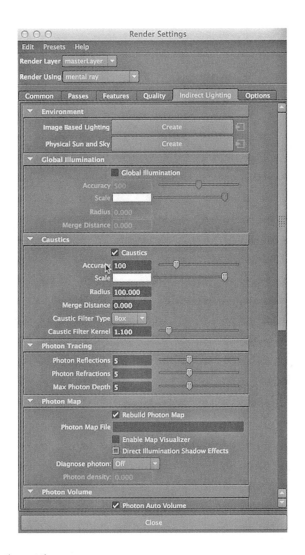

FIGURE 15.18 Caustics settings.

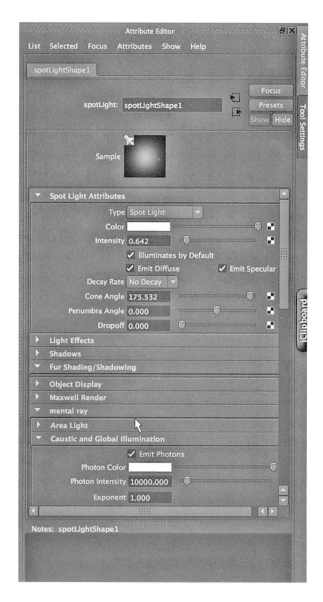

FIGURE 15.19　Emit photon settings.

We go to the list below the words "mental ray" in the Hypershade and create an instance of mia_material, as we have done before (see Figure 15.26). In Figure 15.27, we go to the Main Window, choose the preset GlassThin for our material, and select Replace. Then, in Figure 15.28, we click on the Refraction color and set it to a dark yellow. We Shift-select the four panes on our right-hand door, go to the Hypershade, and then right click on the material and hit Assign Material to Selection.

We render with the mental ray renderer, with the result shown in Figure 15.29.

FIGURE 15.20 **(See p. CI-16 of Color Insert)** Render with Caustics.

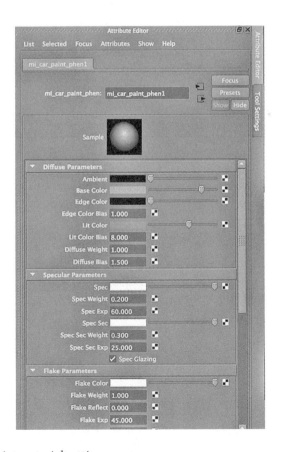

FIGURE 15.21 Mia paint material settings.

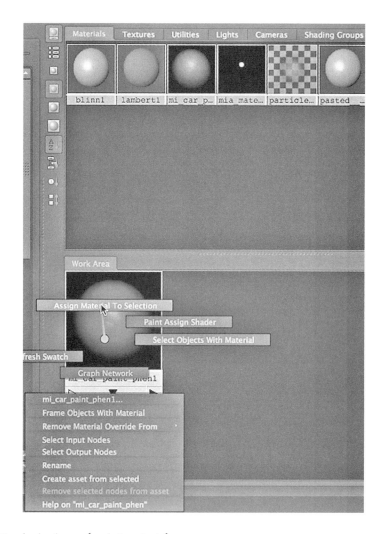

FIGURE 15.22 Assigning red paint material.

FIGURE 15.23 A dim result.

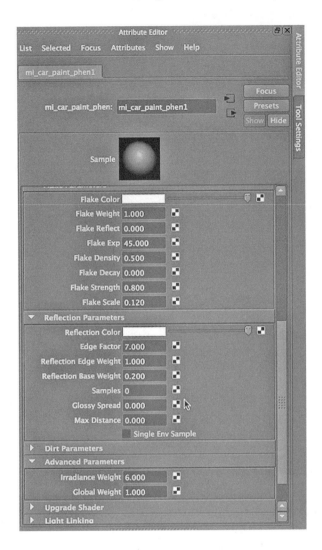

FIGURE 15.24   Increasing irradiance.

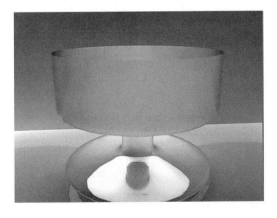

FIGURE 15.25   **(See p. CI-16 of Color Insert)** Irradiance glow.

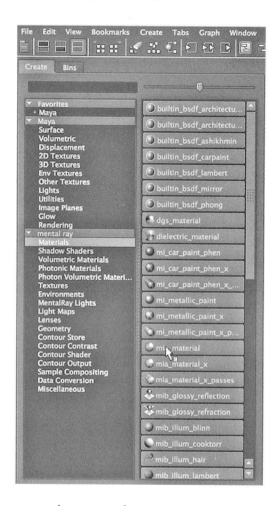

FIGURE 15.26 This shows mental ray materials.

COLORING A MATERIAL WITH LIGHTS

We will color a bowl by using the lights that are shining on it. Figure 15.30 shows the mental ray material attributes; we are using one of the metallic paint materials. The colors of the material are all set to white.

There are two spotlights shining on the bowl. They are between the bowl and the viewer, pointing directly at the bowl. The spotlight attributes are shown in Figures 15.31 and 15.32. We are using two different yellowish colors.

The rendering is shown in Figure 15.33. (Note that the brown background in the Color Insert on p. CI-16 for Figure 15.33 is not influencing the color of the bowl.)

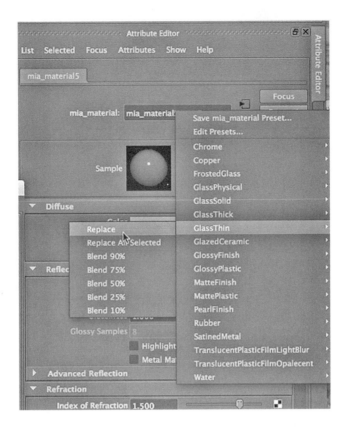

FIGURE 15.27 Thin glass settings.

USING ANISOTROPY WITH MENTAL RAY TO CONTROL
THE TRANSPARENCY OF FROSTED GLASS

We will focus on one particular setting for the frosted glass on the double doors, Anisotropy. Anisotropy is an attribute that can be set in the mia_material attribute box. This controls highlights that run across the scene in multiple directions.

In Figure 15.34, we see the Anisotropy settings for the mia_material that makes up the frosted glass of our doors.

Figure 15.35 shows a render resulting from an Anisotropy setting of 1, meaning that the left-right and up-down values of the highlights are equal, or more precisely, that the highlights are even in all directions. Thus, the glass doors blur the white shelves behind them.

In Figure 15.36, the setting is 10, creating a highlight that is not equal in all directions. In particular, the top-down highlights are softer than the left-right highlights. The effect is to undo some of the frosted effect of the glass, as the highlights do not blur the shelves as much. You can think of it this way: In order for the horizontal shelves to be distorted

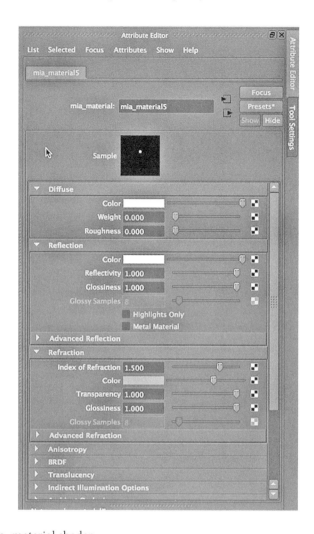

FIGURE 15.28   Mia_material shader.

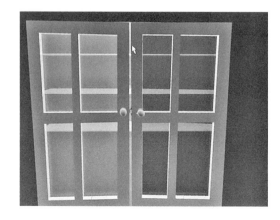

FIGURE 15.29   **(See p. CI-11 of Color Insert)** Rendering the colored glass.

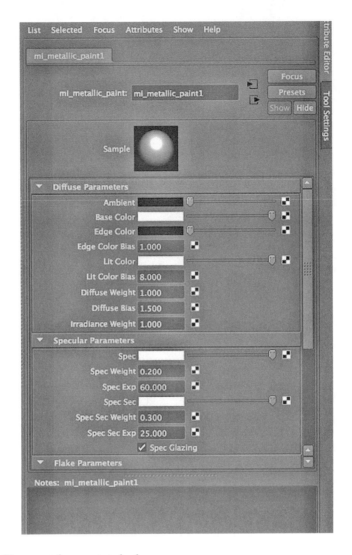

FIGURE 15.30   The mental ray paint shader.

to the point of not being easily visible, the white coloring of the shelves needs to be moved upward and downward.

If we crank it up even more, we see in Figure 15.37, that the highlights are very weak in the top-down direction (compared to the left-right direction). So there is now virtually no frosted glass effect.

In Figure 15.38, we see what happens if you set the number to .1. Now, the highlights are greater up-down than they are right-left, and the doors are distorted again. (See p. C-11 of the Color Insert for Figure 15.38 for various Anisotropy settings.)

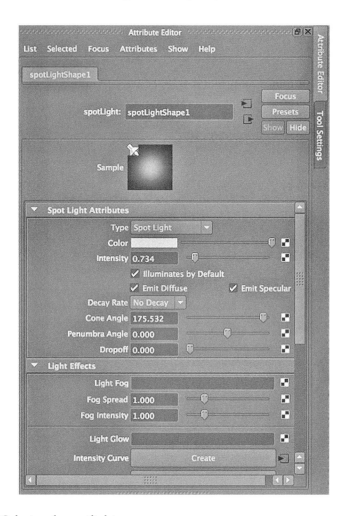

FIGURE 15.31   Coloring the spotlight.

USING THE PENUMBRA AND DROPOFF SETTINGS ON A MAYA SPOTLIGHT

For the most part, we have focused on Cone Angle and Intensity as the key attributes of a spotlight. Here, we will look at two other attributes: Penumbra and Dropoff.

The lights in the scene are shown in Figure 15.39. There are two soft point lights inside the closet, as well as a spotlight positioned outside the closet and pointing directly at it. The spotlight has a cone angle of 94. The Attribute Editor that pops up if we select the spotlight in the Main Window and then hit a Control+A once or twice is seen in Figure 15.40.

The penumbra is the part of a shadow where some light makes it past whatever is blocking light and casting a shadow. It is a softer, gray shadow around the edges. We see in Figure 15.41 that a larger penumbra setting gives us a more gradual edge to the spotlight. And in Figure 15.42, a penumbra of 0 creates a harsh edge to the light. Without a penumbra, there is no grayish zone.

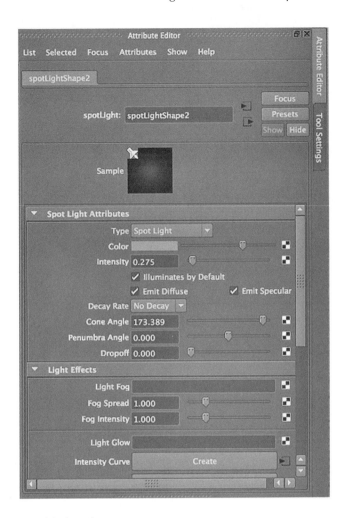

FIGURE 15.32   A second light color.

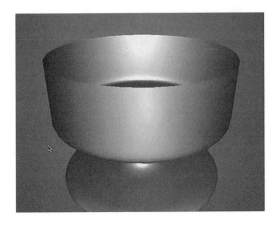

FIGURE 15.33   (See p. CI-16 of Color Insert) A bowl colored by light.

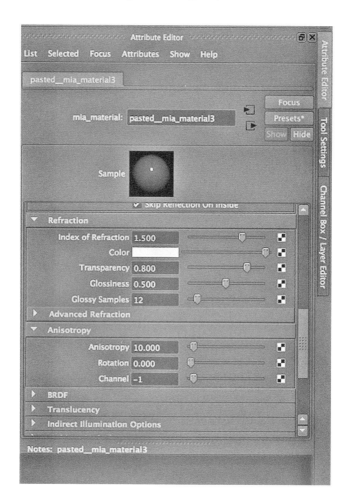

FIGURE 15.34   Anisotropy settings.

FIGURE 15.35   **(See p. CI-11 of Color Insert)** Anisotropy of 1.

FIGURE 15.36 **(See p. CI-11 of Color Insert)** Anisotropy of 10.

In Figure 15.43, the Penumbra is set to 10 and the Dropoff at 94. We add a dropoff set-ting here in order to point out that the rate at which the light degrades as it moves through space also has a powerful impact on the shadows cast by a light. (See p. CI-12, Figure 15.43 of the Color Insert for the appearance of the doors with various penumbra settings.)

ADJUSTING THE RESOLUTION ATTRIBUTE OF A DIRECTIONAL LIGHT IN MAYA

We will look at adjusting the resolution of a shadow. First, we choose:

Hypershade window → Create → Lights → Directional light (see Figure 15.44)

Directional lights are meant to model sunlight, that is, light that is moving in parallel rays across the scene.

FIGURE 15.37 **(See p. CI-11 of Color Insert)** Anisotropy of 100.

FIGURE 15.38   **(See p. CI-12 of Color Insert)** Anisotropy of .1.

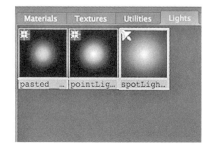

FIGURE 15.39   Three lights.

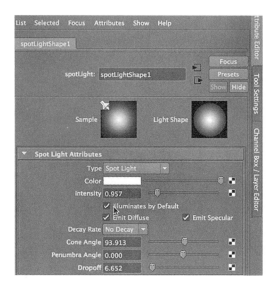

FIGURE 15.40   Spotlight settings.

FIGURE 15.41   **(See p. CI-12 of Color Insert)** Penumbra 10 and Dropoff 0.

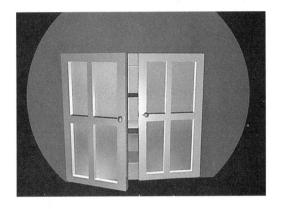

FIGURE 15.42   **(See p. CI-12 of Color Insert)** Penumbra 0 and Dropoff 0.

FIGURE 15.43   **(See p. CI-12 of Color Insert)** Penumbra 10 and Dropoff 94.

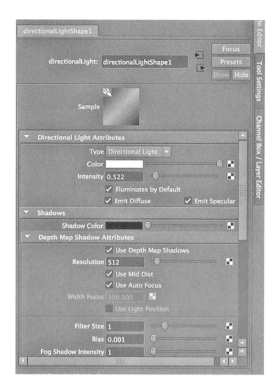

FIGURE 15.44   Resolution 512 with Depth Map Shadows.

With the light selected, we hit Control+A once or twice until the Attribute Editor of the light appears. We set the shadow Resolution to 512 and choose Depth Map Shadows. Depth Map Shadows, as we have seen, are sharper than the alternative, Raytrace Shadows. Then we render with mental ray; our scene, which consists of a glass bottle sitting on a countertop, is shown in Figure 15.45.

We see that the shadow of the bottle is quite jagged. So, we change the resolution to 4096 in Figure 15.46. We render the scene again (see Figure 15.47). The shadow is much smoother now.

FIGURE 15.45   **(See p. CI-10 of Color Insert)** Render with jagged shadow.

ADDING RAYTRACE SHADOWS AND MENTAL RAY SUN AND SKY TO THE BOTTLE

The mental ray Sun and Sky can do a lot more than provide a nice, gradual blue horizon. It is a significant light source and we can use it to create powerful effects.

In Figure 15.48, the attributes of a Directional light are shown, with Raytrace Shadows checked. The result is shown in Figure 15.49, and we see that raytracing

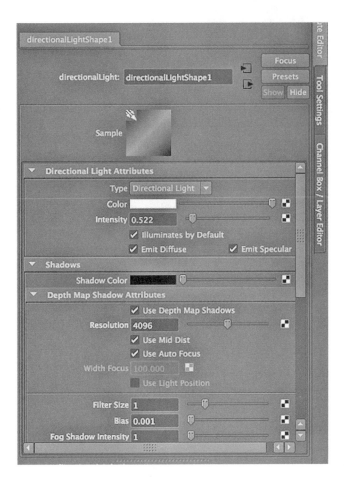

FIGURE 15.46   Changing resolution.

FIGURE 15.47   **(See p. CI-10 of Color Insert)** Depth Map render.

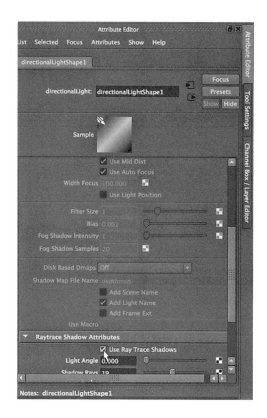

FIGURE 15.48   Raytrace Shadow settings.

FIGURE 15.49   **(See p. CI-10 of Color Insert)** Raytraced Shadow rendered.

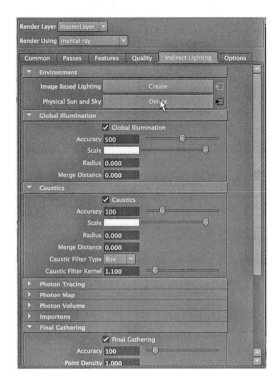

FIGURE 15.50   The mental ray Sun and Sky.

creates soft shadows. Now, we go into the Options settings of the Render View window and click on Physical Sun and Sky (see Figure 15.50).

The result is shown in Figure 15.51. Notice that the added light from the mental ray Sun and Sky material is completely washing out the table on which the bottle sits, giving the scene a hot feel.

FIGURE 15.51   **(See p. CI-10 of Color Insert)** A bottle in the Sun.

II

The Cabana

I N CHAPTERS 2 THROUGH 15, we have learned by doing. Each chapter presented a series of hands-on examples. We did not neglect conceptual knowledge; it's there, intertwined with the examples, because it is best to learn why you are doing something as you learn how to do it.

But here, we step back. The goal is to take all of the conceptual material covered so far and create the sort of framework that will hopefully "stick to the mental ribs" because we already have an intuitive, detailed understanding of just what an application like Maya can do. First, we consider the overall task of putting together a simple scene.

A BEGINNER'S PROJECT: BASIC, TOP-DOWN ARCHITECTURAL MODELING

A good place for a beginner to start is with an architectural scene, either indoor or outdoor. Both are well suited for polygon modeling, as buildings tend to be angular. They are also naturally top-down modeling efforts, with a main scene that can be easily decomposed. When building architectural models, one common approach is to block the main scene out first, with basic shapes like cubes and cylinders to mark the relative positioning and size of objects in the scene. Then, as the models that will be used in the scene are built in separate scenes, we can bring them into the main scene and replace the crude place-keepers.

Reuse

Architectural scenes also lend themselves to component-based designs, with basic building blocks that can be heavily reused in a given environment.

Textures can be reused as well. This makes it easier to put together a complete environment. It is also important to take care not to overdo the reuse of components and textures, and thereby create an overly homogeneous, churned-out appearance. Sometimes it is helpful to use some human characters or critters in a scene to give it some scale.

Reuse of components and textures can extend over multiple animation projects. Sets of cameras and lights can also be reused in similar scenes. Outdoor architectural scenes often need similar sets of cameras and lights. The same is true for interior scenes.

Reference Images

It is a good idea to use reference images (perhaps photos of a building or room), not only to supply details that add realism, but also to get the overall proportions of the objects in the scene correct, and to keep things in proper proportion as detail is added.

Modeling with Texturing and Animating in Mind

We should model with texturing in mind. The natural boundaries of human-made objects like pillars and chairs can make it easy to apply textures. Using the Outliner to carefully build complex objects will make it easier to animate elements in the scene.

THE CABANA

From a modeling perspective our cabana is a very simple scene. First, some of the detailed items in the scene are content that I have bought. These include the palm trees, the gold chairs and table, the potted plants, and the wooden chairs. The sources of these items are listed in the Acknowledgments of this book.

Using Prefab Content to Flesh Out a Scene

The three human models are derived from characters I bought on the Daz3D site. Figures 16.1, 16.2, and 16.3 are closeup images of these three characters. They were very easy to create. Thank you, Daz3D.

Daz characters are also widely used in Poser. The application Daz Studio is currently free but you have to supplement it heavily with content sold on the Daz site. Second-party vendors supply most of the content available on the Daz site.

FIGURE 16.1   A Daz man.

FIGURE 16.2   A Daz woman.

Daz provides a handful of base charac-ters. Outside venders then rework the base characters using "morphs" available within Daz Studio or by using other programs, like ZBrush. Then they give them names and sell them on the Daz site. Buyers fur-ther morph them.

FIGURE 16.3   A Daz girl.

I started with two adult (but young) characters sold by two Daz vendors, along with one (the man) sold on another site called Renderosity. I morphed all three of them heavily, and then added some hair and clothing. I aged the two adults, made the girl look younger, and used some of the facial morphs that I applied to the two adults on the kid, so that she might look like their child. I retextured clothing, but left the skin tones of the characters alone.

The various morphing tools in Daz help the modeler vary physical attributes, like body proportions, body weight, and hairstyles and hair colors. We can apply different skin tex-tures and morph facial features to create multiple ethnicities from a single human model. There are some very realistic skin textures available on the Daz site that were created from hi-def photographs of humans. Freckles, moles, sun-aged skin, and other imperfections have been added. With Daz, we can age characters with wrinkles, drooping faces, bent backs, and so forth.

A subtle but important feature of human skin is that it has "subsurface scattering." Human skin is not completely opaque, and subsurface scattering allows light to pass through the skin. Some of it gets trapped there, producing a subtle but powerful effect that is almost a very soft glow. There are some subsurface scattering shaders on the Daz site.

The Daz site also has architectural (indoor and outdoor) scenes, shaders, textures, cloth-ing, props, hair sets, pose sets, and light sets, and various plug-ins to expand the capabili-ties of Daz Studio.

You can even do a bit of animation with Daz. The Daz characters come prerigged for forward kinematics (FK) and inverse kinematics (IK). There are canned movement cycles, like walking, running, sitting, and standing. These motion cycles can be strung together to create more complex motions. However, there are not many of these cycles available on the Daz site, and so animating with Daz is a difficult thing to do. Both Poser and Daz have made their reputation by supporting the creation of powerful, single-frame renderings of "posed" characters. It is an art form in itself, even if you do not create any new material yourself. And, there are a variety of mostly small-scale professional operations that use Daz Studio to create art for things like graphic novels and commercial advertisements.

Daz Studio has no physics engine and no particle system.

Some of the architectural models sold on the Daz site are extremely cheap, given the many hours that clearly went into their development.

Building the Cabana: Workflow

So, what is our cabana? The cabana arches, pillars, stairs, pool, water, and inside framing of the walls were all created in Maya and imported into Daz Studio as wireframes (.obj). The brick wall, the carpet, and the roof of the cabana are just flattened cubes or planes. I used Daz Studio for most of the materials and textures, and imported a few file textures. There is a Daz Studio plug-in for Luxrender, a very nice raytracing renderer that is free. That is how the characters and the cabana were rendered.

The arches were created by using polygon extrusion. The cabana itself was created out of a cube with Boolean operators to remove the cutaways for the arches. I also put notches in the blue covering where it falls behind the pillars, so that it would look like fabric. The pillars are made out of polygon cubes, cylinders, and spheres. The water consists of a semitransparent layer under which I placed an almost neon green layer. The background is a canned, procedural environment shader from the Daz site that is specifically engineered to work with Luxrender; it proved to be a little tricky to work with, but it got the job done.

Reuse is something that can help simplify the construction of almost any architectural environment. There are fourteen pillars in the scene, but I only had to make one. Perhaps they should have been varied a bit. I could have varied the texture of each pillar so they would not look so identical. Or the texture of each pillar could have been grunged in a unique way by using Photoshop layering, before being imported as a file texture into Daz. The way I made the pillars is by creating three objects: the engraved ball at the top, the etched length of the pillar, and the block it rests on; the top ball and the bottom block are parented to the length.

This scene illustrates how much can be accomplished with just a handful of modeling tools—and how critical it is that materials be carefully chosen and applied. This part of the task was somewhat more tedious than a beginner might expect. And since the materials were not created specifically for the Luxrenderer, it took a lot of playing around to get them to render properly.

A NOTE ON ANIMATING HUMANS

We saw that Maya has a very nice human skeleton generator. A powerful alternative to manually animating a character using an IK rig is to use motion capture data, such as BioVision Hierarchical (or BVH) data. We can let someone else do the big job of capturing human movement and then simply plug their data into our characters.

BVH data is free on the Web, but can also be exported from various applications, like IClone from Reallusion. Maya cannot directly import BVH data, but Maya and another Autodesk application, MotionBuilder, are closely integrated, so BVH data can be imported into MotionBuilder and then exported directly to Maya. I animated the cabana characters by using MotionBuilder in this way.

THE COOL CONCEPTS OF THE CABANA

The detailed charts in Chapter 17 provide an overview of the important concepts that were covered in this book. These are the "takeaways" of this book.

The concepts in these charts are as generic as they can be without making them so abstract that they would not be useful. They were heavily influenced by Maya, but indeed, there is no way to learn 3D animation without diving into the details of an actual professional-grade 3D modeling, animation, and rendering application.

Cool Concepts

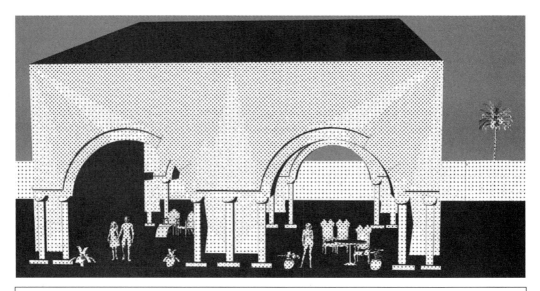

The Cool Contents of the Cabana

4 Coordinate Systems and Hierarchically Structured Models

Terms:

World Space (x, y, z):
The grid of the entire scene space. Its center is at (0, 0, 0) of the scene space.

Object Space (x, y, z):
The 3D coordinate system of a given object. Its center is at (0, 0, 0), with respect to the object, not the scene.

Local Space (x, y, z):
Each object in the hierarchy inherits the Object Space of its parent (as its Local Space). In this way, a complex object will move as a coherent whole.

Surface Texture Space (u, v):
This is the coordinate system for the surface of a given object.

Cool Concept 1: Object hierarchies and multiple (x, y, z) spaces

One of the most critical things a 3D animator must do is carefully place all objects in appropriate hierarchical relationships with other objects. This allows the motion of one object to depend on another object. This is how an object can be moved independently but also be certain to move with respect to its parent. Building hierarchies also provides a convenient way to place different materials on different parts of an object.

Cool Concept 2: What is a model?

Within Maya, there is a semiformal notion of an object—It can be something that will render, like a car windshield, or something that does not directly render, like a path along which an object might move. But there is no fixed notion of what constitutes a model. Models are in the eye of the animator. Often, the root of an object hierarchy is what the animator considers to be a model.

▼ A Closer Look: Examples of using multiple (x, y, z) spaces

Consider a car on a roadway with various Objects hierarchically arranged.

The entire scene sits in World Space.

The road has its own Object Space.

The car has its own Object Space. Its Local is the Object Space of the road.

Each axle has its own Object Space; its Local Space is the Object Space of the body of the car.

A pair of wheels have their own Object Space. Their Local Space is the Object Space of the axle.

Now, the wheels turn independently, but they stay on the axle as the car moves forward. When a sinkhole opens under the road, the road falls and the car follows, and the axles and the wheels go with it. The wheels are still spinning.

And each of these objects can have their own material. The object hierarchy serves for more than just creating hierarchical movement. If we make the windshield of the car a child of the body of the car, it will be easier to give the windshield its own material. It will also make it easier to reuse that windshield on another car or to replace the windshield of a car.

3D Surface Models—Components of Vector-Based Models and Pixel-Based Renderings

Terms: Polygons

The "**wireframe**" of a "**polygon**" object contains "**vertices**" and straight "**edges**" that connect the vertices in the World Space of (x, y, z). But all edges are in 2-space.

polygon faces

Straight edges form polygons, which are called "**faces**," each of which is in 2-space.

A group of "**faces**" form a "**mesh**." One or more meshes form a polygon "**object**."

Cool Concept 1: Infinitely thin surfaces made of faces

Maya is not a solid modeler; models have infinitely thin surfaces, which are defined by how they react to light shining on them. This creates colors and transparency, and refracting and reflecting light.

Cool Concept 2: Vertices/edges/faces are converted to pixels

Although a polygon model is represented with line geometry in 3-space, ultimately it will be rendered as pixels in 2-space, with each pixel having color and transparency attributes. Before it is rendered, each quad is cut into two triangles.

A NURBS model goes through an extra step: it must be turned into a polygon model before it is rendered.

Terms: NURBS

The "**wireframe**" of a "**NURBS**" object contains "**control vertices**" and "**curves**" In the World Space of (x, y, z). All curves are in 2- space.

curves

Curves in NURBS modeling are defined by a set of "control vertices," of which the beginning and the end vertices are on the curve. But the other CVs are not; they are used indirectly to form a specific curved line. A NURBS curve that only has two CVs is actually a straight line.

patches

A NURBS object is a set of connected "**patches**."

▼ A Closer Look: Why both straight and curved line geometry?

Straight line geometry is quick to manipulate, but often the animator uses curved lines to specify particularly "organic" models.

The specification of NURBS curves (and its somewhat simpler cousin Bezier curves) is surprisingly compact and reasonably quick to render. This is largely due to the mathematics that we use to represent Bezier and NURBS curves. With only a few vertices and some polynomials, a curve can be perfectly defined and will scale easily to any size.

3D Surface Models—Diagramatically

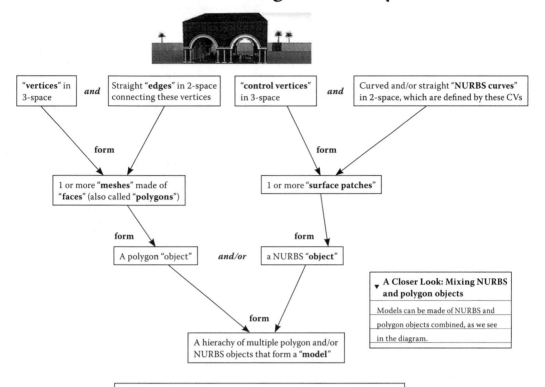

| "vertices" in 3-space | *and* | Straight "**edges**" in 2-space connecting these vertices | | "**control vertices**" in 3-space | *and* | Curved and/or straight "**NURBS curves**" in 2-space, which are defined by these CVs |

form

form

1 or more "**meshes**" made of "**faces**" (also called "**polygons**")

1 or more "**surface patches**"

form

form

A polygon "object"   *and/or*   a NURBS "**object**"

▾ **A Closer Look: Mixing NURBS and polygon objects**

Models can be made of NURBS and polygon objects combined, as we see in the diagram.

form

A hierachy of multiple polygon and/or NURBS objects that form a "**model**"

Cool Concept 1: What makes up a 3D surface model?

Manipulating 3D Models with Translate, Rotate, and Scale

Terms: The big three

"**Transforming**" is the generic term for manipulating objects in order to create models, like turning a sphere into a human head.

"**Translate**," "**Rotate**," and "**Scale**" are the big three transformation tools. These three underly much of the process of building and animating models.

A note on Pivot Points

When an object is rotated, its center of rotation is the object's "**pivot point**." This point can be changed by the animator. In this way, the animator can make a door swing open on its left edge and not in the middle of the door.

The pivot point is not necessarily at the origin (0, 0, 0) of the object's Object Space.

Cool Concept: The versatile power of translate, scale, and rotate

These are the core tools used to create a complete 3D animated scene. As we craft objects that form models, and as we animate the models in our scenes, we are either directly or indirectly translating, rotating, and scaling objects. (We might also be adding or removing vertices, edges, and polygons.) For example:

These tools are used to morph 3D objects into final models. We can scale a cube in two dimensions horizontally and turn it into a long, ranch style house.

We can move vertices and edges in order to morph the polygons that make up the mesh of a polygon object; sometimes this is called "**push and pull**" modeling. We can move faces of a polygon and "**extrude**" new faces as we go.

These three tools are used to animate objects. We can scale, rotate, and translate an object over a series of keyframes. The moon rotates as it goes around the Earth. In Maya, the Graph Editor allows us to carefully hone and reuse an object's scale, rotate, and translation attributes.

We can use the big three to apply textures and materials to the surface of an object. For example, we could scale a zebra's stripes to make them narrower or wider, or we could rotate them to make them horizontal if we were making a fantasy zebra.

We can use these tools to reform the (u, v) surface grid of an object to enable an evenly-applied texture.

We can also use the big three to position, configure, and animate lights and cameras. We can widen the arc of a spotlight by scaling it in two dimensions. We can also scale up the icon for directional light, not to change its light attributes, but simply to see the icon better as we build a scene.

In NURBS modeling, which is focused on manipulating curved lines and suriace patches, (as opposed to necessarily working with prefab primitives like spheres and cubes), we can take a curved line and by moving its edges and vertices in 3-space, revolve it to create a bowl.

Modeling—Approaches to Modeling and Adding Detailed Geometry

Term:

"**Transformations**" change the geometry of an object by changing the location and/or number of vertices, edges, and faces. These operations are used to incrementally build objects and models, and they are rooted in the three big tools of translate, rotate, and scale.

Term:

An "**isoparm**" is a line across a NURBS surface where the u or v value in 2-space is constant. This is a more restrictive definition than an edge in a polygon model, and indicative of the fact that NURBS modeling has a very different feel than polygon modeling. For example, isoparms can be moved to open or close a NURBS sphere or cylinder.

Cool Concept 1: Using polygon and NURBS transformations

In polygon modeling, we perform these operations on vertices, edges, and faces.

In NURBS modeling, we perform these operations on CVs, curves, and surface patches.

Adding or moving vertices/CVs and edges/curves does not necessarily change the rendered appearance of an object, but we still say that its "geometry" has been changed.

Cool Concept 3: The modeling mode

In polygon modeling, tools are used in the context of the current modeling mode. We can work (at least) at the vertex, edge, face, or object level.

In NURBS, we can work at the control vertex, surface patch, surface point, or object level.

We can also work at the isoparm level.

Cool Concept 2: Modeling is never only top down or only bottom up

In polygon modeling, we often start with a single geometric primitive (like a sphere or a cube) and transform it into an object that forms part or all of a model.

Or, in polygon modeling we can start with multiple geometric primitives and transform them into one or more objects, that in turn can form a single hierarchical model.

There are polygon tools that focus on lines being manipulated in 3-space. We can extrude a square along a straight or curved line.

We can start with NURBS surface primitives.

Or we can start with lines, squares, circles, and curves, manipulate them into surface patches, and then use these patches to create an entire object or model.

Cool Concept 4: Controlling the geometry of a model

1. Adding edges and/or edge loops early in the modeling process lays down the framework we will need to add detailed modeling later, and to enable the eventual smoothing of a polygon model later. It is useful to add concentric edge loops around the eyes of a character, or at the end of a baseball bat. This will help create a smooth depression for the eye sockets or a rounded end of the bat.

2. But a modeler has to keep track of the density of geometry in a model. Unnecessary detail, or detail added too early, can make a model difficult to manage. Maya's modeling tools tend to manipulate individual vertices, edges, and faces, and we want the right model to emerge after as few steps as possible.

3. In a way, controlling the geometry of a model is both top down and bottom up. Top down, in that we build the outer form of a model first; bottom up in the sense that early on, we begin building the extra vertices, edges, and faces that we will need later to add detail to the model.

4. Limit the number of edges emanating from any given vertex to 4 or 5.

5. Most of the polygons in a mesh should be quads, and a smaller number should be triangles.

Modeling—Polygons, Sculpting, and Small Granularity Tools

Cool Concept 1: Getting started in modeling

It's best to start out with a small set of tools and learn them well and only gradually extend this set. Most models can be built by using a small subset of the tools provided by an application like Maya.

Basic Polygon Tools

Below is a list of Maya tools that correspond to each category.

Translate, Rotate, Scale
(vertices, edges, polygons)
These stretch lines, extend polygons, and stretch out neighboring polygons

Extrude Tools
The Extrude tool

Copying and Deleting Objects
Copy, Duplicate, Cut, Delete

Create Polygon Primitives
Sphere, Cube, Cylinder, Cone, Plane, Torus
It is important to consider the required geometric density of a primitive when it is created.

Tools that surgically add edges and vertices
Interactive Split, Insert Edge Loop, Add Divisions

A tool that removes edges and vertices
Reduce

Sculpting tools
Sculpt Geometry, Soft Modification, Soft Move

Tools that can be used to smooth models
Smooth, Soften Edge, Convert to Subdiv, Camfer Vertex, Bevel. Soften Edge manipulates normals, not the geometry of the object.

Basic Polygon Tools (continued)

Boolean tools
Union, Intersection, Difference

Deformers
Nonlinear Deformers

Tools that snap polygons/faces together and align them
Snap Align, Align, Snap Together

Tools that combine objects, separate objects, and combine detailed geometry
Combine and Separate, Connect Components, Detach Components, Move to Center, Merge Vertex, Merge Edge, Slide Edge

Tools that fill in faces and create empty faces
Cut/Delete (in Face Mode), Fill Hole, Make Hole, Bridge, Merge, Merge to Center

Tools that mirror geometry
Mirror Geometry, Duplicate Special (will continue to update the mirrored version of the object as the original is changed)

Tools for animation morphing
Blend Shape, the Nonlinear Deformers

Cool Concept 2: Sculpting—An alternative approach to creating organic models

Two very popular 3D modelers, Autodesk Mudbox and Pixologic's ZBrush, can be used to craft the surface shape of an object and give the modeler the feeling of working with clay. In comparison, polygon modeling in Maya tends to feel like a surgical approach, where polygon tools work at the level of individual vertices, edges, and faces. However, sculpting applications make it all too easy to create models with very large numbers of faces.

The Reduce tool in Maya can be used to lower the number of polygons in a model imported from another application. It can also be used to make a polygon model easier to manipulate at a larger granularity.

The soft modification tool and the sculpt geometry tool in Maya provide a bit of this sense of sculpting.

Modeling—NURBS and Its Unique Qualities

Basic NURBS Tools

Translate, Rotate, Scale (CVs, lines and isoparms, surface patches) These stretch lines, curves, and surface patches, but do so in a smooth, organic fashion

Copying and Deleting Objects
Copy, Duplicate, Cut, Delete

Create curves
CV and EP, Create Square, Create Circle

Manipulate curves
Cut Curve, Attach Curves, Detach Curves, Align Curves

Create NURBS Primitives
But remember that you are making surfaces; e.g., a cylinder is three separate objects. It is important to consider the required geometric density of a primitive when it is created.

Tools that take lines/curves and move them through 3-space to create surface patches
Revolve, Loft, Extrude, Bevel, Project Curve on Surface, Move Sweep (done in the attribute box of NURBS objects)

Tools that manipulate surface patches
Trim Tool, Extend Surfaces, Surface Editing

Tools that join or separate patches
Stitch, Attach Surfaces, Detach Surfaces, Duplicate NURBS Patches, Offset Surfaces

Tools that surgically add geometric detail
Intersect Surfaces, Move Seam, Insert Isoparms

Tools that align patches
Align Surfaces

Tools that support sculpting
Sculpt Geometry, Soft Modification Tool

▾ **A Closer Look: Is there a "complete" set of beginner's tools?**

In short, no. The tools on these two lists are really just suggestions for good tools to learn early on. They provide basic, core modeling support. There is no mathematically defined set of polygon or NURBS tools that can be said to provide all the functionality that you need to create basic models. Modeling is an ad hoc, subjective process.

Putting Surfaces on Objects—Materials, Textures, Paint, and Hair and Fur

Terms:

A "**shader**" is an object that determines how the surface of a model (or of an object or an individual face/surface patch) should respond to light.

A "**material**" (in Maya) is the same thing as a shader.

In some applications, a "**texture**" is a bit mapped image that is used to control the colors and pattern of colors on a surface; a texture might be a photograph of a stone wall or of tree bark.

In Maya and in other applications there are also 2D and 3D "procedural" textures.

Cool Concept 1: Textures versus materials

In Maya (and in many other applications), a material (shader) is more powerful and flexible than a texture, because it can have a broader set of attributes. Often, textures serve as attributes of shaders.

Terms and Cool Concept 2: Prepping textures outside and inside Maya

Often, the modeler will use a program like Photoshop, GIMP, or Pixelmator to create "**layered**" textures. By using various layer modes, the colors and apparent shadow patterns of multiple raster images can be blended.

In particular, a texture can be blended with another texture using modes such as "**darken**," "**luminance**," and "**hue**."

Maya has its own built-in facility for creating layered textures, but it is less powerful than those found in professional image manipulation applications.

Cool Concept 3: Ramp as the duct tape of shaders

Ramp shaders and textures can be used in a variety of ways to give multiple colors to a scene. For example, they can be used to color a particle cloud by assigning the various colors in the ramp spectrum to individual particles.

Cool Concept 4: Painting

Another way to put a surface on a model is to paint it on. Skilled artists can create highly detailed textures that would be very hard to create using file textures or 2D/3D procedural textures.

Cool Concept 5: Fur and hair

The surface of an object can be covered with fur or hair.

In Maya, fur is usually laid down in homogeneous patches that can be groomed into various styles.

Hair in Maya is a smaller grained capability and can be animated in very complex ways. Hair can also be used to guide the animation of fur.

Cool Concept 6: The importance of good materials and textures

The materials that are placed on models are key to the way viewers will interpret the models and scenes. Are the models new and elegant and fresh? Or are they neglected and beat up and aged?

Above all else, materials and textures must be applied with great care. Good materials make a model; bad materials destroy a model.

▼ **A Closer Look: Maya's painting metaphor**

In Maya, a painting metaphor is used in multiple contexts. Single objects or meshes of objects can be painted into a scene. The painting metaphor is also used to control the Sculpt Geometry tool and other tools; this gives the modeler a smooth, graceful way of crafting a model. Maya's painting engine is called "Artisan."

▼ **A Closer Look: Dual-purpose textures**

Often a professionally designed texture comes in two versions—One that is a full-color photograph and another that has the same texture as the photograph, but is in only two colors, one of which is black. The second version is used for bump maps and displacement maps.

Putting Surfaces on Objects—Using Textures

Terms:

A material can have various types. In Maya, these include "**Blinn**," "**Phong**," or "**Lambert**."

If we use the mental ray renderer in Maya, there is a large suite of material types.

Some materials come with multiple "presets"—These are collections of attribute values for the material. Often animators create their own presets.

Materials can also have properties including "**color**," "**transparency**," and "**ambient color**" (this influences the overall color of the material and defaults to having no influence). Sometimes "**incandescence**," which allows a material to emit colored light, can also be specified.

In general, there are two kinds of textures. "**Bit mapped**" textures are digital images made out of pixels. To apply a bit mapped texture to a surface, it usually must be "**tiled**."

The second kind of texture is a "**procedural**" texture, which means that it is applied to the surface of an object by a program, and not simply by projecting an image onto the surface.

Maya also differentiates between 2D and 3D procedural textures. A "**3D procedural**" texture can be envisioned as a bucket of texture that the object is soaked in; the texture sticks wherever the surface of it touches the liquid texture.

Terms and Cool Concept 1: Four uses of textures

In Maya and in many of its competitors, the word texture is used in multiple contexts:

1. A "texture" can be applied directly to a surface. When a texture is used in this way, it often needs to be tiled in order to cover the entire surface. It is best to use a texture which can be tiled in a "**seamless**" way, i.e., so that the borders between the tiles cannot be seen.

2. A texture can be used as a "**bump map**," wherein Maya will use the light and dark areas of a texture to create the illusion of geometric relief on a surface that is actually smooth.

3. A texture can also be used as a "**displacement map**," wherein Maya will perform more detailed calculations and add the shadow effects that would have been present if the object had actually had true geometric relief. Displacement maps are typically harder to use but provide better results.

4. A texture can also be used as the color of a shader, turning a simple texture into a more sophisticated shader, with all the flexibility that comes with a material.

Cool Concept 2: Two ways to lay a texture down on the surface of an object

There are two ways to lay down a texture:

1. The normals information of the object can be altered in order to control the way the texture is laid down on the object. In this case, a "**normal**" texture is used.

When using a normal texture, Maya provides a powerful tool, the UV Texture Editor, to help reshape the (u, v) surface of an object.

When a normal texture is laid on the (u, v) grid of an object, the animator can rearrange the (u, v) grid to allow the texture to be put down evenly. This remapping can be done in a variety of ways, including planar, spherical, and cylindrical. The animator can also use tools to surgically adjust local areas within the (u, v) grid.

2. The animator can work from the perspective of the texture and vary its density as it is being laid down. In this case, a "**projection**" texture is used. A projection texture can also be laid down in various ways, including planar, spherical, cubic, and cylindrical. The animator often tries to match the overall form of the object; e.g., if it is almost spherical, a spherical mapping would be used.

Whether a projection or a normal texture is used, the "**normals**" information belonging to the surface of the object must be altered internally. In this case, the word normal is being used in its plain geometrical sense; on a curved surface the normals of that surface gradually change direction across the surface. On a cube, all normals on a given face are parallel. When normal information belonging to an object is changed, this can make it appear to have a physical relief that resembles the texture.

▼ A Closer Look: The special role of the checkerboard texture

As a primitive like a sphere or a cube is manipulated into a piece of a model, the original (u, v) layout can become very irregular with vertices varying significantly from their original spatial relationships. Vertices can become very dense in one area and very spread out in another.

A checkerboard texture can be used to judge the layout of the (u, v) grid on the surface of an object in order to determine if the grid should be reshaped as a texture is applied. In Maya, when this is done, a normal texture is used.

Animating 3D Models—Morphing and Skeletons

Terms: Animating an object

"**Morphing**," the process of changing the shape of an object over a series of frames, can be used as a form of animation. This is frequently used in facial animation. Blend shapes are often used in Maya to create morphing animation.

"**Keyframing**" is the process of providing periodic positions/scalings/rotations and/or morphs of an object over a series of frames, with the animation application filling in the positioning and/or shape of the object between the keyframes at render time. Deformers can be used to animate objects; they can bend or twist or squash an object over a series of frames.

"**Path animation**" is the process of laying down a line (often in a loop) and having an object follow that path at render time.

Terms: Simulating the organic motion of living models

"**Skeletons**" consist of bones and joints that control the movement of a character over a series of frames. Skeletons are laid out in hierarchies; in a human the root is usually at the hips.

"**FK**" refers to "**forward kinematics**" and "**IK**" refers to "**inverse kinematics**." FK means that when a given joint in a skeleton is moved, all joints and bones below it in the skeleton hierarchy move with it.

In "**IK**" the movement of a given joint causes other joints, both below and above the given joint in the hierarchy, to move in a way that is logical, given the structure of the skeleton. To use Maya terminology, this is controlled with IK **handles**," each of which has an "**effector**" which can be moved to adjust the form of the skeleton. As an example, when the effector of a hand is moved so that it reaches out to grab something, the hips and legs might move with it. Adding a complete system of IK handles is called "**rigging**."

The "**skin**" is the outer surface of a living creature, like a human or a cow. This is often actual skin or clothing. The process of making the skin move with and over the skeleton is called "**binding**" the skin to the skeleton.

Terms and Cool Concept 1: Using a graph editor

A "**graph editor**" is a tool in an animation application that maps out the precise movement in 3-space as an object is rotated, scaled, and translated over a series of frames. The graph editor provides the ability to fine-tune movement, as well as to reuse movement loops or segments.

Cool Concept 2: Hierarchical animation

In Maya and applications like it, the movement of a parent object in a hierarchy is inherited by objects below it in the hierarchy. Each object can also have its own independent movement, but remains bound by the movement of objects all the way up to the root of the hierarchy.

Cool Concept 3: Two perspectives of motion

Models (and the hierarchies of objects that form them) can be put in motion. The closer the camera is to them when it is recording them, the faster they seem to be going. When the camera backs away, it's like watching a NASCAR race from the perspective of a blimp: the cars seem to be moving slowly.

Or, the camera that is used to capture the scene can be animated. Rendering from the perspective of a moving camera can be very effective in giving the viewer an intense sense of motion. While riding along with Harry Potter on his broomstick, some viewers will actually have motion sickness.

▼ A Closer Look: Subsurface tissue and painting in Maya

The painting metaphor in Maya can be used to help apply flexing muscles and rigid tissue (like immobile bones) under the skin of a character so that when the skeleton moves the skin is deformed in a natural way. Maya calls this its "muscle system."

Animating 3D Models—Physics in the Large and in the Small

Terms and Cool Concept 1: Two kinds of object physics

In general, there are two sorts of dynamics that are supported by various animation applications. One is "**particle**" dynamics and one is "**rigid**" and "**soft**" body dynamics.

Maya has two dynamics dropdowns on the Main Menu, Dynamics, and nDynamics (which is newer).

Maya can calculate the effects of collisions between objects, between objects and particles, or, in the case of nDynamics, between particles.

Terms and Cool Concept 2: Particles and Emitters

In Maya, "**particles**" are manufactured by "emitters" over the course of some number of frames.

Emitters and particles have a number of attributes that control, among other things, the rate of particle emission, the distance particles can travel, their direction and speed, their color, and how long they "live."

Emitters in Maya can be standalone or attached to an object.

In Maya, there are "**hardware**" particles, which have no geometry and so Maya only simulates the appearance of the particles being 3D, and "**software**" particles.

Software particles can take on various shapes; the animator can also create custom-shaped objects that are emitted.

Hardware particles, because they are rendered by the Maya Hardware renderer, are much quicker to render.

Cool Concept 3: Dynamics effects

Dynamics are heavily used in 3D animation. Particles can be used to model clouds, smoke, and water.

In Maya, we can turn a polygon object into cloth by turning the object's vertices into particles. These particles are programmed to have "links" which control their interaction. We can turn a polygon surface into water in a similar way.

Cool Concept 4: Natural forces

In Maya and similar applications, natural forces can be placed in a scene; they can be used to influence the way particles, soft bodies, and rigid bodies move in a scene. These forces include wind and gravity.

Particle emitters frequently have randomness attributes which can be used to simulate these semichaotic effects.

Constraints and nConstraints in Maya can be used to tailor the interaction between objects, particles, and fields.

▼ A Closer Look: Physics in Maya

Both Dynamics and nDynamics support particle dynamics and rigid/soft body dynamics. But there are significant differences.

Only in nDynamics can particles interact with each other.

In nDynamics, the interplay between fields and particles can be more carefully controlled.

Cloth, which is a dynamics effect, can only be created in nDynamics (it is called nCloth).

▼ A Closer Look: Bounding boxes and object collisions

Each object in a scene has a "bounding box." This is the smallest (perhaps stretched) cube that encloses the entire object. A bounding box is usually aligned with the three axes (x, y, z) in the scene—The World Space.

Bounding boxes serve multiple purposes. They are used, in particular, to quickly determine if two objects with at least one of them in motion are going to collide. If the bounding boxes of those objects will not collide (something that can be calculated quickly because of their rectangular shape), there is no need to perform more complex calculations that will determine exactly if two geometrically complex objects will collide.

▼ A Closer Look: Coding animation

In Maya, as in many other 3D animation applications, the movement of objects and models can be controlled by expressions written in a scripting language. When using mathematically precise simulations of movement. scripting can often be a far more accurate and simpler way to create motion. (In fact, almost anything that can be built with the Maya GUI can be created by writing code.)

Rendering and Lights—From Vector to Raster Geometry, and the Interplay of Lights and Materials in Rendering

Cool Concept 1: Recapturing the 3D feel of vector models

The main goal of the rendering process is to take 3D vector-based-models that are animated and turn them into a series of changing pixel-based images (at perhaps 30 per second). The renderer must also recapture the sense of 3D depth that was present mathematically in the original, internal vector models.

Cool Concept 2: The dependencies between light, materials, and renderers

The process of rendering involves three very closely related technologies: lights, materials, and the renderer itself. The renderer has to know how to interpret the materials and how to use the lights to illuminate a scene. This is why many second-party renderers come with their own lights and material libraries, and their own lights editors and materials editors.

When a plugin is used to adapt a second-party renderer to an animation application, the plug-in is largely in charge of translating materials and lights into a form native to the renderer.

Terms and Cool Concept 3: Light types

Animation applications typically support the kinds of lights that essentially simulate lights as they appear in the real world, including lights made by nature and lights made by people.

Sunlight is simulated in Maya by a "**directional**" light. This is a light that washes across the entire scene with parallel rays.

An "**ambient**" light simulates just what its name suggests: light that has spread evenly through an entire closed area or an entire outdoor scene.

"**Point**" lights can be used to model light bulbs inside fixtures.

"**Spot**" lights can be used to model the arc of a light coming out of a lamp shade.

"**Area**" lights can be used to model fluorescent lights.

An indoor scene can be enhanced by placing a directional light outside so that it comes in through a window, simulating sunlight.

Terms and Cool Concept 4: Light effects and environments

Lights can have many attributes, including color (not to be confused with the color of a material), their intensity, and how far their light will travel.

When using mental ray, "**caustics**" can be used to provide harsh lighting effects.

Specialized lights and shaders are used to create "**environment**" spheres or cubes.

Terms and Cool Concept 5: Picking a lighting strategy

There are many ways that an animator might engineer the lighting in a scene.

One common approach is to simulate the use of lights in live action films. There might be a "**key**" light that shines on the scene from an angle, a "**fill**" light which shines from a different, sharper angle and is not as bright, and a soft "**back**" light coming from the rear of the scene and that accentuates the silhouette or outline of the models in a scene.

Another strategy is to create lights that represent the natural place of lights in a scene, such as lamps, the sun, and objects like TV sets that emit light.

Lights can be constrained to lighting only specific objects in a scene, and thus used for very selective purposes.

It is also possible to control what lights cast shadows and what objects receive shadows.

Cool Concept 6: Keeping your lighting simple

The lighting of a scene should be kept as simple as possible. Introducing many lights in order to draw out various places in a scene will make it difficult to coordinate them in a way that gives the scene the desired look. It can also increase render time and wash out needed shadows.

Shadows are what root objects to a scene, so they don't appear to be floating. There is a delicate balance between lights and shadows.

Terms and Cool Concept 7: Surfaces as the sources of light

Surfaces can have light emitting properties, such as a "glow." In some applications this concept is taken much further.

Rendering and Lights—The Process of Rendering, Controlling the Render Process, and Leveraging the Visual Artifacts of Rendering

Terms and Cool Concept 1: Rendering and raytracing

When light hits objects in scenes, the materials control how the surface responds to the light. This includes color, transparency, reflections, and refractions.

The dominant technology for creating renderings uses "**raytracing**," which follows "**rays**" or "**photons**" as they reflect and refract through the scene.

This technique is used in order to create "**photorealistic**" renderings, i.e., ones that look as much as possible like real life. On the other hand, if we are making engineering models or creating 2D animation, we might not use a photorealistic renderer.

Terms and Cool Concept 2: The live action camera metaphor

In an application like Maya, rendering is done from the perspective of "**cameras**." This is in keeping with its live action metaphor.

While building a scene, we can look at the scene from the perspective of the cameras from which we intend to render it. This allows us to very carefully set up a scene for rendering.

The area visible to the camera sits between the "**near**" and "**far clipping planes**." A camera can "**dolly**" along the z-axis. It can "**track**" along the x and y axes. It can "**tumble**" (rotate), as well. "**Zooming**" the camera changes its focal length but does not move it.

Terms and Cool Concept 3: Baking materials
The complex interaction of lights and materials that must be calculated in order to render the surface of an object can be captured in Maya (and other modeling applications) and then "**baked**" into a file texture so that potentially very long render times can be reduced dramatically.

▼ A Closer Focus: The nature of rendering

The process of rendering a scene consists of creating (usually) 20 or more pixel-based images per second of rendered video. This causes us to think we are seeing continuous movement, not the discrete passage of individual frames. Generally, a soundtrack is synched to the video image series, and the entire rendered video is packaged as a "container" such as .avi or .mov.

Cool Concept 4: Controlling render time

A number of factors can influence how long it takes to render a given frame.

The number of polygon faces in a scene can have a significant impact, because the calculations that control how each polygon reacts to light must be individually managed.

Particle effects can be very expensive, because there tends to be a large number of particles generated from an emitter, and because each particle can change location, as well as its light properties, from frame to frame. Hardware particles, however, render much more quickly.

The level of raytracing in a scene can also increase render time.

As the number of lights in a scene increases, the render time tends to increase.

Highly reflective or refractive surfaces can lead to long render times, while surfaces that fragment light ray and thus create diffuse light are less costly to render.

Terms and Cool Concept 5: Shadows and light

Shadows are a critical part of a rendered scene. They root objects to the ground, to tabletops, etc., thus keeping the objects from appearing to float. If a shadow starts at the bottom of a milk carton, we believe that the carton is on the table.

Shadows also can make a dragon look like it is flying by casting a shadow that hits the ground but does not touch the body of the dragon.

Raytracing by the renderer can wash shadows out, and so can having too many lights. Final gathering and global illumination can also remove shadows, in particular, small ones.

An ambient light can also wash out shadows because it bathes a scene in light coming from all directions. A directional light, because it moves through the entire outdoor scene, can also wash out shadows.

In Maya, there are two kinds of shadows, "**raytraced shadows**" and "**depth mapped shadows**." The first creates softer edges and the second creates harsher edges.

Creating a Scene—The Big Picture

Cool Concept 1: No fixed set of steps and no fixed set of guidelines

The process of building, animating, and rendering a 3D scene is not a linear process. Nor can it be represented as a tree or graph of steps.

Building and animating 3D scenes is an artistic process performed with technology. The animator must have an intuitive understanding of just what the software can do—and the animator must be inspired and find creative ways of using that technology.

Cool Concept 2: Plan the overall feeling of your scene

The scene needs a sense of depth and a sense of scale. Draw the viewer into your scene; focus their attention on the part of your scene you want noticed first. Light and color are powerful ways of attracting your viewer's eyes.

Provide easily recognizable objects such as people and furniture. The more unreal your scene the more the viewer needs to be guided to understand the dimensions of an architectural model or craft.

An overriding concern is the feeling and/or story you are trying to convey. If the interior of a building has been left to decay, put some grunge into the textures and around the edges of window panes. Consider building layered textures.

Cool Concept 4: Some rules for building scenes

1. Make sure that all the models that you build will have the same look and feel when you pull your main scene together. Do you want the scene to be dark and foreboding? Cartoonish? Ultra modern? Is it anime?

2. Make sure your main scene is fully fleshed out. Think in terms of building an environment, not a stage with actors and props on it.

3. Don't fill a scene with gratuitous content that will distract the viewer. Particle dynamics can do more harm than good.

4. Make sure your models are carefully rooted in your scene. Use light and shadows to do this. Avoid straight on shots that will rob your scene of its sense of depth. This is true for characters and buildings alike.

5. An outdoor scene typically has one dominant source of light —the sun. Its rays and the shadows it casts are a powerful way of giving a scene a sense of depth. They also clue the viewer in to the time of day, which contributes to the overall feeling of the scene.

6. It's a good idea to use reference images (from multiple perspectives) or reference objects as you craft a 3D model.

Cool Concept 3: Build in a box or use an environment dome

When building an indoor environment, like a bar or a living room, build your scene inside a cube. That way, you will get the natural reflections of light you get inside a room. You might want to leave one wall out or make it a separate object, so that you have room to maneuver your cameras, if necessary. You can also place a wall in a separate display layer, so you can more easily view your room.

When building an outdoor environment, you can build inside a software-based "environment dome" like the Physical Sun and Sky inside the mental ray renderer. This is a procedural environment, not an image on a piece of geometry, and it creates a natural looking skyline that covers all 360 degrees of your potential renderable area.

An alternative to the Physical Sun and Sky in mental ray is the Env Sky found under the Maya Software Renderer in the Hypershade. Or a scene could be placed inside a sphere, with a ramp texture used to simulate the transition from dark blue to light blue to a whitish brown at the horizon.

Creating a Scene—For the Novice

Cool Concept 1: Steps for the beginner

1. Model deliberately. Think about what you want your result to look like. Don't simply give up at some point and accept whatever your model happens to look like at that moment. Accidental modeling is not good modeling.

2. Build the models that will make up your final scene in different scene files so that you can focus on them. Put your final scene together by importing and scaling the individual models. Build a model to a level of detail that corresponds to how close up you are going to render it.

3. Try roughing out your final scene, including all the components you will import. This will give you a feel for how the overall geometry of your scene will look best. You can use basic primitives like cubes or create very rough initial models for your scene.

4. Create and toss out early attempts at your models. For every hour you spend creating your models, spend two experimenting with the tools your application provides.

5. Save multiple copies of your models so you can return to earlier versions when problems are revealed.

6. Avoid taking on models that are very complex until you are ready. Cars can be very difficult to build. They must be precisely engineered, and at the same time, they are very organic.

7. Grow your set of animation tools slowly—and learn to use them well.

Cool Concept 2: Visual and emotional—But also technological

1. When you express yourself in this visual art, make your scenes convey emotion.

2. Keep in mind that this is both a visual art and a technological field that takes years to learn.

3. Remember that you are not drawing a 3D model. Rather, you are crafting it.

▼ A Closer Look: More on keeping lots of versions

You might also use old versions of models as starting points for new models. Engineers are particularly careful to keep multiple copies of a product design, because a single detail of a model could easily render it useless.

Index